Reactions to
Mind Leap: Intimate Changes and Communication Between Worlds *(2010)*

"Reading *Mind Leap* was one of the most delightful experiences of my summer. First, I found it an absolutely intriguing story of personal challenge and human relationships, exceedingly well told. But second, and most important, I found it highly inspiring. There are many times in my own spiritual journey that I wonder whether it is all worth the effort – whether there really is a greater reality. This book is a powerful incentive to keep going, an inspiration and a source of hope!"

– Joyce E. Ansell, literary editor

"*Mind Leap* is a sincere record of paranormal experiences, highly symbolic dreams [and] encounters with wise entities from the spiritual realm, such as a gentle soul named Moita channeled by Siofra Bradigan.

"Letts presents a fascinating journal of his darkest and brightest moments... packed full of astonishing descriptions and mysterious details from the disturbing to the uplifting. For those who enjoy the pursuit of different realities, Letts will not disappoint. His work educates and entertains, focusing on the extraordinary capabilities of the human spirit."

– ForeWord Clarion review

"David Letts made a huge contribution by helping the presences known as Loria and Moita come into the lives of many of us. He has a marvellous facility for comprehending the channeled messages in the context of surrounding events and has a gift for describing their deeper import for those fortunate to be there at the time or who read about it now. As well, I am astounded at the depth and profundity of David's dreams and the fine uses to which he has put them. Many seem to tap a source similar to channeling and remind me of Carl Jung's powerful dream-life.

"This material is deep and takes concentration; but for those who are ready, it is a very rich reading experience."

– Dr. William H. Wynn, Emeritus Professor of Psychology, University of Regina

Reactions to the Moita material

"I would be most happy if Moita would give me a message as to the opinion of the unobstructed world about the choices we have taken. There are so many hours I would like to sit with you; listen; ask questions; receive answers. I will dream up a place and a time when we can connect. Until then, a big, big hug for all the messages, the love and the support, from your old medicine woman."

– Dr. Elisabeth Kübler-Ross (1981)

Further reactions to Mind Leap and the Moita material

"I would highly recommend *Mind Leap* to all who would be open to the changes we are experiencing as the turning point to a New Age approaches. The messages and learnings that came through David Letts and his associates are prophetic and relevant for this time, and those of us who are less sensitive can learn much from reading this material."

"The information conveyed in these conversations with Moita is comparable to the more famous Seth material. Comparing Moita with Seth, I find her much less bombastic in tone, which one would expect of a feminine being. Much other channeling like Edgar Cayce and *A Course in Miracles* is couched in formal language. In print, Moita comes off as having great charm because of her gentleness, humor, and articulate use of colloquial English. I was very moved by the moment one person tried to embrace this spirit, and her response."

– Elihu Edelson, <u>Both Sides Now</u>

Reactions to participating in sessions with Moita

"She looks right into your soul, and there's nothing that's not there for that look. I've never seen anybody look at somebody with such total love. But at the same time there's this Puckish attitude, like she's having fun with us. Like she knows something really good about us, some really good surprise that's in store for us, and she's kind of smiling and keeping it to herself."

– Frank

"That is truly a mind-blowing experience. There were a few moments there where I could just feel my consciousness being totally drawn in. 'What's going on here?!' *Neat.* I really didn't expect it to be as intense. It felt like somebody who's been helping you all your life behind your back, and you don't know it, all of a sudden stands in front of you and says, 'Here I am.'"

– Lisa

Mind Leap series

THE WORLD CONSPIRES

Weaving Our Energies to Renew the Earth

DAVID W. LETTS

with SIOFRA BRADIGAN *and* MOITA

> *"It is my function to weave together different energy levels...*
> *I help others to weave their energies in order to*
> *make new and fresh discoveries of each other and of themselves...*
> *There are many levels of conspiracy at work here!"*
> *– Moita*

 www.trafford.com

North America & international
toll-free: 1 888 232 4444 (USA & Canada)
phone: 250 383 6864 ♦ fax: 812 355 4082

Contents

Series Preface: MIND LEAP 1960S/2012

Today the gauntlet of crises facing life on Earth is undeniable: from extreme poverty-hunger-disease to financial system upheaval, from religious-ethnic-political fanaticism to massive weapons proliferation, from pervasive ecological destruction to escalating climate change and natural and/or manmade disasters. The Hopi's discerning understatement clearly applies: *koyanniquatsi*, "life out of balance". Indeed, without a fundamental, planet-wide change of course, scientists have warned that within the next decade, perhaps even by 2012, we may pass one or more "tipping points". Thereafter, spiralling events could spell the decline of nature and civilization.

However, simultaneously, many voices around the world have been portraying this same period of years, leading to 2012 and beyond, as a time of rare transformative potential.[1] The collapse of existing structures brings the opportunity to reinvent society on a surer, more resilient foundation. But more than the obvious socio-economic and environmental challenges are involved here. The voices of transformation urge we now prepare for the descent of spiritual energies, and synchronous rising of human energies, that will open up our blinkered view of what is real. For life again to flourish on this planet, humanity's consensual, working reality must expand to include higher dimensions of being.

This opening to higher levels can begin as simply as tomorrow morning's dream. But it has vast implications. It is essential in restoring the perspective we lack: on *who we are*, where we have come from and where we are going, individually and collectively; on our *sustaining relationships* with non-physical energies able to generate inspiration and insight toward solving our many practical and existential dilemmas; and on the as yet *unknowing power* of human thoughts and emotions to reflect outward, co-creating our world. In other words, there can be no lasting solutions to external problems without overcoming our spiritual estrangement and achieving wholeness from within. By reconnecting with our source, we will rediscover what is truly essential in life and how to manifest it, helping to heal ourselves and our Earth.

Not the first new world to be born in the death throes of another, say seers of far ancient days. I include the Maya – by whose Long Count calendar the fifth World Age begins at the December solstice 2012 – and those you will meet in the *Mind Leap* series. While perceptions of what lies ahead vary, it is certain that humanity's future consciousness will diverge from the one creating these crises, and will represent a new evolutionary stage. Therefore a journey of transformation beckons us all – which means opening our minds and hearts and entering the unknown. That will always be the starting point in this series.

Of course, within our collective memory there was another period of widespread change, of leaps in consciousness and alterations of lives, though generally lasting only a few brief years. Yet they were a harbinger, those late 1960s and 1970s – and a preparation. Various groups and personalities spring to mind as representatives of that era, be they cultural heroes who pioneered and clarified the new awareness or self-aggrandizers who exploited and profited from its facsimile. But out of the public spotlight, certain others delved deeply, exploring new territories of experience with minimal distraction.

Today humanity needs to rediscover and share all that we can learn about transformation and the challenges now staring us in the face. To do so, we must move beyond our safe positions, whether of uncomprehending ridicule or understanding silence. Accordingly, you hold in your hands one of the first very public sharings from a couple of those relatively quiet explorers, two of us forever changed by encounters with energies of whom I have spoken.

The names that humanity has given these energies are much less important than how we can connect with them. And now, establishing more conscious relationships with higher levels has become an evolutionary necessity – as inevitable a quest as searching for physical life on other planets, and much more urgent. But far from alien, this connection is the most intimate thing in the world, for it flows from listening to our dreams, feelings and intuitions, perhaps eventually blossoming into more direct forms of communication. It is the fulfilment of our growth, our reaching toward joy.

Such communication has been spreading more widely than many suspect, expressed and understood in whatever ways individuals find most natural. Directly or indirectly, it has helped energize and enlighten movements toward peace, human rights, community and reharmonizing ourselves with nature.[2N] On the other hand, those who wish to preserve the old limits on consciousness, who try to resist the rising energy environment we are entering, may face mounting pressures they are not able to explain.

True, mass culture has made sport of forms of communication called "channeling". And yes, the trivialization and abuses of supposed "spiritual" contact are obvious. But part of the mainstream attitude toward channeling – as also toward the wondrous communications called "crop circles" – is a nervous, adolescent reaction to something important. This is an actual mystery that reaches much deeper than its media image. Perhaps more are now ready to look carefully at the reality behind the caricature and examine the workings of this bridge between worlds.

We must be clear: good communication with the non-physical or "subtle" worlds is a cooperative endeavour between levels of being, both ends of which need to be clear and whole.[3N] That is why information should not be believed merely because it *appears* to come from a higher source, and why anyone wishing to evaluate a body of non-ordinary communications should seek an *inside view* of how it emerged and evolved. One should be on guard against dishonesty and manipulation: those putting on a front of all-knowingness and "spiritual" perfection for influence or financial gain.

One should also look into how the communications addressed the psychic and very human problems of those involved. The true value of a guiding philosophy shows in how it is conveyed and applied, both day to day and in life's emergencies – like the intensity attending the birth and early evolution of our own contact. That is why we have chosen to share these life-changing experiences, and we invite readers to glean from them what is universal and/or useful to yourself.

Through the *Mind Leap* series, we introduce Moita (*Moy*-tuh), a friend and teacher speaking through Kelly (Siofra Bradigan). We convey the manner of Moita's coming: the learnings and choices that opened us to her reality so that eventually we could share her and her own higher levels with hundreds of session participants. Then, we invite you into our sessions, providing verbatim the most revealing conversations with these energy presences – their wisdom and even "cosmic humour" – as well as spontaneous reactions by those who participated.

Future offerings will continue our own journey and share many more communications of an experiential and prophetic nature. The fact is, much that has been happening to our Earth, and is now being suggested may emerge circa 2012 and beyond, was mentioned or hinted at decades ago – and explained to us in the context of human and planetary consciousness evolving toward a new stage of co-creation. Though no definite target date was given, the similarity between the transition as then projected and what is developing and being spoken of now is impossible to ignore. Because of this, however difficult the period ahead, I feel assured that love and growth will be at the root of extraordinary changes to come. Special-effects movies aside, this is not a prophecy of ultimate catastrophe, but of transformation and renewal.

> *For us, this is a labour of love. Instead of man creating only on his own, as an individual self set apart from the rest of the universe, this time he is involved in a co-creation – and we are the co-creators. Those who are here have arrived to help found a new world.*
> *– Moita*

No one yet knows the degree of awareness and commitment humanity will bring to this transition. But today the harbingers of co-creative wholeness are everywhere: as gossamer as sudden intuitions, meditative visions and lucid dreams; as down-to-earth as farmers' fields graced with amazingly complex, inspiringly beautiful "crop circles" (like the one[4N] on our title page); and as bravely outgoing as those prophetic pioneers who would lift present-day civilization from its cynicism and destructiveness toward "One Earth", a green and just "peaceable kingdom".

Without human beings, obviously, no new vision can be incarnated. A high source whom you will meet in this series once put it very bluntly: *"If it was something we could accomplish alone, it would have been done eons ago."* We face tests continually, small and large. Choosing well eases the whole world's struggle toward rebirth.

David Letts
January 2011

Notes: Superscript numbers correspond to Endnotes referring to sections of *Mind Leap* or to other sources by author, date and any page references, linked to the Bibliography. A superscript number followed by the letter "N" indicates that the endnote includes an author comment – for example, this one about ellipses[5N]. These, like a few footnotes at the bottom of pages, provide additional information or clarify the author's perspective on the subject being discussed.

A Letter From Kelly
(Siofra Bradigan*)

Circa 1982

Dear Reader,

I've decided that the best approach is to pretend you have just heard about our work with Moita, and have written me a letter asking me about it. You're curious about how I discovered I had this "gift" and what it's like to be a channel for an energy-presence such as Moita seems to be.

Perhaps you're a little skeptical and somewhat uneasy about asking such questions. After all, you have heard about various strange cults and the dramatic and sometimes deadly effects they have on their members. But that's okay – because skepticism doesn't bother me in the slightest. As a matter of fact, I'm skeptical myself, and *I'm* at the centre of this phenomenon!

Oh, not skeptical that it isn't real – at least, not at the time it's happening. But it's hard to know exactly what to call it, how to phrase it. It refuses to be quantified or pegged nicely. And sometimes, as I don't go into trance at all, I am skeptical about the "truth" of what comes through. Actually, Moita herself has explained that it is a cooperative effort between her world and ours, and that whatever comes through is changed by the nature of the channel – in this case, me, my thoughts, my hidden needs and desires, my perceptions of reality.

So, now that I know you are a real person, just like me, with your own wisdom and life experiences to draw on, I can talk to you as I do to all my friends – straight (*my* kind of straight!). You're free to disbelieve absolutely everything I say – I can't force you to believe me. But, for my own sense of personal integrity (after all, I *do* have to live with myself forever, you know), I'm going to say to you that everything I put down on paper or that comes from my mouth is *truth as I perceive it*. I cannot make any absolute claims. I only know what I see and feel is real for me. What *you* see and feel is real for *you*.

I've always been what is commonly known as a "psychic" – but I don't like the word. I've spent my whole life thus far trying to accept me for me, without definitions that tend to limit me. I'm just a person who is willing to admit to her intuitions and perceptions, and who is trying to understand how the universe *really* works – aside from what I've been told in school, by the newspaper and radio and TV, by friends and relations. I want to be me – and that means I have to let go of preconceived notions of the way things are in order to find out what works.

Yes, I've had many strange things happen to me – only, for me they're not strange, they're normal.[6N] I've had experiences of telepathy (such as with my father while growing up), premonitions and prophetic dreams, unusual "coincidences", and a healing energy that comes through my hands. I haven't as yet seen a ghost, but I *have*

---

* Siofra Bradigan ("spirited elf") is the Celtic name Kelly will adopt later on in this story. She bears her birth name Kelly during all the events of this book.

seen Moita.

Moita has a talent for the absurd. It helps to dissolve the mythos of a spiritual teacher. She is not interested in followers. (I imagine she's already much too busy and too fulfilled to have time or room for them.) So, talented as she is, one of the first times she chose to show herself to me was while I was up on a hydraulic lift at three o'clock in the morning in a big city downtown service station – actually *I* was in a car, and the *car* was on the lift!

It's hard to describe what that was like, but I wasn't afraid. She was obviously a beautiful being to me. There was an exchange of thoughts, but the encounter was brief because I didn't know what to say. I can't remember it ending as such. I guess I just floated out of the space where she was visible.

But I've never forgotten it, either. Seeing her filled me with a desire to see her again – to be *with* her. It was like being an orphan and then finding your real mother – and all the fears you had about why you'd been deserted, what was wrong with you, were dissolved. I knew she loved me, and that knowledge filled me and helped me through some very rough times over the next seven years: life experiences that prepared and strengthened me so that I would finally be ready to let her speak through me to others.

When it began, when she first actually spoke through me, I wasn't even consciously aware that it was happening. I was in the midst of a personal crisis, a painful breakup in a relationship. The words that I spoke gave a larger perspective – certainly not how I would have usually been able to speak of it. (How many of us could talk about our own pain calmly, as if it belonged to someone else?) David recognized a presence and asked who was speaking now. There was a sudden rush of energy to my mind, and she repeated the name that came to me in that earlier experience: Moita.[7N]

It was as natural as breathing after that initial breakthrough. She came spontaneously, sporadically, for short periods of time. Those first few months were exciting as well as confusing. We had to be ready to change our state of mind at the drop of a hat, never knowing when she would come to speak. She came only when she was needed, and said only as much as we could hear and understand at that time.

She has never told us what choices we should make: these, she has said, are our own – and if she made them for us, we would not become strong. That impressed me. She has said that it is important to make mistakes so that we can learn. That is how she got to be where she is, and her level gives ours the same freedom so that one day we can join them. That impressed me, too.

I was upset and worried from time to time about whether it was real. But over the last four years she has proven to *my* satisfaction that she is not a secondary personality I created to fulfill some need within me, and she isn't a demon from hell bent on possessing me for her own evil ends. I was there, and I speak from my experience. Except for the rarest of exceptions, there was never any coercion involved.[8N] I was always willing to let her in, and she was always willing to leave when she was done.

I did realize after a while that, if she so chose, she was powerful enough to "possess" me in a negative sense. But having the power to do something to someone, and *not* using that power, says volumes about her purpose and her sense of integrity and what level she comes from – at least, to me.

There will always be those that see something sinister and frightening in this. That's okay, because they will never *be* a channel – not in this life. But I *am*, and I feel honoured to be able to help in this way, even though I recognize that a lot of hard work on my part went into preparing me for the role I have chosen.

My experience of her inside me is hard to put into words. It's like reality shifts a little. My mind buzzes with energy; the air comes alive; the walls of the house dissolve into insignificance. It's not that they disappear, but that we no longer attach any importance *to* them, so they cease to exist in our reality. What does matter is her presence: the sense that you are really being looked at and listened to completely, maybe for the very first time in your life. I'm carried upward on a wave of energy and "eternal nowness". Time passes, and yet it passes more slowly, or more *richly*.

Each question that is asked becomes the most important question that has ever been asked, no matter how trivial it may sound to others. She shows by her intentness that she believes in *your* reality as well as her own. Though oftentimes the answers are hard to understand for a while, or not what you expected, it's obvious that she cares enough, loves enough, to make the attempt at opening the lines of communication between the levels. She *shares* her perspective – her broader insight into why the question was asked in the first place – but she does not *impose*: "Do not stop questioning or testing the truth of what you receive. In the end analysis, you are the only one who can decide what you perceive of all this and what applies to you directly."

As you read the excerpts from the many sessions we have held since this began, you will note that the quality of the exchange between others and Moita has grown and evolved, and I have become more comfortable with the idea as I have grown to know and accept myself. I do not foresee any *end* to this process of growth. There is always one more step, one more barrier to dissolve, one more discovery to make or remember about the nature of reality and the universe.

Her purpose in coming is simple, really: to make us aware that we are not alone and that we have within us tremendous potential for real love and compassion – for giving back to the universe joyfully and freely the gifts we have received, for learning how to become the co-creators of our world; to let us know we can remake our lives into works of beauty – if we will but take the reins in our hands, be responsible for our own action, and learn from our mistakes.

These words came from me, and yet I can make no claim to them. I am the channel, the vessel, through which they came – but they are more than I know of myself. We are *all* channels, and we are all mysterious, beautiful and worthwhile. If she never gives me another thing, knowing that we all matter is gift enough.

Love,
Kelly

DAVID'S INTRODUCTION

In her reality, Moita can experience any phenomenon at once in all its phases, by *becoming* that multi-dimensional whole.

If we were in that space now, introducing you to Moita and all that flowed from her presence in our lives would be simple – and wouldn't require a series of books! Reality would not need to be broken into pieces, with parts of our story fitted into different publications. But after all, we physically focused beings do have to make some accommodations.

This book is as complete in its own way as possible, while intimately tied to *Mind Leap*, the volume in this series that was first to appear in print.* In fact, this book offers a complementary, alternative pathway into our adventure with Moita, shining greater light on "this great experiment in communication between worlds" – a weaving of energies, giving birth to fresh discoveries, helping to renew the Earth.

Our emphasis shifts here from those personal life changes, recounted in *Mind Leap*, that preceded and surrounded the start of these communications. Instead, you are invited into many, many more of our sessions with Moita and further entities, reading the dialogue between these channeled beings and a great variety of participants, as well as verbatim descriptions of the experience by Kelly, me and others. Along with wide-ranging information offering insight and practical help for inward explorers, this book also presents the critical events and learnings, as these communications developed, that resolved a number of key issues left simmering by *Mind Leap*.

࿇   ࿇   ࿇

But first, other burning questions may be top of mind for many readers:

How can I begin to experience deeper levels of energy and reality?
How can I break through the walls of conditioning – physical, emotional, conceptual – acquired from living in today's society?
In short, how can I free myself and become whole?

As a young man in the summer of 1973, I was asking myself these same questions with special urgency. I had been consumed with writing a masters thesis in psychology; but nearing the end, I felt stumped for a better-than-routine conclusion. Simultaneously, my emotional life, embodied in my marriage, was at an impasse. In fact, my partner Leanne had just departed on a trip to get back in touch with her former boyfriend. Then, the morning after she left, I awoke with the following dream.

Mind Leap: Intimate Changes and Communication Between Worlds by David W. Letts with Siofra Bradigan and Moita (2010, updated readers edition). Reading *Mind Leap* is not necessary to understand and enjoy *The World Conspires*.

"Escaping Ancient Catacomb" dream
David (age 26) / July 11, 1973

It is fairly dark here, as in a dimly lit cathedral. Hanging from the high ceiling is a long cord, around which circles a glowing object resembling butterfly wings. A spherical, gyroscope-like form is created as it spins, ascending and descending. I feel this phenomenon has some mysterious, holy significance. My companions, however, appear not to see it and claim it is only a figment of my imagination.

From this place, we all then pass into a narrow corridor constructed of yellowish white stone. It feels very oppressive, like an ancient catacomb. We have become sealed inside these walls without apparent means of escape. The others seem to accept this prospect. I, however, look for a way out and guess the stone-block door ahead of us may not be as impenetrable as it seems.

I remove a covering from the large rectangular stone in the door's centre and discover holes that will make the block lighter to move. Straining to push, I manage to dislodge the stone to the other side, leaving an opening through which I can crawl. Meanwhile, my companions have been ridiculing my efforts. And now that I have struggled through the opening, they simply stand back amazed, afraid to make any such move themselves. They feel it is their obligation to remain imprisoned.

Then I see I stand in another corridor like the last, with another sealed stone door at the far end. But I can push its middle block as before. And as I crawl through the open centre, the unrelievedly bright, arid hardness of the corridor comes to an end. I smell fresh, moist air and see that around a corner lies the out-of-doors. It is a mild wintry night. I hear familiar voices of children playing out on the damp street, lit by lamps among the shadowy trees.

All that separates me now from freedom is a metal fence. I leap and fly upward through overhanging tree branches laden with snow sparkling in the moonlight. I soar toward the starry blackness above a clearing, then glide joyfully over the snowy forest.

A crisis in my marriage would soon burst upon me, shaking me to my core.[9] But as in this dream, I would one quiet morning find an opening at "the centre". Meditating, a deeper level became present, "befriending" the conscious me. Creative energy lighted a way forward, transforming my outlook; healing of my relationship followed. (The dream also found its way into my thesis. Replacing the expected, prosaic ending that I resisted writing, it introduced three further archetypal dreams that lifted my conclusion to a new level[10] – the academic equivalent of escaping dry, dead catacombs.)

In the same spirit, Part One is entitled "Age of Metamorphosis". The title relates to Moita's words in its Prologue and Epilogue, picturing a caterpillar transforming into a butterfly. Part One ushers you into the world of our Moita sessions, as a variety of people bring concerns like the "burning questions" above. I've arranged these conversations by common theme, progressing from individuals' first meetings with Moita [Chap. 1] through phases of personal-spiritual growth. Topics include:

- *knowing oneself* – letting go of fear; guilt and attachments; emotions vs. feeling; vulnerability; centring; seeing one's own beauty [Chap. 2];

- *wheel of rebirth* – there are no accidents; choosing vs. "falling into" reincarnational lives; fate and freedom; probabilities and one's optimum path [Chap. 3];

- *opening intuitively* – bypassing our conditioning; teachers and structures; meditation and energy sharing, past-life recall and dreams [Chap. 4];

- *vibratory bodies* – grounding and unfocusing; illness and healing; aura colours; chakras; out-of-body experience and materialization [Chap. 5];

- *other dimensions* – meeting entities in dreams and the afterlife; time-hopping; probable selves; co-creating our unique realities [Chap. 6];

- *channeling doubt* – the need to question and discriminate; lower astral thought-forms; a case of channeling abuse and dependency [Chap. 7];

- *universe of presences* – higher selves; focus personalities; trance mediums; frustrated entities; Cayce/Seth/Moita; worlds coming together [Chap. 8].

Kelly's and my personal narrative enters very little into Part One. Session excerpts are presented in the most relevant order – for the point they illustrate or information they convey – usually without regard to participants, time or place. Then, at the end of most chapters, I offer one or more "Illustrative Dreams", all received before my involvement in channeling sessions, all previously unpublished. These not only mirror aspects of Moita's message in those chapters but also demonstrate dreams as a medium for touching the soul and its wisdom.* Readers eager to start dipping into Part One, please feel free to do so at any point . . . or even jump to Part Two.

⸱ᵍ   ᵍ   ᵍ

Part Two, "The World Conspires", has a different format. Here more of our personal narrative returns, but with a new focus: the early evolution and major turning points of these communications, including key dreams and past-life explorations, from the beginning of Kelly's and my partnership.

A brief review of events will now provide some context for new readers. *Mind Leap* began as I was led along a path of growth consisting of a series of transformative passages or "transitus" experiences. Dreams, psychedelics (entheogens), meditation, spiritually oriented psychology and intimate life changes all played a role. By 1975, the

---

* Appendix A indexes all mentioned dreams and regressions (some as told in *Mind Leap*). Session excerpts in Part One are indexed in Appendix B, and Part 2 sessions in Appendix C.

year Leanne and I separated, I had chosen my goal – or perhaps the goal had chosen me. Against my earlier prejudices, but inspired by Jane Roberts's Seth material and the founders of Findhorn Community in Scotland,[11] I knew that I desired somehow to become involved in psychic-spiritual communication, or channeling.[12N]

In 1976, in Regina, Saskatchewan, Canada, I met my counterpart in Ruth, another American expatriate studying toward a psychology degree. Recognizing so many commonalities, we began living together and planned to offer "Sunseed" workshops on dreams, meditation, myths and symbols, and other avenues for exploring the psyche. But before our first group ever met, Ruth discovered that she, with my psychic and moral support, could channel a non-physical presence named Loria. Loria identified herself as the entity of which both Ruth and I were earthly expressions.

We had much to learn about openness and rising in consciousness. At the same time, I endured much ambivalence on a personal level with Ruth, especially after Loria urged that we conceive a child together (consistent with Ruth's dreams about being happily pregnant). But our sessions were bringing such good energy into our lives, I could not deny the magic. So I devoted myself with Ruth to conceiving a child, to be fulfilled in the eventual birth of our son Michael.

There is history behind a further goal Loria urged upon us, that of founding a community and learning/healing centre. In one of her most powerful sessions, Loria told a group of friends about our long-ago life together in the beautiful city of Musili, a city that was alive, built or grown by the ancient art/science of sound. That ancestral group vowed to bring forward the light and love we then shared to a world that was, relatively speaking, dark and empty – meaning today. We would only find joy in this life now, Loria said, by leaving the old ways and creating a path into the future, despite great personal risk. Thus, in tandem with our channeling work, would we play our part within a seeming groundswell of humanity during these 1970s, contributing to a coming breakthrough in consciousness and global culture: the "New Age".[13]

But further surprises were in store for me. In powerful dreams from fall 1976 and fall 1977, I received the message "I won't be with Ruth too long" ("If You Meet the Buddha" dream) and was shown a new goal, symbolized as a high mountain peak, by an unknown woman ("Snowy Natural Bridge" dream).[14N]

Six months after this, Kelly appeared, joining our spring 1978 workshop. Psychically gifted since childhood, Kelly shared with us her tumultuous life story. Afterward, Ruth and I agreed that Kelly had the quick, creative energy of Musili people. For her part, Kelly connected one past life she had always remembered – as an "aura dancer" – with Loria's description of Musili.

This was only one among many strong connections coming quickly to the fore between Kelly and myself. When our complementary energies joined in meditation, even merging telepathically, we both felt transported into a wholeness previously unknown. Our visit to the Indian medicine wheel on Arrow Mountain, lying near a potential site for our community, accelerated the openings within and between us. A week later, toward the end of a past-life regression in which I was guiding Kelly, Moita began to speak through her to me.

These developments might conceivably have blended harmoniously toward the creation of a community, guided by the higher levels of all its members. But given our humanity – our need to grow through challenging circumstances purposefully arranged before birth – the triangle of Ruth-David-Kelly generated forces that could only be healed over a passage of years. Nevertheless, Kelly and I were left no doubt that events had brought us together in order to begin our work with Moita.

ॐ   ॐ   ॐ

As mentioned, *Mind Leap* could not tell the full story. In fact, at least *seven* important issues still lingered, unresolved, at its conclusion. In different ways, each of those, if answered, could significantly affect our view of preceding and future events. Now the chapters cited below will bring closure to *all seven* of these mysteries:

(1) When Ruth and I met Dr. Elisabeth Kübler-Ross in 1977, she told us every group working closely together had an entity as its "guiding spirit". Loria later said an "interesting" step for our community would be opening contact with its "group entity". But by the end of *Mind Leap*, our group still seemed to lack a centring point. *How, if ever, would contact be made with the group entity of our envisioned community? And if it were made, how would that entity view the events that overtook our group?* [Chap. 13, 14, 15 and 17]

(2) Immediately after the meeting with Kübler-Ross, Loria said that "an extended, close relationship will develop between you and Elisabeth this time around, building upon your past associations".[15N] But Ruth and I were to have no further direct contacts with Elisabeth while together. *Would a close relationship develop with the world-famous, controversial Elisabeth Kübler-Ross after all, and if so, how and in what regard?* [Chap. 7]

(3) Our vision of community was said to spring from a vow made by the group in ancient Musili. We also were told of a yet earlier life in Asia Minor (Kyrionis), from which a larger group split in opposite directions, half migrating toward what became Musili. But beyond descriptions of our magical existence and individual talents in Musili, very little was known of group interactions during those two lives. *Would we ever recover more detailed knowledge of events in Kyrionis and Musili? If so, what light would that shed on happenings and relationships now?* [Chap. 13, 14 and 15]

(4) Near the end of *Mind Leap*, a rapid sequence of events combined to threaten Kelly, her children and me with no available house to live in. At the last moment, we were left with a single possibility to rent: a rather dilapidated house in a rundown neighbourhood. *Is there a non-ordinary reason that we were pushed toward this house, and if so, what opportunities as well as dangers did it present for Kelly's and my work together?* [Chap. 10 and 11]

(5) As mentioned in "A Letter from Kelly" and described more fully in *Mind Leap*,

Moita first appeared in outward visual form and spoke to Kelly in rather odd circumstances in 1971. Kelly said to Moita at the time, "You sure look a lot like someone else I've heard a lot about!" – namely, a blond-haired, blue-robed Virgin Mary. *Why did Moita appear in this way to Kelly, and what does it say of Moita's greater role for humanity? Is the Virgin but a conventional religious icon or is she an energy evolving with the times, in tune with our transforming Earth?* [Chap. 16]

(6) From the beginning, Loria stated that in future her own higher self would communicate with us. The next year, Priamo (imaged as an old man) came with overwhelming energy and attempted to speak, but Ruth could not let him through. My own dreams of an elder masculine energy reached a climax around and after the birth of Ruth's and my child. As well, starting with our medicine wheel visit, Kelly repeatedly received powerful images of an Indian brave wearing an eagle feather. *Would Loria's higher self succeed at communicating clearly, and if so, through whom? How far would his true identity extend, and what would it reveal of Loria's and Moita's connections? What would be his message for us?* [Chap. 11, 13, 15 and 17]

(7) Finally, *Mind Leap* ended with a clear sign that our estrangement from Ruth would be healed, but space allowed only reference to a "series of surprising dreams" that assisted that healing. *What were those dreams, and how did they help re-establish accepting communication between Ruth and us? More generally, what lessons in consciousness change emerge from this individual experience of conflict and resolution? How is the fate of personal relationships so intimately tied to spiritual growth, such that healing the former enables a leap in understanding of self and other, our very identity, at this time of transformation?* [Chap. 13 and 17]

On the answers to these intertwining questions, and others that will occur to you as you read, hinges much of the value of sharing our journey with a wider audience.

❧ ❧ ❧

While I trust the details of our individual experiences will hold some interest, the greater purpose in sharing them is to illustrate what is universal: the usually hidden relationships to higher levels of being on which our lives as we know them depend. As well as satisfying the authors' own curiosity, that is why we have put so much effort into finding and making plain the intelligent order revealed by these communications. Having pursued this path, I can assure readers their own rationality as well as intuition are welcome and needed here and in the new world that is coming – as long as we are first willing to entertain a larger perspective on what is possible.

In order to have new experiences in these realms and open up other sides of our nature, we must temporarily suspend disbelief, letting go of our tendency to prejudge and limit reality. But afterward, we always need to look back and question, try to understand, evaluate and further investigate what we have experienced, as the authors and other participants have done throughout this book. Through this balanced interplay of all our faculties, we may enjoy the intrigue of a multi-levelled detective story along with the intrinsic rewards of exploring new realms of experience.

Already, you have likely been pondering a further mystery: What does this book's title, one of Moita's evocative sayings, actually mean? A great deal does lie hidden within both "conspires" and "world". First, let your mind play with the original meanings of "conspire", given at the start of Part Two. Then, "world" suggests how *huge* this all is. To personal transformation, and movements to overcome the many barriers dividing the human family and end ecological destruction, this book adds the non-physical levels of action on which our inner guides, nature spirits and devas, and higher angelic beings operate – all working together in this crucial period for our planet. Similarly, as you read, you will find many specific connections to the subtitle, "Weaving Our Energies to Renew the Earth" – which is as concise a translation of "The World Conspires" as I have found. But let me at least reassure the security establishment this is no physical-level plotting they would think worth worrying about (though its ultimate effects may be beyond their wildest imaginings).

Just as each chapter of this book will add clues for understanding its titles, the authors, too, gained perspective gradually, through a measure of struggle. As Kelly and I dug down into new layers of experience in the course of our quest, we gained glimpses of this little-known "conspiracy". With surprise, and humility, we recognized that forces behind the scenes, invisible to most of us at the time, had been weaving our lives and the lives we were touching into new patterns – patterns contributing, despite others' opposition and our own doubts, to the world's changing tapestry. Then also, at special times when a higher source acknowledged our participation in the "moment of change", there were no words that could express the energy.

Yet, to the extent words *are* possible, many clues to the emerging pattern – highlights from the entire book – are brought together in the Afterword, to be imagined as a channeling for the Winter Solstice Eve of 2012.

We tend to think of spirituality as a search for perfection – rather than as engaging ourselves more deeply in life, becoming open enough to experiment and learn from our mistakes, taking leaps into the unknown to realize new levels of caring and creativity. Indeed, happenings that may be frowned upon socially, and therefore attended by anxiety and ambivalence, may be the very ones planned before birth to serve growth in awareness at this critical time.

Come to think of it: how could the current of transformation *not* run contrary, much of the time, to our conditioning and expectations? The upshot should be that we resist rushing to judgment of individual lives when we know not the full context, the inner significance, of each actor's part in the play of this age – in what Moita means by "the changing of the world".

Yes, Moita acknowledges with a laugh, "There are *many* levels of conspiracy at work here!" Thus the world conspires to save itself. And we are *all* implicated.

PART ONE:

Age of Metamorphosis

Prologue

THE FIRST LEAP IN YOUR MIND

Once the first step is made, the first awareness, the first leap in your mind, the first acceptance of other realities and experience of them in a direct way, [things] have a tendency to escalate very rapidly.

You have chosen this time to come into in order to be ready... Your life up to this point was a preparation for an accelerated experience such as you are having. And to you, this self, it may seem quick, but the foundation for your opening was laid long ago.

It is as if you were a caterpillar who has just spun a cocoon and is going through his metamorphosis. He knows he is changing; he is not what he was. But as yet he doesn't know what he *is* until he emerges from that cocoon and flies away. It is an entirely different experience to fly!

– Moita

Chapter 1

FIRST MEETINGS WITH MOITA

It is interesting to see how my energy affects others. It is difficult to propose that it is their imagination when it does affect them.
– Moita

An intriguing aspect of meeting Moita for the first time is the very idea of personally interacting with a being from higher realms of consciousness temporarily inhabiting a sister human's body. So, at least, the newcomer is *told*, for he or she does not yet know this from experience. It is a concept that takes some getting used to – which is why some shy away completely, and others doubt or resist the situation even while it's happening to them.

Picture sitting with us in a circle as Moita's presence enters Kelly. As the session begins, our bodies may be translating the energy Moita brings into unusual sensations or emotions. And while our minds and hearts respond to the message of her words, intuitive perceptions and knowings may be released through the doorway she opens to our inner selves. Amid all these changes, the quality of the personal encounter reflects our willingness to move beyond the surface of life, our ability to perceive and function on deeper levels without losing our individual centre and grounding.

The first meetings in this chapter show a wide variety of reactions, though some nervousness is almost universal. Certainly the unfamiliarity and ambiguity of the situation has much to do with this. One wonders: "Is Moita here? How will I know? How do I talk to her? Will she be completely different from Kelly?" But another part of the nervousness involves the "interview with God" syndrome – even if, in Moita's case, a "god" who doesn't fit many of our preconceptions. One asks: "How will she feel toward me? Does she know what I'm thinking, and everything about me? Will I be judged – and what will the judgment be?" As Moita summarizes it, "The idea of meeting someone who may know more about you than you know about yourself can be unnerving, but you need not fear."

We begin with the first meeting of one of our community college workshops following my introductory talk. The 14 participants have expressed their wish to meet Moita. To Kelly and me, though, the atmosphere of the sterile classroom seems a long way from Moita's reality. We are still trying to prepare them while Moita's presence becomes, for us, more and more obvious. Kelly, in particular, is feeling hot, her cheeks visibly flushed, her head spacey, making it difficult for her to talk. Thus Moita's energy refuses to be an impersonal, objective phenomenon on the "psychic frontier"! Not sure how the others are reacting to all this, I give a short guided relaxation, after which Moita opens Kelly's eyes.

David: You can begin to open your eyes now. *(long silence)*
MOITA: First meetings are always difficult.
Bob: Excuse me, do you hear us talk in our silence – different things pounding in our hearts?
MOITA: I see *many* things. This is not a quiet place! *(laughter)*
Leslie: Why do you want us to know you? There are so many others that are *hiding* from us – I mean, [that] we're not capable of seeing. Why do we know *you*?
MOITA: Because I am one who *can* be seen, and it is needed for man to see something beyond himself. He has wished for it. We are another world of reality. We are part of your Earth – and we are not the *only* ones that you cannot communicate with.
Leslie: Why do we stay so ignorant? Just that we don't *want* to see?
MOITA: It is more that you are afraid.
Leslie: Do you see us afraid tonight?
MOITA: I see some nervous, uncertain and doubtful. My presence does not usually enlighten the fear, for I am coming through another. I am subdued, if you will. I am not coming as my whole self. I am giving you a part – a part, it has been found, that is easier to handle.
Leslie: How do you feel being here, being called upon by so many different people so many different times? Is this your work?
MOITA: Yes.
Leslie: Is this what you want?
MOITA: It is my desire to help bridge this gap between realities. There is a time coming when the gap shall be less, and my coming now helps to add energy to that future line so that it will be more likely. We have much to share. We have much love to give to the world and to its people. And we are building that bridge so that the energy that has created the universe can shine out from the Earth and its inhabitants.

            There are no accidents. Any who is here wishes to be, on one level or another.
Leslie: You're here to help us learn how to reach those levels?
MOITA: I am a teacher. I am here to help you find yourself and see the beauty that we see in you. *(pause)* This experience is a doorway. When this door is open, more of our energy can come in, and it is the experience of the energy that opens the doors within yourself.

Ꭷ   Ꭷ   Ꭷ

   The nervous energy comes out in a different form in another workshop. In this case, Georgia missed the first group meeting with Moita and during a subsequent session finds herself suddenly plunged into a tub of warm feelings.

Georgia:	I feel so good. I kind of feel silly feeling so good.
MOITA:	Can you figure out why you feel so silly?
Georgia:	No.
Marcia:	Do you have this feeling like you just want to really smile a lot?
Georgia:	No, I just feel good! *(giggling)* Can *you* tell me why I feel so silly about it?
MOITA:	There seems to be an element of almost guilt, or a mixture of surprise, unexpected. Many people feel that when they feel good, there must be something wrong. *(pause)* Some people react to this energy rather violently, depending on where they are at the time, and how much they are able to let themselves flow with the feeling. This feeling is a reality of *my* world, and should be more of yours.

⁊   ⁊   ⁊

Moita obviously enjoys meeting each new group of people, as much as we enjoy sharing in their encounter. The next excerpt is from the night before the start of an "Expansion of Consciousness" workshop, in which we propose to be open to possibly frequent, spontaneous visits from Moita. This is also around the time a young reporter has decided *not* to do a story on us for a local magazine – because others have raised doubts in her mind about "black magic".

MOITA:	How do you think [the workshop group] will take to me?
David:	Oh, I expect it'll be really good – maybe a few uncertainties for a while.
MOITA:	I wonder! I have heard rumours *(we laugh)* that I am not what I appear to be! It is hard to even imagine that I am what I *appear*! *(laughter)* It would be easier if I fit into a tighter slot. Perhaps that is one of my engrained characteristics: I slosh over... *(laughter; long pause)*
David:	I was wondering how long people will take to stop trying to figure you out.
MOITA:	The longer they take, the harder I am to pin down.
David:	*(laughing)* I've noticed.
MOITA:	I can be tricky, and slippery like a fish – for my own reasons. If they could pin me down, what then? They would put me into a nice convenient slot and forget me.
David:	We experience the same problem sometimes.
MOITA:	Of being put into a slot and forgotten?!
David:	Or remembered. Either way! *(laughter)*
MOITA:	But still in a slot. People are very concerned about exactly what things are, instead of accepting diversity and just what *is*. At least *you* do not doubt my reality, even though it changes.
David:	If one doubts one's own, one doubts others' too, I guess.
MOITA:	You have been prepared well. *(pause)* Do you think I should pop in the first night? Or should my introduction be more leisurely and not unexpected?
David:	How can we decide now? I'm all for giving them a taste as soon as it would not be too upsetting.

MOITA: How can one plan?!... It shall be fun.

ക   ക   ക

(After spending the first workshop night "preparing" them, here's how things go the following week:)

MOITA: You can open your eyes.
Hazel: I can? Has everyone got their eyes open? *(laughter; pause)*
Owen: You certainly seem, uh, authoritative.
MOITA: *Me*? Hmm.
Owen: Well, not *authoritarian*. Authoritative.
MOITA: Perhaps a better word would be "knowing myself". I have no doubt.
Owen: I see. *(Moita laughs)* ...I take it you're not really offended by the doubts.
MOITA: If I were offended by doubt, that would mean that I doubted *myself*.
Owen: Exactly. *(laughing)* I find that reassuring in my *own* doubt.
MOITA: Well, if I was an imaginary creature, my existence would depend on others' belief. But I exist...
           (to Steven) Have you anything to say?
Steven: No. Still adjusting to the level, I guess.
     (Long pause. Moita looking at Tim:)
MOITA: Are you feeling put on the spot?
Tim: Yes! *(laughing)* I don't know what to say!
MOITA: There are many sessions that we have where few words are spoken. It is your inner experience that is important. I have been told I have a bad habit of making people uncomfortable... But it is not because I see anything I do not like.
Steven: *(laughing)* It's just very hard to deal with the energy and think of other things to say at the same time. *(laughter)*
Owen: It seems like a very convincing experience. It doesn't answer any of the speculative questions that we were asking, of course. *(laughing)*
Hazel: I feel very playful right now. Is that a normal aspect of this? *(much laughter)*
MOITA: Why worry?! *(laughing)*
Hazel: Well, I just asked the silliest question, so everyone should feel relieved about asking their question. *(laughter)*
MOITA: I must say, I am not always what others expect. I have images of high lofty words, of tight and dangerous energy, of earth-shattering revelations – many things I do not fit.

ക   ക   ക

When an individual, rather than a group, meets Moita for the first time, reactions can vary to either extreme, depending on that one person. The next example comes from the negative end of the spectrum. In this rare instance, the question foremost in the participant's mind becomes: "Who are you trying to kid?!"

Jerry is a young man who has tried a variety of consciousness-expansion groups and techniques, including psychedelic drugs and isolation tanks. Having had sporadic contacts with us in recent years – strangely enough, being the person who brought the two of us together[16] – he phones Kelly this day asking to talk over difficulties he is experiencing with his latest enthusiasm, tantric sex. Kelly soon concludes she alone can't help Jerry too much, given his very uneven energy, so she proposes a Moita session. It proves one of our strangest.

(After a period of silence, gazing at each other:)

MOITA: One who has used energy as much as you does not sense changes?

Jerry: I feel skeptical.

MOITA: Then feel skeptical. It does not hurt us. It is not always necessary to understand exactly what something is in order to change and learn.

Jerry: I feel that you're Kelly, and I should be taking care of my own shit.

MOITA: It is true that you're responsible for yourself. I am more than Kelly. Kelly is not one to use pretense. You could say that this is like the verbalization of your own wisdom, for the world is a mirror and what you see here is sometimes what you hope for and sometimes what you fear. As the same happens to you when you take drugs, the same happens to you when you do not – only, when you are more expanded you are more vulnerable, and more easily hurt, and more aware of change...

The form that you receive your own learning from is not as important as the love you put into it...

(Moita's message to Jerry about the path to spirit continues with the words concluding Chapter 4, including these: "I say that love does not try to control; love flows. And something that attempts control is not love... I have said once before that you cannot get into enlightenment by banging on the door and trying to knock it down. The door opens of itself.")

Jerry: Damn. I feel I'm Jerry, who should be taking care of his own shit. And I feel you're Kelly trying to help Jerry take care of his own shit, but I don't believe that Kelly can help Jerry take care of his own shit.

MOITA: What you believe will become reality.

(Jerry goes on to discuss his path and his view of reality, with Moita adding her comments when able. Finally:)

Jerry: Kelly, I know how to let it work, and there's nothing for me to do but to get into that, and I think I knew that from this morning on.

MOITA: So long as you learn to love, you shall do fine.

Jerry: *(laughing)* I'm going to go now. I've got stuff to do.

MOITA: You must wait, then, for Kelly.

Jerry: *(laughing hysterically)* Come on, Kelly.

MOITA: Goodbye.

(She closes her eyes and Kelly returns, quite mystified by the experience and somewhat upset at Jerry's complete lack of acceptance and grace.)

Jerry is an instance of someone acquainted with Kelly before Moita, and this *can* be a barrier to acknowledging a differentness. Moita once suggests as much at the start of a session with a new group. The first person to speak expresses her excitement and bewilderment by laughing and saying (with a meaning quite different than Jerry's), "I can't *believe* it!" Moita responds, "It is an idea that takes some adjusting. You have a certain advantage – all of you – since you do not know Kelly well. And so, you do not hold her here as much as those who are more familiar with her pattern."

On the other hand, those who do *not* know Kelly have less basis for distinguishing between the levels. Whichever the case, the presence of the medium in these communications can provide leeway for any doubts a person may have about the very existence or accessibility of non-physical beings: in other words, perhaps this is all the work of a good imagination – or good acting. When people are unsure about keeping their own balance amid the energy of the situation, these explanations can provide a handy refuge, a way of shielding out the intensity. Then arises the demand for "proof". But what is proof of reality or goodness to one is not to another. The openness or closure of the heart, and any inner fears, seem to decide how the mind will judge.

(Marion has been conversing with Moita for a long time, asking question after question about the soul, life after death, and religion, when she asks:)

Marion: Could you read that question in my mind? *(laughter)*

MOITA: *(smiling)* That is something you must decide for yourself. Have you another?

Marion: I just keep thinking this is ridiculous. *(laughing)* Like, I don't feel like I'm talking to you. I feel like I'm talking to Kelly. I'd like to see her separate from you, and then I could believe it.

MOITA: It is not so much if it is real that matters. It is if it is *worthwhile*.

Marion: *(pause, then laughs)* That's true.

Phyllis: Do you ever appear visually? Or are spirits that can't accept their own death *("ghosts")* the only ones that appear visually?

MOITA: They are not the only ones. Some have seen me visually, and there have been others that have been seen by many. It does not seem to prove our existence any more than this does.

Phyllis: Right. *(laughs)*

MOITA: There are always ways to talk yourself out of believing an experience if you wish to. Then again, it is also such an individual thing for those who have seen something happen. It can be that *they* believe there is something beyond themselves, but it may not be that they can convince another that what they have seen is real.

ॐ   ॐ   ॐ

MOITA: Sitting quietly, listening intently.

Ella: There's a lot going on in my head.

MOITA: Wondering greatly.

Ella: Right. I don't know why I feel so cynical about things that make so much sense to me. I keep hoping you're suddenly going to tell me something about myself I don't know, so that I'll know it's okay to believe things I believe, so I can let down my guard of doubt.

MOITA: It is not doubt so much as fear. You are afraid of yourself, as so many people are – afraid to find something you cannot face. But we are here to show you the part of yourself you are hiding, and to [show] there is nothing there to fear. There is love in the universe, and it is not hiding beneath the ground. It is there in the open, and you can grasp it.

Ella: I just always feel that my head's getting in the way of my heart.

MOITA: It is true. Love does not need to have analysts for understanding. Love is a force, an energy, a feeling – and not something that can be measured or seen with the eyes. It must be seen with the heart and accepted with the heart. The mind makes a bad master; it makes a fair tool. And if you let yourself be ruled by your mind, your heart will lie in waiting until your mind can no longer function.

Ella: So how do you shut off your mind?

MOITA: You don't shut it off so much as you allow your heart to open. Then your mind no longer rules; it merely serves. We are not here to destroy logic – but logic is misplaced. Because one is so busy looking, one never finds.

Ella: That's why I've never been able to be hypnotized. I'm so busy trying to be hypnotized, I . . .

MOITA: But you see: you *are* hypnotized, for you have hypnotized yourself into not seeing the world as it really is, as it feels in *its* reality. It is being afraid to be *un*hypnotized that blocks you.

Ella: What's the first step?

MOITA: Seeing beauty. Look on the world with the eyes of a child, with wonder. Remember those things you have known and put aside. The child within cries out for freedom – and he is not a tyrant.

Ella: Learn, and do not fear.

MOITA: If you can accept life as it is, fear will have no hold on you. You cannot fear what you understand. And if you do not fear what you do *not* understand, you will gradually grow to know it, for then you will not turn yourself aside...

Ella: I keep wishing you'd tell me something I didn't ask you. *(laughs)*

MOITA: But I am only here to answer questions, those that you know how to ask. For when I tell you answers, and you do not know the question, the answer will not be heard...

Ella: *(laughs)* I was thinking: all these "how to" questions I ask have been answered many times, if we'd only listen. And then I think: did *I* think that or did you tell me to think that?

MOITA: *(laughing)* And will you ever know?

Ella: I doubt it.

MOITA: And then: does it matter? The answers all come from within...

Ella: I always think: it's impossible that I could be hypnotized; it's impossible that I could actually talk with someone not entirely of this reality.

MOITA: You are beginning to see some of your own maze.

Ella: Oh, I do a real number on myself. I've suspected that for some time...

(Ella says she feels down deep she really does believe. Nevertheless, Moita addresses her closing words to whatever small part does not – and to many others:)

MOITA: It does not bother us if you do not believe, but it does please us when you can accept our energy as it is, without trying to worry about what it is. For even *we* cannot explain it to ourselves. To answer that question, you must be able to define life. And to answer that, you must have faith and believe that there is God, a universal mind, love, reality.

You think, you feel, you *are* real. You are not a passing fancy that is born, lives, suffers, enjoys, and knows no more. And you contribute your essence to the universe. Even when you are not aware of it, it works – for it is real.

Ella: Thanks.

MOITA: You are welcome. We hear your thoughts. They are not easy to answer, for many reasons.

ॐ   ॐ   ॐ

Another complication is that Moita and Kelly are *not* completely separate, and that Moita's awareness may merge with hers to some extent at other times than sessions. The more sensitive one is, the more one notices this, and wonders.

(C. is a self-reliant, unconventionally creative woman who prefers that we at least use her own initial rather than a pseudonym. In this group session, Moita looks at her for the first time during a silent period:)

MOITA: Why so nervous?

C.:   *(laughing)* I don't know. *(laughs; silence, then laughs again)* I don't care who you are, I like you. *(laughs)*

MOITA: Your energy is changing a great deal. *(pause)* Yes, you see me well.

C.:   I don't know if I do or not.

MOITA: From my perception, I see you do. *(long silence as they gaze)* Be at peace...

C.:   What do you see when you see us?

MOITA: It varies. You are each different!

C.:   Do you see all of us or a part? Can you focus on our conscious thoughts if we project them, or do you see our feelings and parts of ourselves that we can't see at all, perhaps?

MOITA: I see all of that, depending upon what I choose to focus on. I can focus on all of them at once or on one at a time.

C.:   Can you pick up one's conscious thoughts?

(Moita tells Kelly at this point that C. wishes her to answer telepathically a question that C. is asking in her mind.)

MOITA: Perhaps *I* can. But in order to convey that to you, I must do it *through* another. And so, you see, I am not working just with myself. I am working with myself and someone else's awareness. To come into your world through a body, I must be filtered. You cannot experience me directly in this form, nor can I express myself to you completely. I must use the tool that is available and the awareness through which I speak. Some things I can influence very greatly. Other things are not as easy, and much hinges on the acceptance and the belief of those present.

You can see instances where I have been able to convey the idea of telepathic communication – some very *clear* instances that have occurred in this kind of communication – but they are not things that I can do *directly*. I must be *sneaky*, and subtle, in order to seep through defences that are already in place. Does that explain things?

C.: *(laughing)* Maybe it does. I feel like part of me gets it, but consciously it's a little confused.

MOITA: Things will come...

(From the conversation afterward:)

C.: I was experiencing a sense of conflict between Moita and Kelly when she said I saw her clearly. I was seeing your features – but now you [Kelly] look different... The other day when I was talking to you, there was more of the kind of energy that comes through with Moita – enough so I find it really hard to separate what seems to be yours and what seems to be hers... I always felt like you were sitting there too.

Kelly: That's maybe why she gave you the speech on filtering.

∽   ∽   ∽   ∽

A letter from my own parents prompts this next exchange. Their liberal Christianity has not extended to psychic realities, so they are less than enthusiastic about my continued involvement in these communications.

MOITA: What do you think your parents would think of this?

David: Do you mean just any session, or this particular moment?

MOITA: *(laughing)* The energy at this particular moment is particularly good!

David: I'm afraid they would probably have great difficulty handling it – or letting it happen. But a lot would depend on preparation, and willingness to enter into preparation.

MOITA: It is interesting to see how my energy affects others. It is difficult to propose that it is their imagination when it does affect them. But then, many people think ideas have no effect, either.

∽   ∽   ∽

Speaking of parents, though, one initial meeting of Moita within the first year of our communications is unique: the one with Kelly's own mother. Marlene is living thousands of miles from us in late June 1978 when Moita begins speaking. One month later, Moita comes through while Kelly is in the midst of writing a letter home. Kelly grabs a new sheet of paper and lets the words flow, excerpted below.

My dearest Marlene –

Although it would be better for us to communicate in person so that you too could experience the energy of my essence, I feel (and the others who are with me on this level) that at this point some clarification may be necessary and desirable. Try to realize that words are difficult enough for us to use – and writing even more so because there is the lack of interaction between beings.

Even though you are physically many miles from Kelly, the close connections that you have together will serve as a means of producing many changes in you as well. Right now you are experiencing confusion and doubt about many aspects of your present life – where it will lead, and if it is leading anywhere at all.

As I have told many others since beginning this communication with your level through your current daughter, you also must learn to flow with the life force in a more direct and conscious manner.

At this point in time, many are experiencing the same doubts and openings. The texture of the world is changing, and all those who are already partially "tuned-in" to us will feel the effects at a highly accelerated pace. The confusion will be short-lived for those. However, for the majority of humankind the disorientation and confusion will continue to increase...

As a teacher, Kelly will be entering upon a very different kind of path than she has up until now. As in most of her past existences, she is an initiator of new ideas and concepts – and their application in everyday living...

Do not worry for her – she is in good and gentle hands. She is on the Path of Love, which is not an easy path, but one which leads to the Valley of Peace. Our love goes out from here to all of you in your distress and confusion – and you are doing well.

When next you see her, I shall speak to you in person. Until then, let your love shine on all.

MOITA

ဟ   ဟ   ဟ

Writing a letter is one thing. The following year, when we do visit Kelly's mother, all of us wonder how the transition from "current daughter" to "Moita" will be accomplished, and accepted. After all, Marlene is the person most closely associated with Kelly as a physical personality in this life, the one who might be expected to "hold her here" most tightly.

But Marlene was long ago forced to accommodate herself to Kelly's psychic nature

– one reason she's become involved in an Edgar Cayce study group in recent years. She has not placed barriers in the way of Kelly's freedom to soar. Thus it all comes pretty naturally – easier than for Marlene's friend Frank, who has met neither Moita nor Kelly before. (By the way, Kelly herself often gets nervous before sessions, and this, understandably, is one of those times!)

Marlene: Hi.
MOITA: Hi.
Marlene: It's nice to meet you at last.
MOITA: You have heard a great deal about me.
Marlene: Yes, I have! All good.
MOITA: Fortunate! *(silence; looking toward Frank)* And what do you see?
Frank: I don't know. Not sure. Not sure I understand.
MOITA: What is it you do not understand?
Frank: Whom I'm talking to.
MOITA: *(to Marlene)* Do *you*?
Marlene: Sure. *I* know whom I'm talking to.
Frank: Do you know me, or of me?
MOITA: Everyone knows of everyone. There are no secrets in the universe.
Frank: I don't see any secrets I can keep from *you*.
MOITA: Your secrets are safe with me.
Frank: You can look into someone's soul, obviously.
MOITA: But I may see something you do not suspect.
Frank: What is there is there.
MOITA: But letting it out is the trick...
Marlene: You enjoy being with Kelly, huh? *(Moita smiles)* I'm sure – silly question!
MOITA: She is not the only place I am, though!
Marlene: Yes, I understand that. You must be very busy between trips to Kelly.
MOITA: Even as I am here! Not all of me can come at once.
Marlene: Hmm, I haven't thought about that. Kind of a big thing to hold onto, isn't it! *(laughing)*
MOITA: It takes time to expand yourself to a point where you can take all this in.
Marlene: How would I go about getting to know my . . . what you call yourself – uh, higher entity? I don't know what the term is.
MOITA: Terms are somewhat misleading. A word has a tendency to constrict a thought into a certain form. And then if the thing it is supposed to be describing does not all fit into that, there are many things that can be missed.
Marlene: That's very true. Words *are* kind of a difficult form of communication. Let's see, how do I put this question, then?
MOITA: You want to know how to get in touch with *yours*.
Marlene: Right.
MOITA: You are well on your way.
Marlene: Oh, okay. You mean I'm heading in the right direction? There's *hope*. *(laughter)*

MOITA: There is always hope.

Marlene: Oh, I know that. You're joking with me. Well, why don't you ask a question, Frank?

Frank: I get the feeling that you like to toy with us to an extent. Is that true?

MOITA: "Toy". *(pause)* It depends on what you mean by "toy".

Frank: Not in a . . . I mean, you're kind of teasing us.

MOITA: I admit to having what has been called a sense of humour... *(laughter)* Are you experiencing the changes of energy here?

Frank: Yes, I did, especially at first, before you came. Why is that?

(Afterward, Frank will describe having seen in his mind's eye "these lights flashing in different patterns like checkerboard squares, but differently shaped – really weird.")

MOITA: You have never had this kind of contact?

Frank: No, not that I can recall.

MOITA: As you focus yourself in physical form, in order for me to be here enough, I must also focus a part of myself. The focusing of myself is like taking an expanded light that spreads out in many directions and gathering it together into a pinpoint of brightness that aims only in one direction. So, in some ways my energy is concentrated in one specific area – most of my energy, a part of my energy. This concentrated energy affects those around where I am.

Frank: That is strange. You must give off a different type energy, for I've never experienced anything quite like that.

MOITA: I am a different type of being than those you have experienced, since I have not had a body in so many, many years. I bring with me my view of the universe, and some of my own reality also leaks through.

Frank: This is entirely new to me. It's hard for me to grasp.

MOITA: Well, we are here to let you experience it.

Frank: Why do I feel strange?

MOITA: These are different waters than you are used to.

Marlene: It's like a charge!

MOITA: I am a doorway into your self.

Marlene: I feel like a battery being charged up. *(laughing)* That's what the energy feels like to me. *(silently mouthing the effect on her: "boing")*

MOITA: "Boing" is a good description! *(laughter)*

Marlene: You've got a beautiful smile.

MOITA: Thank you. I make her face sore!

Marlene: *(laughing)* Do you really?! I can't imagine anyone's face being sore from smiling.

MOITA: You have not been inside this face! *(laughing)* There is some intensity to my smile, I suppose. It comes from the energy.

Marlene: Yeah, I would imagine. It's got to go somewhere.

Frank: You seem to draw great pleasure from this interchange with us, is this it?

MOITA: This is part of my work.

Frank: Do we have this same kind of interchange at the spirit level?

MOITA: There are certain reasons why this particular interchange is happening and the other is not at the moment. We are trying to help you understand how you create your reality in a slower fashion, in some senses, than by taking your soul out of your body and having you experience direct communication between souls. There are very few of you who could retain your sense of balance in that kind of an interchange.

If you were on our level now, you would have many things around you that you would not understand: thoughts that would distract you, things that you would see, that you were creating yourself but were not aware of creating.[17N] By our entering your focus and gradually unfocusing you, it makes it easier for you to see these things for what they are.

Frank: Yes, but you're in a complete atmosphere of total love, and on this plane we don't have that. I'm sure that it's much easier to grasp these things when there's such a total feeling of love around you. On this plane, it's much harder to demonstrate these things, too. I guess this is our proving ground here. Am I right in this?

MOITA: This is your school in many ways, but you are here to learn how to let this energy flow through you without blocking it up.

Frank: I've felt many times that there's like a curtain between me and something. I entered from the other side through this curtain and I couldn't see back through. But I know what's beyond that curtain, and sometime I'll go back through. That's the way I've thought about my consciousness: there's this curtain between me and all the knowledge of the universe. Going from one plane to another is for me like walking through this curtain.

MOITA: That certainly is not very difficult when it comes down to it.

Frank: No, what amazes me is the simplicity of it...

(From the conversation afterward:)

Marlene: This was a new experience for me... The energy, it was really tremendous. It was pulsating – and not just my hands. This was like I was getting a very heavy electric charge through my whole body – not a hurting kind, but I was buzzing, and everything else was . . . I don't get that much energy when I meditate. I feel like I've had a tremendous . . . like the best meditation I've ever had!

You almost looked stern, Frank!

Frank: Well, she looks right into your soul, you know. You want to check to make sure it's clean! *(laughter)*

Kelly: Yeah, I could feel a real intensity happening between them.

Marlene: You weren't sure that it was Moita, right?

Frank: That is irrelevant. The look that she has – you don't know, whoever it is, Moita or Kelly – looks right into your soul, and there's nothing that's not there for that look, wherever it comes from.

Kelly: A lot of people get that feeling, that they feel naked all of a sudden – nowhere to hide.

Marlene: I didn't feel at all uncomfortable, though. It was really neat. I felt like grinning like a Cheshire cat all the time. I felt like an idiot, feeling so good.

Frank: She looked at me like someone who hadn't seen me for a long time. She looked at me for a long, long time, and it was a pleasant look.

Marlene: Long lost friends...

Frank: I've never seen anybody look at somebody with such total love.

David: What seems to make that loving possible is the total assurance of her own centre, her own existence.

Frank: But at the same time there's this Puckish attitude, like she's having fun with us – not a cruel fun, you know what I mean? Like she knows there's something really good about us, some really good surprise that's in store for us, and she's kind of smiling and keeping it to herself.

Kelly: Not to spoil the surprise! *(laughing)*

ର   ର   ର

Occasionally, the higher energies of those involved seem to have "divinely manipulated" the possibility of a first encounter with Moita. And as the meeting occurs, some of those energies are released to consciousness. A good example of this comes in the summer of 1980, when we have taken up our rural (and phone-less) existence in the British Columbia interior.

Earlier this year we received a letter from Judi, a staff member at Elisabeth Kübler-Ross's healing centre in California. Having run across copies of our *Rays* journal in the centre's library, she wrote to us: "The communications from Moita are always profoundly moving for me, and I would feel very honoured to have the opportunity to share in this experience with you." Though Judi's original hope to connect with us on an anticipated trip to Vancouver was disappointed, she subsequently wrote: "Please know I feel a very strong drawing toward each of you, as well as toward Moita and her lovely messages, and feel in my heart that our meeting will unfold according to plan."

Two months later, Judi learns that an upcoming speaking tour from her centre will include a stop in south-central B.C. Though travelling has never been part of her job there, she writes: "I...will remain open to the possibility, as the Universe indeed holds some fun surprises." The next month, because we have invited her to visit, Judi is offered the chance to accompany the tour! But then complications of all kinds arise – including how to journey the 650 air miles from a small border town across mountainous British Columbia to our isolated valley, and then, after whatever time is left for visiting, travel many more air miles back to Vancouver for the return flight to California, all between a Friday and a Sunday!

Thus the plan collapses – so we are told. Until, on that Saturday afternoon, a woman arrives at the only lodge in our valley, asking how to find us; and our friend Mike, who happens to be there and guesses who she is, phones another friend's house, where Kelly just happens to be. Mike agrees to drive Judi up to our cabin while Kelly waits for me to arrive back from town. This gives Judi a chance to slow down *a little* on our deck overlooking the river.

An hour later, we are hugging hello and learning how Judi ran into an old friend, who drove her the 300-plus miles from Grand Forks, B.C., to Vancouver all through Friday night, where she caught the morning flight north. (Her friend told her she was crazy to fly to a place she'd never been, to visit people she'd never met, who didn't even know she was coming. But Judi trusted her intuition and went ahead.) And just to prove her intuition right: waiting to board her flight, she inquired of two children, who, being from our valley and knowing us, volunteered her a ride in their family's car for the 60-mile drive from the airport to our valley lodge.

As Judi will describe it later, "The entire journey and visit with you seem almost like a dream. I feel as if I am in some altered state of consciousness the entire time, which is probably greatly due to arriving without having slept for 30 hours!" Referring to the session we hold with her that Saturday night, she also will say, "The transcript continually takes on new meaning for me, and I have truly been touched by the depth of Moita's wisdom."

This session, to be further excerpted in another chapter, touches on many subjects. But the few exchanges below seem to focus the energy of that first meeting, as also the theme of this chapter.

Judi: Moita, I have felt very drawn to being here tonight, and things have happened very easily to bring me here, and I come as a listener to find out why. (pause)

MOITA: You have sought this kind of tangible contact in this life. You wish to be able to set aside what doubts still linger in your heart. In order for you to truly meet a spiritual presence, you must open your heart to the love that we bring, and in this feeling recognize other times that we have touched you in your life. You are opening up a gateway for my energy to flow in, and so the energy changes as your perception opens.

Judi: I felt very touched by the words that David and Kelly sent, and I felt a truth in them when they arrived. But I feel confusion still as to the strength of the pull to be here. I feel a strong inner connection with my own guidance, and yet there must be something being said that I'm not hearing that necessitates this meeting. Can you give me more clarity on that?

MOITA: In my function, I can be the speaker for your own doubts, even those you are not aware of. But to give them a name, to tell you "This is where you fail," will not help you grow towards it but turn you away. There will always be some things left that you do not hear. It is in trying to listen to the unheard that you grow more towards becoming a greater self. It is so even *here*. I am learning to listen to voices that I have never heard before. It is growth: expanding, broadening the scope of understanding.

There is a difference between feeling certain of yourself and feeling certain of your heart, of that touching. You are here, you are drawn, for confirmation.

(While Moita's presence is very clear and deep, she is perhaps taking care not to say anything dramatic, lest Judi lose her own centring in attachment to people so far from home. Her feelings find resolution at a later point in the session:)

Judi: I feel again that my mind is searching for questions in every place but in my heart. I've come a long way. Is there anything else that you can see needs to be said, without me limiting it with my own question?

MOITA: The only path you need is love, and you will find love in joy as well as pain, in acceptance... More helpful than my words is my energy, for it is the *total* – my words are but the part. Language is itself a structure that limits what I can say. But thoughts have no such limit, when they are unbound by love. *(a silence, as Moita continues to look on her)*

Judi: I don't have any questions. *(soft laughter)*

ও   ও   ও

SUPPLEMENT: SESSIONS WITH CHILDREN

This chapter feels incomplete without an example of Moita speaking with young people and of their reactions to her energy and presence. This addition will also settle one issue: it is not Kelly's mother, but her youngest child Arista, who can "hold Kelly here most tightly". Arista proves this, at age five, during the earliest session we allow her to attend, by squeezing Kelly's nose – hard – to stop her from being Moita! Three years older, Donovan – who sees auras and has extended dream adventures, even out-of-body experiences – has proven more receptive to Moita from the beginning.

The following conversations happen two years later when Ben, one of Donovan's school buddies, comes to stay with us while his parents (our friends) are away. Though it is already a change of pace for Ben to be spending a week in our more remote country home, he also asks to see what this Moita business is all about.*

Whatever natural advantages children may hold in terms of openness, there are obstacles to their appreciation of Moita (especially when the medium is "Mommy"!). Physical, personal and psychic levels are less differentiated than they are for adults, so it is more of a challenge to rise above body and ego reactions while interacting with her energy. In the end, though, above a certain age threshold, the quality of a child's soul is able to shine through. The two older boys' experiences during the second of these sessions demonstrate this.

Much must be cleared away, though, during the first of the sessions with Ben (10), Donovan (9) and Arista (7). Arista mainly succeeds in proving she is not daunted by older people trying to be serious – especially when it's all obviously a game!

Donovan: Hello.

Arista: Hello. *(giggles)*

MOITA: We have quite the audience!

David: How do you experience the energy of the younger ones? *(pause)*

MOITA: A sense of freshness, not as many preconceived ideas, a little nervousness. Tell me . . . *(to Arista, who has begun to giggle more and more loudly)*

---

* We only hold Moita sessions with local young people who have their parents' permission.

Arista: What?

MOITA: . . . does my presence make you want to giggle?

(Arista giggles hysterically. Donovan expresses his distaste for how she's laughing.)

David: *(to Arista)* Did you have any questions for Moita? *(Arista shakes her head.)* Maybe you'll think of something. Does someone else?

MOITA: All of a sudden, nobody can remember. I've heard many questions of me... *(to Ben)* You look as if you were about to break out in a cold sweat. *(laughter; then, after a question from Donovan:)*

Arista: Are you out of your body, Mom?

MOITA: Your Mum is still here... She is not completely out of her body... *(pause; Arista laughs loudly, then starts burping on purpose and giggling)* It is hard to talk with other people when you are doing that. Do you know why you wanted to come? *(Arista shakes her head.)* Have you tried to understand why you wanted to come?...

(Both Ben and Donovan deny they have any questions.)

MOITA: That is not true. You just can't think of them right now...

(After some prompting from me:)

Donovan: Was my out-of-body experience really true?

MOITA: Do you mean, was it real? Yes. There are many things that are real that you cannot usually see.

Donovan: What was the light that I followed, floating out through the wall?

Arista: How come you're saying that in that voice, Mom?! Mom!

MOITA: It was your own higher self.

Donovan: It was?

MOITA: Your guide . . .

Arista: Mommy? Mom!

MOITA: . . . and teacher.

Arista: Mommy.

MOITA: *(to me:)* Perhaps it is time for her to retire. She is not gaining much from this experience at the moment.

Donovan: Am I right that this is her second time at a Moita session?

MOITA: She has met me before. The last time we met, she pulled Kelly's nose. *(Arista giggles.)*

Donovan: It hurt you?

MOITA: Not *I*. I have no nose.

Arista: Yes, you do.

MOITA: I will *wait*.

(This said pointedly to me – as I take Arista to bed. Meanwhile Donovan and Ben begin asking questions about Moita's reality.)

MOITA: I am a teacher for *many* souls. Yet each soul I am a teacher for has their own entity too... I am sort of like a grandparent.

Donovan: Are you like a grandparent for all?

MOITA: Not for all. What you conceive of as God is the grandparent for all. I am one step closer to the source than your own higher self...

    (to Ben) What is your experience of the energy?

Ben: Nervousness.

MOITA: Why are you nervous? *(Ben shrugs; long pause)*

    (to Donovan) Are *you* nervous?

Donovan: Yes, a little.

MOITA: What do you see?

Donovan: I don't know. I sort of see into nothingness. I look into the air around things.

MOITA: Am I fading away?

Donovan: A little bit. How did you know?

MOITA: I see into your heart... You are trying to see my spirit.

Donovan: Am I?

MOITA: In order to do that, you must look beyond the body. You must allow it to melt or disappear in some way. You are seeing with different eyes. The soul has eyes too...

Donovan: It's a little hard. *(pause)* Something keeps trying to stop it.

MOITA: Now we are gaining distance! Your depth perception is altered. I look farther or closer than I did before.

Donovan: Right now you are disappearing. You look funny. You fade away, then you get closer, then you get farther.

MOITA: Do you think it's real?

Donovan: Somehow I *do*...

MOITA: You are not frightened?

Donovan: No.

MOITA: Do you know why?

Donovan: No.

MOITA: Do you think you should be?

Donovan: Yes. *(laughs)*

MOITA: *(to Ben)* Are you feeling any more comfortable?

Ben: A little. *(pause)* Do you know why I'm scared? Can you tell?

MOITA: You are afraid of the idea of a spirit that can see you at all times, know you for who you are. You need not fear. I will keep your integrity intact. Your self, your heart, is safe with me. I am not here to reveal to you your failings. I am here to illuminate your beauty. Things that are new are very often frightening – not because they are bad in themselves but because they are unknown... Do you know what I mean? Does that help you feel better?

Ben: Yep.

    (Meanwhile Donovan is becoming distracting as he plays with the idea of leaving his body, physically leaning back out of the circle and interrupting to ask Moita about it.)

MOITA: *(to Donovan)* I have given you a great deal of attention. Now I am giving it to someone else. You are trying to gain the attention back...

    (to Ben) We will talk again... And then I will speak to you of other things,

for by then you will feel more comfortable with the idea, and many of those questions that I see churning within you will have an opportunity to be released. *(laughter)*

Ben: Ha, I might be chicken next time.

MOITA: You will not chicken out on me next time. I am *certain* of it! *(smiling)* I will say good night to you both for now. Good night.

Donovan/Ben: Good night.

(From our conversation after the boys go to bed:)

Kelly: Donovan looked really neat. He looked really clear there for a while. His face was starting to change for me, starting to look like a man instead of a boy. He certainly was getting more light as Moita looked at him. And Ben too. I could hear her talking to him in my mind before he finally asked if she knew why he was afraid. I could hear her telling him he needn't be, that his secrets were safe with her. It was interesting to see that he had the same fears as other people, despite the difference in age. The fear is exactly the same.

David: I never would have looked at it in terms of secrets, but I identified with his space a lot. I could see how "on the spot" he was feeling, and felt uncomfortable myself for him. Moita's presence is so strong and direct, it forces you either to retreat or to really get yourself together – speak out of some strength inside you that a lot of people aren't in touch with.

❧   ❧   ❧

The success of our second session with the boys is partly credited to having them draw up a list of their questions beforehand. I will quote one example, chosen partly because psychic abilities are far less rare among children than we may think. They deserve the same acceptance and encouragement as any natural talent, if not used disruptively.

Donovan: Why do I see auras when most other people don't?

MOITA: Do you enjoy being able to see colours around other people? *(Donovan nods)* Do you know what it can be used for?

Donovan: I think I sort of do and I sort of don't.

MOITA: The colours that you see around others, when you learn more about them, can tell you if they are sick or healthy, if they are happy or sad. They can even tell you what kind of past lives they have led.

Donovan: Oh boy.

MOITA: It is a very useful talent to be able to see auras – or rather, to be able to *interpret* what you see. You have this talent because at some point in the future your being able to see what is going on around a person's body is going to be very important – not only to yourself but to helping others. This is one way in which you can contribute, can give...

But there is a great deal for you to go through first before you will be able to utilize this. That you can still see auras at this age is a sign that you will probably not lose this ability as you grow older. It is also a sign that you have made some advances in your spiritual growth that will come out once you have worked through your older lessons.

(Ben lets himself open to the energy much more this time as well. In the after-session conversation, he says this to Kelly:)

Ben: I was seeing sort of the inside of Moita or you. Like, I could see your bones on the right part of your face. And I was more spaced out than I was before. Whenever I closed my eyes and opened them, I could see an orange sort of sun on your forehead right here *(pointing to Kelly's third eye)*. Like, it was focusing, 'cause it would move around and then stop in the centre. It was on there the whole session, just about. And then it went away just now when she left.

Kelly: How about you, Donovan? What did you experience?

Donovan: I saw a halo around your head. I was all spaced out. I felt like I was about to fall down.

Kelly: Yeah, you looked it too. I'm surprised you're still functioning. Did you really hear what Moita said?

Donovan: Yeah, except I sort of couldn't make them into words.

Ben: I heard every word she said.

Donovan: I heard the words, except she talks a little too fast sometimes.

Kelly: Fast?! Moita?!

Ben: She talks *slow*!

Kelly: I never noticed her talking fast! You must have been in a strange speed place or something. You were so slowed down that stop would be fast.

David: I enjoyed looking at you, Donovan, especially when Moita was talking to you. Because you were listening – even though I'm not sure what you were *hearing* – but you were focused on her instead of going all over the place. And you seemed serious. I like the clown in you, but I like that part too.

∽   ∽   ∽

The ultimate compliment is paid on a later evening, when I remark, "Guess what's on tonight, guys!" Donovan and Ben both ask if I mean a Moita session. No, I say, it's the next episode in the *Star Wars* radio serial we've been following. "Oh, a Moita session is better than *Star Wars*," pipes up Donovan. "Yeah," says Ben. "*Way* better!"

∽   ∽   ∽

Chapter 2

LEARNING WHO YOU ARE

The path to spirit is simple – so simple, few see.
– Moita

In saying this, I believe Moita means the way is not complicated or abstruse – but also, not easy. It can be very difficult for us to become simple and return to the beginning, even to admit that the beginning lies within ourselves. It can be very difficult, when conditioned fears have enforced the opposite, to work that revolution in one's life that makes knowing and being oneself the root of all else.

The attempt to graft ourselves to some external support rather than seek our own deep roots is so engrained that so-called "spiritual development" can become one more distraction from the basic challenge of finding happiness and peace as whole and creative individuals on this Earth. It is not uncommon for people to view Moita as a means to perfecting this form of distraction – and some of her more pointed answers have come in response to questions with this motivation. As she once told us, "It is not always easy to tell who will and who will not be reluctant to learn who they are. Many fear what they will find – they have secrets they are keeping. It is difficult enough to keep a secret. In order to keep one, you must make quite a wall."

The wall that blocks a true spiritual opening of self may also twist into undesirable channels any psychic powers a person may develop. That is why the path to spirit rightly begins here, with the problems we face in our everyday search for meaning and growth as persons and in relationships.

Though Moita is a highly evolved being who, we learn, has not lived in a body nor been limited to a single personality for the last 50,000 or so of our years, she can so mingle herself with our experience that she almost becomes one of us. Her answers to these personal questions, while directed to a unique individual in a unique situation, reveal an extremely consistent philosophy of living – one that may prove as wise and practical in your own life as it has in ours.

Grandmotherly Sara welcomes us to her home – a pleasant enough bungalow that adjoins the appliance repair business she has run for many years with her husband. We spend the noon hour talking about her psychic interests and then arrange this session at a friend's apartment on a day that her husband – a large, red-faced man who is not open to these interests of his wife – will be out of town.

Unbeknownst to her spouse, she has requested us in hopes of realizing her dream: to learn to astral-travel to historical periods that fascinate her, allowing her to develop many new abilities she wishes to utilize in her present life. Her desire to leave her body behind, because she feels restricted by her life circumstances, illustrates the tendency to substitute "spiritual development" for things that must come first.

MOITA: *(to Sara)* You can open your eyes.

Sara: Oh, can I?! *(laughing, but then lowering her eyes, as they will remain throughout the session)*

MOITA: How are you feeling?

Sara: Okay... I don't know where to start. Am I likely to be able to go on astral journeys?

MOITA: Consciously?

Sara: Well, consciously or unconsciously – if I will be able to learn from these journeys?

MOITA: You leave your body every time you sleep, and you learn in the astral. The trick is remembering.

Sara: Mmm. But when I dream, I don't dream about things that I want to learn about. It's usually disconnected and nothing of any value.

MOITA: Ah, your dreams never speak to you of things that are not of value. They speak to you of things you have not seen or noticed, of things you are worried about, of things you are trying to understand. If they seem disconnected, you are not understanding their message.

Sara: Now, will I be able to consciously astral-project, and learn any of the subjects that I want to learn – like, specific things that I don't have to . . . that I can't learn from disconnected dreams?

MOITA: Before you will be able to learn those specific things in a conscious astral experience, before you will be able to leave your body as an aware individual, you must first understand what your dreams are telling you. The things your dreams are saying are those things which are keeping you from being able to leave your body.

Sara: Mmm. But how does one interpret a dream without knowing what the meanings are?

MOITA: Your dreams speak to you in symbols of things that happen around you. If your dreams feel disconnected, it may reflect your own feeling of being disconnected from yourself during your waking hours. It is the feeling that your dreams bring up within you that will help you understand what it is they are pointing to. [Dreams] are where your feelings do not hide from you anything at all – either about yourself or those around you. And dealing with these things will help...take away the feeling of not being joined with yourself.

Sara: Mmm. In other words, I have to know myself better to be able to do these things.

MOITA: When you leave a body behind, ...you are leaving...what you associate as a haven, something to protect you. It is heavy and dense, although it has feelings. But a spirit is light and free, can travel through things that you in your body cannot, can go into space and visit other worlds and visit other times. These are concepts that are not as easily accepted. Just because you leave a body does not mean that you leave yourself. You will bring all those things that are *you* with you when you go.

Sara: Now, is it safe to make astral journeys? What would be the danger, if any? And how would I safeguard the return of my spirit to the body again?

MOITA: If you can leave your body behind without fear in yourself, then no fear can come to you. These non-physical dimensions are filled with thoughts, but they are also filled with *us*. No one has an experience they do not wish to have. So, if for some reason inside yourself you desire to have your body entered by another spirit, it will happen, if you think this will teach you a lesson that you feel you need to learn in this life. I do not perceive that this is your purpose in being here. If it were, most likely it would have happened already, when you were much younger...

(Sara goes on to ask a number of questions about family members. Then:)

Sara: I just can't think of anything more right now.

MOITA: Just let yourself go. If your thoughts are cloudy during the day, it is because your heart is not speaking to you. You must learn how to listen to yourself.

Sara: My problem is, I have so many things I would like to do and I don't know where to start first.

MOITA: When they say "charity begins at home," they mean it begins with yourself. Many of these things may not be essential to your development. Some are your desires to please others rather than your desire to grow more, and others are attached to your need to express creatively who you are without having to please others at the same time. If you take one step, accept yourself and love yourself and let yourself flow outwards into your life. You will see that your life will change in ways you may not be able to anticipate.

Sara: Well, I've always been taught to think of others, and I've always tried to see to the needs of my family to the best of my ability – often not doing what I personally would like to do for myself. Now, are you saying that I should be more selfish and think of myself more?

MOITA: Learning to be yourself does not mean, in the end, letting go of your concern for other people. It does not mean not helping others. But it does mean that your capacity to love, and your ability to help in any more constructive way, is lessened when it is not given from a centre of balance and growth that comes from within. A gift that is given when it is not wished, or when it is not given freely, is not a gift at all.

It is important to start from the moment – not to embroil yourself in the past – for your life begins from where you are, not from where you have been. It is sometimes difficult to explain in words what it means to be whole and able to share your wholeness with others gladly.

Sara: When you say to develop myself, are you talking in a spiritual manner now – to develop spiritual qualities, or to develop my potentialities as a person on this earth?

MOITA: It is best not to separate them – they should both be the same. One should flow from the other and into the other. Developing yourself as a person here in a body, so that you are expressing your inner nature in a physical form, is one of the things everyone needs to learn. It is not healthy nor balanced to wish only to have what others may call "spiritual virtues".

Sara: Well, I'd like to develop my qualities – as you say, doing the things that are creative that I enjoy doing. It would make me a more whole person. But circumstances being what they are, I have to work in a job which I do not like and that causes a lot of frustrations. I simply do not have the time nor the space to do what I would like to do.

MOITA: If circumstances are destructive to you as a person, they will also be destructive to those around you who relate to you as a person. There are always choices that can be made if you can find them within yourself and make those choices. These are yours to make...

Sara: Can you tell me who my guardian angels are?

MOITA: When you open yourself up enough to be able [to hear them], they shall tell you their names. But there are energies around you that help to guide you and give you strength – as much as you will open yourself to it. The names are not important; it is the energy and the love that make the difference. Identify them within yourself as a feeling and as an acceptance, and that will bring them to you.

Sara: I can't think of anything else right now.

MOITA: Since you cannot think, why don't you just *feel* for a while and let us flow into you. *(a couple minutes' silence)*

MOITA: I shall say goodbye to you for now...

(As Moita leaves, Kelly returns.)

Kelly: I saw you glowing at the end. All of a sudden my eyes changed and your sweater got white instead of blue – just like a light that was shining.

After the session, Sara describes one of her typically "nonsensical" dreams. In the dream Sara and her mother-in-law are trying to close the door of the mother-in-law's house, which is being blocked by a huge bear. Outside the house are cane fields. To Sara, looking at it literally, this dream appears merely crazy.

Afterward, though, we wonder if Sara wants to "close the door" to something in her life and feels blocked from doing so by powerful forces (the bear). By Sara asking what she has in common with her mother-in-law, she may realize why they are struggling together in the dream. The cane fields may also be suggestive to her – perhaps of dull, repetitive labour.

The more we think about it, the more it seems to us that the dream, taken symbolically, is describing her personal predicament quite precisely – and posing the difficult choices she now faces.

 ❧ ❧ ❧

Underlying Sara's premature hope for psychic openings lies a doubting of her inner self and its messages as a guide for living – with resulting fear of action to satisfy her own real needs. This fundamental doubting of self is made explicit – and taken to an extreme – in the following one-on-one exchange with a morose young man previously acquainted with Kelly. As well as having once glimpsed a negative thought-form and taken it for his own entity, Gene may be feeling uneasy or guilty about some current relationship issues in his life.

Gene: Why have you consented to talk to me?

MOITA: It was felt at this time in your life it might prove beneficial for you to have such contact. It was discussed before between myself and your entity.

Gene: Aren't you afraid of me?

MOITA: *(laughing)* Why should I fear you?

Gene: I'm evil. I know my entity is evil. I've seen him; I know. Doesn't that frighten you?

MOITA: You are not evil, Gene. No one is truly evil. And on my level there is no fear. When you can come to the point where you realize this, you will have made great strides forward in your development.

Gene: You don't believe in evil?

MOITA: An entity, in its development, makes many mistakes. That is how it learns what is beneficial and what is not. Seeming evil is the learning of this lesson. *(looking with great concern)* Do not think that you are inherently evil. You are not alone in this fear. Many have felt the same way you do. Much of the evil you see stems from your own fear of it. Ask Kelly sometime about the reality of thought-forms. As with everything else, you create your own evil.

Gene: I still call it conscience.

MOITA: Every soul has its own code of ethics and its own method of punishing itself for past mistakes. Do not be overly hard on yourself...

Gene: You know I'm not ready for this.

MOITA: I know you do not believe that you are. It would be easier for you to see me more clearly if there were other people present. Their added energy would make this particular communication easier. The quality of the energy is important.

Gene: Yes, but then I would feel . . .

MOITA: Inhibited?

Gene: Yeah, the same thing. Why are you here?

MOITA: To show...by my presence what it is you are looking for... To show that love is a very real and vital energy. You too have a higher self, as does everyone. You may choose to evolve to that level, to that self. It is, however, not a foregone conclusion that you will. It is entirely up to you. You may reject that future...

Before I leave, I wish to say something to you that may help you through this time of pain. Even though you may not be consciously aware of it, there are those of us on this level who are with you helping you as much as you will allow us. There is a great deal of love here, for you. Please remember that even in your greatest pain you are never truly alone. We are with you. *(pause)* I fear this may be of little comfort, however.

Gene: No, it helps. It really does. *(a warm and smiling silence)* Thank you for coming.

(During the session, Gene also volunteered to Moita that he thinks she is "good for Kelly". "I had thought," he went on, "that maybe you were a schizo something, but I see now that you are not. You seem to have given Kelly serenity – something she didn't possess before.")

ઉ   ઉ   ઉ

This next exchange, during the first dream workshop Kelly and I ever give together, shows the beginnings of movement out of a bind similar to Gene's fears. In the first session of this two-day seminar,[18] Kathy revealed her deep interest in dreams and Moita's reality, and also a strong emotional attachment to someone close to her who has died. Now, on the second day, she voices more directly what she is feeling about herself.

Kathy: Am I afraid to see myself as I really am? Do I hide things from myself purposely?

MOITA: You are afraid to see yourself as you fear you are, not as you actually are. The things that you hide from yourself are things that you think would look ugly to someone else's eyes if you let them out – and to your own. But if you let them out, they are not ugly at all because each one of you is beautiful and has [her] own purity – if you are allowed to touch your self. Everyone is different. Everyone is a different expression of the divine energy, and all true expressions of that energy are beautiful.

It is when they are warped or thwarted and when the energy is stopped or plugged that the idea of ugliness arises. You should not fear yourself. Even emotions and energies that look ugly to start, once they are gone through to their beginning and understood, are transformed and changed. The only thing that can hurt you is something that you fear will.

Kathy: I just feel a lot of guilt and I want to know how I can get rid of it.

MOITA: By expressing your anger – why you feel guilty. You have to let those things out, because by keeping them in you block yourself. By letting them out you can see them clearly and understand them and then deal with them. The emotions that are suppressed are the ones that cause harm. Any feeling you have can be a healthy feeling providing it is not locked in.

You must also learn to take care of yourself. You are just as important as everyone else, and you cannot love another unless you love yourself first. I am not perfect, nor is anyone I know. Perfection means [that] you have stopped and you have reached your goal, [that] you are finished. To me, perfection is death. Once an end is reached, where else is there to go? To learn is the joy of life, and to find new things all the time, always changing. Do not hold yourself in bondage by an idea of who you think you should be. Let yourself bloom.

In another workshop encounter, Moita brings up an irony that is surprisingly common among us.

MOITA: Do not be afraid to be happy. There is that place of happiness deep within, even in times of turmoil.

C.: It's a very strange thing to be afraid of! *(laughing)* I don't quite understand why I am.

MOITA: It is not very unusual for this world to fear happiness.

C.: Because it makes one so open, and then the pain comes down.

MOITA: One cannot love unless one is vulnerable. You must strip away your armour of protection and take the risk of pain.

C.: Mm-hmm.

MOITA: There is strength in this, though – strength of self. Even if you go through pain, if you do not lose that centre, that knowing, it is something you can carry with you... It is all so simple when you believe in yourself.

From Moita's perspective, all the levels of suffering and negativity in our lives teach their own cure – and are there for that purpose. She gives such a message to us below, in the midst of some of our own trials.

MOITA: There are many interesting events ahead. View all these happenings as things that are being shown to you, as something of yourself. You can find out your own weaknesses and learn your own strengths. Pay particular attention to when you feel reluctant or when you feel afraid or when something is not pleasing you. Those are all doors that lead to your innermost self, through which you can travel.

In the following case, a young couple has just described to Kelly the problems with people and practicalities they have been having ever since moving to a new city.

Scott: Can you tell us why we have been having so much trouble here?

MOITA: It was necessary so you could learn to find your own centre.

Scott: What do you mean by "centre"?

MOITA: That place within yourself in which you are in a state of balance... When you are centred, ...outside influences, other people and their thoughts, will not and cannot affect you in the ways in which they have. Not that others will have no effect on you whatsoever, but they will not be able to get you off-balance, to make you lose your centre.

Scott: What do you mean about others not being able to influence us?

MOITA: You will be able to withstand the pressure of the status quo.

Scott: Yes, I see what you mean.

⅋   ⅋   ⅋

This "status quo" is especially hard to withstand when it is an emotional reality –
not just in others but in one's own self. In the following two excerpts, Moita offers her
perspective on an upsetting situation in which we are personally involved.

MOITA: As a person becomes clear about who [one] is and what [one] truly feels,
others may miss the familiar emotions and perhaps accuse [him or her] of
being "cold". Emotions and feelings are two different things. Emotions arise
out of fear and doubt; they are easily manipulated by others. Feelings arise out
of truth. They are what they are. They are the real you and can't be
manipulated.

MOITA: Love is not an easy concept for you to understand on this level. On our
level it is far easier because we do not have the blocks that you do, at least not
the same kind. You must learn to separate your feelings and your emotions.
Emotions have a tendency to cloud your mind, whereas feelings are things that
well up from deep within the soul and do not cloud but clear. It is important for
all of you to be able to distinguish the difference. It is not always an easy thing.

⅋   ⅋   ⅋

The following group interaction is initiated by Helen, a woman concerned about
her changing, perhaps dying, relationship with Jake. Here Moita distinguishes between
projecting emotions onto others and relating directly and deeply with people in the
present. (Due to an error in recording, part of the conversation – and much of Moita's
poetry – are unfortunately lost in this reconstruction.)

Helen: Could you tell me something about confusion – how it happens, how to
deal with it?

MOITA: Confusion happens when you are not clear. It helps you to gain perspective
if you can be by yourself for a while in order to get more in touch with your
inner self and your true feelings. Confusion often results when your thinking
gets in the way of your heart. And sometimes confusion happens when you are
not looking in the right place.

Helen: What do you mean about not looking in the right place? *(pause)*

MOITA: Let us say that you find yourself in a forest. The floor of the forest is
covered with a blanket of leaves...

(As Moita develops her metaphor, Kelly and others are seeing scenes of falling

leaves – some still a bit red and yellow but turning brown, some of them all brown, some already rotting beneath. The analogy Moita makes is that the fallen leaves are the past and the dying leaves on the trees are on their way to becoming past. To focus on the leaves – as in the absurd attempt to tape them back onto their branches – is to look in the wrong place. It is looking back to the past, trying to hold onto it and recreate it, rather than flowing with the changing seasons of life. The forest must go through its fall and its winter sleep before the rebirth that is spring.)

(Moita's last point is that we react emotionally on the basis of past expectations and definitions. The result is that we are not prepared for the changes that, with acceptance, can bring renewal and further growth.)

MOITA: ...If you fear tomorrow enough, you won't want to be here when it comes. Rather, listen to your true self, which lives in the changing moment.

Helen: Thank you.

Jake: What can Helen and I do about our confusion?

(Moita elaborates on her previous answer. She speaks of accepting change with equanimity, of helping needed change to come by dealing with the fear it involves, and thus of leaving the forest below, soaring above it. She suggests that by tuning into the rhythms of change in nature around us we can never feel depressed or alone, and that those same rhythms within us are the source of joy.)

MOITA: Would you be content to always see the sunrise and not also the full light of day or the night with its stars? *(pause)*

Jake: My heart understands, but I have a hard time grasping what you're saying in my mind.

MOITA: I am using images that are designed to help you listen to your heart. *(pause)*

Myrna: Emotions aren't bad, are they? You said something before about reacting emotionally being part of confusion.

MOITA: If you enjoy confusion, there is nothing wrong with emotion.

Myrna: But aren't emotions a basic part of a person?

(Moita stresses that emotions are reactions that do not clarify a situation: they are more on the surface and do not express who you are in a deep way. Feelings, on the other hand, come from within and enable you to see a situation whole, including the effect you are having on those around you.)

MOITA: At first it is difficult to tell them apart. Once you have experienced the difference, however, it is quite clear.

Jim: It seems to me that there is a great amount of individual growth going on lately. But also, there is a great strain on relationships – friendships, romances – at the same time. Is the coming New Age putting extra pressure on these things, or has it always been thus?

MOITA: People in bodies have always been making trouble for themselves. But as our world comes closer to yours, this tension will increase. It is becoming more and more difficult to hide from oneself or others. The walls are crumbling and false games are being torn away. People are searching to find what it is they really want in a relationship and this is frightening to many.

Jim: So will the lessons people are learning in relationships now help prepare them to handle the greater changes of the New Age?

MOITA: Those who can adapt and become strong will survive the changes to come...

Myrna: If emotions are confusing, what about love? Don't people consider love to be an emotion?

MOITA: Much depends on the level of love of which you speak, because love – when it is experienced as it should be – encompasses all facets of existence. It is the force which has created the world.

Myrna: So it's not fair to call love an emotion? Love shouldn't be confusing.

MOITA: If it is confusing, it is not love... But the word is used to describe emotions that are not necessarily connected with the true energy that is love. Love is not a feeling, either. Love is a *force*.

˛   ˛   ˛

In the extended dialogue with a close friend of ours that follows, Moita seems to be trying to allow for all the various possibilities of relationship: the emotions aroused through continuing or abandoning them, losing or preserving them; and the potential for growth either within or beyond them.

Paula: I'm not trusting myself very much, I know that.

MOITA: It is easier to give authority to others than to take the authority or responsibility upon yourself for making choices.

Paula: Mmm, that's been a bad pattern for me. It's been comfortable to stay in, and I've had a good excuse to rail at others when things didn't work out well.

MOITA: Learning to become more open to yourself is very much like being born. You are changing worlds.

Paula: There's no such thing, then, as choosing between one way for the better good and . . . I don't know. It seems I've been making choices between adventure and duty all my life, and choosing duty just about always and resenting it.

MOITA: This is where unselfish love becomes hatred. Love that is not given freely is not a gift but a weapon, and it is not love. Love comes from the heart, and it is given without condition and without regret.

Paula: Where does responsibility fit in with that – as in parenthood, for instance?

MOITA: When you can choose to let love flow, you will understand how that brings responsibility with it. You are responsible to allow yourself freedom to grow as an individual. But there are joint responsibilities, since choices were made about who would be together in a life.

          There are many times when beings choose to come together again in a new life to try to work through hatred or other similar emotions that they have created in another time. The only thing that can uncreate them is acceptance and love. But it must not be confused with duty. It is something that must be found and the doorway opened.

There is regret for duty when it is believed there were other possibilities that may have borne more fruit. But every life situation that you are in or might be in will bear as much.

Paula: Then there is an obligation to go through with previous commitments in a lifetime (?).

MOITA: These are not things that are easily spoken of in generalities, for each life and each case is different. For some it is necessary for them, in order to realize their potential as people, to make new commitments. For others it is important for them to learn how to change their reality where they are. To make a change or a choice of that kind, it needs to come from a very clear place.

If the choice is made unclearly, without understanding of motives, the life situation will not be changed in any great respect – the same emotions will come up in a different setting. But if it is these emotions that need to be worked through, leaving will not change you and it will not help you to uncreate your circumstance. This is what is meant by working from within to know yourself, and give of yourself, and be able to see your path with a clear eye, not a muddy one.

There is no doubt that things cannot change without willingness on another's part to change the universe that you both share. It must come as well from love. Those who are together and do not give the freedom to each other to make their own mistakes and be their own person will always be at odds and will never be satisfied with where they are. It is not easy for many to watch another make what they may consider very grave errors. But by trying to prevent these considered mistakes they may, without knowing it, create greater ones; for then there is a battlefront, and then there is something to fight for or against... You also have a responsibility to let others grow into their own unique expression.

Paula: Have I stopped that lately? Have I been holding somebody back?

MOITA: You must decide that for yourself. Look around you with a calmer eye and a more centred heart and see if you are trying to mould another to your own thoughts...

Paula: I have a large reservoir of anger which I'm very aware of. How do you suggest I get rid of that anger?

MOITA: Forgive it, accept it, know that it is there; and then take steps toward changing it. You do not get rid of anger by regretting it. Then you feed it, for then you are angry at yourself for being weak, or seemingly. The only way you grow is to accept yourself as you are and to know that – even though you may not be perfect as you would envision yourself to be – you have within you the seeds of beauty and what you would call perfection. If you would open that and let it grow, you cannot deny any part of yourself, for then you would not be a whole person. You would be but a piece, a superficial painting for others to look at, and none to know your true self.

The energy that is put into anger can be channeled in other areas and directions. You do not need to lose that energy in order to lose your anger.

Paula: I could channel it into creativity, for instance?

MOITA: That is one possibility, but you must also understand where the anger comes from. If you get rid of the cause, through love, the anger will also go. Most anger is directed inward even if it expresses itself toward an object or a person... Sometimes people get angry at others because they see something in them they do not like in themselves... You are angriest at yourself, for many reasons.

Paula: I know that.

MOITA: If you would lose your anger, you must love yourself. And if you can see ways to improve your own self-image, it is wise to put energy in that direction: do those things that make *you* feel whole and beautiful...

This is a world [in which people need] to make many conscious choices and to become more consciously aware of themselves and their role in creating their world. When we speak of responsibility, we are saying that all of the conditions in your life...are your responsibility – and you are the one who can change them, just as the people of the Earth can change their world...

It is getting on. We have said a lot. *(pause)* Good night.

Paula: Good night, Moita.

        ❧ ❧ ❧ ❧

Karen's session weaves together a number of themes in its own unique way and recalls the issue with which we began: looking outside oneself for self-knowledge.

Karen: I'd like to start by asking you about the exact time of my birth. I've been looking into astrology and wondering if that would be a help to me. My mother doesn't seem to recall the exact time. I wonder if you would know that. *(pause)*

MOITA: If you have lost your time, it has been for a good reason – for *you*.

Karen: A good reason for me to have forgotten it? Do you think knowledge of past lives would be helpful to me? That's another of the offshoots I've been investigating. I'm not placing a lot of reliance on it, but I have been investigating. *(pause)*

MOITA: You have a need to become unburdened with many of these external structures that you are looking to for understanding of yourself.

Karen: I find it very difficult to concentrate in order to achieve self-searching through meditation. I seem to be very mentally scattered.

MOITA: It comes from learning how to relax. Once you can learn how to relax and take things at an easier pace, you will find many things fall into place on their own. When you put much energy into outward things, very little comes back to you inwardly in this kind of search you are on. You put up blocks that we cannot circumvent. Ideas can be used as walls, for when one has an idea that is firmly planted, something that may run contrary to it will bounce off and be rejected out of hand, and sometimes without [your] even noticing that something has been offered.

Karen: What are some of these blocks I've been using?

MOITA: It would be better for you as a person to develop experience rather than learning through others and their experience. You know each experiences everything differently. Some can take another experience and draw it into themselves, and by so doing share in that experience or sensation and take away what fits them and their own path. Others will sometimes take the experience as a whole, a structure unto itself, [as if it were] something that needs not to be [fitted to] individual perception.

Karen: Am I trying to escape my problems, do you think, or am I meeting most of them head-on in a constructive way?

MOITA: You will find your problems not as great if you melt into them rather than meeting them head-on. Many problems are created by the reaction a person has to a situation, thinking there is only one way to react or one choice to be made – we get the feeling of being cornered. When your alternatives dwindle, [when] you see only one road, your perception narrows. There are always choices and no situation is unchangeable.

Karen: Who is Timothy? *(referring to a romantic partner)*

MOITA: *(pause)* Why?

Karen: I want to know. He's had a big impact on me. I want to know if it's a good impact or a destructive one. I'm confused. *(long pause)*

MOITA: Since you know you create your own reality, or at least you accept that this is so or possible, you must also be aware that any person will be the kind of influence that you wish [that person] to be. You are projecting your life onto others and it is coming back to you in different forms. If you are confused within and do not see your path and are not seeing with your heart, are not clear within yourself, then your life also will be confusing, and confusing things will happen to you. There will be elements introduced into your life that will thrust this back at you until you come to the realization that it begins within.

When you work on yourself and you can accept life and your own beauty that is there waiting to be released, your life will also fall into place. There will always be things to jar you from complacency. Otherwise, you would cease to grow – you would become a hermit of within and there would be no outward movement.

But it is important for you to know and understand: even though [all the persons in your life are also individuals and are] projecting their own view of the universe upon you, depending upon where you stand within yourself, you will either see your own view coming back or perceive how they are seeing you from their view.

It is not an easy thing to accept and understand as a reality rather than a string of words. Making these things true for yourself changes you from a very deep place, and change can be frightening for many – or it can be beautiful and accepting and a flowing out of a greater part of yourself. You have within you all the elements to change everything around you, if you will but relax and love and know yourself first. Through understanding yourself you will understand others, not the other way around.

Karen: You think I've been perhaps practising self-deception in my attempts to get to know myself – trying to hide things from myself so that I don't see what I don't want to see?

MOITA: You are practising self-deception not so you don't see what you don't want to see, but because there are things within yourself that you have never seen – things of beauty and light and oneness. It is these things that you are afraid of, for part of you knows that admitting them into your life will change you and your perception for all time, not just in this life alone.

It does not make sense to me that [people are] afraid of acceptance and love and beauty, except that they fear they will find the opposite and do not believe in themselves as true spirit and more than they are. Each one of our universes is different, yet they all contain similar elements. They all are based on love.

Karen: Do you think my love has been selfish in any aspect?

MOITA: It is not selfishness but unselfishness that causes people to lose touch with their own beauty. If they project their love all in an outward way but neglect to help themselves as well, then they are the plant that forever seeks to flower and die but does not seek to grow deep roots so it will strive and grow more. It is like shedding skin to know yourself and be yourself. It is very simple, although people make it difficult for themselves to do.

Karen: I've been accused of being afraid to be happy. Why do you think I would be afraid to be happy?

MOITA: Many of the things I have just said will apply to that, for that is basically what I have been saying. But it is a deeper kind of happiness of which I speak.

There is one way to explain that fear. To believe that you are part of something greater is comfortable to a point. So long as people believe that greater part is separate, it is easy to accept. When one realizes that the opening between your conscious self and your higher self will change your ordinary self, it becomes a fear of losing identity, of losing individuality, of merging with a wholer personality, a larger being, of becoming only one thought within a greater universe.

It is not a founded fear, for that is not how it happens. One does not lose individual experience or expression, but adds this part – the conscious part – to the greater for the benefit of both. You are the only one who can decide what happiness means for you, and where you choose to look to make your decision will also have an effect on how you view your life.

We have spoken of...the Medicine Wheel way of life, where you can take an instance – an experience, a happening – and place it in the centre of many people and then see each one of them viewing it from a different angle, giving a different perception to the experience, until it has made a complete circle and all the different possibilities are one. You are not stuck with this one view of your life or experience. It is within you to change your place within this wheel and therefore change your experience of your life and of life itself. Give yourself more freedom.

Karen: Thank you. *(pause)*

MOITA: There have always been those around you who have wished for an opening to communicate their concern and their love for you and your well-being. They wish to tell you that it is real: that there are other forces, other universes, and you *can* touch them. They are not just words.

৩০   ৩০   ৩০

In the end, and above all, learning who we are demands an attitude of open-hearted trust in the essence of life within us.

MOITA: Listen to your heart more than your head and let the love around you flow outward from your own centre. Embrace life in all its beauty and see the joy in the moment – the future will take care of itself. You, too, must learn to shed your guilt. Learning is quicker without certain kinds of pain. Every one of you can let yourself be a doorway to light.

I experience you on more than one level. I see you not just as you are now but as you have been and as you may be. There are some things I cannot say. If you gained all knowledge about yourself all at once, you would be a very unhealthy spirit. I must leave you to your own growing and only give you enough to help you grow yourself more. I seek your light, and I judge what I say by how it shines for me.

The path to spirit is simple – so simple, few see. Nothing happens without a reason, and you are not responsible for others' actions. Whether or not the pattern is clear to you, things are moving as they should. Try to see yourself as we do and accept your own beauty.

৩০   ৩০   ৩০

Illustrative Dream

Before you will be able to leave your body as an aware individual, you must first understand what your dreams are telling you.

Do not think that you are inherently evil. Much of the evil you see stems from your own fear of it. The things that you hide from yourself are things that you think would look ugly to someone else's eyes if you let them out. But if you let them out, they are not ugly at all because each one of you is beautiful and has [his] own purity.

– Moita

In the fall of 1975, I am in the midst of a major transition. I am in psychotherapy after separation from Leanne, still feeling emotionally attached while recognizing our six-year partnership has ended. I have doubts and fears about my changes – whether my new self, life and relationships will be any better, or perhaps worse, than before.

On the evening of November 23, 1975, I read from Ann Faraday's *The Dream Game* about accepting the "underdog" side of oneself. Our "underdog" traces back to vulnerable, grasping infancy. But as the "dark child", it can also represent suppressed or denied potentialities capable of flowing into a reborn self in adulthood, including perception of other realities and psychic abilities.[19N]

Then, waking early from a dream on the morning of the 25th, I experience a fat, rubbery feeling about my body, especially my fingers, as I've sometimes experienced before at night. I ask for a dream to explain this strange perception and return to sleep.

"Deformed, Split Fetus" dream
David (age 28) / November 25, 1975

After being up all night, Leanne and I wind up in a city restaurant. The cook is lighting the fires for the day. She then pours a molten substance into a spoon-shaped mould to harden in the oven of an old black stove.

Later the cook tries to remove the substance from the mould, but it cracks in the process. She flings the substance on the floor and digs out the remainder. It's like rubbery, soft wax. The cook tells me she was making this for a couple, but now they'll be told it was ruined and thrown away.

I look more closely at the rejected substance and see that it resembles a deformed little fetus. It has elongated legs and a stretched-out, pointed head that has split. It looks hideous, and dead.

After Leanne leaves, a woman comes into the restaurant, asking about her baby. The tiny fetal form is still lying on the floor. So I pick it up, intending to tell her what happened and dispose of it – only to feel it moving in my hand! It is alive! Or maybe it remains limp in my hand until the woman sees it and says she wants it. It is as if made from reddish-brown clay. I see the little bald creature yawn, exposing tiny teeth.

I'm afraid about the possible consequences of letting this deformed creature live and grow up, thinking there may be something evil about it. The woman still wants it, though. So I place it in my hip pocket – to safeguard it for her, but also keep it secret from the cook, as I feel guilty for having shown it to the woman in the first place.

It now seems Leanne and I have been sharing a house with this couple, and today they are moving away. I see them carrying out some large, beautiful plants that Leanne has grown. I give the fetus to them now, but I don't want all these plants to go.

I tell them I must discuss it with Leanne and head toward the house. But I find the sidewalk by the front steps aflame. The couple has poured gasoline and set it alight. Jumping over the flames, I manage to get in and find Leanne. She says it's all right, it was her daughter's idea to give these plants to the couple. I'm upset, thinking I won't be able to enjoy them anymore.

As I understand this dream, the little fetus is the somewhat damaged, rejected parts of me at this point in my life. I may have been unaware of them before, or felt unable to express them well enough in my former relationship. Evidently, I still tend to hide and feel guilty over them. But through my recent changes, they are now emerging into the light. This tiny being comes alive through acceptance and love, as expressed by the new woman, part of a new couple who will raise the child. This man and woman are my own masculine and feminine sides, coming together now in balance and greater consciousness. This couple burns the bridges to my past life and carries forward those growing things I have enjoyed – a message of hope for the new phase of life I am entering.

But further: in answer to my question, this fetus is like living, rubbery wax – flexible, not fit for a mould. It is like the "fat, rubbery feeling" of my body this very morning and other nighttimes. As I will realize later, this strange perception is one of energy expanding beyond the mould of the physical body, on the threshold of exploring other worlds.

෨   ෨   ෨

Chapter 3

FINDING YOUR OWN PATH

It is one thing to believe in reincarnation. It is another thing entirely to discover reincarnation as an actual fact of existence.
– Moita

Since the mid-20th century, a new understanding of reincarnation has emerged as a self-directed learning path toward wholeness and higher consciousness. This concept – that we choose before birth, with varying degrees of awareness, the circumstances of our successive lives on Earth – allows us to see how "learning who we are" is the most basic responsibility of all. None of the external conditions of our lives can be taken as excuses to shirk or disparage growth toward self-knowledge, since we have chosen or allowed ourselves to "fall into" those very life situations. Ultimately, then, we have the freedom to improve on our choice-making, so that our learning becomes more productive, even joyful.

As we journey through many lives and in the course of our present life, we progress from pursuing the external for its own sake to focusing on the inner that is manifesting through the outer. We learn by growing closer to the inner self that laid out the possibilities in the first place – not by elevating external figures, standards or ideologies (including "spiritual" ones) to positions of authority over us.

As mentioned, we may "fall into" a life of pain because we have blocked out other options. Or what appear to be negative circumstances may actually be selected more consciously, for they too can serve growth. Some have argued this view discounts the struggle for personal and social liberation by assuming all life situations, however restrictive or oppressive, are the individual soul's responsibility – if not predestined, as older theories had it. However, the circumstances may be chosen before birth precisely to provoke choices about how to respond to, and hopefully change, inequities in a life.

Still, it can be difficult to understand why potentially free beings would choose or allow the harsh conditions so often experienced during our millennia on Earth, including our present age. We begin, then, with a passionate exchange that provides insight into the early chapters of humanity's wheel of rebirth. Subsequent material addresses individual evolution in its later, more conscious phases, entering into issues of fate and freedom, one's optimum path, what a teacher can and cannot do, and creating one's own reality. As always, Moita's words are tailored to the individual she is addressing, and to what lies behind the person's stated concerns.

ॐ　　ॐ　　ॐ

MOITA:　　The universe is very well-balanced. Nothing that happens in it is done
without love, and no one is manipulated [from our level] into doing something

they do not want to do. You have chosen to be here in this time, in this place, and the other parts of yourself know very well what may and may not happen once you have arrived. You are free to make the choice to leave or stay, to work or not work, now that you are a personality in a form. These are your freedoms. You as a whole self made the choice to be [in a physical body]. You as a partial self will make the choices that will affect what you learn from here...

C.:   I don't know, I find it very hard to believe that everything that happens is chosen. My gut revolts at that thought. Billions are born to starve, die, become ugly and evil, because their lives are so limited.

MOITA: But they become these things in order to become beautiful, in order to learn, in order to grow.

C.:   How does starving over God knows how many lifetimes – because the majority of human lives must have been hell on this Earth – how can that make us beautiful? Generation after generation there is famine, and a few people live in luxury and wealth, and smile and have everything very nice, and rob it all from the rest. How would so many people *choose* to be born as slaves again and again? Why don't people's spirits rebel and refuse to come to the Earth as slaves?

MOITA: Because they have not grown enough in awareness to realize that is not what they desire, not what they need.

C.:   Stumbling blindly is hardly a choice, though.

MOITA: It is a choice. They can choose to understand and see and take a different path. They must make their own mistakes.

C.:   Why *don't* people choose it, though? I can't understand why, through choice, such things would happen.

MOITA: It is not always a choice that is as conscious. It is often a guilt or a desire or a fear that drives a soul back into a body on the Earth. And they do not *always* spend their lives in misery or pain or suffering or starvation. Those who are in seats of power do not spend *all* of their lives in seats of power. Very often *they* become the slaves until they understand what it is they are doing, until they can see that they are making themselves as much a slave as those that they are trying to rule in other lives.

It is not a very straightforward thing, and [it is] difficult for you to understand as a part of yourself in this one particular time. You do not see your past or your future. You see other people suffering, but you do not see their joy when they finally do find that doorway and are free to develop the way they wish. A soul that can have beauty and love and joy, in a life that others see as filled with pain, is a soul that has made so many strides forward in [its] development you would not believe [its] appearance at [its] death.

It is for all of you to understand: no situation is beyond your control; there are always ways out – if not through the body, [then] through the heart or through the mind; and it is given to you to do, with what you have received in this life, what you can to make yourself a more worthy and whole individual, and let the others who are around you, and whom you cannot touch, do their *own* choosing, their *own* suffering, so that they can become free when they so wish it.

One who has chained himself to a rock and enjoys being chained to that rock will not look upon you with kindness if you come upon him with a hacksaw and take him away from his foundation that he has grown to love. There are many who enjoy pain. They must learn through it that there is more to life than that.

C.:   I don't know. I find it terribly hard to accept.

MOITA: You will accept it in time.

C.:   Perhaps – and perhaps another course can be forged. Perhaps the light can be brighter so people can see more choices. Perhaps we don't have to have these blinders around us. Perhaps . . .

MOITA: Perhaps if you did not want to *build* them... There is light in the universe. There is light everywhere. There has always been light and there has always been love.

C.:   Well, why can't a chicken in a foot-square cage see that it can be a grouse? Can it?

MOITA: You are looking only at this one time period.

C.:   The history that I know is pretty much the same. In that sense, most of humanity have been slaves, have been kept by external institutions from growing in any kind of awareness. I can't feel that that's right.

MOITA: I am not saying that it is right, nor am I saying that it is wrong. I am saying that it *is*, and that it can be *learned from*. It need not be, in this world's future. *I* can see where the world is heading, and the possibilities for growth and advancement and awareness. And in this world's future, when man has changed, these conditions do not exist.

C.:   I *hope* they won't exist.

MOITA: There are few souls who can take the pain of the world upon them and survive. Your own pain is enough. Leave the world's pain to itself for now. Your suffering for them will not make them free. It will only bind you to this Earth more.

C.:   Perhaps I don't desire to leave the Earth but simply to see the Earth become something one can live as a reasonably free being upon.

MOITA: You must first become free yourself before you can learn how to show the light to others. It is time for "the blind leading the blind" to cease. First gain your sight and then speak from knowledge, not from blind groping. You fear the dark too much at the moment to learn to light the way for others.

C.:   I perhaps don't so much seek to light the way to that for others as to get some dark things out of the way.

MOITA: That will not be done in this way. It can only be done from within yourself.

C.:   Yet materially, physically, the world has changed and improved in some way. There is less slavery, perhaps, than there used to be. By working in this way, things *have* improved on this plane.

MOITA: By working on yourself you will affect the world around you, and things will improve. By working on others, more walls will be built.

The universe begins from within, and it expresses itself without. If your road is not what you wish it to be, look to yourself first before you look to man and the things he is keeping as slaves. Because most men look to others and not to themselves, the world is as it is in this moment. If you would change this cycle and pattern, you must start first here.

Being filled with the love of the Earth does not mean you have no compassion for those who are separated from this love. It does not mean that you are better than them, nor worse. It does not mean that you are setting yourself upward from them. It means that you are getting in touch with the real world and the real Earth, at least for yourself; and so, some beauty is preserved for the rest of man to find another time.

There is no sin in happiness or joy, and there should be no guilt in it, either. To feel that you are in a perhaps better position than your fellow man, and to blame yourself for being in that position, will not make them better or clearer – or yourself. If you worry about your thoughts creating realities you do not like, do not dwell so much on ugliness, for the world as you see it now is very ugly. See its beauty – help it to flower...

(Later in the session, a younger member of the group wants Moita to clarify the issue of choice.)

Erica: When we leave this world, do we have a choice what we want to be next? Or do we come back as what *they* send us to be?

MOITA: No one sends you to come back; you send yourself. And the amount of choice you have will depend upon how free you are to understand that choice. If you are unfree within yourself as an individual spirit, you will make a choice based on fear. If you have gained an awareness and are free within yourself to take each lesson as a lesson to learn and grow from, you will be able to make a better choice – one that will probably permit you to grow more than one you would have made through fear... From going through this life with more awareness, making a conscious connection with a higher self, you can set about the process of unchaining yourself from the rock. It is something all of you can do.

Would you like to unchain yourself? *(Erica nods)* Keep it before you. If you can accept freedom, it shall come your way.

Erica: How would I go about trying to get free?

MOITA: Open yourself and let the love of the universe flow through you into the world. This is how anyone becomes free.

ာ   ာ   ာ

Here are two more exchanges relating to those whose personalities in this life appear to be relatively unwhole or closed to love.

Sylvia: I wonder about individuals who seem to us to be totally lost, people who are psychopathic or appear to be quite deranged, for instance. What about the ultimate destiny of these souls? Do they too have a spiritual centre, or is there such a thing as people who are really "beyond redemption"?

MOITA: You see in any one life only a part of an individual. How can one understand something without having experienced it first? – that is one [reason for choosing such a life]. And those who feel guilty over having done something in a life that was not very aware, was against the grain of creation, will sometimes put themselves in situations such as this for punishment – which is not healthy either.

And then there are those who have a reservoir of anger and are expressing their anger in a life because they are afraid of themselves: they do not want to accept their own death; they do not wish to accept their wholeness.

And some of those things happen because others believe they are not "high". If you have an individual who feels himself to be different and yet is told he is not allowed to express this differentness, his energy can go into these areas as a way of striking back at the walls others have placed around him that he is not understanding enough to dissolve.

But all of these things are learning experiences, and all individuals have a central self that they will someday discover, regardless of how slow their path may seem, or how crooked. We can only help them when they make a discovery, when they allow us the freedom to help them on their paths, to show them the shorter, sometimes harder road. It is not within any of you to change these people from without. It is only in your ability to change yourself from within.

∽ ∽ ∽

Jean: I feel as though my mother needs me right now. Is this true? And I'm wondering how I can help her. You said yesterday she might not be able to accept or understand where I'm at, but that I need to . . .

MOITA: You are trying very hard to work out a *great* many things that may not be essential for you to work out! You are placing more guilt upon yourself than you deserve, for a great many things. And some of the things you are doing are, for you, atonement for that guilt that you feel.

Jean: I guess that's true.

MOITA: You cannot accept responsibility for another's way of life, another's view, or another's learning or not learning. Many have the desire to wake up everyone around them. But it is through the blindness that many people experience in a life that they learn how to wake up later. You cannot know for certain what stage of development those around you are in. You only have the appearance of their present personality to guide you, and appearances can be very deceiving. Look beyond people; look beyond their personality. Know that they are whole and complete, whether or not they appear to be to you because they are working on their own individual development.

Jean: Mm-hmm. Yeah, that's good... I guess I feel sad that in this lifetime we never became close as I would have liked. Are you saying I shouldn't feel sad about that – I should be willing to let that go?

MOITA: You can offer love, but you cannot make that love accepted until the other is ready herself to accept it as a gift, for what it is. It is not wasted, though. There is a *part* that always is aware of this energy that you can put out to others. And when the life is finished and the remembering is done, the love will be seen and it will bring much joy. I know this is hard to accept.

Jean: *(crying)* Yes, it is.

MOITA: But there is much love around you in other places, too. None of you wish to stand alone, and you all feel you do. Until you can learn to stand by yourself, and to feel you *do* stand alone in a strong centre, you will not realize how little you *can* be alone at all because of all the life that is around you. Love is in everything, even in those things that do not *appear* to contain it.

                         ∾   ∾   ∾

As souls grow in consciousness, the interplay between pre-birth choices and choices during the life grows in significance. The next four excerpts illustrate this interaction.

Amelia: Is it our decision in what body form we come back?

MOITA: Yes. You are your own reward and your own punishment. No one imposes those things upon you. It is your own free choice.

Amelia: At the time we choose, do we know what lessons we have to learn, or do we find out during the lifetime?

MOITA: In the cycle of rebirth, when you die, the first thing that happens to most – not all – is you remember your pasts. Then you look on the life you have just led and see what it is you have learned from that life, and fit it into the other things that you have learned in others. Then you look on yourself as a whole and see where you lack experience or strength or humbleness. Then you choose a life and a circumstance that will most probably teach you what it is you see that you lack.

          It is not always true that you will learn what it is you set out to learn – not always as much as you would hope. But there is also the [chance], depending on where you are in your own development, that you may come back not with the idea of teaching yourself something but with the idea of punishing yourself for something you feel you have done that needed to be punished. It grieves us when you do that.

Amelia: Yes, I would think so.

MOITA: But we can do nothing, since yours is the choice. And for each who recognizes the fact that punishment is not the way to learning, we are very joyful. When you learn you are here to learn love and joy and peace and acceptance of yourself with all of your inequities, then you have made a conscious choice of letting yourself bloom, and the rest of your lives from then on are lives filled with more conscious lessons.

ے   ے   ے

Owen: I frequently dream of events that happen anywhere from a couple of months to years later. Something happens, and I suddenly remember dreaming that this happened. The question in my mind is: How much of our lives is mapped out by ourselves, and we're just trying as skillfully as possible to go through the motions of that script? How much do our choices represent really decisive turning points? That's a very traditional question, of course, but no less puzzling.

MOITA: Let us say that before you are born, you choose circumstances for your life that will most likely bring about the desired lessons you want to learn. In any life there are many possibilities; there are many probable future lines. At certain points in your life you are faced with many choices. The choice you make at that point decides which future line you will take. There are some people that dream about happenings in the future that do not happen, not necessarily because they are not happening somewhere else, but because they have made a choice that has carried them along a different future line. You are the one who chose the life. You are the one who chose the circumstances. And you are the one who makes the choices.

Owen: How many significant turning points are involved, then? I suppose you're saying there could be any number.

MOITA: It all depends on how you have planned it out. If you are trying to learn a particular lesson in patience, you would choose a life where you would have many, many choices all the time – and try not to make them, perhaps. But if you made them, you would end up in circumstances where there would be even *more* choices that you would have to make. And it would accelerate the life till, when you got to the end, if you hadn't stayed on a single track, you would have become very entrenched in the idea of not making choices, because you would look back and see how many wrong choices you made. That is a very sketchy example.

Owen: *(laughing)* It sounds very appropriate. I'm not sure I fully comprehend.

MOITA: There are instances where you plan a life so there are fewer possible future lines that you could take, because it is a more intense life and one that is filled with more purpose. That way you preclude many mistakes that you might make.

You see, you can choose the circumstances, but before you are born you do not fully know how the personality you have chosen is going to react to those circumstances. So, it teaches the part of you that made the choice in the beginning more about the whole, in seeing the reaction that actually does occur when sometimes the life is not led *at all* like the entity would have wished.

Owen: What is the difference between patience and procrastination?
MOITA: *(laughing)* Perhaps *you* shall have to figure that one out!

శ   శ   శ

Faye: You mentioned there are several paths that may be taken. I have difficulty understanding that because I have felt directed to take one path, and if I don't choose that path I will cause myself much pain.
MOITA: Before you are born, you choose what one can call an "optimum" path, one that will teach you the lessons you have chosen to learn in the shortest length of time or in the best possible way – they are not always the same. But when you are born, your consciousness is born within you, and it does not always choose what is or can be the optimum path. That is why there are other possibilities.

          The spirit is always working to make sure you get as much as possible out of whichever road you choose, if you do not happen to choose the one it would like. So there are always circumstances and lessons that are thrust in your way to make you stop and look and see and try to understand.

          Each of you has the desire to follow the one path that was decided before your birth, but you are also free to choose not to. It is entirely your choice. You are not predestined to walk on one particular road, each stone and each fall set before you, before you start. It is a living process, not a stagnant one.

శ   శ   శ

Caroline: Can you give me an idea of how to go about my life? Say, the purpose of my life would be eventually to become one with God, and one way of doing that is not to let fate govern my life [but] to choose my own reality. How can we choose our goal and head straight for it without letting that sort of fate govern our lives?
MOITA: By giving your essence into the hands of your own self, with faith, [knowing] that although you may look on your occurrences as fate, they are *not*. The workings of the universe can be extremely tricky, because sometimes what seems to be an occurrence...out of the blue – something [unexpected] that has dropped in on you [that] you would consider a bad turn [of] fate – is not that at all and [is] your own inner self trying to awaken you, trying to show you that perhaps there is something you are missing, a lesson that you are not learning, a path that you have taken the wrong turn on.

          Make your own choices, but do so with an inner awareness. Strive towards being that expression of yourself to the best of your ability.

శ   శ   శ

When we believe we have received our first bit of reincarnational information, we may tend to overestimate its importance and seize upon it as prescribing a certain path or view of ourselves. For instance, to discover reincarnational links with another individual or group may lead us almost automatically to conclude we are predestined or obligated to share paths in this life as well. In the following extracts, Moita insists it is always our choice how to *react* to such information.

Ted: I'm interested in how and where I'm connected with this group here.

MOITA: At this moment in time, you are here because you need to be. At the moment there are threads that pass between you all – some more, some less. You see, it has been given you to make a choice in this life which threads you will take up and which threads you will cast off. You are coming in contact with a great many different types of groups for that purpose. In the end, the choice is yours.

ϡ   ϡ   ϡ

Joan: We have a friend that came up to live with us. We were wondering if she would be staying with us, each helping the other grow?

MOITA: I see another crossroads here. There is a possibility she will branch off to another place, but a bond has been created and it will continue.

Joan: Has she been with us in another lifetime? She feels that she has.

MOITA: It is quite possible. Of course, sharing a life with another does not always mean *(laughing)* that the next life will be good. There are levels of contact and commitment. As always, it is *this* life that is most important at the moment.

ϡ   ϡ   ϡ

The "soul mate" relationship is frequently seen as highly significant, though its exact definition varies. It is often equated with twin souls – persons who are part of the same higher entity; in the extreme case, it could mean a single soul's simultaneous lives. Or, it may mean souls that have shared very close relationships in numerous lives, who are either very similar or who deeply complement each other. But whichever way, one shouldn't assume the connection prescribes some definite form of relating here and now.

A young woman named Jill once asked Moita if her friend Darryl was speaking truthfully when he told her they were soul mates – and if he wasn't, Jill wanted to know whether she *would* meet her soul mate in this life. Using the first definition above, Moita replied that sharing a life with one's soul mate may not always be something to look forward to. She laughed as she said it, reminding us of her comment a few days earlier about Ruth's and my being "soul mates" in that sense: that such encounters are fairly rare and most turn out to be "intense learning experiences" that are not necessarily pleasant.

Another piece of supposedly crucial information is the age of one's soul: how many lives, or how far back they go. But once Moita has brought in the nature of time, of creation, of purpose, as well as issues of learning speed and quantity versus quality, this too turns out to be a much less straightforward prescription of attitude than first appears.

George: How many times have I been here?

MOITA: *(laughing)* You are here as many as you want!

George: You were saying our past lives were important.

MOITA: And so are your future ones!

George: Right. But my future is open.

MOITA: That depends on which lives you speak of. Some of your future lives are already in your past. *(laughing)* You see, we can also speak of time along your particular line of development. When you are trying to develop a soul in one way, at one point it may be good to go back before written history and experience something there, and...directly afterwards it may be wise to go forward into history that has not yet been recorded! So: so much depends on which view you wish to take.

Chris: There's more sequence to our lives than there is to history? Is that what you're saying?

MOITA: *(laughing)* It is possible.

Mike: Were we created at the same time – I mean, you and everybody in this room? Did it all happen at once, and we all created our own paths?

MOITA: No, it is a constant happening. It is not something that has happened or has stopped. It goes on and on. There are various ages here. I will not pin you down to who was here first! Of course, I could safely say *I* was! *(laughing)*

Mike: Well, I'm only 28. You're 50,000 years old!

MOITA: But you can have roots in older times even if you as an individual soul have not been here that long. Each one of you can – at some point – go backwards into your own history, and then into the history of your creation and your creator. But it is up to you.

❧   ❧   ❧

Joan: Do you know how many times each one of us has been reincarnated?

MOITA: You all have – *are* – incarnated different amounts, depending upon what aspect of the life-force you wish to nurture, and depending upon how quickly you choose to learn what lessons you come here for. It is hard to put numbers on lives. It can be many; it can be few. And sometimes the many can be not as important as the few.

Arthur: Mm-hmm. We're after quality, not quantity. *(laughter)*

MOITA: Right. One would think that after so many years *I* would not be here any longer. *(laughter)*

Joan: Arthur says this is the last time.

MOITA: Each time *is* the last time. *(laughter)*

People often hope that Moita, or any other teacher with whom they come in contact, will be able to define for them their purpose or proper path in life. Moita responds by suggesting that we are here to learn to be our own teachers.

Joe: Why have the five of us come together tonight?

MOITA: This is a meeting place on your path. Each individual has his own road to take; and walking that road, he sometimes comes to a place where others meet. Oftentimes these places are there so that choices will be made, things that decide what a future path will become. There is the potential for change in any meeting, and these are usually for purposes of growth – to increase understanding in one form or another. Experiences can be brief or long, feel very good or unpleasant. It is the end product that matters: what you become, how you understand yourself. That is why *any* come here.

Joe: Hmm. Are you able to be more specific in reference to each of us as to purpose?

MOITA: Purposes are not things that are easily defined. They are things that are felt within each individual. We do not communicate to give purpose but in some way to give hope and to share that there is more, and it is real...

Debbie: You said that we were all here for different reasons on different levels, that there is a lot more happening here than there is on a physical plane. I'd like to know more about that.

MOITA: You create your circumstances from another level first before you manifest them. You have choices. There are possible lives you could lead that you may not, because of conscious choices you make here when you arrive. *(pause)*

The main purpose any of you have is learning to open to your other levels, learning to be yourself and learning to flow. If our level came to yours and told you exactly who you were or why you were here, you would not learn for yourself and soon what we said would be forgotten.

This is your teaching place. You are your own teacher. We lend a hand where we are able, where it is deemed fruitful for your development, for your own teaching. We are here more to help you learn to teach yourself than to tell you what it is you are trying to learn.

The child who is born without a problem, who lives a perfect life, has no strength; and if he should meet on his road a problem that he has no experience of, he will very often fall, not to rise again. Those who live and fall and rise continually grow stronger as they travel, fall less far and rise more quickly, until they need to fall no more.

No one can teach you strength; no one can give it to you. It must come from within.

Debbie: So it doesn't really *matter* why we're all here. *(general laughter)*
MOITA: Except for how you view it yourself.
Debbie: Right.
Vic: Moita, I get a feeling that you would make one helluva good politician if you were really interested.
MOITA: I have been told I am good at straddling fences! *(laughter)*

               ∾   ∾   ∾

MOITA: We do know the right path, but we arrived here by our own mistakes. We give this freedom to you, so you too can grow. If we led you around by the nose, none of you would ever learn.

               ∾   ∾   ∾

The next four exchanges deal with a closely related issue: asking Moita not what *should* happen in one's life, but rather what *will* happen. Being anyone's fortune teller is something Moita politely refuses, and in such a way that we're unlikely to ask again!

Lois: I've been trying to write a novel. I want to know if I'm going to do that kind of writing for the rest of my life. Can you see anything about that?
MOITA: If you wish to write, you will write; and if you choose not to, you will not. Your life is not set out before you as a book. There are still many changes in store. You may find that there is a time when you will not have time for writing. You may have many other things that will occupy your time or your energy. And there will be times when you will have a great deal of time for it. If it is something that you love, something that is within you, it will come out in its own time and blossom.

               ∾   ∾   ∾

Art: Do you predict the future?
MOITA: The future is still malleable. It exists, and yet where it exists there are many possibilities to it. There is still the ability to change what may come... Oftentimes, if the future is predicted, the prediction helps to bring it about, because then people put their energy into believing what will be.

               ∾   ∾   ∾

Gil: Could you tell me some things that would be beneficial for me?
MOITA: You could also tell yourself a great deal that would be beneficial to you.
Gil: I know that. I believe that you might have a clearer awareness or greater access.
MOITA: Then speak your thoughts clearly.

Gil: What's the best advice you could possibly give me?

MOITA: Not to ask for advice. If you have a question, a most specific question, you may get a specific answer. [Otherwise] you shall continue to dwell in generalities and not get the answer that you seem to think you seek.

Gil: Well, I could ask questions, then. It doesn't seem like it's very important, but when will I drop my body?

MOITA: "Your body" – you want to know the moment of your own death?

Gil: Mm-hmm. *(pause)*

MOITA: The information that you ask for is not what you should be looking for. You should be asking, rather, how to live your life *now*, instead of wondering when you will expire. It will serve you no purpose to know times and places. That kind of knowledge could make you fearful; it could make you lose your path and your way; it could make you preoccupied with your endings instead of living now, which is what you are here to do.

This moment is where you exist. When you die, you will exist in that moment as well. But I cannot give you the lesson of that moment until you have reached it.

ھ   ھ   ھ

Gene: Can you tell me what will happen in the future? I know *you* know.

MOITA: There will come a time, not far distant, when man will become aware consciously of his past. But he still will not be able to know of his future. If he did know at that point what his future was, then he would stop striving and reaching, therefore not gaining that future for himself.

Sometimes precognition can be useful and even helpful. But usually it is far better for an entity to live through his life without knowing what his future holds. It is sometimes necessary, and a great learning experience, to take a step not knowing where it will lead.

ھ   ھ   ھ

This chapter moves toward a conclusion by drawing together the themes of learning who you are and finding your own path – which is at the same time a choosing and creating from within.

C.:   How can one know that things are real? I so much find myself doubting everything so very often.

MOITA: You can only use yourself to decide what is real for you or not. Those things that you choose to be real *will* be, and those things that you choose not to accept – if you are choosing not to accept them from a very aware, conscious state – cease to exist for you. This is what is meant about creating your own reality and choosing your own path. But it must be done consciously, for you will be affected by all of those others who are around you.

Duggan: Who are you?

MOITA: To describe who I am, you would have to experience how I view the universe. Individual perception determines who you are; it is identity. What I do and experience is not easily put into words. If I were to ask you who *you* were, what kind of an answer could you come up with?

Duggan: I was going to ask you that one, too! *(laughter)* – 'cause I don't know. I couldn't begin to answer that.

MOITA: I have no doubts as to *my* existence, if that helps to alleviate the doubts you may have about *yours*. Any name I choose to speak would be merely a label of a part of myself, of an energy that I can be associated with.

Duggan: Sorry for asking such a complicated question!

MOITA: It is important to learn which questions are answerable in words and which are only answerable in self-knowledge. This is that kind of a question. You are the only one who can know who you are. And it is extremely difficult for you to express to another exactly what your perception of yourself is, for they see you not through your own eyes but through theirs.

Duggan: What is the real me, or the real anybody? Is it how you see yourself, or how others see you, or both?

MOITA: You could say the real you is determined by your *reaction* to the universe. Whether it be your reaction to others' views or to your own, it is the reaction that you have that makes you unique, for no two people will react the same way in any situation. If you could determine the core of that reacting part of yourself, then you would come closer to knowing what it is that you feel is your identity.

You grow by interacting with others, and you change your perceptions of yourself by trying to see their perception of you. And so, you are always changing, always being reborn and becoming new. There are so many selves that you can have. If you would speak of who you are now, would you determine that by this moment, this experience, or would you draw on past selves, on a childhood self, on a five-year-ago self, and maybe on a projected self into the future, on your hopes, your dreams and aspirations?

Duggan: You can only talk about now.

MOITA: In this moment, I am a doorway.

Dan: What am I . . . what are we supposed to be doing here? *(laughter)*

MOITA: Do you mean in this life?

Dan: In this life, in this place.

MOITA: The answer is the same for all of you. You are all here to become whole and to find out what love means in a *real* world. The answers are simple, but the questions are not always so simple. They all lead to the same place on different paths. Learning to accept other people's paths is one way of manifesting love. That is the energy that will change a world, and that is how you become whole – by opening your own heart and connecting to the greater you.

This is where remembering your other lives comes in, and this is *when* it comes in as well. You have a legacy of experience and understanding and humility in your other lives; and, remembering them, you understand from a deeper place that no life is more important or less important than any other, and that you have been a saint and a sinner and are learning to become balanced. To be able to remember your past will help you shape your future. It broadens you.

Chris: It's not necessary, is it, to actually remember the incidences? Can that be something you can comprehend without having to . . . ?

MOITA: You are, at the moment, a sum of your past experience. When you reach a certain level of growth, your own pasts begin to open up for you. While you are caught in a physical form and cannot reconnect with your higher self nor remember your own experiences, you are not as able to make clear choices, and it is easier for you to retain the need to return in a physical form. Those who believe in karma and a wheel of rebirth trap themselves on it in a never-ending cycle. And when you can remember them all or enough of them as you live in a physical form, many can let go of that desire to come back and try again to be perfect in one life.

Chris: Maybe sometimes that can be a really conscious choice to come back, and not just something you can't let go of.

MOITA: Yes, in some cases those who do not need to return *choose* to, in order to help others make their own choices.

Mike: Why are we caught in this physical form, anyways? How did this all start? *(general laughter)*

MOITA: You could say that it started with the desire to experience other forms of reality, and there was not a great enough awareness of what that desire might lead to. It has been a necessary journey, for it has broadened the spirit of man in many ways. *(pause)*

You could, in some ways, call the descent of the human spirit in physical form the "fall" from the Garden of Eden. But in so doing, when the form returns, the Garden will be changed too: it is not only a place to experience things that fill you with wonder, but now a place to bring your ability to create *to* it. This way you can form consciously that with which you feel most comfortable – before, you were stuck with what was there. It is like suddenly being grown and recognizing that your parent once was a child as well, and now you can go off on your own road.

Mike: That's why we're in this body – to learn to use our creative powers to get out of it?

MOITA: To learn to recognize yourself as a creative power, and to discover as a first-hand experience what your own creative energy can do to you, so that you will use it wisely.

❧ ❧ ❧

MOITA: Nothing keeps you in a wheel of rebirth except your own sense of guilt or your own desire to come back.

Jean: And what after that?

MOITA: After that the whole universe is at your feet.

Jean: When each individual decides they don't need to come back, is there no place in common that they all go? They just develop in many, many ways?

MOITA: Many, many ways. You create your own universe. And you may meet others that are in a universe that is close to yours, and then change yours and theirs as well and make a new one. But there is no one place where everyone goes. Each chooses his own place, a place that is an outer reflection of his inner being.

Jean: Is it still individual?

MOITA: It is individual – or many individuals. You do not lose your uniqueness when you reconnect with yourself, but you also gain all the other selves that you have temporarily forgotten. You see, your soul learns from your experience here, and then together you will add to the direction you are taking. It may sound complicated in some ways, but it is not really. It is all very simple.

❧ ❧ ❧

Joe: Is it true to say that we're each on different levels at different times?

MOITA: I would say: As your thoughts change, your level changes with them. It is not something that is so easily defined. There is the image of the onion. Each time you come to understand or think you understand all there is in your existence at any one moment, you pass a certain point which is, in a sense, entering another plane. You can see that the layer you were on has shrivelled and dried and fallen away, and now you are on a new layer and you are understanding that.

The process continues onwards and inwards until you reach your core or your centre. For each individual, the process is different; the timing is not the same. My expressing that your plane now is different from the plane you were on when you were ten is something that is obvious to you, because in your experience you can see directly the difference between your old consciousness and yet know that you are still the same. It is only your awareness of life that has changed, not you yourself.

But to tell you that you are also aware in another part of yourself what your consciousness will be when you are sixty-five – it is not so easy, because you look at things running from one point to another in a line, and I look at them all being together at the same time. I do not have the same concept of time as you. I can be at one and the same time newly created and wholly evolved, in your estimation.

Vic: Is it not possible for us to achieve the same understanding at this level?

MOITA: One of the reasons you are here is to be able to do both at once: to be here in a body, to love your Earth and your fellow man, and to be with us on our level and understand your own place in creation, your own responsibility for using energy. It is when you reach this kind of point that you no longer feel the need to return.

œ   œ   œ

Illustrative Dream

There will come a time, not far distant, when man will become aware consciously of his past. To be able to remember your past will help you shape your future. It broadens you.

– Moita

What can we learn of our other lives while we're in this one? Can we actually come into contact with them? Several pathways to past-life experience are illustrated within this book and elsewhere in the series. Of these, dreaming is a spontaneous, altered state of consciousness all of us share every night, yet its full potential is rarely appreciated. The following dream, mentioned in *Mind Leap*,[20N] is unique in my journals: not only providing information about at least one past life (later confirmed by Loria), but also ushering the dreamer into a level of participative consciousness that brings these alternate realities to life.

"1845 Chesterfield Woodcut" dream
David (age 28) / January 7, 1976

A woman asks if I've seen the new dictionary that's been delivered. She hands me what seems a large, heavy book. But I find it is a folder containing the "display pages" from a famous encyclopedia. As I leaf through the sheets, I'm reminded of old Edwin Curtis photographs of American Indians.

But then I come to a picture of an old-fashioned woodcut. A caption states it was made, or found, in the upstate New York town of Chesterfield in 1845. The woodcut reveals a large room with rows of pews as in a church, or perhaps rows of long tables and chairs, on which people are sitting while others stand. One standing man reminds me of a young Abe Lincoln.

Mysteriously, then, as I watch this very detailed picture in sepia-like shades of orange, brown and grey, the people come alive! They move, their expressions change – and yet so subtly and smoothly that I am not totally sure at each moment whether only this image is the way the woodcut has always been. It is as if each moment lies potential within the woodcut, and its various aspects will become manifest depending on the observer.

Now a narrator points to a man and woman entering through the back door and slowly walking up the centre aisle past the Lincolnesque man. The couple are described as being asleep and in trance, though they stare straight ahead with wide eyes. It is further suggested they are making this scene happen, or perceiving this room as I myself am perceiving it, via their trance state. There seems to be a great awareness among the others in this room of what is going on with these people and what this scene is all about.

As the couple passes out of view to my right, I see a large, orange-leaved tree overhanging the meeting-hall, from which leaves begin to fall more and more thickly. At this point, I recognize I have experienced this before. Focusing on the tree, I expect to see many faces of people or animals appear among the branches, as when faces are disguised within landscape pictures for children to find. The faces don't appear now. But as leaves continue falling from the tree, I spy an older man in the hall smiling knowingly at me. A dim orange light casts into relief the wrinkles on his brownish grey face.

Now I turn the page and see what becomes an old movie, dim and flickering at first like a newsreel. The film depicts the brutal execution of an Indian brave, as by soldiers in the American West. (Crazy Horse comes to mind.) I understand this book is special due to its historical authenticity, including these pictures of sometimes shocking content.

I watch a few more pictures of Indian faces. As with the first scene, I sense they depend on and are somehow inside me, like eidetic images. I know I must focus my attention in order to see them at all. At the same time, I feel surprise and wonder at the spontaneity and seeming objectivity of the scenes.

Turning back to the woodcut page, I want to share my experience with the woman who gave me this book. I expect that if anyone looks with the right frame of mind and allows themselves to sink into the picture, they will see what I saw – the potential scenes will come to life for them also.

I ask the narrator if there are more of these books in stock, so that others can look. He replies, "Oh yes, we have about thirty right now." As pictures dim, I gradually realize that I am waking from a dream.

Months later, Loria will identify the couple in the meeting-hall as myself and my wife during a trip to New York state during my 19th century "Kentucky life", an incarnation that included migration across the American West after the Civil War.[21N] However, I still do not know why the meeting-hall scene should be the first memory to surface from that life, nor can I presume any "newsreel" authenticity to the particulars of the Indian's execution.

What is more important, though: this experience of examining a "book of lives", which Kelly too will encounter during dreams and regressions (as described, for example, in Chapter 14). As well, the tree in which I sense, without actually seeing, many faces amid the branches is an image of interconnected lives (similar to another dream image in Chapter 11). Here the images do not flow unconsciously as in normal dreams. I am aware of subtle moment-by-moment changes as long as I maintain my focus, sensing the link between my consciousness and that of the participants. Meanwhile, observing my efforts, the narrator and man who smiles "knowingly" undoubtedly represent higher-level guides.

ॐ   ॐ   ॐ

_____

Chapter 4

THE DOOR OPENS OF ITSELF

You cannot get into enlightenment by banging on the door and trying to knock it down.

– Moita

The feeling is widespread that something is missing – or rather, actively shut out – from the "modern world", the objectified routine that reason has built. People try innumerable doors to find the missing element. But every door leads back to the same prison, unless we work free of the conditioning that maintains the walls. Think of it: we have surrounded ourselves by an artificial civilization for convenience, based on external authority, specialized analysis, technological gimmickry; then we try to apply those same controlling methods and ambitions to all of life, to understanding self and others, to reaching beyond the physical. Usually, *it doesn't work.*

A totally different approach is needed to loose the fetters that have bound the human spirit in our culture, so that we may think, sense, feel and intuit our way toward becoming centred, whole and free. We may rejoice today that increasing numbers are finding their own flexible routes to greater awareness, enabling us to nurture clearer, well-rounded relationships and a healthier society. To assist in this, Moita points to habitual attitudes that can sabotage us in what we think we most want, and communicates a simple "path with heart" to spiritual growth in general and three openings in particular: meditation and energy-sharing, past-life recall and dreams.

The first three questions are from individuals who are becoming aware of the constraints we assume when we take our civilization's premises for granted.

Betsy: Moita, why are most human beings – and I include myself to a large extent in this – why are we so caught up in lower energy levels? Why aren't the intuitive levels of our brain functioning more? Why aren't we more tuned into these things?

MOITA: It has a great deal to do with the atmosphere of this part of the world. You are not permitted to develop your intuitive nature when you are children and there are more openings available to you on that level. They are closed off through training. By accepting the reality of the others that is most prevalent in this time, you accept their limits as well. And theirs is a very limited world, one where intuition does not play a very important part. Intellect is the attribute that is most admired and cultivated. And so, the culture is overbalanced on the side of the intellectual. You are not centred enough between the two to be able to travel from one to the other without difficulty.

Intuition has become a very foreign thing to this time. That is why it takes more energy to open yourself up to the intuitive side. In order to do so, you must restructure your concept of the universe and your belief in that concept. You can very easily say, "I believe there are other energies in the universe. I believe I have a higher self and an intuitive nature that I can contact if I wish." But before you can make that belief a reality, you must break all of those walls that have been placed around you by your own perceptions from childhood: of seeing that intuition does not work, of seeing that intuition is not considered favourable, that others do not appreciate insight. They want to have things that are provable, seeable, "real". And so, you have to in a sense enter a condition of unreality, from their point of view, to develop intuition.

        ∾   ∾   ∾

Leslie: I've often wondered if we're much more spiritually limited in our fast-paced civilization than, for instance, a primitive tribe way out in the Amazon somewhere that doesn't have all these demands for every minute of their time. They have more chance to sit back and think and get in touch with their feelings and the simple natural environment, instead of all these manmade demands. It seems to me, if you have more time, you'd probably be able to reach a higher reality of thinking and feeling.

MOITA: It is not so much that they have more time, but it is that they live within and around the energy of the Earth. They surround themselves with a different form of energy and they do not become distracted. All of the things that man has made he has made not much for his convenience but to distract him, because in the end-analysis he is afraid of spiritual perfection.

Leslie: Well, what made us change like that, though? We seem to really want to limit ourselves. We seem to rather go to a show, or just go out with a noisy bunch of people, just so that we don't have any time to ourselves.

MOITA: Man is afraid to think, and afraid of being alone. He is more afraid of himself than he is afraid of anything in the universe... When you are aware of [these tendencies, they] will have less of an effect on you. There are ways that you can change your own world so that you have the time, but it takes a great deal of energy and a great deal of courage to make that kind of a change.

        ∾   ∾   ∾

Mary: I seem to be having a hard time getting off this Earth the way I've seen it to be. I wonder if I've been here for an awful long time, or if I just won't let my mind travel in different levels.

MOITA: You travel in different levels without realizing it. The only thing that keeps you from realizing it is the fact that you aren't supposed to be there – so you think. And there is a fear involved in changing your reality and in making yourself appear different to yourself and to others.

This is something that you will work out in time. It takes time to work on those things. To be able to be here in a body on this Earth, and also to be able to touch the energy that comes from our level, is what you are here to learn – not to lose touch with the Earth. Otherwise, why would you be in a body? There is nothing wrong with being in a body, if that is where you are...

As long as you're not impatient, things will come along quite nicely. If you can learn all there is to learn at the instant, you will have much to work on for a long time!

∾   ∾   ∾

The widespread use of psychedelic and other psychoactive substances since the 1960s and continuing today – whether with the goal of experiencing higher levels of consciousness, or just escaping the normal one – reflects the alienation many have felt in these times. Drug use also demonstrates the modern preference for external, physical, perhaps synthetic agents to produce rapid but usually temporary and superficial change, sometimes at great cost to the human beings and natural systems involved.

This can be said without denying the very positive, even supremely benevolent role that entheogens may play at a certain stage for people who regard them as sacramental way-stations along a path of holistic growth. Moita's responses to the following questioner, however, emphasize the ways a drug can disrupt and hinder one's natural evolution in consciousness.

Caroline: Moita, can you recommend drugs as one way of breaking down barriers, or do you find it quite dangerous? If I was debating whether to take LSD, just for the experience or to gain a different insight or be more aware of my intuitive side, would you think that would be a good idea right now for me?

MOITA: I would say that LSD is a more dangerous drug than some others. The energy that it releases is not very easily controlled, and one can become very confused with this new reality. Much depends upon the individual person and their own concept of reality beforehand. It can be very disruptive to break down all of your walls at once – for they are there, in many cases, for good reason. They are things that need to be understood more slowly, broken down with a great deal of awareness. Much is learned by breaking down your own walls, and that learning experience can be lost when it is done too fast. And in some cases it can retard your progress, for then you do not have those barriers to protect you as you grow toward awareness. You have to, in a sense, start from scratch.

Caroline: Protect us against what? Our fear, or what we think is our reality?

MOITA: You are born into a body with a very single-minded focus, focused in just this instant, in this moment, in this "real world" that you have created. You can open yourself up to other worlds that do exist beside the one you are in, and you can lose your ability to focus in this one. Then others will not be able to communicate with you, for you will be speaking to them from other realities. And some people who have put themselves in this situation and have lost this necessary barrier have ended up in institutions, because no one can understand what it is they are saying. They have no common basis for communication.

In this world, you have many things that you have all decided are true, are real. You can speak a word, and everyone around you will have the required image so that you have something to communicate with. But when you take away all of these common symbols, what is there to communicate? I must use your common symbols; otherwise, you would not understand anything I said.

Caroline: Say someone was really spaced out, like in an institution. Would they themselves know who they were and where they were and understand what they were saying, though no one else would?

MOITA: Sometimes it is true that they know what has happened. Usually they are unaware of it as well, for they have not gone into it gradually, have not allowed themselves to flower into other awarenesses, to learn the rules that govern other universes; and so, they are lost. And sometimes it takes a great many lifetimes after such an experience for them to find their central core again and be able to communicate with their own higher self and understand this experience from a different perspective.

Each case is individual; no two are the same. There are other drugs that are easier on the mind and less dangerous, for they open you up to lower energies, but still energies that are higher than what you are used to – if you put yourself into the right situation, so long as they are only used infrequently. For they, as anything else, can become a crutch and you can stop your growth, for then you are not willing to go through the work it requires to break down barriers.

Progress that is made more slowly is usually more substantial. It is somewhat [like] Christ spoke of in building upon rock or sand. Great revelations can be learned in short times, but the importance of them can be lost very quickly, and you can be swept aside by a breeze that comes along and speaks of other things.

Caroline: And meditation would be one way of achieving this slow process of opening up to your intuitiveness? Would that be the best way?

MOITA: That is the safest: becoming aware of the world around you, being conscious of the things that you do, without judging them; gradually making your meditation a living experience rather than just a moment taken from a hectic day. Sometimes taking a drug is like taking a man without a spacesuit and throwing him into the universe. It is a great expanding experience – but one he does not survive for long. *(laughter)*

Caroline: So you don't recommend it. Taking LSD, for instance, is not a good idea.

MOITA: There will be enough body changes without creating them chemically. Your own mind can change the form of your body. That drug does affect the natural processes of healing that are within each of you, usually detrimentally.

෨   ෨   ෨

Beyond the issue of drugs, there remain numerous pitfalls in our culture along the way to opening inwardly. Moita addresses some of these in the next seven extracts.

Sylvia: It almost seems like there's a state of balance somehow in the universe, but I seem to be overreaching. I have to use very inadequate words, but the more I reach to overcome my "lower self", it pulls me down with such a vengeance.

MOITA: Your lower self is not there to be overcome.

Sylvia: I don't understand.

MOITA: By trying to overcome something, you are giving it more energy. You are creating, as I have said, a battlefront, something to fight for, something to fight against. You are fighting against yourself. There are things that you do not like – those things that you consider your lower nature. They are part of your being, part of your energy. They may not be expressing themselves in forms that you would approve of now. But by denying that energy, that part of yourself, you are trying to split yourself into pieces. You are becoming an unwhole personality. You can endanger your evolution.

You are here to accept yourself and others, but you must start with yourself first. And that means loving *all* of you, even those things that you do not like. It is easier to say than it is to do.

Sylvia: You've given me a lot to think about. Am I erring by trying to observe my own progress too much or becoming too self-conscious? Is this all sort of a twisted ego thing I'm getting into, because I seem to waste a lot of energy thinking about how I'm really not manifesting anything, and any time I come even closer to trying to purify myself, what I'm really doing is building some nice little self-image?

MOITA: Do not think that great spiritual endeavours come with bright music! The things that you think of as your greatest strides may not be strides at all. We come in the quiet of the night and in the stillness of your mind, unawares and unexpected. What you are here to do is to learn to love yourself and those around you. *(pause)*

Sylvia: I have a great deal of learning to do. Thank you very much.

MOITA: I will say something to you: that the way to yourself starts in very small ways and may not be noticed at all for a very long time. But each life you live, you are given the opportunity in that life to start on this road to yourself. Do not downgrade your own essence or the essence of your soul. Do not think that you are unworthy of anything at all. Each of you is as worthy as any other, and you only hold yourself back by thinking you cannot do it.

It is not an easy road in some ways, for it forces you to look at yourself and it changes your life and your perception. But it is a road that will bring you much joy and great reward in that you will bring about your own freedom. *(pause)* Relax and let yourself love life.

Sylvia: It sounds simple, but I keep on losing it.

MOITA: It is easy in times of great strife to overlook the simple things.

❧   ❧   ❧

(During a silence, Kelly hears a phrase repeating like poetry in her head. Her eyes close.)

MOITA: This time we shall say it. A phrase is coming to thought: "Wherein shall we look to find our heart's desire, except within ourselves?" Close enough. *(pause)*

So many search so far, and never look at home where all their answers lie. They will not stop until they realize that they will not find it in that way – and in not looking, their answers will come up from within themselves. Some souls spend many, many lifetimes learning that, and some spend only a few. It depends on each individually how much they see and how soon. They are not necessarily [growing] when they seek. Oftentimes they are hiding and delaying the moment, because they are afraid of it and hope there is another way. I feel a great deal for those who seek and do not find..., for I have walked that road myself and know the fear.

ॐ   ॐ   ॐ

MOITA: You can touch this energy at other times.

Helen: Yes, I have been trying. Sometimes I think I just try too hard, try to force it, and then it doesn't seem to come. But I'm probably blocking it, I suppose.

MOITA: It is a trick not to try. It is very true that when the student is ready, a teacher will appear; [but] as long as the student seeks the teacher, he is not there. The universe flows in many unseeable ways.

Helen: Hmm. That's very beautiful.

MOITA: The energy makes it better. The centre of knowing, of understanding the ways of the universe, is within each of you. It is not something that has to come from without.

Helen: It seems hard to get in touch with it sometimes.

MOITA: That is why there are beings such as I to help you become more acquainted with its feel, so that it is easier for you to find it yourself.

Helen: To keep an open heart and not shut down (?).

MOITA: When you can touch your own soul, you give it the ability to assist you...and to help you grow in your understanding of life. It is not connecting to an outside source, as some people think. It is connecting to yourself – a greater part, a part you have not been aware of for a long time, but still you.

Helen: What about little thoughts going on all the time? Your inner soul doesn't really speak in your head all the time, does it?

MOITA: Usually that is your consciousness. But there are thoughts just below the surface of that stream. Thoughts that come from your soul usually are very clear, unclouded, vivid thoughts. They may not always start as vivid; they may be nudgings in certain directions, vague intuitions. But they are usually persistent, unless you have closed yourself off from them altogether.

Harold: Is it good that we're going to visit [a certain spiritual teacher]? Is this part of the plan? Are we reading it right, or what?

MOITA: Anything is right if you take your own rightness with you.

Harold: I'm not sure I follow that.

MOITA: If you see it as right, if you experience it as right or good or as positive, or as learning or as growing – they're all the same – then it *is*. If you go there expecting not to learn, it will not be right.

Harold: I go there very *definitely* expecting to learn and grow, but I also feel or believe that there is such a thing as an initiation and that [the spiritual teacher] can initiate us. I don't know what that means, or whether I'm even on the right track. Can he take us to higher levels?

MOITA: No one can take you except yourself. Do not depend on him to take you somewhere. Depend on yourself to open to perhaps where he can go. He has his limits too. None of you are perfect channels. None of you are totally pure. You must also remember that you are all each individuals and all each persons.

Harold: I feel like I could become like God.

MOITA: You *are*. But you must become a god which travels with, and not against, life. The gods who travel against life are thrown down. The gods who travel with life do not care if they are gods. It is a tricky path for some, because they can believe that theirs is the only way and forget that theirs is only one part of an important whole. *(pause)*

     This is why so many teachings speak of humility. It [does not] mean feeling unimportant or unworthy in yourself. It means to understand and accept with grace your part, your importance, but also knowing that yours is not to impose that sense of oneness on any other. Humility gives you the freedom to be yourself, and gives others the same freedom.

❧ ❧ ❧

Curt: Colleen and I have received the information that we each are one of twelve selves within an energy gestalt; and that as we find completion in our uniqueness, that helps the other selves just as they help us. Is Kelly on a similar journey?

MOITA: You are getting into a structure of reality that may or may not hold true later. Each one of you [has] different parts of yourself which may make up more or less than twelve. The possibilities for individual expression are endless, and the only limit is that which you place on your own mind. If you choose this structure, it will manifest for you, become reality. If you decide to keep yourself open to other possibilities, you may return to your soul-self and change its concept of the universe.

Curt: So the structure that we created was a step up at a certain time, but now it may be a step back down – it may limit, it may restrict, our growth or advancement?

MOITA: Each structure that you create hopefully is one that brings you forward. And when it has served its purpose in creating more energy for you to work with, and you grow to the point where you no longer require a structure, then that structure hopefully will fall away and leave you limitless. This is how I view the universe. I have many of what you might call "friends" whose reality is nowhere near what mine is, and the only reason...our realities are different is because of the perceptions we bring to it. You will create for yourself the universe of your choice.

Curt: So our focus is on God, on oneness, in the now of existence, and any structure that comes along is simply a stepping-stone to that goal.

MOITA: I have lost many structures. This is also a structure right now. And the concepts that I present using Kelly as a channel are also structures in their own way.

ം   ം   ം

MOITA: The form that you receive your own learning from is not as important as the love you put into it. There are many forms on Earth – forms of learning, structures of paths. Each chooses the structure he feels more comfortable with, but the structure itself is of no consequence. For every structure, you will find some who can transcend their awareness and some who are destroyed by their own lack of stature, their own weaknesses or their own fears.

ം   ം   ം

Shelley: We've talked about opening ourselves up to different things, being more sensitive and learning more, being able to do more because we're aware of more. Say I'm here *(gesturing at a certain level)*, and I want to get up here *(raising her hand)*, what do I do next? I really feel I'm ready for another step, but I'm wondering what might be a possible step to take. Can you advise me?

MOITA: If words weren't such a tricky thing, it would be so easy. Everyone needs to develop a sense of humility – which is a very difficult word to express how it is meant: being able to put yourself into another's hands, in a sense; knowing that your development will be taken care of; trusting. When the step is ready to be taken, it will present itself. And many times a person will take the step and not recognize it until [she] has the benefit of time to change [her] perspective on [her] past. Important changes may not come with loud, blaring trumpets. They very often come in the quiet of the night, when you are sleeping and most open.
           Disappointed?

Shelley: No.

MOITA: Keep yourself aware and let yourself flow, and all of those steps shall be there for you to take.

❧ ❧ ❧

Door #1: Meditation and Energy-Sharing

Many forms of meditation involve a delicate balance of concentration on a non-conceptual focus (a repetitive activity, a point in the body, an image, etc.) and non-judging openness to experience. The meditative state can be a joy in its freedom from conventional limits. It can also be a stepping-stone to mingling energies with others and to creative and psychic activity. An extended conversation with one couple touches on various facets of what has been called a priceless jewel.

George: Can you tell me how I can improve my meditation, or maybe tell me what is wrong in my methods?

MOITA: *(after a long silence)* There comes a certain point in meditation where you seem to reach a wall or a block – you feel you can't go any deeper than that point. The way to get beyond that is what some people have called surrender to your self. It's not giving anything up; it's more opening an inner door and letting yourself out. It's a feeling of acceptance, or quiet and [stillness], of not letting your focusing on certain things get in the way of receiving that greater part that's in you. When you focus your thoughts in a certain direction, you sometimes block out what would be given to you in other areas – similar to how words box things in and keep other things from letting themselves be known.

George: I usually practise what's called "seeded meditation", where you try to implant thoughts of love – something like that. Or do you think you should just clear your mind of all things and be receptive?

MOITA: That intrigues me: "implant love". You see, love is always *there*. There is no need to put it there where it already exists. There is only a need to open yourself up to it, to let yourself be aware of that energy – to be receptive, if you will. Love is an energy by itself. It is not a thought. It exists independently of all thought.

George: But you could meditate with a feeling of love to bring it forth from you. Is that right?

MOITA: When you open yourself up to your universal inwardness, it's there. It is also in the air around you, and in the sky and in the grass and in the trees. You do not need to sit still in one place in order to meditate. You can make your life a meditation, one of joy and beauty. We are in everything.

George: I can accept that. God is omnipresent, when we're with God.

MOITA: In order to find these things, there are many things you must let go – unimportant things that seem important. *(pause)* Worry, for one.

George: I accept that intellectually, but demonstration is difficult.

MOITA: It takes time to learn to let these things go. It is like peeling off layers of an onion to get at the heart. Each layer, when it turns brown and crackles and falls off – as it does that, you realize that it was not important and that there was something underneath. But then that new, fresh layer that's there is clear and seems to be "it", the lowest layer you can go to, until it also turns brown and falls off, until you finally reach the core. These things will happen in their own time.

George: I'm comfortable with the way things are moving now.

MOITA: So long as you don't try to rush things, things will happen much quicker than you would expect otherwise...

Jane: Is there anything that we can do individually to help raise the consciousness generally?

MOITA: By raising your own, you will do as much as you are able.

Jane: Uh-huh! Not necessary to try to raise other people's (?). Work on my own first. *(laughing)* That's a good point.

MOITA: By raising your own, you *are* working on others'.

Jane: Oh!

MOITA: You affect those around you. And if you see yourself as a flame that grows [brighter] as you grow stronger, others are aware of the warmth and the light that you are projecting, and then they too become brighter and learn their own lessons, until they are also a flame...

George: I'm looking forward to experiencing the things that you're experiencing. I know I have many friends there already that are special to me. I long for their companionship.

MOITA: You can feel them near you when you wish. I know it is not the same.

George: I know, because my thoughts dwell on them quite often. I send out love to them and I receive it.

MOITA: Your gifts brighten our world. We notice the tiniest thoughts of love sent out from anywhere. And the energy is used to help bring about changes in others, so they too can feel it.

✤   ✤   ✤

MOITA: Even though you are far from your family, your energy will affect them, since there is no such thing as distance except in the mind – as your energy affects many others too, even when you do not see them.

✤   ✤   ✤

These sessions, of course, are rich opportunities for moving through what usually appear to be walls – between levels, and between each other.

MOITA: You can feel the energy in each thought here as it leaves...

(Taking advantage of the extra energy present, I am experimenting with focusing on different people I know and sensing the quality of the link between us. Meanwhile, as Kelly will describe later, "I know a thought is someplace. Then all of a sudden I can

feel this whoosh! – like a rocket taking off, a surge in a certain direction."
Interestingly, the image of a rocket also comes into my mind near the end of this silent
period.)

MOITA: It is nothing mysterious to read your mind... It is easier to tune in another's
              thought when yours are not cloudy. Sometimes, receiving someone else's
              impulses, you interpret them from your own viewpoint, from your own
              prejudices, rather than receiving them in their true form. Fears and doubts play
              a great part...

(From conversation afterward:)

Kelly: Right after seeing your thoughts, I felt this energy coming out of the back
              of our heads and coming around and meeting, and then continuing and
              mingling, making this circle of energy going back and forth and around, in
              both directions at once. *(gesturing behind each other's head and crossing in
              front)* Almost like a figure 8.

୬   ୬   ୬

Door #2: Past-Life Recall

People sometimes ask what the purpose of remembering past lives could possibly
be, usually mingling their assumption that incarnations are linear and separate (rather
than simultaneously interacting) with a deal of doubt that any valid memory is even
possible. Moita has said such knowledge is not, in fact, always beneficial. And only
rarely will she simply inform a person about a past life. Most times, it needs to be
worked for oneself.

Jill, however, comes to us at a time when opening to her memories clearly *is*
indicated by present need. In the last chapter, it was Jill's friend Darryl who told her
they were "soul mates". In the exchange below, we get a fuller picture of connections
between Jill and Darryl that are not as positive as they first appear – and more material
on Jill's predicament awaits us in later chapters.

After introducing Jill's situation, we'll look in on people seeking methods of
remembering under less pressing circumstances. Hypersentience (from Marcia Moore's
book of the same name) is a technique of guided regression in which a deeply relaxed
subject perceives happenings, images, feelings, etc., that may be from another life and
brings them back through dialogue. The problems in opening sufficiently and then
evaluating the results of these experiments are also explored.

Jill: Can you give me any thoughts on what's the best way to deal with Darryl?
              I feel as though I need to go there. I feel that if I don't do that, I'll be missing
              something.

MOITA: Your need stems from a different place..., from the past.

Jill: Hmm. Another life?

MOITA: Yes. There is a danger sometimes in fulfilling a need from the past when
              there have been too many changes between those involved in the intervening

space. You should become more clear on your reasons and find their roots. A thing that happens very often in a physical life with someone who is beginning to [remember other lives] is that recognition of a past acquaintance or friend or close soul is not always easy to distinguish. You cannot always tell, from that ringing inside your mind that says "I think I have known you before," exactly what way that knowing was done. And in the beginning it is so easy to misinterpret the desire to find someone whom you have known. You *must* be wary.

Jill: Mm-hmm. I will be...

MOITA: There is also the side that sees things from the past only, does not see them clearly in the present, places old values or old associations on present ones and sees not the changes that may have occurred. It is like having a very close friend when you are younger and then not seeing that friend for fifty years – and in the meantime that friend has changed a great deal and gone on another way – and then meeting that friend again, and expecting things to be as they were and placing those things that you saw then *on* him, whether they are there or not...

Jill: It's just a few more days till I visit [Darryl's city], and I'm feeling very vulnerable. I feel as though perhaps some knowledge of my connections with Darryl would help me deal with the situation at present.

MOITA: There is no doubt that being armed with further knowledge, you would be better able to make decisions as far as what you wish to do with it. They say ignorance is bliss, but it is not true.

Jill: Right.

MOITA: Although truth is frightening to many, you have the courage to face it. It is your fear of what it *might* be that frightens you far more than the actuality when you remember. You colour the unknown with large, dark shapes that loom on your vision, and when you get to yourself you will find that those shapes have disappeared. When you learn and accept yourself as a whole instead of a piece, there is no ugliness. So there is nothing to fear...

Jill: Can you tell me about my connections with Darryl?

MOITA: This is something you should try to find out on your own. I can tell you, but it would be better for you if you discovered it for yourself.

Jill: Then do you have any suggestions for my doing a hypersentience session on this?

MOITA: Try focusing on your past connection with Darryl that creates the need to help him in this life.

Jill: I guess I need some reassurance. I don't know if you can give it to me. Will I be okay after? I'm scared!

MOITA: Being frightened does not take away your inner courage. You have much of that in reserve when you need it, and you have many here who are willing to help you through it, if it gets that bad. Providing you have love around you, you have nothing to fear.

Jill: That helps. *(pause)* Are you with me when I'm away from here?

MOITA: If not me, then someone quite similar.

(Later that evening, Jill is able to open to certain information about a life in which Darryl was her son. She does not go very deeply into it, however, presumably because she does not feel ready. A later chapter will reveal more on the source of her understandable fears.)

ॐ   ॐ   ॐ

Jane: I'm trying to find a way to remember my own pasts myself in meditation. Is that possible to do, or do I need a guide?
MOITA: It's quite possible.
Jane: Takes a little longer, huh?
MOITA: It all depends on the individual. Many do remembering on their own without help. Just so long as you do not seek the experience of remembering for its own sake, but remember you are doing it to learn and that you yourself may not be aware of what would be the best thing for you to experience, you can open yourself up to that energy that can guide you into the best experiences so your [memory] will flower in its own time.

ॐ   ॐ   ॐ

Betty: You said that we have threads from the past coming together and we should recognize them. How can we do this?
MOITA: One of the first things that you can do is try to recall those innate and inborn traits that you possess. Those interests which you have been drawn to are usually an indicator of another existence which has leaked through. After you discover these, you can then concentrate on them in a state of meditation similar to the hypersentience state and see what flows from there. All of you have teachers on other levels who are working toward opening you towards yourself.

ॐ   ॐ   ॐ

Sam: Would it be advantageous for me at this time to know something of my other lives?
MOITA: Have you been given any sign from within?

(Sam describes a dream series he's experienced regarding a particular city, and also recurring feelings throughout his life of being a hermit in the woods – a life of joy and also sadness that seems linked to his present.)

MOITA: It will be better for you if you can experience these lives more directly than through my explaining them to you right now. The experience of remembering is a very good opening.
Sam: This is through dreams?
MOITA: You can do it through David.

Sam: Good. *(laughter)*

MOITA: He is becoming good at guiding, and of course you never go into this experience alone. There will always be your own guide there to help you.

ᔥ   ᔥ   ᔥ

Bob: I seem to have a personal block about other times, past lives. I'd really like to know about another time, but it seems to be only a hope or speculation or just daydreams.

MOITA: And where do daydreams come from?

Bob: The imagination, I would assume.

MOITA: And your imagination?

Bob: Self.

MOITA: The trick is to decipher which level of self your imagination comes from. That is how you can tell to a certain extent if a memory of another time is speculation or memory – and if you get details (things your conscious awareness has not been shown or taught), vitality in a memory, or a memory that does not change when you think of it again. Very often in a dream world if you see something, the next time you look on it it is not the same. A real memory would not alter its state.

ᔥ   ᔥ   ᔥ

When past-life information is blocked, the block may act either in support of a person's long-run growth or against it. Here are two examples.

Mary: Could you give me any hints as to a previous life? I don't seem to be getting much indication from the group hypersentience session.

MOITA: Usually that's a good indication that you don't want to know yet.

Mary: Oh, I have a feeling that I'd like to.

MOITA: In remembering a previous life, by remembering it you also bring to you the energy that was around you at the time of the life. And till you have prepared adequately and are ready to accept those changes that remembering will bring, you will keep yourself from remembering. It is your own intuitive blocking so that you do not go too fast too soon. It would do you no good if you would backslide.

Mary: That sounds reasonable.

MOITA: Keep going in your own direction. You shall find amazing things.

ᔥ   ᔥ   ᔥ

Despite progress in guiding hypersentience sessions, I still have a lot to learn and practise as a subject. During my first session, I experience a number of interesting scenes – for instance, a group of elves dancing around a fire in a clearing (very common in faery lore). But my skepticism at the time as to their being any more than fantasy holds me back. During this session, Kelly, acting as my guide, hears Moita noting my reluctance to open to deeper levels. I talk to Moita directly after I return.

David: What is my reluctance?

MOITA: You are reluctant to let go of yourself, to immerse yourself in an experience, forgetting yourself as you go. You try too hard to take your objectivity with you, instead of becoming one with the experience and then being able to be objective about it after you have come out the other side. It is sometimes the way you live your life as well. The lessons that are in life for you to learn cannot be learned by being objective... One of the largest lessons you need to learn [is] to let go of your expectations. You saw it in the man [who saw the elves], because he found something he did not expect. Sometimes by looking too hard for something you expect, you do not find anything at all.

David: My problem is not always being as conscious as I might of what you call my objectivity and expectations.

MOITA: Since Kelly has been born, she has been on a search. She has been looking for me, or that contact, in everything that she has seen and everything that she has done. However, until she reached the point where she lost her expectations, when she stopped trying to find me, when she stopped looking to see me in everything . . . It was at that point that she allowed me to do those things that were necessary in order to bring about that realization.

When the contact is not there, when you are searching in your life for meaning, you are actively looking; and whether or not you can consciously realize it, you are expecting or hoping that something will happen. And this state of looking does not let you see clearly, causes blindness, a kind of blindness that you are not aware of having and therefore is hard to get rid of.

You are beginning to let go of some of these things. But you have a very analytical and critical mind and sometimes see things that are not there to be seen. It is important at a certain stage in your development to have these qualities. It is the paradox of the universe that when you stop seeking, you find.

David: What happened in Kelly's life when she stopped seeking? Were there things in her outward life that brought that about, or was it an inner change?

MOITA: All of the outward events that have happened to her have had something to do with the inner change that has taken place. It is her viewing of the outward events that has changed, not the events themselves. She has been able to reach down lower into herself without interfering with it, and she does not know how she has done it. Sometimes it is not necessary to understand.

It is possible for you in this life to link up with the past. Many of the things that you saw were accurate from the time they came from.

ॐ   ॐ   ॐ

Door #3: Dreams

Once when Kelly told a hotel clerk we were in town to lead a dream workshop, she received the astonished reply, "Whatever *for*?" The incredulity of many in our culture that dreams might actually be taken seriously reflects a massive split between night and day, conscious and unconscious – and an underlying fear. Our first excerpt sheds light on this phenomenon through C.'s willingness to explore her reaction to the psyche's dark underside. The two following deal with degrees of dream awareness.

C.: What do you see when you look at a person?

MOITA: I see many things: their emotions and feelings become visible, and their pasts and futures are also standing there to be viewed. Much depends upon what I seek. I seek to see you opening and to touch your centre, what I call "your light", that place within you that has a steady, pulsing energy.

C.: Is the energy really steady, then? Sometimes it seems to be far from steady, and I sometimes wonder whether the energy fluctuates.

MOITA: It is not the energy itself that fluctuates. It is only your awareness of it that changes. Sometimes you are closer and other times you are farther away, so you see it as brighter or dimmer.

C.: Sometimes I feel very, very dark.

MOITA: It happens when you turn your back on yourself, when you try to shut out that light, or when you try to protect it from others. Many fear their light will be blown out, as if it were a mere candle flame. Regardless of the winds of life that may buffet you, that inner flame cannot be extinguished. It can only be forgotten for a short time.

C.: Is the light always there, then, even right when one goes to sleep? It seems there is a darkness before one begins to dream, and a period when one doesn't exist. Does one, then, always exist?

MOITA: You are always existing, and yet sometimes you are unaware of it as existing. It is like you have the ocean, and you look on it, you know it is there. Then you take your eyes away from it and look to the stars. You see not the ocean anymore and may even forget it exists, and yet it has not moved. All you need to do is look at it again to know it is still there.

C.: I don't understand where one is when one isn't conscious.

MOITA: One is conscious of other things.

C.: In the periods that seem to be totally unconscious or dark, is it just forgotten what one was?

MOITA: When you are in the darkness and cannot see the light?

C.: I guess I was wondering why the light fluctuates sometimes so much, and experiencing the darkness when one is asleep and not dreaming makes me more inclined to think that the light would indeed go out. How a light that can seem so bright sometimes can be gone at other times I find very hard to understand.

MOITA: When you are going to sleep, it is like you are turning around. You are entering into another realm, another world. That moment when you open that door, the shadow of the doorway is what you experience as darkness. But when the door is fully opened and you walk through, then you can see and you experience your dream-creation. You are afraid of the transition, the in-between space.

I do not know if this will clarify things for you. I can only say again: you must learn for yourself what happens when you are unaware of light from within, what seems to close that door for you when you are awake.

∾   ∾   ∾

Rita: Do you take Kelly on journeys when she's sleeping?

MOITA: She travels out of her body a great deal – not always with me – but she does not always remember. But then, so do you.

Rita: Yeah, that's what everybody says, that you always go out of your body at night.

MOITA: Some go to a place where they make their dreams. There are special spaces for certain things... Some who go to the world of dreams are more aware than others. Some are not aware that they are there at all. That's why they don't remember their dreams.

(Meanwhile Kelly is seeing a plain covered by mist. People are sleeping and dreaming on this plain. Some are curled up in a ball, totally unaware. Others are having different degrees of awareness, with some walking around and helping to create their dreams consciously.)

∾   ∾   ∾

Nora: What happens at night?

MOITA: Everyone leaves their body at night. Much depends upon them how far they will go to learn. If you have a person who cannot remember [her] dreams, [she] has not gone very far. That is the first step, the first plateau after you have left your body in sleep. You do not become any more open asleep than you are able to become open while you are awake. You bring those personality traits with you. And if you are afraid of finding out about yourself, you will close down your doors even if they are open. You will do all in your power to lock them.

Nora: How does one deal with this fear? Is there anything a person can do to open themselves more and not be afraid?

MOITA: Changing your perspective of what it is you are doing: not being afraid of truth, not being afraid of making mistakes; *embracing* your mistakes, for that is why they are there. If they do not do their service, if they do not teach you something, you will make them again. So the sooner you embrace them, the sooner you can get on with something else.

As a person becomes more able to react and participate in a dream world,

[her] dreams gain more depth and teaching can come through. Experiences from other levels can start to trickle down through the layers of reality. It is extremely simple, although many people make it very hard to do. It is very much like turning around and seeing what is behind you, instead of looking on it as a shadow that is trying to overtake you. Once something is seen in full view, the fear almost always disappears. It is more the fear of unknown things that holds people back – the fear of finding something they will not like.

ဢ ဢ ဢ

Nightmares are what people most fear to dream, and what convinces them their inner self is no friend at all. But threatening images in dreams are there for a purpose; and when they are confronted, that purpose is revealed.

(Before this session, group members are discussing their recent dreams. Andrea says she was having a number of frightening ones, and that since then she has had trouble remembering any.)

Andrea: Are there reasons for every dream? Is every dream trying to tell you something?

MOITA: Your dreams are important to you as a developing spirit. They help you understand your feelings, and they show you when you are afraid of things. If you did not know, you would not be able to do anything about it.

  When your dreams come back, if you find that you are frightened, try to remember that your dreams cannot hurt you. They are only there to help you; they are a friend. And if they are trying to frighten you, it is because your inner self feels they are most important for you to understand. If you can, confront a fear in a dream, force it to stop and talk to it. It will tell you what it is. And then, [having been understood], it will go away.

ဢ ဢ ဢ

Interestingly, this advice about confronting a fearful image in a dream, and Moita's next suggestion to treat dream antagonists kindly, strongly parallel the reported cultural wisdom of the hunting-gathering Senoi people in Malaysia, practised in both the waking and dreaming state.[22N]

MOITA: *(speaking of waking emotions)* It is like in a dream experience, where part of yourself that has been neglected will present itself as an antagonist until you try to show it kindness or affection or care, and quickly it will forget its antagonistic role and become a fast friend.

ဢ ဢ ဢ

Of course, for many people (like Sara in Chapter 2), dreams carry little significance, appearing relatively trivial, meaningless or inscrutable to the extent they are remembered at all. Once Moita is asked, "What are the steps to remember or find meaning in dreams?" Her one-word answer: "Interest!"

Larry: What do dreams mean?...
MOITA: They usually reflect things that you are not seeing – unconscious thoughts, your own feelings.
Larry: They usually don't get reflected in a manner you can understand, though.
MOITA: Dreams have their own language.
Larry: I don't have a dictionary. *(laughter)*
MOITA: Ah, but you do: *yourself.* For when you can understand your own feelings in your own dreams, then you will reach closer to your true self and open up other things as well. Dreams are only incomprehensible if you look at them from the wrong angle. The important thing is to experience the feeling *behind* the dream.
Larry: Does the amount or lack of dreams you have mean anything?
MOITA: A lack of dreams can indicate a lack of interest in them, or a block between your waking self and your sleeping self. When you are asleep, you are more open, more aware of other realities – of other times and dimensions of your whole self and your road. When you are awake, you are more focused. If you have a strong desire to stay focussed, do not enjoy (from your focused point of view) the experience of freedom in a dream, then you will blot out the experiences so they will not disturb your waking life.
Larry: Do you still have them when you're blocking them, or do you block yourself off from having them?
MOITA: You always have dreams, whether you want them or not.
Larry: You're just blocking off the memory of them, then.
MOITA: You leave your body when you dream, and sometimes there is a definite trick to remembering what you have experienced when you come back. What experiences come through when you are asleep depends [a great deal] on where your conscious is focused during the day. You do not stop learning in your dreams just because you don't remember them, but it is important for you to connect these parts of yourself. You cannot become whole if you are a different person when you sleep than when you wake.

Dreams do not lie, and they are a very clear road to your inner self and higher realities. Even without a teacher of any kind, you can teach yourself when you understand your dreams, and they will guide you safely through any hazards.

∞ ∞ ∞

Where interest exists, a commitment to keeping a dream journal is key to reaping the full harvest of one's dream life. Training your will to write down dreams as soon as you wake, even in the middle of the night, will provide the accurate detail and associations you need for a full interpretation. But even when only fragments are remembered, much work can be done with them.

Dawn: My dreams haven't been opening up – at least, my sleep dreams. Do daydreams have the same kind of significance as night dreams? May as much be learned?

MOITA: There is something to be learned from everything, but daydreams are usually not as deep. You are not dipping down farther into your awareness. When you have dreams at night, there are many levels of awareness that you can descend to, and it is experiencing these things and then interpreting them and bringing them back to the surface that makes a dream.

It is somewhat like meditation. When you first start, there are many thoughts that fly through and distract. As you become more practised at it, you descend below this stream of thought and find there are fewer thoughts and they are more clear and have more meaning. Being fewer does not make them less.

Even though you may only get a face to remember in the morning, study the face that you *can* remember and see how you feel [about] it. Many things can be written in the lines of the face and in the soul of the eyes. You try to speak to yourself succinctly in your dreams. Since you remember few images, the images you do remember have more import. Being one who works with words to create an image within a mind *(Dawn is a poet)*, you should know that you usually start with the image first and then try to find the words to fit it. It is a cycle that flows from one to the other. When you wake up with an image, try writing down how you feel about it in the instant.

ৎ৹   ৎ৹   ৎ৹

Jane: I wish I could remember all that was said in those dreams, but I can't remember *anything* except that it happened. I often know I've learned something in my dreams, but when I wake up I can't remember what it was I learned.

MOITA: Sometimes it is more important to remember the feel of something that you have learned than the actual words that you have used to teach it to yourself, because you can get bogged down in words. This leaves you more freedom to explore what it is that you are learning. By leaving some things out in your memory, you are instilling an intense curiosity in your present self to fill those apparent gaps in your knowledge.

Jane: That's true, no question. *(laughing)* I guess it *is* piquing my curiosity. I keep trying to figure them out.

MOITA: And that is how you expand and grow!

ৎ৹   ৎ৹   ৎ৹

And what do these dream learnings have to contribute to life in the outer world that today gives them so little recognition? How do they relate to why we're here in bodies in the first place, and the long evolution in consciousness of which the passing "modern" era is such a small and recent part?

MOITA: The whole point of being here is being able to bring *to* the world your awareness; to be able to open up enough to your own self to know what you are doing, to become a whole being instead of one who is one part in the day and another at night – or one who changes his character more than he does his clothes, depending on the people he is with.

❧   ❧   ❧

Paul: Is there a particular time of day when we're more in touch with our higher selves? I've heard it said that just when you've woken up is when you're closest to enlightenment. But I don't know if that was a joke *(laughter)* or a conjecture.
MOITA: I have also heard it said that, if you are rudely awakened, you are closest to murder! *(laughter)*
        When you sleep, you leave your body. You go into other worlds, other realities. You create your dreams and react with them. You meet teachers, you go to classes, learn lessons, some [of] which you bring back in dreams, some [of] which you bring back in intuitions and hunches. The problem is the separation of the two forms [of consciousness] – the one in the day and the one at night. It is a very artificial separation, and the one thing that man is striving for is to bring these two worlds back together, so that the one can work with the other – not so the one you are missing will replace this one.
Paul: So part of our being on Earth is to develop and integrate our rationality with our more intuitive parts?
MOITA: You were separated from this level of feeling and intuition in order to create in you the sense of the ego, a rational mind, the intellect. And now that that has been accomplished and you are hopefully seeing many sides of what it can do, it is time to bring that quality together with the spirit so that you will have more purpose, more understanding of the creative forces of which you are a part.
Paul: And what is the purpose of the ego?
MOITA: To make you an individual expression, and a unique interpreter, of all of your experience.

❧   ❧   ❧

Now Moita lets the fruits of all these ways come together, effortlessly.

MOITA: Our teachings – the way the world speaks to you – are very silent and still and quiet. We do not speak in a loud voice; we speak in a small way, but an important way.

You need peace. You have looked for it and, looking, have not found. Peace is around you if you will relax, if you will let love flow into you and then allow it to flow out in its own form. Do not try to structure your world too much. You limit yourself and you interfere in your own flow, your creativity...

I say that love does not try to control – love *flows*. And something that attempts control is not love. You gain more by not trying to gain than you will ever gain by putting your energy into [trying]...

I have said once before that you cannot get into enlightenment by banging on the door and trying to knock it down. The door opens of itself. Embrace life, and enlightenment comes.

Þ   Þ   Þ

Illustrative Dream

You can touch this energy at other times. The centre of knowing, of understanding the ways of the universe, is within each of you. It is not something that has to come from without. It is a feeling of acceptance, or quiet and [stillness], of not letting your focusing on certain things get in the way of receiving that greater part that is in you. [Surrender to your self] is not giving anything up; it is more opening an inner door and letting yourself out.
– Moita

This dream neatly illustrates the difference between true openness to higher states and the walled-off attitude of a skeptic driven by unacknowledged emotions.

"Lotus Meditation Being" dream
David (age 27) / Summer 1974

I am among a few students attending a seminar. The guest speaker is a tall, thin man credited with recording a huge number of indigenous folk tales. We were to have read an Alan Watts book (on Zen?) in preparation, but another student tells the speaker he couldn't make any coherent sense of Watts. The speaker responds by mentioning meditation, on which he has written extensively.

Now an aide to the speaker opens a door, and a strange little all-metallic being scurries in! It's shaped like a stick figure, with a long tapering point for a head. It scrambles across the floor as a cat or toddler might, only to stop in the centre of the room and assume the lotus position for meditation. We understand this is the speaker's "child", a type of purely spiritual being who is born to humans from time to time.

The male student questions this being as to the effectiveness or worth of meditation. The being says how simple it all is, if one just assumes the proper position. Sitting in my chair, I bring my legs up and cross them, as do all except the questioner. Suddenly, energy is coming over me in pulsing waves of great power and warmth. The pulses unlock laughter and joy. I wave my arms in circles, showing the energy revving up. We are all transported by the energy, except for the one questioner who walks curiously around us, incredulous and embarrassed.

Waking, I feel a warmth of energy within me, which lessens as the dream fades. I hear a steady, rushing sound outside and muse about a flying saucer of "lotus beings" stimulating me to dream and get in touch with this cosmic energy.

Chapter 5

CROSSING ENERGY THRESHOLDS

That is part of that subtle, higher vibrational body that people have called your soul or your spirit – the inner you, the one that does the thinking and the feeling, that can separate from the body to make journeys of its own.
– Moita

As we grow in awareness, another level of perceiving begins to open up "within" or "behind" or "above" life as normally experienced – bringing a new vocabulary in its wake. From this larger perspective, the material bodies of our ordinary world become but relatively dense islands in a sea of vibrating energy. All levels of potential experience have their own reality within this unobstructed, interacting universe, as determined by their rate of vibration, their fluidity or density. Whether or not this non-physical dimension becomes visible, tangible experience for an individual, its vocabulary meshes well with the dynamics of inner evolution.

We now continue our tale of metamorphosis by describing energy-flow patterns to which a person can attune in order to negotiate safely new thresholds of reality. A more conscious approach to spiritual development inevitably means taking greater responsibility for the well-being or dis-ease of our bodies as well, lest there be a breakdown in either realm. For many, the pursuit of inner wholeness naturally involves departing from conventional but unhealthy lifestyles. For others, a physical ailment may be the initial impetus for recognizing an even more serious spiritual debility. Thus the body can serve as a mirror of, and vehicle for, an individual's growth in awareness.

We begin with two people experiencing the physical symptoms of a blockage of energy as they stand on a threshold in their lives.

Kelly and I first meet Howard when he asks her to try healing the painful "tennis elbow" he has developed in his job as a meat cutter for a chain grocery store. This ailment has been leading him to question the viability of orthodox medicine (which hasn't helped him, short of proposed surgery) and his acquired trade as well.

Howard comes back a week later, saying the pain returned after a single shift. Kelly suggests Moita's perspective may be of help in exploring the broader background to the problem. Howard agrees to the idea, but in the newness of it all he keeps his eyes closed and head bowed during most of the session.

MOITA: Are you nervous?
Howard: A little bit. *(laughing)* No, I'm not worried.
MOITA: You don't have to keep your eyes closed.
Howard: That's okay. I'm relaxed... *(pause)*
MOITA: You have a lot of energy coming from you, you know.

Howard:	Yeah, mm-hmm.
MOITA:	You seem to be trying to keep it in.
Howard:	*(laughs)* Is that good or bad to keep it in?
MOITA:	It is never good to block a great deal of energy.
Howard:	Right. *(laughs)*
MOITA:	Perhaps I should introduce myself. They call me Moita.
Howard:	Mm-hmm. *(long silence)*
David:	Can you put anything in the form of a question? Sometimes that helps me when I'm trying to converse.
Howard:	I don't think of anything – except for my arm, what's the problem with it... *(pause)* I guess that's really all I'm concerned about, is my arm.

(Kelly and I are both surprised at how suddenly Moita responds with the larger picture.)

MOITA:	There are many changes that are coming to this Earth. And there is not that much time left before they start.
Howard:	What's the changes?
MOITA:	There are many levels: physical as well as spiritual, and social and economic. The world is in a state of flux, getting ready to change over.
Howard:	For better or worse?
MOITA:	That depends on those who go with it.
Howard:	Right. Yeah.
MOITA:	It is a necessary change. From our view, providing enough energy is put into it, it will be a very good change because these energies will be able to come more together. But since there is not much time before these changes happen, many are choosing...a position where they must look farther into themselves to find the answers they are seeking.
Howard:	How does one look into himself to find the answers? *(laughs)*
MOITA:	That is a very individual search.
Howard:	Yeah. Where does one start?
MOITA:	You have already started. Seeking is the first step, and then taking what you experience into yourself and learning how to become still enough to hear yourself speak. You have within you the answers.
Howard:	It's *finding* them, knowing that that is the answer.
MOITA:	That is the trick.
Howard:	Yeah. *(laughs)* How does one know when one finds the answer?
MOITA:	There is a certain feeling that goes with it. Once it is felt, you won't be able to mistake it. Believe that there is a feeling and let yourself open enough to the possibility, and you will find what you are looking for without looking. When you open yourself more completely to this energy, you will find it much easier to handle.
Howard:	I don't know how to start. *(laughs; pause)* I can't think of any questions to ask you. *(laughs)* How does one go about finding these energies?
MOITA:	There are some techniques that others use.
Howard:	What are they?

MOITA: Different forms of meditating to reach inside yourself, learning to become quiet.

Howard: Something like yoga.

MOITA: Yoga is a form of meditation, not suitable for all.

Howard: Yeah. And what are the other ways?

MOITA: There is finding something in life that gives you peace and gives you joy; or a place that makes you feel at ease where you can be yourself; finding out who *you* are first and what that means; touching your greater part in small ways at first; letting your intuition bloom. You are here to learn joy.

Howard: That's right. *(pause)*

MOITA: This is all I can give you for now.

Howard: So I have to search within myself for the answers.

MOITA: That is where you will find them. You need not do it alone...

Howard: If a person doesn't have any worries, does that help?

MOITA: Not always. Sometimes worries are there to spur you on. Your life is a way of teaching yourself what you think you need to know. Learning how to understand those things is what you are here for.

Howard: Not many people do *that* – really understand it.

MOITA: That is why there are so many people *here!*

Howard: Yeah, that's it. *(laughing)*

MOITA: The energy of life is in *all* creation, and we can draw on that. Remember your simple things. Remember all those things that are given without any demands.

Howard: You mean from other people, or through life in general?

MOITA: Both. That is where you find the key to yourself.

Howard: If a person's feeling happy, does that not help?

MOITA: If a person is free to be who he is, that is what counts.

Howard: You mean free without obligations, or free without anyone else?

MOITA: No, that's not what I mean. That all depends on the individual. Freedom is not necessarily free *from.*

Howard: What happens if he can't have the happiness he wants because someone won't give it to him, won't let him have it?

MOITA: Sometimes it is difficult to see that the happiness one thinks one wants is not always the happiness he needs.

Howard: He's just kidding himself.

MOITA: When you look too hard in one direction, you may miss it coming *for* you in another. *(long silence)*

Howard: I can't think of anything else to ask.

MOITA: I shall leave you with what has been said, and felt...

(As Kelly returns, and she and Howard unclasp hands, she exclaims, "You had all that tension on your elbow there! I can see how that really . . . !")

Thus, Howard's meat-cutting is only the most obvious situation in which he binds up energy in his arm. More levels of his vitality are now seeking release.

The second example arises from an essentially similar context and need, but closer personally to us. In the summer of 1978, our group of friends is being challenged to work through its barriers, and the members to open beyond their individual comfort zones.

Betty: I want to know why my ankle is causing me trouble. I think it's more than just physical, because it's not going away. *(long pause)*

MOITA: The reason [for] the difficulty in having it go away has a lot to do with what is happening to all of you right now. You are all having a difficult time being healed at the present moment, and this effect is very widespread – not just for you. David and Ruth also are feeling the effects of this, and Kelly. Partly it has to do with the changing of your energy, your openings and the blockings that you create to prevent those openings from happening. And whenever you block a flow of energy, you create a great tension in your body which then manifests itself in a physical form. If only the physical difficulty is treated, then the injury will manifest itself again, because the root has not been cured. It will take some time for you to discover the root cause within yourself, and when you do, then it will stay healed.

Betty: Yes, my energy was definitely changed when I was at [name of a growth centre], and that's where this started.

MOITA: It is not unusual with changes of energy to have this happen at one point or another.

Betty: Is there an easier way?

MOITA: Sometimes many things can be learned through pain more quickly and more readily. A lesson learned in that way is not one easily forgotten.

Betty: What I have to do is try to find out what I'm blocking.

MOITA: You have to try to let yourself be more open with the people around you – although you are a very open person. We all have much growing to do in that respect: being able to *express* those openings and not *hiding* them from others or from ourselves, being afraid that others will find our openings distasteful or reject them. It is not easy to make yourself vulnerable, but you cannot give completely unless you are.

The more we accept that "there are no accidents" on the physical plane without an inner cause or meaning, the more readily physical ailments will serve as positive spurs to growth. This may often require us to become more involved in the work of healing body, mind and spirit. In the next two exchanges, I and another man in our group ask about threats to the health of our female partners.

Gerald: Eileen has seemed in danger of becoming blind for some time now. Are her eyes in this condition for a reason?

MOITA: Eileen understands more about her eyes than you. She sees them as a way to learn about herself, to learn acceptance of what she has chosen, and a mirror to show her how she is going. It is difficult to explain all of the workings in this. But in some way, not being able to see as well on a physical level forces her to see things more clearly on another. There have been many great seers and healers who have been blind themselves, and have shut out the physical world to see the inner one more. That is *one* side. Will that help?

Gerald: Yet our guides have both told her that her physical sight could be perfect.

MOITA: When the learning is done. There is no such thing as an unchosen illness, and there is in a sense no such thing as a sick body.

❧   ❧   ❧

David: Is there anything we're not yet aware of that will help Kelly's hands to heal?

MOITA: Becoming more clear on how to use energy. *(pause)* It is in the process of becoming.

(The words are deceptively simple. Afterwards:)

David: Did you get any meanings out of what she said about your hands?

Kelly: Some. There was certainly a lot of energy in her answer, even though it was just a couple of words. Part of it seemed to be about forgiving – I'm not sure about what or whom, me or somebody else.

What she said earlier in the session about opposition had a lot of significance for me in a way: understanding more about when people come to you, trying to undermine your confidence or your beliefs or your view; and how, if you don't feel the need to justify it, it works better. And that has to do with healing energy, how you use your energy. I must say that what she said really had an impact on *me*. I couldn't believe how gorgeous she was, how much real good energy there is there. It just sort of burst in on me. At least I'm "becoming"! That's encouraging.

❧   ❧   ❧

While Moita emphasizes the inner changes, this does not mean physical remedies and treatments are irrelevant. Indeed, the search for appropriate methods may be part of the learning, and completing the inner lesson may enable those methods to succeed. Moita does not see her role, however, as prescribing in physical terms. Here she has some difficulty getting across to a lab biologist what she means by saying, "Healing...is not my specialty. I am a teacher. However, very often the two cannot be separated."

Ivan: Would it be fair to say that your concerns are not really of health but of learning and loving?

MOITA: No, because they are all connected. I said I was not here to impart specific information. In an instance – if someone were ill and you would say, "What do I do for this person who is sick?" – it is not in my purpose to say you should take this person to the South where the air is dry and warm, or change their diet.

Ivan: Then your purpose is not one of curing people that are ill.

MOITA: That is not what I said.

Ivan: No, that's not what you said, but how can you help people as a generalization?

MOITA: I have a broader view, for one thing... I do not see you, or others like you, as one life. I see you as your entire self, together with the history of who you are, what you are here to learn, or where you are going. And all these things have to be taken into account. If a person dies in this life, that does not mean that they have not been helped, because it may just be that that particular kind of death is exactly what they need...

Ivan: Would it be fair to say you're here to help people, with respect to health, by helping them become aware of themselves?

MOITA: It would be fair to say that when a person becomes himself, he is healthy; and in that respect, yes. It is the only true healing, the only one that stays. It is a by-product of becoming *whole*.

ళ   ళ   ళ

In the next excerpts, Moita shares her perspective on why the simple, natural, whole things that we take into ourselves – or their opposite – affect not only physical but spiritual health. It is in terms of that sea of vibrating energy in which we live, move and have our being.

Bob: How can we help receive the energy from our higher levels?

MOITA: By being open and being grounded.

Bob: By "grounded", do you mean as with electricity, completing a circuit?

MOITA: You could say that that would be a good analogy.

Bob: Aside from being open, does it take a certain amount of self-discipline? Okay, I smoke, you know? I have all my bad habits, and they're bringing their barriers – so I'm told. I can believe that.

MOITA: All right. If we can speak of cleansing the physical: Everything is made up of vibration, different levels of vibration. The physical form is a very dense vibration, and all the physical objects around you are dense vibrations. That is why they feel solid. As energy becomes less dense, it also becomes less solid, so you get into the liquids and then into the gases. And after the gases you get into thought-forms – which are less dense than gas; and then you get into spirits – many different types, many different levels of spirits. Their level depends upon their vibration rate. What universe they occupy will be determined by how well their vibrations match any given universe.

So when you have a person in a body who abuses his form, what you have is a body that is much more dense than it should be. And by releasing what I call "toxins" from the body system, you raise its vibrational rate until it can experience these more subtle realities. You see, the realities are not less real because they are invisible from *here*. They are just less dense; and so, they are harder to *see*.

By "grounded", I mean not just the toxins in the body. I am speaking of the mental processes to a greater extent. If we speak of this from the electrical point of view, an electrical circuit that is not grounded, when it meets a greater energy-source, it explodes or catches fire, it overheats. There is nothing there to drain off that excess. So, in that sense, yes, you must be grounded to complete the circuit or you would be frazzled *(laughter)* and we certainly have no wish to frazzle anyone...

Anna: Why don't we use all of our brain?

MOITA: You don't use all of your brain because you are focused very pointedly, intensely, in one place. As you unfold, as you begin to experience the other vibrational rates, begin to see them, you will also begin to use more of your brain capacity. You will have more energy to fill it with.

They say there is a fine line between genius and insanity. A genius uses much more of his brain. And sometimes if he is not, as I have said, grounded, he will overload and become what you call insane, because he will be unable to relate to this reality. So it is something that must be gradual, if it is to be lasting.

               ɕ   ɕ   ɕ

(Near the end of another session:)

MOITA: You all look quite wiped.

Mike: *(laughs)* How do you sustain *your* energy?

MOITA: I have an unlimited supply.

Mike: You don't tire.

MOITA: No. I *change*.

Mike: And the energy-release during the change sustains you?

MOITA: It brings about a change in my awareness. I do not need *rest*. I do not have time! I am very busy. The density of your form lowers your energy. That is why *you* need rest. I do not have that kind of a form. My form *is* energy.

Mike: I should ask about diet. Is it wise to follow a particular diet?

MOITA: The wisest thing is to find the foods that harmonize with your own particular body. There are general rules of diet that are very simple and basic that all can follow. But apart from that, there is as much variety in reactions as there are people. Much depends on where you get your energy from. If you get it from food, you must be careful what you eat! And as your body changes from dense to less dense, you must watch the vibration of the foods that you put into your body. For if you put something heavy into a body that is light, it will have a bad effect – unless, of course, you desire to lower your vibration rate.

Mike: By not being discriminating all the time, I'm probably impeding my progress (?). Is that a fair assumption?

MOITA: I will say: from here, sometimes your body energy level appears as a yo-yo. *(Mike laughs)* It is not steady in one or the other. It leaps back and forth – which can be *hard* on you: the adjustments that you must make to accommodate each energy change.

Mike: I do seem to be a person of extremes.

MOITA: Many of your extremes are merely mental adjustments to a physical form. As you smooth out your body's rate, your extremes will smooth out too.

Mike: The optimum would be to eat food grown in your own garden, using no pesticides (?).

MOITA: And the right kind of earth. In many places, when things are grown, there is not the goodness in the soil that the plant can take and make part of itself to pass on to man.

అ   అ   అ

As for healing itself, the non-physical aspect of it – which sometimes can be all that is needed – takes many forms: for example, psychic or faith healing, laying on of hands, visualization and voluntary control of inner states. The essence of the healing act, however, is something that many have performed intuitively, with love – bridging the gap between two islands in the sea. Not only can healing help another over a threshold; letting one's own energy flow and be focused in this way is a step in one's own unfolding.

Arthur: I've started to do healing, and I wish to develop it further. Can you give me any advice as to how I might be able to improve?

MOITA: The best way is by practising. You will meet others who are also healers. There are many methods that can be used in this kind of healing; not any one of them is better than any other. Each healer finds the system that suits him well. As long as you remain open to yourself, you will receive what guidance you need in developing your own system.

         The most important thing a healer does is sharing his energy with another. And if the other is ready to be healed, they will heal themselves. Healing acts in a way as I do, being a door. It brings the awareness of the body to another level so it can see what needs to be done.

Arthur: Yeah, I have understood this and I have been working to that end. It's a beautiful experience.

MOITA: And it will keep *you* healthier.

Arthur: Oh! Good! I *feel* very healthy. *(laughing)*

అ   అ   అ

Betty: We've been wondering about the responsibility that goes along with healing, changing other people's bodies and energies.

MOITA: Those people who cannot be healed will not let themselves be healed, so the responsibility for the healing always goes back to the one who is ill. The only thing a healer *can* do is to help the person heal himself. If a healer approaches a healing with that in mind, knowing that there are some things that have deeper roots than he may be aware of, and that there will be some who do not wish to get well, then the energy he puts into the other person will have the right to be accepted or rejected by that particular entity depending on what it was the entity came here to experience.

So, in that respect, one cannot put blame or responsibility on a healer for either a success or a failure, because in the end there is no such thing as success or failure in healing. There is only acceptance or rejection, the right time or the wrong time.

Does that help to clear your mind?

Betty: Yes. Very much.

MOITA: You have more potential than you give yourself credit for.

Betty: That's good. I never think of myself as a healer.

MOITA: Everyone is a healer, or can be.

Betty: I guess everyone has the potential to be anything they want to be.

MOITA: And there is more to healing than meets the eye. There are many aspects of healing. It is a very broad field, because one heals not just a body; one also heals a mind and a spirit. And the thing that heals the mind and spirit is the energy that you all call love.

Betty: That makes it more complicated.

MOITA: And why should it make it more complicated? Because people fear it?

Betty: I guess they do.

MOITA: *(softly)* And why do they fear it?

Betty: *(pause)* Because it makes them vulnerable, maybe.

MOITA: Definitely. It definitely makes them vulnerable. There comes a time when one must be able to take chances and not judge all people by one person's reaction. Not everyone will accept love, just as not everyone will accept healing. And the two are very *closely* connected, in many ways.

❧   ❧   ❧

(Here I wish I could reword my own question, for it assumes the body is a thing separate from "psychic energy".)

David: I want to ask about healers like those in the Philippines who perform apparent surgery with just their hands or ordinary utensils. How are they doing things which appear physically impossible? Are the visible actions and results – which can even by photographed – manifestations of psychic energy, or are they actually going into the body itself and removing tumours and such?

MOITA: The body is just composed of energy.

David: Well, how would you describe the process?

MOITA: Learning how things work: those who are doing it correctly, believing in the impossible, creating your own reality.

David: And I guess they're very good at inducing everyone else to believe in that reality, so that the results are valid on a physical level.

MOITA: They create a great atmosphere in which to work, and those who become part of the atmosphere are affected by their belief. They are not as effective with those who are extremely skeptical, and they are the first to admit it. Faith is important in using a reality that has no [physical] scientific basis.

᪣   ᪣   ᪣

Psychic diagnosis and healing are possible through a part of the energy field surrounding and intermingling with the physical form of the patient. Many can begin to perceive one or more of these progressively subtler "bodies", whether by touch, outer or inner vision, or feeling/intuition.

Leslie: Can you explain to us a bit about what we call "auras"? What do the light and the colours that are radiated off of a person mean?

MOITA: That is part of that subtle, higher vibrational body that is yours, and that people have called your soul or your spirit – the inner you, the one that does the thinking and the feeling, that can separate from the body to make journeys of its own. The body, although it is dense, does not contain all that you are. So you overlap, extend beyond, your physical body.

The colours vary, depending upon your development, where you are along your road, how clear you are about yourself. If you are unclear within, your aura will be unclear without for those who can see into that vibrational rate. The purity of a colour will change its meaning; and in some cases it is not universal, for colours can have different meanings for different people.

This is where other people read your own thoughts as well. You are all connected together on this level. Even though an individual in a body is not aware of knowing what his friend or neighbour is doing, on another level he *is*. For there are no secrets in the universe, and you tell the tale yourself in this energy field that extends beyond.

᪣   ᪣   ᪣

Colour is significant to healing in various ways, including both diagnosis and treatment. Some of Kelly's most dramatic healing experiences are to occur with Sharon, who is herself striving to become a healer. Here Moita elaborates on hints Sharon is receiving from her guides and from a past life as a healer remembered through hypersentience. Retired and recuperating in her modern home, one would not expect a person like Sharon to be embarking on a study of ancient esoteric healing methods – but then, her doctors did not expect that she herself would be healed, either.

Sharon: I have a funny question, Moita. I have been told that I am to take up this old knowledge from past lives in working with stones and jewels for healing others. And I'm at a loss. I'm wondering if you have any knowledge to help me.

(Moita looks away and closes Kelly's eyes.)

MOITA: We have been working on this one for a while. Each soul has certain affinities for different stones during a part of its development. Using the stones as you have before is what you are after, [but] you do not know how you used them. You need to investigate the area of colour healing, and then of using colour refracted through [the essences of] different stones to produce different waves of vibration: different heats, different intensities, different kinds of energy. As you experiment with the process, the knowledge that is already a part of you will begin to come to the foreground, and you will receive more detailed instruction in your dreams and your [automatic] writing. It is an old form of healing.

You have also used the technique of dipping stones in water and then having your patient drink the essence of the stone – the vibration of the stone that is transferred in the water. There is information still available on that process in this civilization. It is not a technique that has been lost in the mists of time, although those who have used it before can gain...more specific knowledge of how to use it again... It is an Eastern tradition. Your attraction to India has a great deal to do with this particular aspect of healing. There are some who are in the process of using it now in India, and perhaps your desire to visit that place is also a call to discover this person and learn directly what you have forgotten.

Sharon: Thank you very much! I was afraid to ask, and yet I was so aware I must. I have a feeling that it's there, and it's just so close.

MOITA: It is good for you to use different stones for meditation. They can tell much about themselves.

Sharon: Can you help me with what vibration of stone would be good for me to use?

MOITA: The ones you are wearing and have been told about.

Sharon: My topaz.

MOITA: If you take a stone and place it on your forehead, you will know instantly if it is a good stone for you or not. You will have a reaction. You know which ones are good now, and you can put them on your forehead in order to know what kind of reaction to expect, so you will not be taken by surprise.

Sharon: I feel very earthy with these. Thank you, Moita.

 confidence ❧   ❧   ❧

Sharon: Do you have anything more to give me on vibrations, because this is an awareness I have: learn all about vibrations.

MOITA: There are different kinds of auras... The quality of a healer is to be able to adjust [her] aura to the aura of the person being healed. You will find that different stones correspond to the different types of auras, and you can use these different stones to change your own aura in order to use it as a healing element, after you have discovered which stones are for yours. You will use these stones to increase your own energy and your awareness. And then when you change levels, you will be able to use other stones as well for brief periods of time. Then, use the stones that you know are for your *own* aura to get your energy back, so you are not depleted. This is the type of healing that you are entering upon.

Sharon: It's so interesting, and it sounds so exciting. I'm really looking forward to it. I'm just anxious to get on with it.

MOITA: It is good to have direction at last, isn't it? The more you learn, the more you will remember what you have learned.

               ❧   ❧   ❧

Some idea of the general meanings of aura colours is given in the following two excerpts.

Joe: How do you see me?

MOITA: I see a golden light that extends far afield and encompasses many...

Joe: How is the energy around me related to the energy around you?

MOITA: *(laughing)* I have a flash of something so simple. My colour is predominantly blue, yours is predominantly gold. Mix the two together and you have green. Green is symbolic of healing and balance.

Joe: And gold is symbolic of . . . ?

MOITA: It is usually associated with the higher intellect.

Joe: And in this case?

MOITA: *(pause)* The Sun is a good image.

Joe: And blue?

MOITA: Blue is spiritual endeavours, balanced endeavours – past the need for great searching...

Debbie: I'd like to know what the colour of my aura is. Can you tell me?

MOITA: You have a fair amount of violet, which indicates searching. You also have a good share of green, which is your healing. There is some red, which seems to indicate stress – abundant energy not channeled. Those are the main areas of interest.

               ❧   ❧   ❧

(In the above session, I missed my chance to ask about my own aura, so on this

next occasion Moita brings it up herself.)

MOITA: I know you wish to speak of your colour.

David: Hmm. Right.

MOITA: When Joe asked me that question, he said, how is it that [I see him]? And I saw him not just as he is, but as a whole spirit. That is by way of some explanation to the grandeur of his goldenness. There are certainly many things that must be done before he could hope to reach the purity of colour of which I spoke. So, one must be careful how a question is asked. Which answer do you want?

David: I want both. *(laughing)*

MOITA: On your whole level, your light is much more of a whiteness. *(pause)* On this level, you have your share of green, and a fair amount of gold. You also have some blue. Most of your violet has disappeared, which is a good sign. And in this kind of situation you do not have any red.

David: Hmm. *(pause)* How do you understand the significance of the white?

MOITA: White is purity, spiritual perfection. It encompasses all colours in balance. It is the light of love.

David: Why would your colour be blue, then? And would the colour of Kelly's completeness be the same as yours?

MOITA: I have said that I am mostly blue coming *into* this level, and that is how I am perceived *from* this level, for those who seek my contact seek it in order to develop their own spirituality; and so, for them that is what I represent. Most do not wish to see perfection, or they would be in church seeking God and afraid of being blinded by His brightness.

It is not easy to say exactly what my colour is – or anyone's – since so much depends on where you are looking from, and where you are going... Most all of you are seeking to be the pure white in your search.

❧   ❧   ❧

Within the body's overall energy field, there are various circulatory pathways and junctures of special importance for outer and inner healing, including the numerous acupressure or shiatsu points and the seven energy centres (chakras) rising up the spine. Each of the latter is associated with a certain colour and emotional, mental or psychic potential. Spiritual growth involves a progressive opening and balancing of these centres, starting at the base of the spine, then even with the genitals, solar plexus, heart, larynx, "third eye" and crown of the head. Being in the middle, the heart chakra is a balance point and fulcrum for the whole, related to feelings and to healing.

Moita sessions often involve the activation of these centres, leading to some remarkable shifts in perceived reality, as in the following two examples.

(As we meditate to begin this session, I feel a definite pulsing of energy at my heart centre, and then at my crown chakra too, which is accelerating. When Moita opens her eyes, Kelly sees my heart chakra glowing and feels Moita altering my energy pattern.)

David: I've been feeling a pinging in my heart centre, which is getting faster.
MOITA: It is a good indicator of how others affect you: your testing stick. *(i.e. showing which chakra is activated and in what way)*

᭐   ᭐   ᭐

Mike: What are the little blue and white lights that . . . ?
MOITA: That you see?
Mike: Yeah.
MOITA: Now or at other times?
Mike: It's a little different right now. I was just noticing it in the middle of the group, but I was thinking more of other times, where a really rich violet would just sort of burst into the air and move across from me and go out or away. It would be either like that or white, luminescent. It can happen with eyes open or closed.
MOITA: You are beginning to see what reality is composed of. Your eyesight is being changed. You could call these things your interpretation of energy.
Mike: Hmm. My mental image of energy is more a continuous thing.
MOITA: And your eyes tell you different. The image you have in your mind is not always what reality turns out to be. You know that very well.
Mike: So then . . . I don't understand energy, then.
MOITA: *(laughing with him)* The only thing I can say is it is like the pulsing heart of the Sun. Energy is always in motion. It does not stay still. For if it stayed still, it would be...matter, perhaps, but not energy. The Earth has a magnetic field. It does not stay still, either; it is in constant motion. It extends and contracts; it pulses. Everything around you is active. It is either in one phase or another. You cannot make a sunrise stop changing colour, so why would you think that energy was continuous when all of its manifestations are in continual change?
Mike: Mm-hmm. Something that's not really like a flow of invisible stuff that permeates every square inch of everything? It can be more isolated?
MOITA: What you are seeing is near its more physical form. You are not seeing in this reality that kind of oneness that connects all things. You are seeing its manifestation, its giving of self – not the reservoir from which it comes. There *is* a continuous energy, a universal energy, a source – and you call this energy "love". And things are continuous or discontinuous depending upon your ability to see them or to turn away from them. But this particular phenomenon that we are speaking of is this energy in its active form, in its creative form.

᭐   ᭐   ᭐

On another occasion Mike is less curious than he is overwhelmed.

(Moita laughs first, aware of the changes that Mike is seeing.)

Mike: I'm lost for words – one of the rare times...

MOITA: I am able to see you more as a light. *(pause)*

Mike: Uh, sorry! I didn't even hear what you said. It was just too – uh, go ahead! Tell me again.

MOITA: I was commenting on the visual effects of the energy, in that I am able to perceive you more as a light or an energy-presence than a form in a body. And perhaps this is in some way as an explanation to some of the changes you are seeing.

Mike: *(clearing throat)* Well, I don't really think I'm seeing things the way you're seeing things. It just seems like spaces and sizes and qualities I don't really have words to describe. Reality seems to be shifting, if I let it.

MOITA: When you change your focus, you find that things are different. Those things that you measure your perception by are no longer steady. You must find new things to use as focus points. It only seems chaotic and disorganized because you are unfamiliar with its rules.

Mike: Hmm!...

          (Then, later in the session:) How are you different than Kelly, or me, or anybody else?

MOITA: My main difference lies in my ability to perceive, to be what you call unfocused.

Mike: Huh! Hmm. That answered my question really well. So we're more rigid, not as fluid as you?

MOITA: You are not very good time-hoppers or reality-hoppers. And you are aware of the differences when I am here. From your own experience of my presence, you know there's a difference.

Mike: Well, that's for sure. A difference in focus makes sense.

ço   ço   ço

MOITA: The change in structure of reality in the room is in small part how I experience the flow of time and the flow of life... This place where I sit and speak from is very much like a nexus, a place where realities meet and mingle. So it should be almost normal for this area, when I inhabit it, to flip in and out of "reality".

ço   ço   ço

"It is like learning anything. You learn the basics first, and you learn them more slowly than you do the rest of this lesson." So Moita tells Mike another night. A month later he describes how he is beginning to get a handle on some new "focus points".

Mike: The first thing which I've been doing the past couple of sessions is to get in touch with my heart as much as possible, without any strings attached in other parts; and then to try to focus in, tune in on everybody else's heart sitting in the group, try to imagine through my heart and head connecting with all that.

MOITA: A line of energy going through everybody's heart?

Mike: Right... I can feel physically the change happen in the way I perceive the energy when I've finally gotten around the whole circle and I can get centred enough to where I'm seeing it as a whole. Then the visuals that were happening on the fringe – the start of facial changes and luminescence around the body – become more controlled. I can have more control over how far I can go. I can move around and experiment – not really knowing what's going to happen, but *allowing* what's there to happen instead of making it conform to my focus.

           So what happens is: the qualities of textures, dimensions, things, would get really super-small in strict detail, and then they would get big, and things would get wide. But those words don't describe it. It's not just three-dimensional things. Colours change, but they're not everyday colours. I can only relate it to the way Rudolf Steiner talks about sensing colours psychically, not the same way as physically. It wasn't as much of a surprise this time. I knew what I was doing more. I knew the process to go through to allow it to happen.

∽   ∽   ∽

The threshold between sleep and waking is another opportunity for consciousness to focus in subtler realms than the physical.

Lee: Sometimes, when I awaken from a dream, my surroundings appear snowy, filled with white particles, and it's emotionally intense – a warm, pleasant, full emotion. I don't understand why I would be able to perceive, seemingly with my eyes, something I don't normally perceive.

MOITA: And this is as you are awakening?

Lee: Yes.

MOITA: So, since you are part-way into *my* realm, you are still seeing some of it when you open your eyes. Your eyes are one of the tools that can be trained to see into other realities, so it is not unusual for them to be involved. And the snow is your visualizing of energy. Energy has *form* here. Do you also get a buzz?

Lee: In my ears? *(Moita nods)* Yes.

MOITA: That would be hearing it. It is like you are not all the way into your body yet. You are in the process of returning. And so, the part of your spirit that is outside of you sees all of this, and you see some of what it sees through your own eyes.

∽   ∽   ∽

Rita: One morning I could not believe! I felt like I was leaving and coming back to my body over and over. I would feel light, and then I would feel solid. Then I was listening, and I could hear a real hum, louder and louder. I could even feel it in my ears, too.

MOITA: Some have termed that hum an "astral build-up". You can travel on the hum. *(pause)*

Rita: I'll have to think about that one for a while.

MOITA: The hum is like a bee that shows you the pathway out of yourself. You increase the hum, you come closer to the bee, grab its tail, and it takes you out – humming all the way!

෨   ෨   ෨

"Astral", of course, refers to that part of the higher vibrational body that, as noted earlier, "can separate from the [physical] body to make journeys of its own". It is also the name for the plane on which it travels. This is a very simplified description, however, as illustrated by one of Mike's meditations in which he feels himself splitting into three different types of bodies. Moita comments below.

MOITA: You were experimenting with your different vehicles of travel... Each one has a different realm of experience that it travels through, and each one is lighter or less dense than the last. As you gain in acceptance of your higher realms, you find that there are even more bodies, more vehicles, [with which] your consciousness [can travel].

෨   ෨   ෨

Aside from dreams, this area has always seemed a bit foreign to me, so I am rather unprepared for the happenings during two individual sessions with Moita.

MOITA: How are you feeling?

David: Strange. *(long silence)*

MOITA: What are you seeing?

David: *(laughing)* You seem very small.

MOITA: Or is it that you are taller?

David: Something like that, yes. *(laughing)*

MOITA: Am I distant as well?

David: Yes. Why is that?

MOITA: Perhaps you have moved away from me?

David: In what sense? *(knowing my body has not moved)*

MOITA: In distance, literally.

David: Hmm.

MOITA: Have you not wondered, as your mind wanders around the room, if your eyes could see from that perspective, what they would view?

David: I also seem larger. *(feeling expanded all over)*

MOITA: And why is that?

David: My body extends. *(quoting Kelly from her life as an "aura dancer")*

MOITA: You are without a doubt taller without the one you wear now. Most are – while they are not restricting themselves to a specific form – elongated. *(pause)* *My* size has not changed. What has changed is your perception of *your own*.

❦   ❦   ❦

David: I seem to be leaning out of my body. *(feeling strangely off-balance, but fairly sure my physical body remains erect as usual)*

MOITA: Mm-hmm! In which direction?

David: Backwards. *(with a laugh, then a pause)* Or upwards.

MOITA: Or perhaps both? . . .

(Then later in the session, as we look towards each other:)

MOITA: And you are seeing . . . ?

David: It starts to be a man's face that comes over, with a moustache...

MOITA: Interesting, since we are seeing a woman.

David: Hmm. *(laughing)* Describe her.

MOITA: She has long dark hair. Can you guess what is happening?

David: Are they another life of Kelly's and mine?

MOITA: *(laughing)* At the moment, what is happening is you are exchanging bodies, and seeing each other through the other's eyes.

David: *(laughing)* Let's try that again. *(long pause)*

MOITA: And how are you doing?

David: It keeps coming in and out. *(feeling the same odd familiarity in the eyes I see, as when looking in a mirror)*

MOITA: It is not something that is easily maintained. It is a question many people have. Many wonder how they look to another.

❦   ❦   ❦

For one like Leslie, who has enjoyed conscious astral journeys in her sleep, it is natural to feel some frustration at being back "here" again.

Leslie: I find my body really limits me. I try to meditate and talk to you and reach other levels of thinking in my mind and my soul. But my body won't reach those levels – that's not going to go with me. And I really find my body and the physical duties that are demanded of it day in and day out really limit my time. I find it *frustrating*, I really do. I would like to...leave the physical behind and get on with the mental, I really would. And I'm just wondering why we saw it necessary to create these physical bodies in the first place.

MOITA: You could say that when physical forms were first experimented with, it was not realized that they could entrap the energy of the soul. The ability to go from one level to another was lost in becoming too focused in a physical plane, for the energy level is lower in that it is denser. But it is not true that when you reach a certain stage of development you cannot take your body with you. Your body is pure energy.

Leslie: Okay, I can see what you mean. I was limiting my imagination by saying my physical body couldn't go...

Shelley: I used to have these dreams... It was an autumn morning, and all these leaves would be falling. My friends and I would be on the street. And we'd be running, and sort of jump up a bit, and then you would take off, you know?... But I never believed we could actually *do* that. *(laughter)* I mean, it would be *nice*.

MOITA: It is true that right now you would not be able to do that, because you do not have the energy, the awareness, to change your physical into something that would be capable of travelling through realities and travelling through time. But there have been those on your Earth who have been able to do that. The thing is that once they have refined their body enough, it disappears from your view.

Leslie: Why does it have to disappear?

MOITA: It does not have to at *certain* points. It can be (what is called) "materialized", made more dense for a short time. But in order to use the body to travel through other worlds, it must be made lighter. It must change its structure... It still exists as itself; it is transmuted.

๛   ๛   ๛

There is an issue that arises with the prospect of transmuting the physical, becoming free of its weight, its slowness, its constrictions. "Since that should solve all our other problems as well," one might think, "why not make that our goal? If we only could, why not develop the new powers to release ourselves from this frustrating existence sooner rather than later – or, if we prefer, learn to manipulate the physical world to suit our every desire?"

Here is the paradox of power and control. Humanity encounters it in all forms of magic, both technological and psychical: the power that seeks to overpower the conditions of its power becomes powerless; control over the uncontrollable is a self-defeating and illusory control. At this point in our development, the way of knowing and achieving more seems to involve accepting how little we can know and achieve purely of our own conscious will. We may strive to become our own teachers, but the nature of the universe still determines the lessons to be learned.

As always, there is a middle way. The solution of the paradox seems the one Mike comes to: "I can have more control over how far I can go..., not really knowing what's going to happen, but *allowing* what's there to happen instead of making it conform to my focus."

Joe: Is this altered perception, the changing images I see on your face – is it connected with being clear, being in the "now" of existence?

MOITA: More being closer to other realities and the opening of latent senses. There are many there.

Joe: Is there any way to facilitate the opening of those extra senses? Or is it necessary or advisable to even think about that?

MOITA: They open more quickly when one does not try to open them.

Joe: Mm-hmm. So just leave them.

MOITA: It is a by-product of . . .

Joe: Right action. Cause and effect.

MOITA: Not an important thing in itself.

Joe: Right. So what I'm experiencing now is an effect of some earlier cause. Just simply delight in the experience.

MOITA: And the experiences come more easily when they have been allowed to flow...

Joe: So tell me what it's like where you come from.

MOITA: Mmm. Something everyone wishes to know.

Joe: Is it a place I would enjoy?

MOITA: *(near whisper:)* Oh yes! *(aloud:)* If you were here completely, there is nothing here that cannot be enjoyed. This is what we fill our own universes with. We have our purpose. Not all of us have the same one. And we have experience in many forms.

                                                           ❧   ❧   ❧

Now an exchange of perspectives that weds many of these ideas together. Spread out before us are spirit and matter, shadow and reality. But the way we'll someday recognize "heaven" is through living where we are now – till the shadow becomes the clearest crystal reflection.

C.: Can you materialize?

MOITA: I have done so.

C.: And it's difficult to do so?

MOITA: It requires a great deal of energy at this time. Our worlds have drifted apart somewhat. There is in a sense a barrier between my world and yours that must be crossed. And the energy it takes to cross this barrier into physical form is much greater than the energy it takes to enter into your world through this doorway. *(pause)* It would be easier for you to see me from this world into mine.

C.: How would one do that? *(pause)*

MOITA: It is difficult to describe. *(laughs)* Your eyes are so accustomed to seeing physical matter. Our energy is a much less dense energy. It is like tuning yourself up, becoming aware of different, more subtle vibrations. Those people who see into other worlds are able to unfocus themselves, to let the trappings of this world fall off of them. It is similar to dream creation, and you can see me in your dreams.

C.:　　　*(laughs)* I wonder if I *have!*

MOITA:　　Each would see me somewhat differently.

C.:　　　What's it like where you're at? Do you experience anything resembling material reality?

MOITA:　　I manipulate form and energy and colour. I do not have the same kind of senses that you do, in that I am not limited to experiencing one sense at a time. When I experience what you might call an object, or what I might call a thought, I *become* it in all of its perspectives. The senses you have, the physical senses, are a reflection of higher senses that you possess. They are the less refined senses...

C.:　　　The visual things one sees, such as glimpses of auras or the blue light we've seen around your face – are those an illusion, or are they a scrap of higher senses being interpreted through visual senses? Are these things really visual?

MOITA:　　They are visual in a different way. You see with a different eye when you see into these worlds – what the ancients called your "third eye". There is a great deal of colour in the universe. This Earth is a very deadened or dulled place as far as its experience of colour and the range of colour, the depth of colour, that is available.

　　　　　To me, this world that you exist in is the shadow, not the reality. It is the reflection of the mountains in the pool that is so easily disrupted when one sticks a foot in or throws a stone, and as short-lived as that reflection. It is not the substance of the mountains themselves. You cannot climb a mountain seen in a reflection.

C.:　　　Where I am, the material world seems to have an extraordinary persistence and inability to change simply by looking at it differently. I mean, I can forget that a stone is in my path, but I'll still wind up flat on my face if I trip on it. Is there any way one can see it differently while in it, as a demonstration that it might be otherwise? I find it very hard to believe it's otherwise, because I keep running into the stone on my path or whatever.

(Moita first responds as if the stone is a metaphor for life obstacles, perhaps reflecting what she sees at a deeper level within C. and to which she wishes to direct C.'s attention.)

MOITA:　　When you become more aware of the reason why there is a stone in your path, there will be no need for you to trip on it. You will learn the ability to walk around the stone when its purpose is known. The way you have set your life out, you have done so to learn certain things that will round out your own soul and experience. And the only way one can change the road you walk upon, and not have these things seem to control you, is through understanding of yourself and what it is you are missing, what you are not seeing.

C.:　　　What I mean is: If there's a stone, and to me it's a material, physical stone that's there, there's physically no way I can know to get it out of the path rather than pick it up and set it out of the path; but if the stone is a thought, I should be able to make it into a rabbit and let it hop out of the path. Yet I don't find instances of this sort of thing happening. So it makes it hard to believe that matter is that, because it seems so hard for this end to manipulate it that way.

MOITA: Do you mean in a true physical way?

C.:   Mm-hmm.

MOITA: There is still too much distance in understanding between man and matter. He manifests it and creates it, yet he does not understand it. He does not understand how he creates it; he does not believe he is its creator. And he has not tapped that reservoir of energy that is in the universe for him to tap. He is still learning who he is and the dangers of learning too quickly how to use this energy.

The physical world is here for you to accept as physical for now, not for you to try to manipulate. In trying to manipulate it, it will take much longer for you to learn how this is accomplished. When you accept and can understand it, and do not worry if there is a stone on your path and are willing to walk around it, it will be able to teach you what it is, why it is here...

C.:   It's very hard to believe things with no proof or evidence. This is the problem. Like, there's so much I really want to believe, but without a shred of being able to demonstrate it to myself.

MOITA: ...That kind of understanding will come through experience at later times... And you will grow, through understanding, to know when it is necessary for this kind of [direct energy] manifestation to occur, and when it is a folly, a need to prove something.

It is not necessary for you to believe that energy and matter are connected. It is necessary for you to accept the Earth in the manifestation it has chosen at this time... It is not asked of you to believe in something without seeing first. It is asked of you to believe in yourself, in your beauty, in your Earth, and in how you can relate to it as Earth. That is a path to spirit.

∾   ∾   ∾

Illustrative Dreams

Our energy is a much less dense energy. It is like tuning yourself up, becoming aware of different, more subtle vibrations. Those people who see into other worlds are able to unfocus themselves. It is similar to dream creation, and you can see me in your dreams.
– Moita

Shape-changing beings who betray their higher-level origins may appear in dreams as guides. Often they teach the primacy of consciousness: that the world we encounter reflects ourselves, so our success and well-being depend on where we focus our heart/mind/spirit. In this early example, rising through levels of awareness is depicted as psychically controlled flight toward space, where we enter a world of vivid colours and destinies may be revealed.

"Flight to Space Station" dream
David (age 25) / May 13, 1972

In scenes from the Vietnam war, a young woman appearing in different guises avoids being shot in creative, acrobatic ways. I'm a soldier at first who assists her in hiding. Her pursuers then come after me as I run barefoot over sharp stones, not making headway.

Suddenly I spy an orange, bat-like shape (resembling a sideways figure-8 or infinity symbol) flying toward me from one side. I think it may be a warp in space-time, an energy field opening to another dimension. Does it merge with me? All I know is I too start to fly – or at least "swim" through the air by kicking and waving my arms.

Now the energy assumes the form of a beautiful woman who floats along beside me. I am still low to the ground, unable to go higher, jumping to avoid obstacles. But as a skyscraper looms ahead, the woman says my movements are unnecessary and only hinder me – that flying depends on one's state of mind. By thought now, I manage to veer between buildings. She and I begin to soar together, rising gradually over the city. In the sky above us, in vivid green and blue, a sign appears reading "LIFE GOAL:". I wonder what may follow, but then realize the answer, too, may reflect my mental state. With this thought, I read: "TIMES CHANGE".

Our effortless flight now reveals a vividly green platform or "space station" floating and rotating in the sky above us. We're not in space, but I know whether one sees it or not depends on one's level of consciousness. We fly upward and land on this, the woman's home base. I realize that she only appeared earlier as she did in order to contact me. This space station is very luxurious with glass-like furniture in green and blue. Soon we're sitting down to an elegant meal. The atmosphere resembles the ending of 2001: A Space Odyssey, *as I wake up.*

∾   ∾   ∾

Another symbol for rising energy levels – an elevator – is used in the next dream, depicting human beings learning to become their own teachers. This remarkable experience unfolds in (or from) the dream-state following the last meeting of the social psychology class I teach in spring 1975. I created the course to examine how consciousness is affected by technological society and to indicate pathways beyond those limits, drawing upon the likes of Aldous Huxley, Theodore Roszak, Krishnamurti and even Seth. The interest level of many students and the creative energy I feel coming through me as teacher point to this being a very successful experiment.

"Elevator of Consciousness" dream
David (age 28) / April 10, 1975

I am acquainting a small group of people with an unusual elevator. Depending on which buttons are pressed, the elevator rises to floors that have each their own character as media for creating experience. All experiences that various people have on any floor, though, reflect thoughts, feelings, preoccupations, expectations – literally, their own mental furniture. So we experiment with this elevator, visiting several floors according to an inner logic of associations. We are tracing spontaneous, multi-dimensional ideas, memories and feelings through their various levels in a Hesse-like "glass bead game" of the psyche. [23]

One woman creates a pattern of experience that involves some beautiful but also conflictful, frightful or chaotic events, likely originating in childhood. Our small group is sharing what she experiences. But then the woman panics and abruptly terminates the sequence, returning us to level "0", the main floor lobby.

Fortunately, we are not faced with a crowd of strangers. While I'm aware that reaching floors 4 and 5 at the right time might have resolved the woman's tensions, I now quickly press "2", a floor that previously offered a peaceful setting (a quiet meadow in the woods). As the elevator door opens, we find ourselves in an open forest of tall evergreens. My spirit soars to the treetops as I relish the clear, fresh morning air.

We walk down a path through these woods, viewing to either side the prototypes of experiences that we or others have had at this level. As we pass, their bare outlines (like printed electronic circuits) are filled in with colour, taking on momentary reality.

We evidently choose to enter one of these scenes, because the woman and another man and I are next seated in a living room, listening to an elderly woman playing the piano. I explain to my companions that only certain people are receptive to those like us on "the other side" (almost as if we are ghosts, but meaning the rare state of consciousness we are in). It seems the pianist and her living room are in the everyday world, yet she is aware of our invisible presence on her sofa.

I am also reviewing how the woman's experiences in the elevator followed a chain of associations, each experience containing an element in common with what preceded and followed it. I explain that once someone has made an association by travelling in the elevator, that link becomes a persisting reality that others can travel on also.

Then the man decides he must leave, so he walks over to a door or window and steps out. The woman and I trade impressions of his reality status, wondering: Was he a creation of the pianist, or a more independent but somewhat disoriented spirit? Since his manner suggested "time to go", I check my watch. Strangely, I see two watches superimposed, one showing a few minutes before the other. I guess that once they coincide, it will be our time to depart.

Lastly, the woman turns to me, saying that by sharing her inner experience in the elevator she senses an imbalance has been resolved between us. We both feel good about this, as I now recognize her to be one of the most interested and intelligent students in my class. Then our time must run out, for I awake – on the main floor.

℘   ℘   ℘

_____

Chapter 6

ENTERING OTHER REALITIES

The invisible energy that surrounds the Earth and all things that are created on it [is] able to retain imprints of energy and thought. Nothing is ever forgotten. All things are remembered somewhere.
– Moita

When I observe the cynical reductionism, the materialistic tunnel vision, that still holds sway in much of today's world, despite many people's growing openness to other levels of energy and meaning, I wonder how long the established order and its trained media can continue pretending there is nothing real beyond our five senses. Like the dwarves near the end of C. S. Lewis's Narnia tale *The Last Battle*,[24] will "true unbelievers" continue perceiving (and huddling together inside) a mangy stable *in the very same space* where others are savouring a joyful homecoming?

Each of us does get to experience the reality that, at some level, we have chosen. But the handiest means of denying that freedom of choice is to insist only the lowest common denominator of authoritatively observable "hard fact" is reality. All else – thought, imagination, intuition, feeling, individual perception, creative artistry, dream, vision, mystical union – is merely entertainment, self-indulgence or mark of instability. This chapter foregoes these blinders, showing that the furthest reaches of imaginative, visionary experience may sometimes reveal, quite directly, the ground-plan of human existence – and may provide the insight and inspiration needed to transform even those apparently "hard facts" of today.

Rather than be confined and controlled by our ignorance and fear – as with the ancient map designations "Here Be Monsters" – perhaps the time has come to openly explore these uncharted waters, progressively making them our own. The time may have come to trust each and every inner happening as a reality of its own, growing out from the centre of all things, with a reason for being exactly what it is in this moment.

MOITA: I would like to take you all on a trip! – or at least an experiment of a trip. For this trip, you will all close your eyes and let yourself feel first very still and free within. This is a trip into your imagination, and you will get to this trip by letting the back of your head open, and then imagining yourself flowing out as a little bright sun of thought and awareness.

Beside your head there is a doorway, just the size for you, and you will float through this door into a new world. Do not try to make this world something you know. Leave yourself open to all possibilities. You are perhaps entering another planet, one with rules that you are not familiar with. You are here to explore without judging, just to see what happens, whatever form it takes. So, step through the door.

ও   ও   ও

Moita's words one evening to the members of our "Expansion of Consciousness" workshop may awaken us to the vitality of our own imaginative worlds this very instant. Sometimes these worlds become shared – as when some literary characters become more real to millions than the people physically around us every day. Is this a mere semblance, a subjective illusion resulting from a writer's skill, or can we say those characters and events *are* real but in a different way or on a different level? Kelly's own novel-writing experience suggests the latter.[25N]

David: Kelly seems to be doing well allowing the scenes of her book to come to her. She can be surprised at what happens next, and sometimes receives pictures of events and hears conversations as if they were independent of her. What is she drawing on here?

MOITA: In a sense what is occurring is like dream creation, when the images that you dream come alive and have their own reality. She has, in a sense, a reservoir of creativity in a certain place; and by giving life to characters in the books, she can let them develop their own situations, continue the creation, and she adds to it. When the pictures come, it is because she has given them enough life and has connected with that place long enough and sees what it is they are developing into. It is a part of herself now; and so, many past experiences and some future ones are drawn upon. She is the reservoir from which the characters take their development.

ও   ও   ও

The dreams we create in our sleep, on the other hand, are the souvenirs – and sometimes guided tours – of landscapes foreign to waking consciousness, though not to the rest of ourselves. They are a doorway to participation in learnings and interactions of which we will become conscious sooner or later, at the end of physical life if not before. Here Moita invites Kelly and me to make the most of an opportunity.

MOITA: You will be getting some very important information in your sleep... Both of you are becoming very open to *me* in that arena... This is what you may call a dream quest. You have learned to let your dreams lead you, and have been rewarded by the results of that journey. It is a more intimate way of pointing you in certain places – more adventuresome, also more productive, as far as your own individual growth is concerned. In some ways this is a sign of direct participation – more direct than *this*.

ও   ও   ও

Hazel: When we dream of someone we know, is that an actual emanation from that person, or is it our conceptualizing of that person to fit a role in our own inner drama?

MOITA: A lot depends on the dream. They come from different levels. There are times when you are actually experiencing the other person travelling in the dream world too. More often it is your own creation.

❧ ❧ ❧

David: Can you tell us why Kelly dreamed of Karen last night?

MOITA: It *was* Karen: one of those instances of meeting another... In order for such a dream to take place and be remembered, many things must weave together at the right time in events, in thoughts – to trigger the retaining memory, not the experience itself.

❧ ❧ ❧

C.:   Are the people in dreams real? I mean, do they have an existence which goes beyond the particular focus of your dream?

MOITA: Sometimes they are other people who are having dreams of their own.

C.:   And if they're not other people from this plane, do they have an existence that extends beyond that tiny little snippet that you participated in? Is the dream still going on after you're no longer in it?

MOITA: The energy that is created in a dream continues on after, and other entities or energies can utilize that energy and change it. You may not recognize your dream, but the energy that you begin is in itself an act of creation. And it will continue, just as each thought you have does not disappear if you no longer have it. You have put energy into creating the thought, and it goes on, either affecting other people or being changed and growing into something else.

C.:   Maybe I'll remember to ask some people in my dreams who or what they are.

MOITA: You may get some interesting answers!

C.:   I hope I can remember to do it. *(laughing)*

MOITA: Becoming more aware in the dream state...is in itself an altered state of consciousness, and within a dream you can do many things.

C.:   Is there any particular trick to doing that – being aware when you are dreaming that you are dreaming, without losing the dream? I have some tendency at that point to begin to wake up. It's really frustrating.

MOITA: Not to get too excited *(C. laughs)* because your excitement brings you back. It is a delicate balance to stay *between* two states. You can only hope and practise, and each time you have an experience you will get better at it.

C.:   What *is* the dreaming state?

MOITA: A little death. Leaving your body as you do, and reconnecting with your higher self, you experience every night what it is you can experience when you die. Flying in your dreams, being able to manifest instantaneously your thoughts – it is a world of your own creation, and this is the kind of world you live in when you die, if you can accept it.

C.:   Does it have a reality such as this plane here does, or is it an utterly different sort of reality?

MOITA: It is a reality where things are quickened, results are more instant. Here an action that is released, or a thought that is released from you, in some cases may take years before it comes back to you in another form. Then you have to try to understand why this is happening to you now, where are the seeds to this experience. In a dream state, or in that kind of world, you can *see* the results.

ഇ   ഇ   ഇ

The next two exchanges continue the theme of meeting people in dream or astral states – the first, with our own group in mind at a time of parting.

David: How can we continue to grow as a group, express our purpose, even though we may go in different directions physically?...

MOITA: A group can stay a group even if it is apart, because of the thoughts that flow from one to the other through distance. Distance has no real meaning, [though] physical contact helps create better energy-flow between people and certainly intensifies [the links between them].

Steven: Who directs that level of communication?

MOITA: This is a cooperative thing. Your own other conscious [does]. You can do it on a conscious level and call it telepathy, or on an unconscious level and be affected by things that come up – sometimes in your dreams. You do not really know exactly where they come from. Some dreams are teachings, are communications with you, helping you to open and grow. You can dream together as a group. When you are asleep, you are a much more aware individual. And many differences [between people] that are seen when you are awake do not seem so important when you are asleep and out of your body.

There are many places of teaching that can be reached in an out-of-body experience. People clothe these places in different forms. Some add their own trappings, create their own dream places. And sometimes they meet together with others who are there to learn similar things, or in a group setting where they are working out difficulties. These things don't always manifest on a physical level. Sometimes they're not *learned* about until after you die, and then you can *remember* these night journeys you have made, recapture your knowledge of other lives. It takes some time; it is a bit of a *shock* at first. The more conscious it is, the stronger it is, though.

ഇ   ഇ   ഇ

Jane: I dreamed I was in a bare room with three men I didn't know, who were dressed in business suits. I became aware that I was teaching them how to die. I thought to myself in the dream, "Why am I doing this? I'm not an expert on dying." But I watched the dream unfold, and the men began to walk around the corner of the room, leading to a hallway, as the class ended. I realized that as each man did so he was passing over to the other side. The third man hesitated, however; he was afraid. I put my hand on his shoulder and told him he didn't have anything to worry about; it was okay. Then he walked around the corner, and then I did the same. That ended my dream, and I've been trying to figure it out ever since, because it felt important. *(pause)*

MOITA: When you go to sleep and you dream, you enter another reality – one that has less limits than the one you are aware of when you are awake. There are others who also go into that reality with you – some consciously, some not, some in many states of in-between awareness. You are one in that level who helps to teach others how to become more aware of their own dreaming and their own changing of reality. You have just now started to become aware of that fact, and you have caught yourself helping others learn how to change their own level of awareness as they are dreaming.

ॐ   ॐ   ॐ

Repeatedly, Moita has compared dreaming to the after-death state, in that one's creation of reality becomes more obvious and complete. That death is not an escape from oneself, from consciousness or from future lives, comes as a bitter pill for some, while others feel joy at the prospect of such creative freedom and growth without the shadow of the traditional Judgment Day.

As Dr. Elisabeth Kübler-Ross famously stated, "Death" – in the conventional view as the end to life – "does not exist."[26] The implications of that realization can transform our world. Knowing how to be open to the dying process is a major step in living fully today. Here we give Moita's descriptions of this great transition, preceded by two excerpts on the intriguing phenomenon of in-between.

Tim: What are ghosts?

MOITA: Usually when someone dies, their spirit moves on to other levels. It frees itself and goes into different realities. Sometimes . . .

(A window falls with a bang, startling us.)

David: A ghost!

MOITA: . . . an after-image is left behind. Your spirit forms itself in the shape of a body when you are alive. When the body disappears, that energy pattern still exists. There are many kinds of ghosts; there is a problem. Very rarely is it the actual person, or his spirit, that is returning to the Earth. A relative's desire to see someone who has left can give life to that after-image, reanimate it for a while.

Hazel: Will it then have a life of its own for a while?

MOITA: When those on this plane release their desire to draw it here, whatever
           individuality it may have gained will be rejoined with its original spirit.

           There are also times when one dies and does not believe in other realities
           even after death, and those [souls] can let themselves become entangled in the
           world that they should have left. It is usually their desire to do something that
           has been left undone, or their fear of accepting that they are free. You create
           your own reality in life and in death, and whatever it is you wish to find, or
           fear to find, will await you. And the worlds that you will not or cannot believe
           in will not exist.

                              ∽   ∽   ∽

(As Peter asks his question, Dora is seeing a ghostly presence surrounding his
body. She says nothing about it, however, until well after the session.)

Peter: I'd like to know where my brother is. Could you help me?
MOITA: Can you give me some detail?
Peter: Well, he went missing in a boating accident and was never found. It must
           be close to 15 years ago.
MOITA: You do not believe he is alive.
Peter: Um, there's a possibility. *(pause)* What do *you* believe? Is he alive or not?
MOITA: Everyone is alive! *I* am alive.
Peter: Is he in a physical state, as I am at this moment?
MOITA: Yes, but not in the same body.
Peter: Not in the same body as I am (?).
MOITA: Not in the same body as *he was*!
Peter: Oh, I see. Is it possible for him to influence my character in any way?
MOITA: That all depends on you. I can influence your character as well – if you *let*
           me. I can see that he is close to you, in *many* ways. His spirit does not dissolve
           just because he is born again. The energy that you knew him as still exists.
Peter: Are you saying that he was born again as a baby, or that his spirit is in
           some other form – something to that effect?
MOITA: I said both. He is spirit, and he is body. You see, each of you [has] a soul,
           and this soul sends out parts of itself to be born in different times and different
           places. And when the experience has come to an end, that part goes back and
           another part goes off to have a different kind of experience. The parts that go
           back are still identifiable as a personality that was once on Earth, and can
           interact with those who are still living and are familiar with this particular
           energy form. In fact, it is easier for, say, the soul of your brother to
           communicate with you through the personality that was your brother rather
           than presenting itself as a more complex, and more whole, entity. You have
           already opened doorways within yourself by being familiar with it. These are
           doorways that are easily opened...
Duggan: Is it possible for you to contact the energy that was his brother? Does that
           energy have anything to say, maybe, to Peter?

MOITA: Well, I feel the energy *here*, at the moment. And I also feel his energy was with you in your near-death experience. I see that clearly. *(i.e. Peter's own boating accident)* What I get is, "What does it matter?" *(laughter)* I think he is having a good time.

(As Dora tells us later, she thinks so too. What she is seeing, from the beginning of this excerpt, is the figure of a 12-year-old boy reaching his arms outward from Peter's body, gesturing in welcome first to Moita and then to the others around the circle. While Peter has felt this spirit's presence as an influence to take on some of his brother's extroverted personality, Kelly knows immediately that Dora is perceiving the spirit's new form, in which it incarnated about three years after Peter's brother's death.)

      ❧   ❧   ❧

Marcia: How many dimensions *are* there? Like, when we die, how many do we go through?

MOITA: There are an infinite number of dimensions. When you die, much will depend upon your ability to accept experience, your understanding of death and its transition. Some who die do not go any farther than out of their body and become what man has called "ghosts", who haunt because they do not understand what has happened and they cannot accept their own death.

If you can accept your death, you can have either a dead relative or two come and greet you and show you around whatever reality you have chosen to live in between times. If you are beyond expecting relatives, if you can accept the idea of teachers, then your teachers would come to you more as themselves instead of in disguise as a relative. And if you can experience a teacher, very often from there you can go on to reunite with your entire soul-self, and from there the possibilities are endless.

You live in the universe that you create for yourself, in life and in death. If you choose a universe that is filled with pain or guilt, you will experience pain or guilt. You can punish yourself, send yourself to hell. You can go to heaven and stay until perhaps you become bored with it, until you have a desire that draws you back into a body, until you find a need that you think must be fulfilled and that brings you back again. It is not an easy question to answer.

Marcia: So you're telling us there *is* a heaven and a hell?

MOITA: I am saying each makes his own. There is, and there is not. It all depends upon what you have created for yourself. For some, it is what they wish; for them, it is real. For others, it is not; they bypass it and go on to something else. And there are different kinds of heaven and different levels within that kind of experience.

Barb: I can't see how we couldn't accept our death, because it is a part of life.

MOITA: You would be surprised how many people cannot accept their own death.

Barb: And so they have no choice after that?

MOITA: In time they will grow to understand what is happening to them, and efforts to arouse their ability to experience other things do not cease even if they are not aware of the help that is always pouring down to them. It is not that they do not have a choice. It is that they have *made* a choice that is difficult to unmake, or that takes a long time to learn from. You are allowed to make as many mistakes as you wish in order to learn. That does not mean that you are always stuck inside *one* mistake.

An eternity of wandering the Earth will eventually become boring, and somewhere that spirit will say, "Why am I here?" And when he recognizes there is a question, then he may get the answer and find out that he does not need to be there at all. Until that recognition takes place, that knowing that it is not necessary to be where he is, he will continue to stay behind. This does not mean that the rest of his soul does not continue to develop. He has not put a stop to it. It is only his particular part that he is plugging.

჻჻჻჻჻჻჻჻჻჻჻჻჻჻჻჻჻჻჻჻

Don: Can you assist us if we come over to the spirit world – any of us?
MOITA: When you leave your body?
Don: Yes.
MOITA: There are always those there who can help you, if you are in trouble and if you ask. Sometimes you may not be aware of the help. You may not be aware enough to see us, but the help is there...
Dorothy: Carrying on with Don's thoughts, then, when we are ready to leave this physical body and go into the other reality, what we find on the other side is the reality we take with us – is that right?
MOITA: More so there than here. This is why, also, many times when people die or have near-death experiences and bring back their memories from that, ...they see those that they have known in this life waiting for them – for those are people or energies they are more familiar with and they find an easier time accepting in transition.

And after they have grown more in a spiritual sense in that kind of reality, most of them gradually become aware of the fact that those friends that they have around them are also a part of themselves – a projection from their own higher self in order to relate. And then those forms can disappear and become something more. Then a step along the path of evolution is taken, a step towards your reuniting with the soul, becoming a part of a whole again. It is for many a very gradual process. And there are some who do not, after death, reunite with their soul but immediately find another body.
Dorothy: This is because they don't want to go on learning?
MOITA: It is because they are afraid.
Dorothy: They're afraid, so they come back into a physical body (?). At what point does the soul, after the physical death, look back on a life that it has lived and choose the type of life it wants to go into next?
MOITA: Again this will depend upon the soul. Some will immediately review their

life. Usually when it is immediate they are not well-prepared for understanding, and they will usually take on a course of punishment or guilt. If they are totally unaccepting of the idea of being born again as a means to compensate for the life they have lived, they will put themselves into, essentially, a hell for punishment, until that reality wears thin. And then they will be taken and *put* into another body by their higher self – sometimes without their knowledge or awareness. In that case that personality does not participate in choosing the life or the circumstances. It is more drawn *to* that life and circumstances – depending on its development, what it has and has not learned.

If you have a soul that does *believe* in reincarnation but still is not accepting of what it has learned in the life or its inability to learn it well, it may choose a life as a punishment to repent of its mistakes. Many times this kind of concept backfires on the soul-self, for it can be a downward spiral going from one life to another that is lower and lower in energy and in opportunities for understanding self, until something of a bottom is hit and the soul in a sense comes to its senses and begins to rise again through those same levels, until it realizes that it can accept mistakes through growth and [does] not have to punish itself or feel guilty for unawareness. What it has to do is become more aware in other lifetimes and learn the joy that is healing.

Does that answer your question?

Dorothy: Yes, yes. So the more we become aware – mm-hmm, that's beautiful.

ℤ ℤ ℤ

As we linger yet a while between lives, it is appropriate to become aware of the different perception of time that is possible here. While in a physical body, our narrow consciousness leads us to assume reality is stable, "out there", something that we can easily grasp. We take real time for granted as an orderly, linear progression. Yet even in physical existence we can travel quite freely through time via memory and thought – though we dismiss this as a "subjective" mental capacity saying nothing about the "objective" nature of things. This is how our either/or, single focus blinds us from seeing the larger whole at which the capacities of the human mind can but hint.

Again, the creative act provides one of our better hints. And we have a very immediate example – the composing of this book.

MOITA: Your putting together things that have been said in orders that are different than how they have occurred in your experience is showing you very much what it means to have fluid time. You change your concept of the past and restructure your inner self by doing this.

ℤ ℤ ℤ

But what is the reality at which our familiar consciousness can barely hint? It's time to go to the source. In the following excerpts, Moita uses various images to convey *her* reality, which our souls may only begin to approach between lives: where the potentials of consciousness *are* the universe, so that all times are co-present at the flick of a focus.

Leslie: Something else I've been wondering about: It's been weeks since we last talked to you, and we've all done various things in our lives. It's been a period of time for us. Is there any element of measurable time where you are? Like, I want to know, "What did you do this morning?" There *is* no real morning for you, is there?

MOITA: As far as this kind of communication is concerned, I have said before that for me it is continuous. There are no gaps from one session to another. It is rather difficult to describe time-hopping, or changing focus, becoming more than one, spreading myself not just through time but space – but all at the same moment.

ॐ   ॐ   ॐ

MOITA: For me, your past and your future are all the same, in the same now, because in this dimension there is no such thing as time flowing in one direction. Time exists in all, at once.

Rita: Somehow that's really hard for me to grasp... How can you put all that time all in one?!

MOITA: Our question is: how can you separate it?!

Rita: *(laughing)* Ah, no!!

MOITA: It's like taking a many-sided jewel with many facets and showing only one facet at a time.

Rita: Ahhh! I like that one. That's kind of neat.

ॐ   ॐ   ॐ

MOITA: I have a certain sense of time because I deal with *you*, or rather, I have a time *reference* – but only for while I am here, and only for this part.

David: What is the relationship between the part that is speaking to us here and parts that are doing other things now?

MOITA: In some ways it is like a jellyfish, composed of individual parts but making one body and working together as a unit. All of the parts of myself are in touch with the others, yet they do not interfere.

David: They're consciously in touch?

MOITA: Not *all* of the time, but yes. I can shift my focus at will, and it is only a matter of focus. *(pause)* If you have a person with six faces, all facing a different direction, with one mind, they each see a separate part of the world but they conceive of it in one thought.

David: But they don't see each other.

MOITA: They do when they meet in the centre of their thoughts – or if they stand before a mirror. It was a poor analogy, but it is also a complicated thing to explain to one with one focus. *(laughter)*

David: There are times when one focus, then, loses conscious touch with another focus?

MOITA: Are you speaking of mine?

David: Yes. Forgets that there are other focuses, perhaps?

MOITA: No.

David: All right.

MOITA: *(laughing)* Always *knows* that there are other focuses, but does not *concern* himself with them.

David: Is not aware what they're doing?

MOITA: No *need*. I can always find out quite easily, by turning my focus back again. And I can participate as this focus in what is going on by drifting through time.

David: An interesting life.

MOITA: Or *existence*. *(pause)* There are some still in bodies who can do what is known as "bilocation", being in two places at the same time. It is a *step* in this direction. Have you not ever had the experience where you suddenly notice that part of you has returned from somewhere?

David: Perhaps.

MOITA: You do it as well! A part of yourself goes out of your body and does something else. You have a thought; it travels to where your thought came from or where your thought was pointing. You think of a person; a piece of you leaves and goes to the person you think of. You have a whole network of things drifting in and out of your head all the time. You merely lack control over the phenomenon and cannot recall where you went. Although, sometimes one can notice when you come back, because there is a change – there is more of you there; your focus is stronger.

℞   ℞   ℞

Bill: I guess my greatest problem right now is being limited by my perspective of time. It's hard to visualize time as a fluid thing, when we operate on a very structured concept. I guess it's going to take *(laughs)* quite some . . .

MOITA: Time?

Bill: . . . to break those walls down.

MOITA: The focus is necessary, at least for now. You do not have the ability to tap the amount of energy yet that is necessary to keep yourself centred and balanced when time no longer exists at a single moment. I too practise focusing and being able to determine which period of time I will send a certain part of myself to. It is like having rows upon rows of movie reels. And you can pick any one you want, and you can put three or four on a projector at a time, but you can also only put one if you so wish.

Bill: So you can focus your attention to more than one?

MOITA: It is like I split into more than one being. There is enough energy where I am for me to do that.

Bill: Do you gather all the information from different times simultaneously, or do you recollect it when you return to your whole self?

MOITA: That depends upon which way I choose. It is mostly a matter of turning your attention *away from* other things, so that the one particular thing comes into the foreground. But it is a matter of a moment to bring your attention back to those things that you have temporarily turned away from. This is the hardest concept for anyone to understand: the idea of simultaneous lives...

Bill: I guess I'm having a hard time *(laughs)* visualizing all these. Very abstract.

MOITA: That depends upon your viewpoint... The invisible energy that surrounds the Earth and all things that are created on it has the quality of being able to retain imprints of energy and thought on it. Every moment in a life has a certain quality of energy to it, and this energy imprints itself. If you could travel to a point where this energy was imprinted, then you could re-experience the incident that made that particular energy pattern. Nothing is ever forgotten. All things are remembered somewhere.

It is this ability to travel through this substance and tune into instances of energy release that explains [how] many people...are able to see – either into the past or into the future – things that they ordinarily are not able to perceive. There are many proofs around you that time is fluid. If it were not, you would not be able to see things of the future, for it would not exist. You could still see things of the past, for it has already happened in your perception. It is like removing yourself a short distance away from that energy imprint, so that you can see them all.

Many have described time as a river, and you are on a single bend of it. The future bend goes around one corner and the past goes around the other. So you see only a small part of the river, but that does not mean that is the only part of the river that exists.

ೞ   ೞ   ೞ

Jim: Could you clarify for me the nature of time?

MOITA: It is hard to believe that all times are occurring at once, but that is what is happening – not just all times and all of your lives occurring at the same moment, but also all of your *possible* lives are also occurring in that same moment.

Your view of time passing from past into future is [due to the fact that] you yourself are focused in a single instant in one particular place and are blocking out the rest of time. And when you change your focus from one moment to the next, you see that time has *passed*, when time has not moved or changed – only your perception has moved. If you could change your perception of time, you would lose your sense of balance in this moment and become confused –

which is something that does happen to some of you, from time to time. *(smiling, laughs)*

It is a gradual process: learning to reach outwards around you to include part of your supposed past, and then to include part of your own future. This does not mean that on a physical level all things that will come to pass in your future have been determined. This means that all possible futures are laid open before you as you travel in your focus from one moment to the next. So, depending upon where you place your focus, you will bring one or another of those possible futures into your reality and experience.

                                                           ∽   ∽   ∽

Todd: Are you timeless, or do you perceive time in the way we do?

MOITA: I do not see time flowing in one direction. I see it as a simultaneous moment, although there are different flavours to direction and there are many ways the directions can go. It's more like a sphere that starts at any moment so that it goes in all ways. And depending on which path I choose to follow, I will end up in one place or another as I travel along one particular line. Some of this gets into what you would call parallel Earths or lives.

Todd: You mean parallel Earths forming when something happens in one and something else happens in another?

MOITA: Any place where there is a point of choice in a life or for a planet or a nation, where the one choice was made on this Earth, in another Earth that choice was not made or a different one was made. And it goes along to develop what the consequences of that action or non-action would be.

Todd: So that it would branch out in what we see as the future. Do they ever come together or interact in any way?

MOITA: There are some that are very close in their development, and there are places where the worlds touch and some instances of people that have accidentally travelled from one to another and come back with amazing and confusing stories. It is easier, however, to travel through these worlds with your mind than it is with your body.

Chris: I'm having a hard time understanding that the future is happening right now, and it is still yet to be decided – we decide it.

MOITA: From here, all possible futures are happening on a non-physical level for you; and [whatever] choices are made in this life in this future will decide which future you make physical for yourself. And since this is the reality that you are dealing from, and you have not made those choices as yet, your future is still subject to change.

                                                            ∽   ∽   ∽

Ivan: Is reincarnation not a sequence of events, from one life to another?

MOITA: No, it is not. It appears that way because that is how you think of it. But reincarnation does not happen in sequence. One does not necessarily live once in each century in a linear way. One may live at the same time in all centuries or only look at it as going from one time to another, depending on where you are in your line of development – if you wish to look at it as a line.

Ivan: Would it be true to say, then, "I exist now as a man; I also exist now as a boy?"

MOITA: As far as this one particular life is concerned, yes, you do...

Ivan: Would it be also true that I could find that boy and meet with him? Is he a part of me, or am I he? He exists as I exist?

MOITA: You can look on this kind of thing as the flow of your conscious: where, at one point, it is focused as the boy; and at another point it is focused as you now; and then at another point in time it is focused as an old man. It is where your conscious focuses itself that determines where your "now" is.

Ivan: Is there not still a conscious me focused on that boy?

MOITA: Not as [far as] your conscious here now is concerned... If you could expand yourself to a certain point, and you could touch the consciousness that was the boy and make him aware of your existence, you could knit the two together and make them one.

Ivan: But have I not done that by becoming a man?

MOITA: Were you aware of you as a man when you were a boy?

Ivan: No.

MOITA: Then, no, you have not done that... Do you remember being an old man?

Ivan: I don't think so.

MOITA: Then you haven't done that, either.

Ivan: But that is possible, is it?

MOITA: It is possible. It is not always advisable. Some people who have done that have ended up in insane asylums, because they couldn't handle the reality of the difference.

ॐ ॐ ॐ

With a greater appreciation for the mode of being available to us between lives, we may understand a little better what it feels like to find oneself reborn into a new physical body.

(A few weeks old, little Eva cries off and on in her mother Catherine's lap.)

David: What can you say about the consciousness of babies?

MOITA: There is a period of great adjustment in the first few years: taking away things that are to be forgotten, and deciding which things are to be remembered. As with everything, each is individual, depending on purposes.

Chris: I guess some things get remembered later?

MOITA: It is usually decided in the early years which things shall be remembered later. Also, much depends upon the parents, what kinds of thoughts they bring to the surface in a child. Some thoughts are links to different pasts. They form a bridge, and it makes the memory more vivid, more easy to recall later on.

૭   ૭   ૭

(Over two months have now passed. Eva lies in the centre of our circle, crying periodically, then falling asleep. This question comes from her father.)

Joel: At this point in her life, is Eva more responsive or more able to feel the influence of her higher self, compared to us who are more affected by our society's conditioning?

(Eva lets out a cry.)

MOITA: The child is more open to influences, not just from other levels but levels of influence around people – your thoughts and the thoughts of those around. But a child that age has difficulty discriminating between [them], and experiences in some cases a certain amount of frustration in not being able to communicate *(Eva cries again)* what is being received, [for she] cannot use others as a mirror.

૭   ૭   ૭

(This question involves a boy, about seven years old, who during a family gathering was aware that Moita had silently become present in Kelly.)

Jane: Recently you told Kelly that my little nephew was slipping in and out of his past. Is that a kind of thing that may make him a little unstable in this life?

MOITA: He has been born to grounded parents. He has the right background. And it is not so much his pasts that he's slipping in and out of but different forms of reality in his present. He sees *our* world – which is not that uncommon for a child. Many children see until they know they are not supposed to. Since [his father] is more open about these kinds of experiences now, [your nephew] may not have to go through losing that awareness and then trying to regain it later.

Jane: Ah, I see – and still keep touch with reality here, *this* reality.

MOITA: There's always a *chance* that one will slip away, but he has a good opportunity for coming out whole. It's his own experiment.

૭   ૭   ૭

Growing older, people can systematically attempt to enter other realities including past lives. Certain memories are more beneficial than others, however, depending upon purpose, and all of them will reflect the perspective of one's present self.

Owen: The other day I was trying some of the visualization exercises recommended in Marcia Moore's book *Hypersentience*. I feel relatively confident about what has been left in me from the experience, but how seriously do you think we should take the images that come through in these exercises?

MOITA: You could say that when you dream you are using your imagination to create form. You do that not just when you sleep, but whenever you utilize your mind – even when you do not see the visualizing of your thought. So, what you have seen has its own reality. It exists in some way independent of you once you have had the thought. Depending upon the experience, you can be connecting to thought-forms that were created in what you would call a "past" experience. Or you can be recreating certain thought-forms and sometimes in some ways re-forming those thoughts to suit your present personality...

If you would take a life that you have lived in the past... – if you were a monk, for instance, in the Holy Land – and then you would take a life that you were living as a bootlegger in California, and then you would take this life, the memories that you would have of the monk would be different. The bootlegger's view of what the monk was like would not be the same. So this is one thing to remember, to consider, when you go into past experiences: that just as you are viewing the world around you through your own lens, you also are re-experiencing your past lives the same way.

Steven: When I deal with my past lives, they always seem to be very "high" lives in the sense of political or spiritual power. I'm sure that from the number of incarnations you go through, you must have a substantially greater number of "low" lives where you didn't accomplish anything or just lived for one certain goal. Why is it that I can't remember those?

MOITA: In this particular life, when you have come here at this time, you have come to bring forward from the past other "high" experiences that you have had. It is not so much the remembering of the "low" ones that is important, when you remember that what you are now is an accumulation of all those lessons that you have already learned. And you also are trying to bring that energy, that difference, those two worlds, together in one place. This doesn't mean that you won't at some time remember what you call a "low" life.

Steven: Well, you know, a peasant existence. They always seem to be much more grand, which leads me to believe that they're manifestations of what I would like to believe rather than some kind of reality.

MOITA: There were some that probably are what you suspect them to be. But if you can take what you have experienced and integrate it in your present, their reality and truth is not quite as important because that will sort itself out later. What you do at this moment makes your tomorrow. *(pause)*

I can see many images of you out in country, being very simple. When you do get into the country, those experiences are closer to the surface. *(pause)*

Owen: I'm wondering how certain historical periods and milieus seem to be exceptionally vivid. Often when I'm reading about them, I feel very in rapport with them, and yet there seem to be far too many for them all to represent results of experience in a body. I wonder what is the nature of that kind of sympathetic insight and interest about a historical period.

MOITA: That would be a particularly strong incarnation that you lived in that time period, one that would be important to you now, one that's closer to the surface. There *are* some individuals who specialize in particular time periods. When you don't think of your living one life after another, it is possible for you to be living many lives in one time zone. If you have a particular thing you are trying to work through, or a particular desire that continues to draw you back to a certain time space, you *can* incarnate there many, many times. And the more you do that, the more important it becomes in your other incarnations...

Sometimes you can connect to another part of you that is living in a different time area. That kind of a connection can also bring up many strong impulses.

∾   ∾   ∾

(Moita sees C.'s face going through many emotions.)

MOITA: You seem to be in great turmoil.

C.:   I've been wondering if some things I've been through in this present lifetime have had roots going quite a ways back – and ties between people.

MOITA: I can tell you there are ties, but now is not the time to unveil them. The most important thing to remember is that each life can stand alone, apart from all others. And if there are experiences in a past life that have led to destructive feelings or actions, you do not have to let them enter this one when you make the choice of letting you be yourself.

I have said that the most important life you will ever lead is the one you are in at the moment. This one can shape all the others. It is not always wise to dwell on the past. Sometimes [that] is helpful to understand the present, but sometimes it can be harmful if you look too much in the distance for understanding, for reasons.

C.:   You mean the reasons are not from the past so much as part of the present?

MOITA: I am saying that the past will only affect you and your reactions to the present if you allow it. Being too much in a past, if it is an unpleasant past, can make a very real connection in this life with that one, since all lives are lived concurrently. You can give this life over to another you, which is not your purpose. *(pause)* This moment shapes your future. Choose your reactions and let go of the past and be free of it.

C.:   Sometimes it's easier to let go of something and be free of it when one knows what it is. It seems a little hard to brush a shadow away.

MOITA: It depends upon your reasons for being here. For you, knowledge has been a dangerous tool in pasts.

C.:   Which wouldn't keep me from looking forward to futures, although it might be nice to know how I wrecked up in the past so I wouldn't repeat the exact, identical error.

MOITA: You could not repeat the error if you lived for wholeness... The error was made in living a different way.

C.:   Was it a fairly recent thing, or was it something way back, many lives ago?

MOITA: Its roots are deep. But you are here to learn to put that shadow behind, so that other experiences of a different nature can come up.

C.:   I don't know what the shadow is.

MOITA: Part of you knows. You are aiming in its direction, striving to reach it, and by so doing blocking other energies and other memories. Just as you can sometimes bring forth from the past something you may not wish, you can connect to a past where you were aware of your self, of the Earth. You can bring that energy forward into your present. Those are the experiences you should be seeking – the ones that are whole and complete, for they will help heal you, if you will let them. And then the past can be seen at its proper time and be understood.

           I am not trying to be mysterious.

C.:   *(laughing)* You're succeeding!

∽   ∽   ∽

Shelley: You said that past and present and future are all existing, only on different levels, right?

MOITA: Yes.

Shelley: So does that mean we are living different lives right at this very moment, and getting subliminal feedback from those experiences?

MOITA: It is an interaction. That is one reason why some people use reincarnation to explain current personality traits and relationships with other people... So it is something that is more than just a concept. It is a living reality that people are beginning to learn how to live with.

Shelley: So a lot of things that we talk about as being instinct or our nature, or the way we're feeling a particular day, do not just have to do with that one particular reality. Perhaps other things are happening in other lives, and all these different levels and times are sort of with us?

MOITA: Yes.

Shelley: I think that's *neat. (laughter)* I really do.

MOITA: I can tell!... *(laughter)*

Shelley: Is there any way to have a better idea – this has really intrigued me – who we are and what we're doing and what kind of relationships we have in other times? Not outside of dreams and memories, right? – which I'm *not* getting. *(laughter)*

MOITA: The only way you can get the kind of information you would like to experience would be to open up to the fluidness of time, being able to connect to that. If you have not, you are not quite ready. And it is not something many do while they are still in a body. There are ways that you can get deeper within yourself to try to remember a life, thinking of it as a past at the time. But then, when you are finished, you can relate that to now and know it is a present influence.

           It would be very difficult to remember *all* of the lives you are living, particularly the ones in the future. Mostly you would remember the ones that related most closely to this life. Amongst all of your lives you have different lines of development, different things you are learning, different types of experiences. And there is a tendency to break them up into categories, if you will. They each have their own flow. If you were going through a series of lives that dealt with a certain fear, then each of those lives would be more affected by the ones that were happening on that fear itself. If you were in this life without having to learn about that fear, those lives would become secondary in their impact.

When it is time for you to be able to open to these things, circumstances will lead you in certain directions. It will be up to you to follow them if you want to have that experience. You must do so trusting yourself, trusting the inner beauty that helps you to unfold, that will choose what experiences are best to help that unfolding.

Shelley: You know, the reason I was so thrilled when you were telling us that we have a whole bunch of "nows" is, you know, the typical question: If you had one wish that would come true, what would it be? Well, my wish was always: I wish I would have seven or eight different lives when I was 15 or so; then all seven of me could all split up and go our different ways; then when we were about 99 years old we'd all get together and have a tea party, and we'd say, "Now, Shelley, what did *you* do? Remember when we had to make that decision and you went that way and I went this way? What did you do and whom did you meet and what did you learn?"

That's always been a really special dream, and even now I yearn for that. I don't know if we'll have our tea party; but from what you're saying, we're all experiencing it on one level or another anyway.

MOITA: And at a certain point you shall be able to remember them all together at one time.

Shelley: Huhhh! *(laughing)*

MOITA: You see, what you have just said is another thing that goes on. It is not just other lives that are happening simultaneously, but also all the possibilities that are happening in this life are also happening on another level. Each time you make a choice, on another level a part of you goes along the road that you did not take, to see what would happen. And so, when you die you can put them all together and you can have your tea party! *(laughter)*

Shelley: Gee.

MOITA: It is a matter of which possibility of the future you decide to make a physical manifestation. But it does not make *any* of them less real; it just makes one of them physical.

Bill: Does that mean that all through your life, for every decision that you've made, the counterpart of that decision is being taken somewhere else?

MOITA: And you are learning from that other part as well.

Bill: Like, that would mean millions of splits. Does it really go that far, split into just thousands and thousands of fragments?...

MOITA: In each life, the way it is planned will decide how many splits occur, because in some of those choices many other parts of yourself may have made the same decision, and then you would have less of a split. They are also free making their own choices. There are some lives where that does not happen at all, because the entity is so together in itself there is no doubt in making a choice. There is no desire to know what would happen if another choice were made. There is no wondering what that other part might be doing now if you had not made the choice you had. In cases such as that there is one life and one line – although those lives are very rare. But you see, ...when you split yourself up, you can learn from mistakes you have not yet manifested, and save yourself some time.

Bill: *(laughs)* Quite a bit. On a world level, would it be the same, or would there be more?

MOITA: There are *many* universes.

Bill: I read a book about people travelling between different timelines. People in our reality, in the world that we think of as ours, were somehow affected by the knowledge that, at any times that they made a decision, millions of reflections of themselves were doing things just about the same or the opposite. It seems to cause a real chaos.

MOITA: ...Chaos is not a necessary reaction to that... Much would depend upon your ability to be whole.

ఎ   ఎ   ఎ

Being whole may seem quite the test in a vast, eternally shifting kaleidoscope of realities. And there are surprises "out there" awaiting any explorer that challenge one's current idea of self – as illustrated by "scares" that come to both me and Mike.

David: Last night, as I was waking from a dream, I felt some sort of presence that – in the state of mind that I was in at the time – I was not very comfortable with. In fact, I was in a panic. Can you tell me what was happening there?

MOITA: You could say it is similar to the magician's darker side of himself. There are times, when you leave your body in sleep, when you meet your opposite – or what you consider your opposite. It has been called a *doppelgänger* in other literature. It is not uncommon for those on a spiritual path to have encounters with this "anti-you".

David: Is this related to what Rudolf Steiner speaks of as the "Guardian of the Threshold"?

(Steiner's "Guardian" is a representation of all those aspects of your soul, through its many lives, that you have not accepted or assimilated, and which must be faced at some point.[27])

MOITA: A *doppelgänger* is something different than a Guardian. A Guardian is something that is with you throughout your lives and in-between. A *doppelgänger* is something that is with you only when you are here in a body.

(pause) It *is* in a sense a warning that you present to yourself: a warning of what you *can* become if you are not conscious or aware of your path. It is there to help.

David: Why was it last night I had that experience?

MOITA: When you sleep long, you are more apt to have those kinds of experiences, because your consciousness does not require that amount of turning off. So, when you reach a point of saturation, when you have had many dreams, you will often go on to something else, try a change of levels. It is not uncommon for those who sleep a great deal to have more dreams, or more lucid dreams.

(I had taken an afternoon nap and then went to bed by 10 o'clock because of working early the next day.)

MOITA: And, when there are doubts that are brought up closer to the surface . . . There are *always* doubts.

David: Mm-hmm! In recent days I have been experiencing doubts about how I'm living and relating, especially yesterday afternoon. Can you say a little more about how this is an "anti-me"? It's the opposite of my conscious, or of my ideals?

MOITA: When you choose to be born, you are given two "blueprints", if you will – something to follow. And the personality that you're born with chooses which of these blueprints it will try to make manifest in the life. Usually you are aiming at something in between, something that has more balance than either the one end or the other. But, by having both in opposition, you try to force yourself into a more middle road.

When you come here, you enter a world of opposites, and you also bring this opposition with you and know that this is what you are working with. They are short-lived. They are a type of thought-form, but a thought-form that is bound to your physical. It gains energy from your physical form. *(pause)* You may be assured in some ways that the more upset it becomes, the better you are doing. *(laughing)* When you can free yourself within a life, it ceases to exist.

David: And last night it was showing it was upset?

MOITA: It is more your reaction to finding it – and *you* were somewhat upset. You were travelling along very prettily *(laughing)* and bumped into it, and were startled and confused, not knowing what it was. And so you made a hasty retreat.

David: So I'm nowhere near freeing myself, I guess.

MOITA: It is still there.

(It remains unclear to me how this doppelgänger may relate to what Jung calls the Shadow. If it is the same, one would "free oneself", presumably, by absorbing and integrating it, with the result that it would not be there as a separate opposite. Then your former ego would indeed be upset!)

            ❧   ❧   ❧

Mike: After leaving Kelly and David's the other night, I had an unusual meditation. I felt my bodies split into three different types and then saw my organs hanging in the air. Next an extremely brilliant light scared me, got me in touch with my fear. I withdrew from it, and then saw scary faces which were part of myself. Was that the purpose of that light?

MOITA: You do not mean to say that the purpose was to scare you.

Mike: I thought it might be one of two things: to get me in touch with dark parts of myself that give me fear, and to learn to accept them in time; or maybe it was the energy of my soul made visible from a different perspective.

MOITA: Your reaction to the experience dictated what happened later. That was not the purpose inherent in the offering. That was something that you brought about by your inability to accept at the moment. And so, you threw yourself into a lower vibrational plane where those fears have their existence; and having opened yourself up sufficiently to experience the light, the denser vibrations were very clear to your perception, and so you worked through it on that level.

          It is not necessary to bring you up to a higher vibrational rate before meeting your own fears, since that is a realm that you pass through first. You could say that your fear of accepting the experience awakened the fear within you and made it more immediate. It drew you to that experience...

Mike: What was the light?...

MOITA: It was your visualization of your own creation.

Mike: And that's why I felt dissolved and made a grab *(laughs)* for something vaguely familiar? Although, I guess I couldn't get any more familiar than my own creation.

MOITA: Much depends upon where you begin the search. You are focused here, and to your conscious awareness the things you can touch in a physical focus are more familiar even than your own soul. There is a fear of losing identity when you encounter such an experience.

Mike: In essence, then, I was perceiving the energy of my soul?

MOITA: More than just that, for at the moment of creation it is not just you alone.

Mike: You mean that . . . Whew! Hmm. No wonder I was scared.

MOITA: It is a very rare thing to see when you are still in a body. *(pause)*

Mike: You don't mean that it was the Creation creation.

MOITA: No. *(laughs)*

Mike: That's good.

MOITA: But I think your creation was enough.

Mike: Well, you said more than my soul was . . .

MOITA: Do you think you created yourself?

Mike: No.

MOITA: Then who do you think would be there at your creation?

Mike: Well, I just don't know. *(laughs)* I guess other levels of being, thought, God. I don't know how I was created. You said it wasn't just my soul.

MOITA: I was saying it was not just your soul that you *experienced*, for you were not there alone at your creation. If you went back in this life to the moment of your birth, you would not see just yourself. You would see your mother and the physicians and nurses in attendance who were helping you to become born. In this experience, they may all have blended together into one light, but it was not just one energy.

ॐ   ॐ   ॐ

There are religious concepts, of course, that many want to impose on experiences such as these (God and the Devil, the bible story of Creation, etc.), with the claim that they represent absolute, universal truth. Moita's view seems as far as possible from this dogmatism.

MOITA: There is no single universe. It is different for each individual. There are as many universes as there are souls to perceive them. Some are close enough in how they see the world so it seems they live within the same universe. They can communicate with each other, but still their universes can never be the same. There are some who can no longer be seen because their concept of our universe has become so alien. For them, our universe has ceased to exist. So, you see, there is a great deal to "reality".

ॐ   ॐ   ॐ

Yet within all the multiplicity, there is still the urge to define an underlying, fundamental unity.

Ivan: Is this universe part of any other universes?

MOITA: Mm-hmm. There are many universes. Each one has to deal with the one he has created.

Ivan: What can you tell me of collective consciousness?

MOITA: Nothing is ever forgotten. Each moment in time is itself its own reality. And so, everything that has ever been said or has ever been thought at any moment in time still exists in its original state in that moment. Those of you who can go out and expand yourself to a point where you can either travel in time and go backwards or forwards, or where you can just touch the "now" moment where all of these thoughts are in existence, can sometimes tune in and see those thoughts as they happen (or happened, depending on how you wish to view it) and gain that information. That is one of the explanations for inventions being invented at almost the same time in different places, because the same thoughts are all there and being picked up.

Ivan: Is it true that we are all part of the collective unconscious?

MOITA: In that you contribute your thoughts to it.

Ivan: But our universe, is it not created by a central consciousness?

MOITA: Are you asking me of God?

Ivan: I suppose I am.

MOITA: We are *all* a part of that consciousness.

Ivan: If that consciousness were to have a different belief, would the world not be different?

MOITA: The world *is* different for each one of you, so in that respect, yes.

Ivan: But it has norms which are the same for all of us, or similar (?).

MOITA: You have to have some basis to work on.

Ivan: But what is giving us the basis? Is it the central consciousness?

MOITA: It is more all of you together deciding what it is that you all believe – a collective consciousness.

Ivan: A confusing question! *(laughing)* The question is: If the consciousness that creates the universe as it is were changed by some means, would the universe then take a new shape, a new *physical* shape, new norms?

MOITA: Are you asking me if this is possible, or if this is likely?

Ivan: Yes, if it's a probability: that if the one would change, the other would also change.

MOITA: You are in the process of doing that now.

෨   ෨   ෨

What higher truth should guide such change without at the same time predetermining or constricting it? In the Epilogue[28N] to *Mind Leap*, Moita named what force unites all the universes. Here she asks us to discover it ourselves.

MOITA: Where I exist, I have no name; and the things I speak of here do not have names, either. They are thoughts, concepts, that we can see as reality – not things that we need to name. If I were to show what time was to another being on the same level as me, I would not try to explain it to him. I would put him *in* it, and he would understand *from experience* what I was speaking of.

I have warned others of the dangers of naming things. It is a real danger because in naming something, in trying to focus a concept so that it fits neatly between four sides, one may miss many points. But it is necessary, unfortunately, to *speak* in order to be heard right now. And in order to speak, I must use words, and the words themselves are limits. So I try to use words that are less limiting and less defining than what others might choose to say. And so, people may see some of the things I choose to say as having gaps in them. But the gaps are there on purpose, in order to force the individual to fill the gap with his own experience.

෨   ෨   ෨

(A questioner asks if a certain "spiritual" book, presenting its version of history, is to be believed.)

MOITA: Truth is something that you must discern for yourself... Historical facts may or may not be true. It is a very fine line, and much depends on where you are looking for information and what kind of information you are seeking. If you are not looking for something, you will not see it if it is there. Or if you do not *wish* to find it, you will also miss it.

Everything that you discover in this Earth...you see through your own perceptions and biases and prejudices. This is what I mean when I say that nothing is true – it is only "true" for you, and your "truth" will not be another's. If you can take all of your "truths" together, and see where they are pointing, you will come closer to *a* truth.

ᔓ   ᔓ   ᔓ

(During this "trip" Moita has taken us on, Kelly has been experiencing a great deal of bright light and swirling energy, with Moita's presence growing stronger and stronger – almost too much for her to bear. But now it is time for us all to step back through the doorway Moita had us create in the back of our heads.)

MOITA: This is not a very long journey. Gather yourself back to the back of your head and all your concepts of this world. Come back into yourself, and try to remember the feel of that other place.

Gail: Why come back now? Is it harmful to overindulge?

MOITA: Let us say, there are times when going too far too fast may make you lose your sense of focus in the here and now, and it is usually better to take small tastes at first so you do not lose your sense of grounding. Providing you leave with the right frame of mind, and so long as you reorient yourself when you return, things usually work out in the right way.

ᔓ   ᔓ   ᔓ

Illustrative Dreams

You are focused [in physical life], and to your conscious awareness the things you can touch in a physical focus are more familiar even than your own soul. There is a fear of losing identity when you encounter such an experience.

Where I exist, I have no name; and the things I speak of here do not have names, either. I have warned of the dangers of naming things. In naming something, in trying to focus a concept so that it fits neatly between four sides, one may miss many points.

– Moita

Two dreams, less than a month apart, appear closely related attempts to open me beyond my normal reality limits. The first seeks to expand my understanding of self through merging with a passionate feminine partner (Anima figure), who then leads me into a world of higher energy, beyond words and egos . . . until my conditioning brings me back down.

"Game of Identity" dream
David (age 25) / December 14, 1972

I'm sitting with many students in an auditorium when a professor announces an hour-long program on Krishnamurti. An assistant then distributes dry spaghetti strands to everyone. As part of a game, we are to moisten the ends and weave the strands into a circle. After difficulties, I find how much to overlap the strands. Meanwhile, the assistant explains that our circular weaving will reflect our particular nature, helping us guess each other's identity.

A young woman in the row ahead now turns and says that though we don't know each other, she would like to be my partner in this game of identity. I point out that the assistant previously spoke my name, but the woman treats this as irrelevant. She begins embracing me with surprising intimacy as we sit together on the floor. Utterly entranced, I return her passionate kisses. She whispers in my ear, "We are one person . . . one person." Our separateness has dissolved into this marvellous experience of sensuous closeness.

I urge her to go away from this crowd with me to make love. We walk toward and through a grove of trees in the dark. But likely recognizing a conditioned desire on my part, she points out, "There are more things in life than sex." "Okay, then let's dance!" say I. So, arms on each other's shoulders, we jump and twirl joyously around what is now my childhood backyard. As we dance, we notice the sun is bright red. At first low on the horizon, this red sun climbs high in the sky, impressing us with its mystery – surely, some sort of omen.

Seeking a better view, we run hand-in-hand down the driveway. She doesn't seem to mind the stones under her bare feet. Out on the street, I greet a woman on a bicycle who knows my wife Leanne and me. But what will she think of my being with this other woman? As I react with guilt, the bicyclist chases faster and faster after us.

My companion asks if that is the woman I live with. I say no, she is another woman with a similar name. She then reminds me I was warned earlier not to do one thing or she would vanish and leave me as I was before. I vaguely remember this warning about using names to distinguish people, with attendant conflicts. She informs me I will now be sent back to where I came from and be "ruled by biology", without remembering my experiences in this other reality.

The two of us lie down some distance apart, she to my left, face up – except that now she is changing, beginning to resemble Leanne. As my mind is overcome by a dizzy unconsciousness, I wake . . . to Leanne, sleeping face up, to my left. But I remember.

Naming in this dream is a symptom of my lack of openness to the greater wholeness that is being offered. And because I am thinking of these women in the separate, egoic terms to which names refer, I develop a guilt reaction here that blocks me from uniting with my inner feminine, with my soul's entirety, and beyond. I will treasure this dream, though, for its moments of high union – as the mystery woman so intimately part of me, and through her, my entity, echoing down the levels, whisper, "We are one person . . . one person."

∾   ∾   ∾

You do not have the ability to tap the amount of energy yet that is necessary to keep yourself centred and balanced when time no longer exists at a single moment. It is like having rows upon rows of movie reels. And you can pick any one you want, and you can put three or four on a projector at a time.
– Moita

Similar images (a turning circle, a red sun) crop up in this second dream to reveal higher dimensions beyond the physical. Miraculously, I am opened to the gifts of an energy source that transcends this world. Eventually, the energy drops as "normal" thoughts and physical concerns intrude. But I will retain the secret to that larger reality – for "the cat has been let out".

"Who Let the Cat Out?" dream
David (age 25) / January 10, 1973

During a reunion for members of my high school band, I examine a very old phonograph that's playing a recording of ours from long ago. As the music ends, the needle travels onto the label, producing harsh static. I and others try to turn it off, but the arm keeps returning to the label area. Finally I pull the plug, but strangely the arm again slowly moves back toward the revolving centre.

As if tapping some mysterious energy, the turntable gradually accelerates. And we're amazed to hear faint music now, as if the needle is tracking invisible grooves at the centre. Simultaneously, the record shrinks to the diameter of the label and assumes an extremely warped form. The needle travels up over high crests and down into deep troughs, as if riding a roller coaster.

I don't know why, but it comes intuitively that since the machine is functioning on some unknown energy, it may in fact be travelling through time. The warped disk may mirror a helical pattern, one intrinsic to the time dimension, passing through our normal three-dimensional world. Thus the disk presents a frozen image of this spiralling energy pattern moving perpendicularly to the turntable. As well, the strange music we hear could be a by-product of the time travel. All this is now taking place in my boyhood home, where my relatives have gathered round. I explain my intuitive theory to the others, but they are unsure and unresponsive.

As the music continues, a narrow, translucent strip like movie film now curls off to the side from where needle touches record. Examining the strip closely, I catch hints of pictures that become quite clear when viewed at the right angle. I see black-and-white snapshots from my early childhood. The filmstrip lengthens and progressively widens into an ever larger matrix of increasingly colourful scenes. As the turntable continues to accelerate, additional pictures can be unfolded, lengthwise and breadthwise, in a seemingly endless array.

Beautiful natural landscapes follow, including tropical vistas and a huge red sunset that seems to pervade everything in sight. I am filled with wonder at the vivid freshness and indubitable reality of all these scenes. Their startling beauty seems self-evident proof of a larger dimension of life somehow connected with freedom in time.

While I am poring most closely over these pictures, my family is deeply impressed as well. But then a change begins, as I wonder whether this is "really" happening in waking life. Could my relatives be just elements in a dream, who won't remember what they've seen? Yet we do seem to be awake in normal fashion, so eventually I decide against this. In a further change, the pictures seem now to be in a high-quality book or magazine. Did I just imagine the movie film? Are the pictures even about to disappear? I have to focus steadily on them to assure myself otherwise.

At this point, though, my father calls excitedly from the door, "Who let the cat out?!" I'm forced to abandon the photos in my hurry to see what's the trouble, only to find there isn't any. But there is no returning, as I gradually emerge into waking consciousness, realizing no one else will remember these miraculous events.

Chapter 7

THE ART OF DISCRETION

A great many lives are spent in learning the art of discretion, in knowing when others are trying to manipulate you and when they are being true.
– Moita

The view of metamorphosis in these chapters, while influenced by the varying experiences and concerns of many session participants, inevitably reflects Kelly's and my own evolution in this life. Partly for that reason, the major area remaining to be explored is channeling itself. Here this means psychic-spiritual communication that results in verbal messages, often surrounded by other energy manifestations. Moita emphasizes, however, that this particular form of "giving voice" to higher levels is not the final goal, for an individual or for humanity. Rather, in her words, it is only a "temporary arrangement" in this era of transition towards a new world in which communication between levels will be widespread and *un*mediated.

Of two chapters devoted to psychic-spiritual communication, much of this first one is devoted to an issue that channeling often brings to the fore most acutely: the need to question and be wary when people and situations do not feel right, when they do not show themselves worthy of our trust. This lesson, even if well-learned in mundane situations, can escape us – and has escaped otherwise sophisticated professionals – when someone opens us to what appears a new level of other-worldly contact. Especially if we have been treading a solitary path, the desire to stay intimately associated with a person seen essential to our own openings can blind us to their less-than-spiritual, human failings.

As an introduction, we will look at how one can become more open to inner guidance and learn to discriminate among sources. The first exchange brings home the idea that *everyone* is a channel. Despite distinctions between psychics or mediums and the rest of us based on forms of communication and degrees of consciousness, all of us do draw in our own ways on higher levels within, and those abilities will continue to evolve.

Anne: When I have special trials or troubles and I summon special help from what I consider to be myself, am I actually summoning a higher power?

MOITA: You are contacting your own higher self. You are opening that doorway between the worlds, and you are allowing help to flow through *you*.

Anne: Okay, do you feel it should go further than that, or is that enough?

MOITA: It is a step. Eventually you will no longer have to be *here*, and then there will be another step. Growth is always moving and changing. Everything leads to something else. There is no *end*. If it is enough for now, it is enough. Someday it will not feel like it is enough anymore. And then, if you have grown enough in this step and have laid a good foundation, another step will take place. And you will unfold; you will open to more experience and closer contact.

ლ   ლ   ლ

Nevertheless, many of us can often feel that we've been left behind somewhere. This next exchange occurs during one of our workshops.

Mary: I'm not as sensitive to these things as an awful lot of people in this room are. I don't see things, hear things... Not that I wouldn't like to. Sometimes I wonder if I'm blocking unconsciously, or if it's just a case of I'm not ready enough or I would get busy and perhaps do a better job of meditating and things like this. I don't know if I'm not putting the right energy into it (?). I think I have the right *feelings* for it, but I don't seem to be getting anywhere. Give me a clue.
MOITA: You need to be able to go deeper within yourself.
Mary: Yeah. But how? There seems to be a mental block somewhere.
MOITA: It is only a door that can be opened on your end. *(pause)*
Mary: Which means I'm not applying myself properly?
MOITA: It is not a matter of application. It is a matter of being able to relax, letting yourself flow, letting go of expectations, letting go of structures, trying to see the world through new eyes without any idea of the meaning of what you see, discovering it for the first time.

It is hard to express it in words. There is a depth to everyone's soul, a place within that touches not only themselves but others, a wellspring of beauty and joy and love that can be tapped and let loose. That is the basis for intuition, for spiritual growth: finding that place within yourself.

It is not so much a matter of seeing things or hearing things. It is a calmness and a peace and a joy of life. And when these things are known, all of the other things fall in place. They are consequences of an inner development; they are not the development itself. The emphasis is not on phenomena; it is on experience of self, on love.
Mary: Thank you. I'll work on that.

ლ   ლ   ლ

Norman: If we each have an energy-force that is available to us, is it within most of our grasps to be able to have it "help" us, should I say?
MOITA: It is within everyone's grasp. The greatest thing it takes is the ability to relax and let go of your ideas. When you decide what form this help should take, you are forcing it into certain areas where perhaps the help it can offer is not as great.
Norman: So by having expectations I would not make the situation easy to deal

with?

MOITA: By having expectations you place blocks within yourself, and being open is the art of relaxing... There is a fine line between focusing energy that is being channeled through you and expecting energy to act in a certain manner when it is channeled through you... There are many ways to learn to be open, but the openness must be there.

Dan: What do we open to?

MOITA: Be open to the form the energy wishes to take. The best and most fruitful manner in which the energy can manifest itself *through* you may not always be the way you would envision it...

Carol: Sometimes there's a lot of energy. Energy grows, and sometimes it's really hard to contain or to know what to do with it.

MOITA: Do not try to contain it. When you try to contain it, you attempt to become the vessel, and by becoming a vessel have already set limits about how much energy you can accept. When you become a light that shines out the energy that comes *to* you, there will never be more than you can share with others.

✎   ✎   ✎

During the 24 hours preceding this session, Amelia is guided through a rather inconclusive hypersentience experience and given a Tarot reading.[29] The "In" card, around which her reading revolves, is The Seeker. A man stands on a pathway, blindfolded so he will not be diverted from his true goal, mistaking it for something that might appear to fit his desires or expectations. Only by following his heart can he eventually attain to the divine fire on the mountaintop.

Amelia: During last night's hypersentience, in trying to discover from my other self some message or purpose to my life, I did not get any sort of clear answer. What would be the purpose of that?

MOITA: You must look on us not as a being who has all power, over you or your life or your destiny, to lead you where you need to go. Your answer lies within. It is there for you to find, and we can only teach and show as much as we are let.

Our worlds are different in some ways. I revolve around a different thought than those who have a body. And so, there are gaps between my world and yours that are sometimes difficult to [cross]. You must become in a way part of ours before we can touch you enough to let you hear what we speak.

Amelia: How do we make those gaps smaller? How do we become a glowing light for you?

MOITA: I see you are well on the way to doing that, letting your heart open and becoming more accepting without giving up any part of yourself. All we need is for you to be yourself.

Amelia: Have I just begun being myself?

MOITA: You are beginning to come closer to your own centre, and finding out what that really means.

Amelia: What is that journey like for me from here on in? Is it a time-consuming one?

MOITA: Time consumes all. If you view this as a small part of your wholeness, a small piece of your eternity, how can one life be a long time?

Amelia: One life is not a long time for me. I do not mean as in this lifetime.

MOITA: You mean in others as well?

Amelia: Yes.

MOITA: The search for self goes on forever, and it never finishes. I am in the process of becoming more myself and will continue to grow for as long as I can see. But the process of becoming yourself is a very joyful thing.

Amelia: Yes, I'm finding it so. I think I would like to form a strong bond, however, with my entity. I have obstacles – imposed by myself, I realize – that come in the way. And yet I would say at the same time I have this desire to become as one with my entity also.

MOITA: It is your desire that blinds you, not your blocks that get in your way. I know I have said it before. Our words and our ways can be easily missed. We come to each differently, speak to you in many ways. Our world is around you, and it is always there. When you strive and look and expect, and think you know what you will find, you are not The Seeker.

� ⋧ ⋧ ⋧

The danger in desiring to emulate particular models is that we miss the very individual way our soul seeks to emerge through us.

Will: Are there more like you that can communicate by the same sort of means through us?

MOITA: Each of you has an energy that can manifest itself in this form, if it is within your own purpose. The means of communication vary from individual to individual. Some receive our teaching through different mediums, like writing or painting, or sitting quietly by a stream and listening to the world speak.

⋧ ⋧ ⋧

Lisa: Is it possible for individuals to clear themselves enough that they are able to experience all forms of psychic communication on their own, or do we come here only prepared on a soul level to be able to handle certain types of experiences?

MOITA: Each soul has its own affinity for certain kinds of channelings. It is the soul's desire to perfect one form, and all the experiences that you have serve towards that end. It is in letting go of the desire for one form or another that the true form will come forth in you and others, giving the soul free rein to express its wholeness.

Lisa: I understand. It's hard not to desire.

MOITA: We understand too. And oftentimes, when you leave a desire behind, you find on the road ahead that it is fulfilled much more than you could have imagined on your own.

Lisa: Through letting go, you can have.

MOITA: That is how it has always been.

❧   ❧   ❧

As mentioned earlier, the emphasis here will be on contact with non-physical levels at least partially resulting in verbal messages, as we have experienced with Moita. Ouija boards and automatic writing are two ways in which people have encountered this type of communication for the first time. It is true the source of such messages may not be the medium's own higher self but a lower, fragmentary part of oneself or of another spirit who has some need to communicate. So, it depends greatly on the frame of mind and quality of energy of those involved whether these contacts, and others developing from them, will prove intriguing and gratifying – or not.

Margaret: What do you think of my playing at the Ouija board this week? *(laughing)* I suspected myself a hundred times of pushing the silly table! But I kept getting such interesting answers...

I felt my energies were really fully concentrated on what I was doing. I think I was as close to meditating as I've gotten in a long, long time.

MOITA: Like anything else, much depends upon what you put into it... For the moment, it is not necessary to determine what the source of the words is, as long as you are open-minded enough to accept the possibilities of either your own projections through your subconscious or perhaps even exterior manipulation. But in the end, how you perceive it, how you learn from it, will determine what effect it will have on you, be it a good one or a bad one. Any experience is a potential mirror into yourself.

I do not make any judgments on how you choose to use your energy. It is the effect of how you use your energy that will tell *you*. That is what you are here to learn, each of you. By seeing your energy in motion and then having your energy come back to you in one form or another, you can determine whether it is a wise use or an unwise use of energy.

❧   ❧   ❧

The fact that a Ouija board can be "played" merely as a parlour game – *or* can be utilized by entities, as Seth did in opening communication with Jane Roberts – indicates a manifest need for *discrimination* in any experience of this nature.

Alice: Can you tell me if my Moses figure, who appeared as my teacher in the hypersentience session, is there to guide me? Is he the real one?

MOITA: For now, he is the one – providing you keep in mind that, now that he has been recognized, you will be able to recognize him each time in the same way. [Then] you will not throw up for yourself any false images to give yourself guidance you may think you want, rather than the guidance you would get if you were just open to him alone. There was a special feeling that goes with him, one that you now know.

Alice: Yes, that's right.

MOITA: And by that feeling you will be able to identify when it is real and when it is not.

❦   ❦   ❦

Dora: There are others here! I can feel others behind you, around you, around us all...

MOITA: Many of those who come are your own entities.

Dora: Some tend to lean on others, and they in turn lean heavily on us, trying to impress what they feel. Is that right?

MOITA: That is very good. We speak not well with words. We communicate much better with feelings.

Dora: Yes, it's much easier. I think that's why I shook! *(laughing)* Somebody was leaning on me awfully hard! *(laughter)* And then somebody else came along and sort of said, "No, don't push so hard," and then I was fine. *(laughing)*

MOITA: So long as you hold no fear of them.

Dora: No, I don't think I do. I have trouble letting go. I know somebody's there, but I have trouble saying, "Okay, go ahead and let me know what you're doing or what's happening – whatever!" I think it's my barriers I've built up, and I have trouble saying "The barriers aren't there anymore" to myself. Am I improving any?

MOITA: Everyone is improving, from my eyes. The greatest key is relaxation, and faith in yourself.

Dora: That I'm trying to learn.

MOITA: It is good to keep discrimination, even after you have learned the others. Open yourself up on a higher level, and there will be no fear at all. There is none where *I* exist.

Dora: No, I feel it must be very peaceful.

MOITA: Peaceful, but busy.

Dora: *(laughing)* Yes, but in a different way than we consider busy.

MOITA: *Very* different.

❦   ❦   ❦

Joe: I have been told the name of my guide. Is he here?

MOITA: Your guide is here. Do you feel?

Joe: Mm-hmm.

MOITA: Then you are asking me for confirmation only?

Joe: Not entirely. I've been told that I've had other guides and have felt them. I have trouble distinguishing – like, I feel a flow of energy, and that's what I sense here, but I haven't learned to discriminate specifically.

MOITA: Mmm. The sword of discrimination. Providing you are tuned into a centred place without desiring to fulfill a gap in yourself, you will not have any difficulty in reaching the right kind of energy. When you reach out to us with a desire that is already defined, there are other forms of energy that can be attracted to you. We are always there as well, but, depending on you, we are closer or farther away.

 co   co   co

The last chapter discussed lower levels of experience available on non-physical planes: thought-forms and various kinds of spirits that have temporarily lost touch with their higher natures or are unclear or obsessed in their motives. These are included in the "other forms of energy" mentioned above. To show the workings of this, here are three situations in which a lack of clarity in the people involved could cause lower astral manifestations to come forth.

David: About a decade ago, Kelly was part of a group that was experiencing many strange manifestations, including apparitions and psychic communications[30]. Can you shed any light on who the spirits were and what all was going on there?

MOITA: Their appearance has a lot to do with the quality of energy that was present. None of [the group was] well-centred. It is difficult to be centred when you are doing so many expanding drugs. In that state it is easy to lose your sense of balance. And there are many energies of self that are available. If there were not, there would be no black magicians...

David: Would different levels come through on different occasions, so there might be some valid information at times?

MOITA: We will say that this is very much like a Ouija board. Whenever there is an opening, the [higher] entity involved can interpose and interject information, concepts, or slightly change the concepts the other [lower] energy is trying to propagate, so that growth takes place along a slightly different path which eventually leads where the entity wishes. Although it may be these experiences were not desired on the entity's part, once they are there they are utilized as much as is possible for maximum growth.
           It is a measure of [Kelly's] stability that she went through those experiences and came out whole.

co   co   co

The second excerpt focuses on Ike, a young man who has outspokenly attacked our group work with Moita as sorcery and manipulation. Yet he remains interested in the psychic field due to recent visionary experiences of his own under the extreme stress of near-starvation. Since Ike has never actually attended a Moita session, others have suggested he be invited to one. We have doubts about the value in doing that, especially if Ike comes only to observe and not to share himself openly.

David: Do you have anything to say on the possibility of holding a session with Ike? What conditions would make it worthwhile?

MOITA: Much would depend on Ike. It could be a useful experience for him. It could also be a useful experience for *you*, and any others who participated in witnessing an exchange of energy between us. *(laughing)* The possibilities are amusing!

He is more open than he appears, at least from this level – or *to* this level. This is one reason he seems to have so many barriers [on yours]. The experiences that he has had with our level have left him feeling vulnerable and insecure. He was unwise to let himself become so open so fast, and he is now learning the wisdom of going slower.

David: And trying to convince everyone else to go slower.

MOITA: He is trying to convince them to *stop*. Then his progress will not seem so slow. He may think I will try to trap him. Fortunately I am stronger than that; for if he went with these attitudes to another, it is quite possible he would force a lower energy to come forth.

David: Hmm. How would that work?

MOITA: With one who is open..., but who is not balanced or centred..., the expectations and desires of those present in a circle can affect what energy can manifest itself through a channel. And so, if the channel is uncertain, and those present are more sure of their desires, that can serve as a doorway, sometimes to the harm of the channel.

Most interestingly, Ike will report this dream a few weeks later: on the one hand, Moita as a very open and accepting presence; on the other hand, a number of us here on the human level feeling hostile to him for judging us manipulators or manipulated. Moita will then confirm to us that it was she herself who appeared in Ike's dream.

৯০   ৯০   ৯০

Channeling, we have seen, is far from simple and straightforward. The level of the source or sources, the clarity and awareness of the medium, and how intimate and voluntary their relationship is, may vary greatly, depending on the development and purposes of all concerned. Here, another warning sign emerges about Jill's friend Darryl, as previously discussed in Chapters 3 and 4.

Jill: Darryl never knows when someone is going to speak through him, and he doesn't remember anything that is said during that period of time. Why is this? Are there entities that enter into his body, speak through him, and cause him not to remember?

MOITA: Regarding entities and how they communicate, there is no set standard. For some, there is no recall. They go into what is called a trance state where they are not consciously aware of what is happening. Sometimes it is not truly a trance; sometimes it is not truly an entity. Sometimes it *is* another part of the person, and the one part recedes into the background as the other part comes forward.

∾   ∾   ∾

The previous three excerpts relating to the possibility of lower astral manifestations in channeling are crucially linked to another continuing story, that of our involvement with Dr. Elisabeth Kübler-Ross. Most of the remainder of this chapter is devoted to Kübler-Ross's strange relationship in the years 1976 to 1981 with Jay and Marti Barham. This would become a very public debacle that no doubt turns some away from anything to do with channeling. But it contains many lessons.

Elisabeth, born in Switzerland in 1926, volunteered as a youth for extended relief work in war-ravaged France and Poland and then overcame her father's obdurate resistance to her training as a medical doctor, eventually specializing in psychiatry. Moving to America with her new husband, she achieved remarkable success by giving loving attention and active encouragement to the most withdrawn, neglected, long-term patients in a state mental hospital.

Then, in the 1960s, Elisabeth broke through the social and professional wall of silence around death by interviewing terminally ill patients about their experience. Her work eventually revolutionized treatment of the dying and inspired what became the Hospice movement. Inevitably, she also received thousands of reports of near-death experiences from such patients. By the 1970s, these reports and other evidence convinced her, against her own scientific preconceptions, of a spiritual life after death.

Besides worldwide acclaim, all of Elisabeth's pioneering work provoked much opposition and criticism from the medical establishment. And in response to her expressed convictions about the afterlife, including descriptions of her own other-worldly encounters, came aspersions about her sanity. Even her neurologist husband would reach his limit and divorce her.[31N]

During Ruth's and my treasured visit with Kübler-Ross in her home in spring 1977,[32] Loria spoke of heavy storm clouds then gathering around Elisabeth. Nevertheless, she said that rays of sunlight would continue to shine through the negativity. The next evening, Loria told me "an extended, close relationship will develop between you and Elisabeth this time around, building upon your past associations." At the time, I did not guess that close relationship would involve helping her deal with one of those dark clouds.

The next installment of this story follows – with more to come in future.

The first hint that something may be terribly amiss reaches Kelly and me in July 1979 on meeting Lara, who has recently studied and worked at Shanti Nilaya. This is the retreat centre Elisabeth founded in late 1977 near Escondido, California, for terminally ill persons, their families and members of the helping professions.

Lara alludes to a scandal that is causing many people to leave Shanti Nilaya, a scandal involving the very man Elisabeth credits with facilitating her first "incredible" contact with materializing presences back in September 1976. That contact was the reason Elisabeth acquired the centre's land, which adjoins property owned by Jay and Marti Barham. Marti is a licensed psychotherapist, while Jay bills himself as a psychodramatist and channeler as well as founder of a Church of the Facet of Divinity.[33] Lara's report lacks detail, but in essence she tells us the materialization of entities is *not* as it appears, or as Elisabeth believes it to be – rather, that Jay Barham himself is creating the illusion of such contact.

When Elisabeth first described to me how her entities materialized, it's true that I was amazed, not knowing what to think. But having seen how inspired and inspiring Elisabeth became in the wake of those first encounters – both at the holistic healing conference the day after, to which she gave her famous "Death Does Not Exist" address, and during my visit the following spring – I have difficulty crediting what Lara is telling Kelly and me in the summer of 1979. At first, it seems far more likely that people are denying or twisting very beautiful events because they cannot let go of their own fears. Having ourselves experienced unfounded charges of manipulation, we are not in a rush to reject Elisabeth's view of events just because she is facing more opposition. Of course, we are also curious to discover why such controversy has arisen.

Near the end of July, when I am able to ask Moita about Lara's report, my words reflect these initial assumptions. But then Kelly and I are surprised how seriously Moita takes the darkness of this latest storm cloud in Elisabeth's life. (Note that the question I ask – which limits Moita's response – concerns experiences directly involving Elisabeth, since I am as yet unaware of reports involving other people's interactions with Barham.)

Moita Session #103 (Kelly and David / July 28, 1979)

David: We want to ask about the version of reality Lara told us: what she has heard or feels is going on at Shanti Nilaya with Elisabeth and Barham. Her version, as she's gathered from others, suggests that what Elisabeth said about the events of Labour Day weekend 1976 was not accurate, that her contact with entities is somehow being created by this man. This seems a case of people reacting with quite different views of reality, and my tendency is to share Elizabeth's. But I'd be interested in your view of what might be going on here.

MOITA: What I can say on this . . . would be more, in a different place.

(Both Kelly and I interpret this to mean she could say more if Elisabeth herself were present. In the following, Moita looks away from me, as she sometimes does when dealing with a difficult or very personal subject. The deep feeling behind her answer is

evident to both of us.)

MOITA: Elisabeth feels she is going through another test, a test of her faith and her ability to withstand criticism, to see her world crumble, to have no one believe in her and her perceptions.

It is true that after a contact with an entity, the communication can deteriorate if the person involved in it becomes unclear with her own purposes, or ungrounded in the world; and there are those who can take advantage of someone who is not as grounded as they should be. Deception does happen, not only from a physical point of view but also from a spiritual point of view, when one forgets to question.

On the other side, if the belief is strong, the experience will be valid, whether or not it is what others would call a "true" experience. It is not that common for an entity to materialize. It takes a great deal of energy, a great deal of purpose, in order to do so. It is feasible that it happened more than once. It is not likely that it happened a great many times; and, in the wake of non-materialization, others whose purposes were not clear to them could make it appear that something was happening that was wished for.

This still does not wipe away information that comes through. For even those who are masquerading are influenced by their own higher selves and by others on our level, whether they are aware of it or not. And the expectation of those who are present, and the energy they add to the experience, will lend a helping hand to us in getting across the message that we feel needs to be given.
(pause)

(Looking toward me now:)

MOITA: You see, there are many places I must go in order to fit together pieces of things that can be or might be.

(Kelly later says: "I can really feel Moita going far afield to gather data, like a real stretching, trying to get in an awful lot of different angles to the situation, so we don't see it from just one point of view.")

(Looking away from me:)

MOITA: If it is found that a deception is occurring, the reaction that she has to its discovery will make a great impact upon her future. If she chooses to believe that it means nothing was real, she will go into despair, for she has given her life over to the search and the contact with us. If she sees that there is still truth, that we are still there, then she will be stronger. She will be wary. She will have more discretion. [It] will be not as easy to [make her] believe in something.

(Looking toward me again:)

MOITA: A great deal of life, a great many lives, are spent in learning the art of discretion, in knowing when others are trying to manipulate you and when they are being true. It always hurts when one is found to be manipulating, if he was considered a friend and your trust was placed in him.

David: Yes, I know it does.

MOITA: The world is full of imperfect instruments striving towards being clearer.

But because you are all unclear in one way or another, there is no "truth" to what we say – not as far as *we* would consider truth. It all hangs in a mist, a mist of perception.

There is also the side that Elisabeth can see to a certain extent *into* our reality, and by being able to do this can transcend, change her viewpoint, see something real in our world where others may see nothing. In a crowd of people, one person sees a spirit floating through the air, speaks – and others say, "There is nothing there." But who has seen the reality, and who are those that are blind?

❧   ❧   ❧

Despite Moita's acknowledgment that people's differing perceptions are factors in the situation, her use of "deception" and "masquerading" and "manipulating" leaves no doubt in our minds there is substance to this scandal. While Moita agrees that Elisabeth is indeed open to higher levels and that one or more materializations may well have occurred (though not the many that are purported), she also says Elisabeth's unclarity or lack of grounding has caused her not to question things that cry out for it – such as the behaviour and statements of this very close associate on whom she has become dependent.

In view of Elisabeth's exhausting schedule and total emotional commitment to her pioneering causes, plus her recently feeling abandoned by her husband, this is not too surprising. In fact, I suspect Loria had this possibility in mind back in April 1977 when she urged Elisabeth to take time for relaxation and self-care – to give herself some of the love she gives others.

It takes me a while to gather my thoughts after our July 28th Moita session. But during August I do write to Elisabeth: partly to describe the controversial changes in our own lives and work as Kelly and I prepare to move to British Columbia, and partly to ask about the disturbing reports we have received about Shanti Nilaya and Jay Barham. Not wanting to close off communication with Elisabeth, who at this point continues publicly to support Barham to the hilt, I do not state either Moita's views or my own thoughts. But I do tell Elisabeth we have asked Moita for her understanding of what is going on and that we will share Moita's answer if Elisabeth wishes to hear it.

Then, a month later, we receive the letter below, written or dictated on the third anniversary of Elisabeth's first meeting with entities appearing visibly before her. I am relieved that she senses my essential support for who she is and for her work, despite not automatically endorsing her view of the current situation, and that she wishes to receive our Moita transcript. Though she gives no hint of a change of mind or of doubts about Jay Barham, I am glad to hear she is setting aside time to relax, centre and ground herself in a comfortable, natural place of her own.

September 4, 1979

My dear David and Kelly,

It is Labor Day weekend and I'm taking...the night off, to read my letters. And among them is yours sharing with me where you are at in your new space, your endings and your beginnings. And I thank you very much for your sharing as it is a special gift today in the midst of newspaper articles that are most derogatory, attacks from left and right. But also today being the anniversary of my very first visit with Aenka, Mario and Salem. And nothing and no one can ever take those memories, those gifts, away from me. I will treasure every moment I have spent with our entities and every hour I'm spending now and in the future with them.

And though we are going through enormous tests, each one of them has helped to separate the wheat from the chaff and has strengthened us in our conviction that we are on the right path...

I have now moved to a log cabin Swiss house chalet type home on top of a mountain a very few minutes away from Shanti Nilaya. Here I do my work, weed my garden, cook a few meals, see a few friends. But mostly just sit and be, watching the sunrise and the sunset and recharge my batteries between workshops and lectures.

I'm enclosing a newspaper of the San Diego Union for you, but I will send it by separate mail since there is no rush about it. Just so you have an idea of all the gossip and negativity that comes our way. I'm sharing this with you in the hope that you will know that if you start something beautiful and meaningful, there will always be negativity and people who try to destroy your credibility. Do not be disturbed by them as negativity can only feed on negativity. And if you stay clear and without fear and guilt, and know what you want, you will succeed as we are growing and succeeding in spite of all the storms.

I would be most grateful if you send me any transcripts from your own entity. But make sure you write "Personal" on the envelope so that I'm getting it. And I'm naturally most curious what Moita had to share. I am still in touch with my own guides who help me to grow, who understand and don't criticize and judge, who recharge my battery when I need it, and who are aware of my ups and downs so that I never feel abandoned and deserted even when I'm totally alone now.

I do hope that our paths cross this coming year and that we'll be able to share a visit and to dream and to sing together one day. Until then be well and happy, and keep in touch.

Lots of love,
Elisabeth

Despite our relief at this letter, it is with trepidation that we then read the forwarded articles from *The San Diego Union* of September 2, 1979:

> Elisabeth Kubler-Ross, the Swiss-born psychiatrist known worldwide for her work with the dying, is in the middle of a controversy involving alleged sexual misconduct and cruelty among leaders and members of her Escondido area retreat fueled by...allegations that during seances there were sexual encounters between individuals and afterlife spirit entities...[34]

The newspaper articles are based on interviews with Elisabeth, Jay and Marti

Barham and a number of participants in Barham's "darkroom" psychodrama seances (or whatever they should be called), as well as with investigating authorities. They leave us shocked – not shocked that people are making wild accusations – rather, shocked that the charges seem in large part so very likely, though incredibly, true.

Thereafter I respond with a letter sharing our own most recent news, the transcript of Moita's words on July 28th, and our thoughts in the wake of all the new information. Those unfamiliar with the details of the scandal can glean a fair idea of the happenings – and of the opinions then being expressed by Elisabeth and Barham – from my letter, most of which appears below. (A few bits of information are added in square brackets for completeness.)

September 24, 1979

Dear Elisabeth,

Because we are attempting to be engaged in work along *somewhat* similar lines to yours at Shanti Nilaya, we are aware of some of the same difficulties in encounters with those who are new and perhaps closed in some ways to the experiences and energies we can make available (e.g., people not taking responsibility for the effects of their own attitudes and beliefs; people looking for an authority and/or womb to protect them from the necessity of individual choice, faith and work; and so on).

At the same time, since we have not been directly connected with your work there, but rather experienced contact of our own with higher level entities..., we may bring an additional perspective that might be of use to you at this time, just as yours has already very much done for us. At least, that is the hope behind my trying to write the remainder of this letter.

It's difficult for me to weed out the essential from the non-essential, to see so many viewpoints at once, to be open to experiences that are strange to me, to find the right language to express my many feelings, to humbly let the truth be my goal (wherever it leads) while I take responsibility for expressing what sides of it I feel I *am* able to see at present. So I will try, and, knowing you, you will not let the ways I fail get in the way of what truth remains.

Kelly and I did not know what to think when we heard some of the rumors about events at Shanti Nilaya – except, as I wrote earlier, a deep faith in you as a person and the wish/expectation that things were not as some were making them appear. In that spirit, we held a session with Moita on July 28th partly to inquire about her view of the situation. As you requested, I am reproducing the transcript of Moita's response verbatim below. There was much feeling underlying her words, and Kelly could sense Moita stretching far afield to include the various angles of the situation...

[transcript inserted here]

Moita often speaks with a certain indirectness, and it is in noticing what she chooses to say and chooses not to say that we arrive at her meaning for us. We had not expected nor wished to hear her speak of masquerading, of deception, and of manipulation. Yet the implication seemed clear to us that, from her perspective, there was a certain degree of truth to the reports we had heard, unclear and exaggerated in some respects as they might be...

We deeply appreciate your sending us *The San Diego Union* article, despite its painfulness, as it provides what we assume to be more accurate information about what is being said, for us to respond to. We feel the reporter did an excellent job at being impartial. I am all too aware that we do not know the true situation or the people involved, as we have not experienced them for ourselves. We *can*, however, respond in a limited way, ...sharing with you the thoughts and feelings that come to us upon reading the articles you sent...

1. You seem to regard the criticisms directed at the Barhams and Shanti Nilaya as more of the same testing you have been through so much of before. You were told several years ago, however, that you had passed your tests of fame and negativity. Criticism will no doubt continue from those who are not ready to admit larger realities, but withstanding that will probably not be much of a challenge to you anymore... This leads me to think that, divine economy being what it is, the present situation is a *different* kind of test.

2. From the way you appear in the article to be linking yourself so absolutely and inextricably with Jay Barham's work, it occurs to me that discrimination might well be part of the test. You decline to discuss the allegations against him and appear to deal with all criticism as more of the same that has been directed against *you* in the past... I get the sense that perhaps your link with Jay – because he was instrumental in your own spiritual opening – has come to feel beyond question for all time; that his importance in your own development makes it appear unthinkable that your association with him cease or undergo radical change, and therefore unthinkable also that he should be acting in a misguided fashion.

It is as if the reality of your own spiritual experiences has become synonymous with Jay Barham's activities. If this is so, I would see parallels between this and Ram Dass's experience several years ago with Joya...[35] In [both] cases there would seem to be a person with obvious gifts and unusual energy that attracts others and comes to be perceived as indispensable. Yet the presence of the power in itself is no guarantee it will flow out in perfect harmony with the universe or the needs of the time, since its human channel is never perfect. Thus the necessity for discrimination, questioning, evaluation of what is actually going on in everyone's experience, the taking of responsibility for the form of expression these energies are given on the human level.

3. One of the more disturbing things for me in the article was the ease with which explanations were given that discredited or disregarded other people's perceptions. For Jay to dismiss charges out of hand on the ground that everybody else is responsible for their own selective, subjective perceptions ignores his own responsibility for his own behavior and for the manner in which he channels certain kinds of energy through him.

Jay claims he doesn't know what goes on between the entities and participants in the darkroom sessions, and yet he doesn't appear to give any weight to those who report what *they* know to be happening. How then can he exercise his responsibility to know and evaluate the results of his work? Session procedures (darkness, switches taped, phosphorescent paraphernalia, etc.) are given ready explanations ("Light would harm the channel" [or the materialized entity itself] – something we and others have not found to be true so far in our work), as are reports of masquerading – not to mention cruelty and sexual misconduct ("You see what you expect to see" or "There must be a positive lesson or the entities wouldn't do it") – which leaves me wondering what sorts of deception and abuses could *not* be made possible and then justified in these very same ways!

4. Underlying these concerns is a deep questioning of the value and appropriateness of what is even *purported* to be going on, in the private darkroom and sexual therapy sessions particularly. The supposed entity materializations appear to be being used as a cure-all for human-level problems that would best be handled through personal interactions with a therapist or whatever. The proper human responsibility to use our own capacities to heal, to make choices, to freely and consciously participate in arriving at decisions, values, and directions for our lives, would seem to be short-circuited in this overemphasis on contacts with entities.

Inevitably, the people that are attracted to such sessions would seem not to have the right grounding and centering within themselves to make best use of such an experience; at least, this would apply to those described as coming out of insecurity, fear, desperation (needing to fill a void in their lives, with the result that they become "hooked" on the sessions). Indeed, such motivations would directly affect the nature of the experience, in that lower, more negative entities would be attracted to such groups.

(A relevant quote from Moita: "The sword of discrimination. Providing you are tuned into a centred place without desiring to fulfill a gap in yourself, you will not have any difficulty in reaching the right kind of energy. When you reach out to us with a desire that is already defined, there are other forms of energy that can be attracted to you. We are always there as well, but, depending on you, we are closer or farther away.")

The quotations from some participants clearly show overdependence reactions of addictive proportions, and a surrender of individual responsibility and freedom of choice to the "authority" of the entities ("I felt that I couldn't go against what the entities were asking me to do.") Far from taking care to correct this misapprehension or be selective about the participants, Jay's own comments seem consistent with this neglect to question and evaluate what the entities say or do. This attitude plays right into the hands of lower astral spirits and thought-forms created by the participants themselves, while blocking the effort of higher beings to nurture true individual spiritual growth.

So, I repeat that even the purported activities seem inappropriate to us. That a higher being would manifest in material form for the purpose of telling someone her sex life is unsatisfactory and offering to make love to her is in no way consistent with our understanding of the nature and purposes of such beings. Moreover, such activities would obviously open the door to tremendous abuses on the human level and/or at the very least great confusion and doubt – which is clearly the case when the "entities" are reported to look remarkably like Jay Barham [including a naked Jay Barham]. The whole account of [entities] "cloning" [themselves from Barham's body] palls in my mind before the realization that no entity from the proper level would choose to come in materialized form if the energy of a group were not sufficiently prepared so as to avoid the confusion evident from these articles. The alternative, then, is to suppose lower spirits or thought-forms are involved – as well as outright masquerading, as some of the other participants conceded was done at the "request" of an "entity". If the "entity" favors deception for others, it is not difficult to suppose the "entity" itself may sometimes be a deception.

5. Finally, I find a certain immodesty in Jay's attitude toward the power to which he has gained access. Speaking of "harnessing" the energy, and saying "It's just a matter of using it," avoid the issue of self-purification necessary to becoming a clear channel for the Spirit – which is much more than the power to work certain effects *on* another. In this regard, we are including [an] issue of *Rays*, entitled "Power – to Use, or How Not to Use", which for me places things in their proper order and discusses some of the possible abuses (physical and psychical) when they are not so placed...

As the spiritual world moves closer to ours in this age, many of us are having to deal with the danger of glorification of the human channel, and the dogmatism, competitiveness, paranoia, and disillusionment that often flow from that. Whether it's mediumship, or healing, or anything else, I feel emphasis has to continually be redirected to the One Source on the one hand, and [to] the openness, faith, etc., of the individual participants in the session on the other, as well as to the clarity of the channel.

Furthermore, as far as evaluating my work goes, if I take seriously what is said about the subjectivity of perception, I must include myself under the same rubric as I do my detractors. That allows me to see myself and others more clearly as the individual human beings that we are – with our different experiences, based on our different needs, corresponding to the different stages we are at – so that *my* experience of something does not keep me from a sympathetic understanding of their perhaps quite opposite experience, and from adjusting my behavior to help promote whatever growth others may need most at the time. I recognize in writing this that this is one of my own biggest problems in working with people: wanting to assume that everyone else is or should be where I happen to be (or think I may be), and blaming them when they don't react as I do (or as I think I might in their position).

Having written all of this, I have many doubts about whether I am doing the right thing – both whether I am right in what I say, and whether I should be writing it to you. It is very hard to send this; it would be much more comfortable to keep quiet about my many misgivings. I am afraid of being regarded an enemy, or at best as having no understanding of the truth. But we share a faith that the truth will prevail, so I will surrender...to that, whichever way it eventually may point us.

Kelly and I both very much value your work, your friendship, your light. We share your faith in and knowledge of the Spirit within all life, and in the reality of that wisdom, love and truth as it increasingly enters our lives during this period. If you ever wish more contact with us or Moita, we would be delighted to hear from you, or perhaps even to welcome you one day to our doorstep...

With lots of love,
David

We do not receive back any direct response from Elisabeth to this September letter. However, the following brief, indirect response a few weeks later is sufficient to the time, assuring me our friendship will continue.

November 17, 1979

Dear [David and Kelly],

I love you and I am enclosing $10 for a year's subscription to be sent to Shanti Nilaya so that we can put it in our library and everybody can read it.

Keep up your good work and your good spirits, and know that this is the time when nothing will be hidden and that we all work together for the benefit of mankind.

We are in stormy times here and have gone through many trials and tribulations, but it has been a blessing in disguise as it separates the wheat from the chaff. And we turn the negativity into a positive experience for many who touch our lives.

We send you love and support from Shanti Nilaya.

Elisabeth

Years afterward, Elisabeth's autobiography (Kübler-Ross 1997) will fill in some of her interactions with the Barhams during this period. The chronology is a bit confusing, perhaps due to the series of strokes Elisabeth suffers in later life. But it becomes clear that between 1979 and spring 1981 Elisabeth's assessment of Barham's integrity is plummeting.

One major blow is discovery of a book written twenty years earlier (*The Magnificent Potential* by Lerner Hinshaw) that contains all of the purportedly new spiritual information that Barham has been teaching, and much of what the channeled beings have been imparting as well. Stunned at this betrayal, Elisabeth is bewildered what to do.

While Kübler-Ross maintains her public support of Barham, second-hand reports of less-than-spiritual darkroom activities at times or places Elisabeth is not present are also taking their toll. Barham's excuses that he cannot know what materializing entities do when they purportedly "clone" themselves from his body while in trance are wearing thin.

As many of the original session devotees depart Shanti Nilaya, Elisabeth and those who remain begin paying more attention to goings-on in the private rooms adjoining the main darkroom and take steps to prevent Barham from being there alone with anyone. They even arrange for Barham to be handcuffed during sessions, and Elisabeth herself plans to switch on a light during a session, despite many warnings against this. Still, while "seriously conflicted" over what she is learning about Barham's "creepy behavior" both past and present, Elisabeth continues to have wonderful experiences connected with visibly appearing entities both in Barham's darkroom and independently.[36]

In March 1980, I write to Elisabeth describing the early stages of this writing project. In April, with Kelly, Moita and me in mind, she responds more enthusiastically than I could expect:

> I am very excited about the outline of the book, and I hope that many, many people will be able to read it. I would be happy to look at the final manuscript and help you in whatever way I can. I will be back in the middle of May and have a strong urge or need to connect with you in person for some reason. Maybe some time during the summer I will be able to do that.

A future chapter will relate what happens to this exciting idea: the attempted "in person" meeting of Elisabeth, Moita, Kelly and me. Unfortunately, it's possible that Mr. Barham has a hand in the outcome.

We have heard that one of the bonds between Kübler-Ross and Jay Barham is what he and the entities describe as a past life together at the time of Jesus. According to the entity Salem, Elisabeth was then "a wise and respected teacher named Isabel".[37] Given also Loria's reference to "past associations" with Elisabeth, Kelly and I will later use hypersentience to investigate any reincarnational background linking us with Elisabeth and Barham.

As late as May 1981, I am amazed to find Elisabeth quoted in a high-profile interview giving full, unquestioning support to Jay Barham.[38] Of course, the actual conversation must have taken place many months previous. That is obvious, because the final rupture between Elisabeth and Barham occurs that same spring.

Elisabeth's growing, well-founded distrust of Barham eventually provokes him, or whatever possesses him, to strike back. Thus a series of very suspicious, life-threatening events – or "attacks" is likely more accurate – finally convinces Elisabeth she must break all ties. As she will later write: "The series of freakish incidents threatening my life – the spider bites, the brake failure and the fire – was too close for comfort. I believed my life was in danger... I felt I had to get away from B. and his evil energy."[39]

We do not learn of these events until the end of August 1981, when a letter Elisabeth dictated back on June 30th finally arrives:

> Since I have talked with you by letter the last time, many things have happened. I had an almost-fatal spider bite on my face. I recuperated from that. Four weeks later, on the day before Good Friday, part of my house burned down with many of its beautiful contents. And later on yet, on Father's Day, my two partners, especially Jay, had to be dismissed from Shanti Nilaya... The details of this are much too cumbersome and difficult to describe... I just wanted you to know what big windstorms...we have had here at Shanti Nilaya and that you know we are in very, very good spirits, that we are also feeling a

sense of new beginnings and incredible growth and peace...

I would be most happy if Moita would give me a message in terms of her opinion about all the new growth, the new changes, the new spring cleaning, as I call it, here at Shanti Nilaya, and give me some message as to the opinion of the unobstructed world about the choices we have taken.

In a session within a week of our receiving this letter, Moita does have substantive messages that we pass on to Elisabeth. Beyond the specific information conveyed, though, Moita's basic message does not waver from what it was the first time we asked about the rumors from Shanti Nilaya.

Back in that summer of 1979, Elisabeth was sure that her association with the Barhams was simply bringing more tests of her strength in the face of opposition from others. But Moita's words pointed to quite a different sort of challenge: "If it is found that a deception is occurring, the reaction that she has to its discovery will make a great impact upon her future. If she chooses to believe that it means nothing was real, she will go into despair, for she has given her life over to the search and the contact with us. If she sees that there is still truth, that we are still there, then she will be stronger. She will be wary. She will have more discretion."

Happily, as expressed in her autobiography, this will also be Elisabeth's eventual understanding of the lesson from this tumultuous period of her life:

Much later, when I was able to communicate again with Salem, Pedro and other entities, they acknowledged having been aware of my doubts and constant questioning whether they came from God or the devil. But going through the terrible experience was the only way to learn the ultimate lesson about trust and how to discern and discriminate. [40]

ॐ   ॐ   ॐ

Illustrative Dream

Discrimination, of course, is a two-edged sword. Whether it brings clarity and promotes growth, or builds walls that close off possibilities, depends on the purposes and perspectives – and the art – of those employing it. Context is also key, as the right steps along one pathway may be doomed to failure along another, especially where other people are involved. Consciousness change cannot be forced or really even argued, in the case of individuals or social structures. As Moita says, true change can only come freely, from within.

This dream arrives on the morning after my 29th birthday. On the surface, it appears fairly ordinary – until my life context is factored in, revealing its symbolic richness and relevance to this chapter.

At this time, I have been in difficult discussions with my faculty Ph.D. committee over my choice to research lucid dreaming – philosophically, psychologically, experientially. Even members who are supportive see many obstacles to my turning this into a viable dissertation in the accepted scientific mould. And while my writings have provoked interesting exchanges among us about academia versus actual mystic experience, the existing professional protocols will be maintained. And so, in time, I will withdraw from the program – but not before embarking upon what seems to me at this point a more promising path to understanding the psyche, in company with Loria and then Moita.

Given this context, I believe "water" in this dream stands for consciousness or spiritual understanding: as in clear, fresh water to replace old, dirty water that has even flooded a classroom; as in a large supply of our own deep well water, rather than piped-in foreign water subject to established power structures. And just as it makes sense for a city to enjoy free access to its own bountiful water supply, I believe the dream is saying that spiritual growth, expansion of consciousness, knowledge of the psyche, etc., comes best by digging deep within oneself. This holds true despite opposition from within and without: fears of inner pollution and instability; charges of arrogance and wild impracticality; resistance from forces of the status quo, even as huge planetary changes are on the way (as in the opening of a "world's fair").

In both waking and dreaming, then, resolution lies deeper than the level at which these conflicts are playing out. I believe that is the meaning of this birthday dream as I approach a crossroads in my life.

"Advocating Our Own Water Source" dream
David (age 29) / March 15, 1976

This seems to be happening near the end of the 19th century, or we may be re-enacting an historical event from that time. A world's fair is going to be held here in Regina. I am among students discussing the water supplies and storage facilities that will be required to serve the city and all the visitors.

I suggest that a deep well be dug to fill a reservoir – given that our biggest water tank so far only holds 29 gallons (!). The others are skeptical, so I outline the advantages of a large supply of fresh water. For instance, we could let dirty water drain away and replace it with clean water. As I say this, I see a bathtub draining. Then I see the whole classroom filled with several feet of water. We're swaying around in the currents until the water drains out.

Our classroom discussion evolves into a town meeting. A woman responds to me, saying Regina has been offered water rights to a cove in a Minnesota lake, which seems more practical to her – an established route, at less cost. It's suggested that Regina water is polluted or that geological problems hinder local well-digging. Then a group of older men express their grave doubts, especially about creating deep wells here. They come on very heavily to me personally, saying I'm making irresponsible proposals without knowing their feasibility, creating wildly visionary plans without any practical foundation. Almost everyone seems to think drawing our water from the U.S. is the obviously correct and only possibility.

I try to respond, speaking slowly and calmly despite my emotions. I deny that I'm claiming to know more than I do or that I would force my plan on everyone else. I have only raised a possibility to be explored, and nothing is going to be done unless people freely decide to try it. But I don't seem able to affect this group of men in particular. They are not really hearing what I'm saying. They will not consider the possibility that we might go to the hard work of creating a large water source of our own, when it is easier and so much more conventional, in terms of established power arrangements, to get water from elsewhere.

In the end, I still think my idea should be tried. But if others don't agree, they can just continue as they have before.

The alternative to this level of conflict is an inner opening and exploring that frees and transforms, along a path that is whole and truly chosen – even if solitary at times.

Often a birthday dream prefigures and prepares the path that will unfold during the coming year or longer phase of one's life. So it is that three months after this birthday dream, just one month before the Loria channelings will begin, I am given a first real feeling for a deep "water source" within. Waking from the dream-state, still floating weightless in endlessly reflective depths of pure knowing, I hear a young woman's voice infused with clear, warm, serene immediacy, saying: "Yes, this is the discovery of my deep centre."

Chapter 8

A UNIVERSE OF PRESENCES

There are always the presences here of your own guides, your own higher selves, your own souls. The purpose [is] to help you reconnect with that self, so that [connection] can last throughout your life, so that you do not need a mediary between the worlds such as I. This is a temporary arrangement.
– Moita

Many people dogmatically assume that the source of all purported channelings is either the medium's own personality or a split-off part of it lacking true independent existence – no matter how "high" or "spiritual" that supposed subpersonality may appear. Others will only go a bit further, admitting that disembodied spirits of other personalities may use a medium to communicate on this plane after physical death. These latter experiences may be merely distracting or can be quite meaningful, depending on the purposes of those involved. Below, one of the rare instances of such contact during Kelly's and my time together provides our chapter title.

David: Kelly felt a presence last week that appeared to be my grandfather, who died 3 years ago [and was of the same entity as son Michael]. Was that indeed a communication from his entity?

MOITA: Your grandfather, as himself, still exists. That personality is not gone even though another part of the entity has reincarnated. And as being the most familiar aspect to you of that entity, it would be the easiest to receive impressions from... It is...a way of saying that the contact is never broken..., and a way to let you know that his thoughts are with you and he is watching and learning from your decisions...

David: I enjoyed his thoughts that we received – his garden, picnics on his lawn.

MOITA: It is nice to live in a universe that is filled with *presences*, and one that is not just bodies that are being manipulated from spot to spot. It gives it more cohesiveness, more unity, more meaning – where nothing is wasted.

❧   ❧   ❧

But limiting the source of channelings to the medium's subconscious or to spirits of the dead fails to allow for contact with the higher self, the entire soul, of the medium – a being encompassing the many personalities it has worn through the ages – not to mention yet further evolved beings, the sources of inspiration and revelation since consciousness began incarnating on Earth. Without the possibility of contact with such "entities" (as we are calling beings from the soul level upwards), there could be little relief from the relativism of human personality, and little point to developing discrimination. But because entity contact *is* possible, the true seeker can aim for the very highest within, and eventually be rewarded.

It may take a while for participants in our sessions to realize how inherent and intimate is the connection between Kelly and Moita, ensuring the integrity and depth of these communications.

Mike: Are you part of Kelly's personality?

MOITA: A personality is a part of a whole soul. So, being a whole soul myself, I could not be a part of anyone's personality.

Mike: Okay. Did you get attracted to Kelly because she was a good channel?

MOITA: Remember I spoke of your being able to investigate your past by becoming that greater part of which you were created? *(Recall Mike's witnessing of his own creation in Chapter 6.)* I am that greater part of which Kelly is an expression.

Mike: Which is different than being part of her personality? You're linked with the energy that is Kelly?

MOITA: I am linked with the energy of the soul that is Kelly, and Kelly is an expression of that soul. If you wish to take analogies, Kelly would be the child, her soul would be the mother, and I would be a grandparent...

C.:   Is Kelly very close when you're here?

MOITA: Not very far away.

C.:   I sort of seem to feel Kelly here, too.

MOITA: She is a participant *(C. laughs)* in much of what happens – sometimes willing, other times uncertain. *(pause)* As you are sometimes uncertain.

C.:   *(laughing)* Perhaps.

MOITA: Perhaps.

෯   ෯   ෯

Will: I'm interested in knowing *you*, and your relationship to Kelly. Who was instrumental in getting you two together? *(pause)*

MOITA: I do not believe there was a who... I know you have heard of my history somewhat[41N], of our connection to each other. As part of myself, in a way you could say she, and the energy of which she is a part, is a child. I have a connection and a responsibility to assist in her development. And by helping her, I am also learning more what it means to co-exist with those who have a more limited view. I am learning much about communicating my own view of reality, and she is learning to open herself up to other realms – not just in my reality, but in hers.

I try to bring a feeling of acceptance. We do not feel any of you as different, less or more. We do not live in a world of contradiction. We see things in a pattern, and the pattern fits the whole.

෯   ෯   ෯

Carla: Will you eventually merge with Kelly? Are you a separate energy from her, or are you a part of her higher self?

MOITA: I am in a way both. I am representative of that which she is working towards. I am also my own entity and an individual energy-presence that will continue to exist and grow.

                                                    ❧   ❧   ❧

MOITA: I am one of Kelly's possible futures. I am what Kelly is trying to become – or something like me.

                                                    ❧   ❧   ❧

Asking the question in a different way brings out additional aspects of a healthy relationship between source and channel.

Will: Moita, can you communicate in this same manner through other people?

MOITA: In order to communicate like this, there must be some affinity between the energies. It is possible, but it would be rare to find another part that I would be able to tune myself into as well. If there were another part that I was connected to, then it would be possible.

                                                    ❧   ❧   ❧

Leslie: Can you come to us without Kelly being here – speaking through someone else?

MOITA: It would be very difficult. There would not be the same sympathy between me and another. In this kind of communication between levels, communicating through a vehicle changes the energy of the presence. It is an interaction: it is not my reality superimposed over Kelly's or yours; it is the two realities mingled together in the same place. So, without one component of this merging, the end-product would not be the same. It would have a different feel. There would be different things I could or could not say, depending upon whom I spoke through. In some cases it could be harmful to the person involved. They would not have as much of a willingness to experience this merging.

                                                    ❧   ❧   ❧

Ann: Can you go through people besides Kelly?

MOITA: There is a possibility – at this time, not very high. If I came through someone other than Kelly, the feel of my presence would be very different. I would in a sense have to use another part of myself in order to do that.

Sometimes it seems Moita uses several different "parts of herself" in communicating even just through Kelly: the gay, stern, tender aspects of a being that participants soon come to regard as an old friend. On the other hand, some believe a proper spiritual being should be impersonally far removed from us – as was, for example, the source that spoke through America's "sleeping prophet", Edgar Cayce.[42] But different forms of channeling each have their advantages, depending upon purpose. Moita's description of handling her many selves tells us much about her reality, and to a certain extent ours as well.

David: The source that spoke through Edgar Cayce has been described as the "universal subconscious". Was the source speaking through him of a different kind than you?

MOITA: The source that spoke through Cayce did not wear the veil of a personality. Everyone is connected and every*thing* is connected. Cayce tuned into his time, the men of his time and where they were leading themselves, and the Earth of his time. *(pause)*

David: Can you say more about "the veil of personality" as it may apply to you here?

MOITA: The personalities that you choose when you live a life are coverings, ways of interpreting your surroundings, smaller doorways and openings into one particular aspect of yourself, focuses on smaller points. You do not shed a personality when you die; you absorb it. When you have lived many lives, you have absorbed many personalities, and you can change them to suit circumstance – those parts of yourself which seem most appropriate. None of them are unreal, but they are tools of focusing.

Cayce did not have a focusing problem, since he was asleep. If I did not use a personality to impress myself in your present, it would be more difficult for me to communicate. It would also be more difficult for *you*.

(And we know part of what she means must be the comfort and joy that her "personhood" has brought to us and others over the years.)

❧   ❧   ❧

In her letter introducing this book, Kelly describes entering a meditative state and consciously "inviting" Moita's presence. On sensing Moita's energy, she partially "leaves" this focus so Moita has a place to "arrive". Below Moita discusses several aspects of their collaboration.

Pat: Are you with Kelly all the time?

MOITA: She can reach me anytime. It is like having a telephone that has an open line all the time. I don't have to be actually present in this sense to be present in other ways, to be aware of what is happening or Kelly's thoughts...

Pat: What do you like Kelly to refer to you as? Her "guide" or her "oversoul"?

MOITA: As "Moita" – since she has given me a name. It identifies me for her. We have many names. If someone who knew my name sent out a call through the universe, my name would find me and I would know where the name had been started...

Pat: Will Kelly remember, when you leave?

MOITA: Yes. She remembers most, vaguely. *(i.e. about as much as anyone!)*

Rita: Have you taught her to remember?

MOITA: No. She has never been a trance medium.

Rita: What is that?

MOITA: A trance medium is one who leaves their body completely, and their conscious goes with it. It is like being asleep and having no memory of what is going on, or very little; sometimes a rising up and down of consciousness happens.

           Kelly is fully conscious, but things are still hazy.

Rita: Oh, and *she* has taught herself to remember.

MOITA: She tries not to, so she interferes less with what is going on. When she is more present, I am less present...

Rita: How can I get in touch more with my higher self?

MOITA: Learn to grow still within yourself so that you can listen to us. When you can still your own thoughts, then you can see others coming up from deeper within. When your thoughts are racing, it is like a traffic jam, and then we are not heard above the roar. It is also a stillness without expectations. In some ways, it feels empty but without emptiness, or being alone without being lonely.

ക   ക   ക

Ann: Where does Kelly's mind go when you enter her?

MOITA: It is like having a sliding panel within your mind, a partition. And when I am present, she closes this partition between herself and the part that I am visiting in. She does not truly leave.

ക   ക   ക

Gil: When Moita's present, what becomes of the personality we understand as Kelly?

MOITA: It can be explained in a number of ways. One is that she becomes, in herself, still enough of her own thoughts to allow me to pour my own within her. I raise the level of her vibration enough to allow communication that is clear enough, as well, to serve my purpose. This certainly is not all of me, nor would she contain that. I am selective as to what part of my being is placed in this particular place and time. Some can say that she steps aside for a time and watches, forgets her own ego, but does not lose her individuality or her uniqueness.

Gil: Right after I asked the question, I got an image of a drop of water inside a cup.

MOITA: You received my mental image well.

ॐ   ॐ   ॐ

Anita: I'm very curious about you personally, as a being. Are you a single whole entity by yourself, or are you a part of all the other entities out there, or in here, or wherever?

MOITA: *(laughs)* It may be confusing, but I am both.

Anita: Okay. I think maybe it's the names that confuse me the most. It seems that every piece and every whole and every group of pieces has a name. And I just start to wonder, "Oh no! Which name is right?!"

MOITA: You are learning the names are not as important.

Anita: I think I'm learning that I don't really care if the names are there – that names are just something that we invent so that we can contain something.

MOITA: It is limiting having a name.

Anita: I should think so! That's why I can't understand why you've *got* one!

MOITA: I never said I did.

Anita: Okay.

MOITA: For this, it has a purpose, in that it identifies a part of my energy that Kelly is familiar with. You could say, in a way, it is a pattern of energy itself, and the energy calls this part of me to this place. It is like a beacon when it is set in motion, so that I can see it in the swirl of other times and other places and identify it as *this one*. That is its purpose.

ॐ   ॐ   ॐ

On this next occasion, Moita sums up her own existence quite succinctly.

Caroline: How do you perceive your reality? Like, we, you know, get up in the morning and go to work, with things pretty concrete. What is your reality like?

MOITA: I could only describe my reality in a general way and by using symbols that you are familiar with, for you have no words that fit what I might consider my concrete doings. A great deal of my work is with energy, and I would say that the work I am doing to help bring [our] realities closer is one of my prime purposes. It is what I have chosen as fitting to how I perceive my own energy.

I do not work just in one moment or time, but through many. I have different selves or energy-presences that I use in my work. You could say, in a sense, that I am a being that evolved with some talent for becoming pieces and using those pieces as whole selves. All of my selves revolve around a central core, yet each is independent in its action and reactions, and each represents a different aspect of my being. And they are also spread out through time and space.

(Meanwhile, Kelly has been receiving the image of a solar system, with Moita's central core being like the Sun, and all of the whole personalities that she utilizes being different planets. She can travel between these planets, with their differing perceptions of reality.)

MOITA: There is great joy in what I do, and great beauty – not just with those I interact with, but in the reality that I have chosen to exist in, for I have mingled joy with work.

Caroline: So we should all!

                                ॐ   ॐ   ॐ

Questions about Moita's reality inevitably lead to wondering about other entities, especially one's own – how they relate to and differ among each other, and the various perceptions that can occur between the worlds. The following is from a community college workshop.

Leslie: Can you see what we're doing every day?

MOITA: When I am not here in this focus, I am spread out through many time periods. There are some that I am more close to, whose development I am in some way responsible for, and those individuals experience me at other times. It is not essential for me to be able to watch a soul in its daily activity, for when contact is made all parts are laid open. I *can* see others when I am not looking through eyes. I experience a being in ways that are not really describable, for you do not have the same senses in motion now that I use. Some of those things you could relate to light, to feelings, to density, to vibration.

Leslie: I had vision of a guardian angel almost, you know, looking down on all of us. And I was wondering, could you see us before we actually opened ourselves up to you? Could you see us as a body where we are?

MOITA: I was here for a long time. It is your energy that brings me – your desire, your openness, your curiosity, your searching. And when there are many people together with the same type of energy, it creates on my level something similar to a whirlpool, and it draws into itself more energy and presences – your own higher selves...

Leslie: Are there many guides such as yourself who want to come into our state of reality and make themselves known as you've made yourself known?

MOITA: Yes, there are many.

Leslie: Do they find it hard to enter?

MOITA: Some of them are *extremely* frustrated! *(laughter)*

Leslie: I bet.

MOITA: But you see, it *is* an art in this time to open up someone enough so that they can hear our voices, so that we can share our perspective, and so that we can give guidance when it is asked. We cannot guide a soul through its life, even when it *is* aware completely. There are only certain things that we can guide. But we can lend our energy when the individual is open to receiving it. We can help them flow with the universe rather than against it...

Leslie: Are there other presences standing beside you right now taking in this session?

MOITA: There are always the presences here of your own guides, your own higher selves, your own souls. This energy draws that contact to you... The purpose [is] to help you reconnect with that self, so that it becomes not just something that can be done on an evening for entertainment or for curiosity, but something that can last you throughout your life, [with which] you can nurture yourself, so that you do not need a mediary between the worlds such as I. This is a temporary arrangement.

      ❧   ❧   ❧

Debbie: Moita, I'd like to know who my entity is. Is he or she here?

MOITA: He would be missing a great opportunity if he was not. *(laughter)*

Debbie: He doesn't do things like that?

MOITA: He would be a very slack entity. *(laughter)*

Debbie: And there are such things as slack entities? *(laughter)*

MOITA: In a world of infinite possibilities?

Debbie: What kind of person would attract a slack entity? *(laughter)*

MOITA: A person who was looked upon by his entity as inappropriate.

Debbie: Inappropriate?

MOITA: Some entities also have egos, and do not appreciate being connected to individuals they do not appreciate...

Debbie: Well, do you stay with Kelly when she's reborn?

MOITA: I am with her throughout her lives...

Your perceptions dictate how we appear to you. Your attitudes, preconceived notions and ideas decide what means we can use to communicate with you. If you would take a memory for each life and see what you thought your entity looked like and what he was composed of, you would find each one would be different. Each one would be tailored to that individual experience of that life.

When you die and see your entity for the first time, if your beliefs negate the possibility of other life than yourself or [of] higher life forms, if you have immersed your personality in a system and you have expectations that you wish to have fulfilled, then your entity will present itself to you in this guise. He can be in the form of an old and dear loved one, if this is what you need, or he can be in the form of a terrifying energy, if this is what you think you deserve. He serves your own purposes. If you wish to meet an entity as he is – or as near as you can [to] like he is – you must not have any expectations.

Debbie: Except I didn't really think about having one at all. Does he have a name? Is he a he or a she?

MOITA: I have called him "he". You would say his energy is more in the male mode. His name is something you can receive on your own. For us, names are used to identify the individual's perception of our energy. The name you would give your entity would be far more meaningful to you than one that I would receive. And you could use the sounds of the name to contact – to touch – the deeper parts of yourself.

Debbie: Is he about all the time – about me?

MOITA: Let us say that we are no farther than a thought away.

                         ❦   ❦   ❦

MOITA: *(amid strong energy)* You have a prompter behind you.

Joseph: What is that? *(having difficulty speaking)*

MOITA: Someone who is trying to communicate...

Joseph: Communicating to me?

MOITA: To you.

Joseph: Hmm. "Someone" in what sense?

MOITA: In my sense. *(laughter)*

Joseph: Hmm. *(pause)* Who is it?

MOITA: Your own guide.

Joseph: Hmm. *(pause)* I had a dream some time ago that perhaps I'm blocking my guide out. I feel a presence coming and . . . I used to have them – not so much now. Is that what you're talking about? It's hard to describe. *(laughs)*

MOITA: I can see that in this life you will establish direct communication with your guide.

Joseph: Hmm! That's very nice to know.

MOITA: He's not too sure. *(laughter)*

Joseph: Oh well, tough luck. *(laughs)* Hmm. *(pause)* Why is he not so sure?

MOITA: It often happens that when you are too close to a situation, you fail to see improvements.

Joseph: Improvements that need to be made, or that have been?

MOITA: Improvements that have been made. I am not speaking of you so much as him.

Joseph: Hmm. What's his name? *(pause)* I guess maybe I should let him tell me. *(pause)*

MOITA: *(nodding)* Right. He feels he needs that kind of sign from you, so I will leave it for him.

(From the conversation afterward:)

Joseph: I could only focus on her eyes. Everything else was really blurry and changeable. I was trying to keep my heart from going . . . *(pounding his chest rapidly)*

Kelly: I had a conversation with you on another level. I said, "You're not going to fall over, are you?" *(laughs)* You said, "No, I don't think so." And I said, "Oh, that's good. I'm glad to hear it." *(laughing)*

Just before Moita said that about your higher self standing behind you, I could see this definite energy-form and these hands that were on top of your head. Then I could see another hand – I think it was Moita's – with her finger on your eye. She was directing energy to your third eye, and these other hands [were directing it] to the top of your head. It was almost like they were trying to crack open a nut *(laughter)*, like they were trying to open it up and pull something out.

It seemed your higher self had something it wanted you to ask. Like Moita said, he's so close to you he couldn't see that he actually got something accomplished. When you asked about his name, she looked over there right at him *(laughs)* and I could really tune into his feelings. There was this real sense of frustration, a lot of energy, and a little disappointment – like, she tried out what would happen if she said his name, and there was this definite sense of . . . His colour drooped. *(laughter)* Your getting his name will be a real lift; it'll give him some confidence. We have to take into account that guy's development as well as yours. I realize this sounds crazy, but that's what was happening.

❧ ❧ ❧

Doreen: I know I have a spiritual guide, but I have never been in touch with him or her. How do I know when he or she is around – just by feeling it?

MOITA: *(trying to contain her laughter)* First, your guide is extremely disappointed, because he has been with you all your life. He thinks you mean that you have never felt him – which I know to be untrue.

Debbie: I have felt it at times, but I'm not sure if it's . . .

MOITA: Communication from my level is almost constant. Reception from your level is sporadic. This is the difference he needs to see. As you become more clear in yourself, your reception of these intuitions, feelings, teachings, will become clearer and less sporadic.

It is a different feeling with each of you. For some, they feel the heart opening as a physical sensation. For others, they feel it in the eye or in the brain. Some just feel this as a peace, calmness, a certainty; others, an inner strength and vitality and energy. And it can be different each time. It is never exactly the same, for as you change and your guide changes, the touch changes with it.

(After the session, the conversation goes as follows:)

Kelly: Well, listen: that was the funniest exchange I've seen in a while, because *(laughing)* as soon as you said that you'd *never had any communication* from your higher self *(laughter)*, I could see this guy behind you going "WHAT?!!?" *(hysterical laughter)* He was *really upset*! And Moita: "There's something here we must explain to him!" *(laughing)*

Doreen: Well, I know he's around. But, I mean, I would like to *see* him...

Kelly: Not everybody's a see-er.

Doreen: Well, I guess my guide may conk me pretty good on the head tonight.

Kelly: It was so funny. Talk about cosmic humour. We were having a little cosmic drama happening behind the chair. I didn't actually *see* him, you know – it was just a mental knowing that somebody was there and that he was reacting. The *emotions* coming off of him were very clear.

Doreen: Oh my gosh, I'm sorry. Wherever you are, I'm sorry. *(reassuringly:)* I love you.

∽   ∽   ∽

David: I've been reading Jane Roberts's second *Oversoul 7* book[43] – and he's a curious character. Are our higher selves having a hard time learning what their job is, like Oversoul 7 is, or are the novels sort of comic relief and not all that accurate?

MOITA: This is very difficult to explain. *(laughter)*

It is extremely confusing to try to relate to many lifetimes simultaneously, and there certainly are varying degrees of this ability. There are many frustrations involved in trying to communicate with parts that are in different lives, depending upon the personality that was chosen for that life. And each soul has a different flavour to it. Some are naturally more calm, and some are naturally more frustrated. *(laughter)* If they are the ones that are naturally more frustrated, they will have many more incarnations that are difficult to connect with, for that will overspill into the lives. It has to do with basics, a basic soul trait.

Souls are far from perfect or all-knowing. They are in the process of learning, first, that they are a soul. And from there they can develop more and find out what it means to *be* a soul. Then there are the possibilities of changing levels and finding out there is no end to development. Each one of you in a life finds it extremely confusing just dealing with *yourselves*! *(laughter)* Try to put yourself in *their* place! *(laughter)* They do have a broader view. And certainly not all of them are like Oversoul 7. *(laughter)*

David: Is the way it works that, after our incarnation cycle and [after] we get a bit oriented on a non-physical level, we start taking on responsibility as an oversoul for any parts of ourselves that were left behind?

MOITA: Each being in the universe is responsible for his own creations. *(pause; much energy being felt)*

David: I guess that sums it up.

MOITA: On many levels, since thoughts are creations too.

∽   ∽   ∽

(After I return from taking a half-asleep child to the bathroom, Moita contrasts such physical reality with our sessions:)

MOITA: I wonder which is more real, this or that. Much depends on where you are.

(pause)

David: Man has been called the "bridge between two worlds". Sometimes it seems harder to straddle them than others. That's when you forget which comes first.

MOITA: Some who exist on this level look on your lives as shadows without substance, and they wonder how you can give your experiences so much importance, especially those who are so caught in webs of their own making. There are not that many from here who truly remember or can understand some of what happens in this life, or grasp its significance to their own. Not all of us work in this way.

⤸   ⤸   ⤸

Paul: Can an entity make a mistake?

MOITA: Yes.

Paul: What sort of mistake would that be, or is that way beyond comprehension?

MOITA: An entity can make a mistake in judgment – may say something too soon, depending if they are into this particular kind of communication.

⤸   ⤸   ⤸

Jim: Other communications have spoken of four families of entities according to whether their energy emphasizes thinking, feeling, sensation or intuition. I was wondering if you were part of the feeling family.

Chris: Does it have to be one?

MOITA: No.

Jim: Do those labels not really apply at all?

MOITA: Sometimes they apply to aspects of entities, and there are some entities that specialize in one particular aspect or another. It depends on which level you are speaking..., for on one level we are all the same, and it is only in projecting parts of ourselves that we seem different. My goal is to become balanced in all aspects... It is like taking a jewel and a small light, and choosing which facet of the jewel to make bright. It is not as important. It is one more division that needs to be dissolved between people.

⤸   ⤸   ⤸

The ease and suddenness with which Kelly was able from the beginning to let Moita through reflects similar experiences in other lives and preliminary steps in this one, growing out of a soul-nature particularly suited for this kind of channeling. Most who try to develop this ability are likely, then, to find it emerging more slowly, or in a different form, depending on their soul's unique path of development. The following conversations, revolving around a brief slice of my own experiences in this area, convey the quality of a more gradual process of opening – its cycles, its ups and downs.

Moita Session #40 (Kelly and David / November 11, 1978)

David: I have been increasingly feeling the presence of someone or something else since we've been talking – this hardness, which first came in a dream.[44N]

MOITA: And you are just as *reluctant* when the possibility presents itself! It is the fear of losing one's self, even if for a while – giving up one's spot, as it were.

(Long silence, as I close my eyes, trying to open up to the entity to see if it wishes to communicate. The sense of hardness increases.)

David: I don't know if it's my reluctance, or that someone is just feeling out my body and is not coming to talk at the moment. But can you explain this sensation of hardness?

MOITA: Exactly where is it felt?

David: It's getting to be everywhere. Especially in my hands right now, but I can feel it all around my head. It seems to be wherever I feel boundaries, both within my body and between my body and the world.

MOITA: Kelly feels a hardness in the back of her head when I come. Concentration of energy into a tight ball makes it feel hard. That is pretty well what it is. Some of it is what I called "reluctance" – what one can call "fighting it", making it feel much harder than it is in actuality. And by sensing the hardness and concentrating on the feelings, it makes it more hard, too. It's almost a tension, and there *is* a tension between your aura and energy field and the being's energy field, which is why you can usually tell when someone is near. Even if they are only on one part of you, you will feel the difference in that energy in that spot as a tension – sometimes as a heat, depending on how close they are standing. But in order to protect yourself, sometimes you make yourself like a shell – which is a useful thing to know how to *do*, when it's necessary. *(pause)*
              What are your feelings towards this energy?

David: I'm sure there is reluctance because it's strange, but I also want to invite its coming.

MOITA: But what are your feelings towards the energy itself, without your *possible* reluctance or not? *(pause)* Do any thoughts come to mind?

David: There's a strength... The experience reminds me of my dream about rare metals and higher levels. It's a feeling like that: something very powerful, and very clear.

MOITA: And as you were going through this experience, what kind of thoughts popped into your head?

(In reply, I mention a question I intended to ask during the session.)

MOITA: And while you thought of this, did you get an answer? What kind of thoughts did you receive on that subject?

David: I didn't receive anything this time. I didn't go far enough into it. I could try again.

MOITA: It would be an interesting experience for two entities to sit across from each other and speak, and for both of you to be on the sidelines and *listen*! I wonder what we would talk about. Probably *you*!!

(From the conversation afterward:)

Kelly: There certainly was a lot of energy there. I could feel all that stuff around your head, could feel all of this energy pulsing through your hands and my hands, flying back and forth, with her like helping just by being there and throwing her energy at you to help this thing happen.

David: It's useful to know about the hardness, that at least part of it is resistance. I didn't know if I should even concentrate more attention on it to help the entity come closer.

Kelly: I feel the back of my head open up in that kind of energy. It's a similar kind of feeling that I get when I'm hooked up to the Mind Mirror and my lower frequency delta waves go right off the end of the scale. There's sort of a tingling, stretching, tight feeling in the back of my head.[45N]

ʕ๏   ʕ๏   ʕ๏

Moita Session #44 (Kelly and David / November 24, 1978)

MOITA: I *am* very present today. . . .

(We take this as a cue to tune further into her energy. There is a long silence, during which Kelly grows aware that several entities are present – that our room is "crowded".)

MOITA: There are a number of us here tonight who wish to know something of you. We have a question.

David: Am I to try to answer for both Kelly and me? *(feeling rather surprised and nervous at the tables being turned, now that they are going to ask me something!)*

MOITA: If you wish. *(slowly and deliberately:)* How do you experience our energy which we have named "love"?

(I close my eyes and feel their energy streaming toward and flooding over me. I also remember hugging Kelly earlier in the day.)

David: I experience it as a radiating out of light, and joy, and warmth, and being free because one is in touch with one's centre.

MOITA: What do you feel for us?

David: What does the Moon feel for the Sun's light? It seems the love you radiate toward us – when we're open to it and aware of it – naturally makes us want to radiate it back.

MOITA: Am I straining you?

David: No.

MOITA: There are many things happening here. *(long silence)* So you feel a touch?

David: I feel the radiating, which is a kind of touch.

MOITA: One stands behind you.

(I close my eyes and attempt to open to this "one". I feel a prickling starting at the top of my head and gradually working itself around and through the rest. There is some warmth and much feeling of changing levels, of more depth opening up inside my mind,

of travelling through space almost. There isn't a real tingling sort of rush, but rather a feeling of mystery and depth, similar to the "Discovery of My Deep Centre" dream.)

(Meanwhile, Kelly is experiencing a subtle change in energy, a flowing sense of Moita leaving and someone else coming in – not masculine – and a clearing of her sight. She is aware of this other entity, who both of us feel is my entity Loria, saying to me, "You must learn to relax more before I can come." There is also the suggestion that when communication is first beginning, it is sometimes necessary to say the first thing that pops into your head, in order to get things going.)

David: *(opening my eyes)* Yes.

MOITA: You feel? *(pause)* You know now you are not alone?

David: More than ever.

MOITA: Are you able to let words come?

David: I guess not.

MOITA: Have you looked around to see your mind, and see if there are words there?... One who meditates is usually aware of his own mind and what thoughts belong to it. You should be able to detect the taste of another. *(long silence)* How are you feeling?

David: I can't get anything now.

MOITA: Everything comes in time. You are doing more than you know.

(Another silence, during which our Siamese cat Silkie comes in and sits down in my lap – instead of his habitual place in Moita's lap during sessions.)

MOITA: There are signs. You must be able to look without searching. You may have a few surprises in store.

David: A few *more*?

MOITA: Like everything else, they come in cycles.

℆   ℆   ℆

A month later, on the day after Christmas 1978, we come as close as we ever do to that "interesting experience" of which Moita spoke: two entities, as it were, sitting across from each other and conversing. That session is given here in Chapter 17, because it relates more to the particular connections between Moita and Loria than to the opening of communication in general. Included here, however, are excerpts from two other sessions in which the issue of my channeling potential again arises.

<u>Moita Session #89 (Kelly and David / May 20, 1979)</u>

(This session is unusual for being held out on our front porch, as it is a warm, sunny spring day. Midway through, we close our eyes during a very long silence. Kelly feels a distinct pressure on her third eye, and sees a green energy pattern float from the corner of the porch down to my shoulder. The way the air shimmers reminds her of oil on water, though without the iridescence. "What's that?!" she thinks. Then, "Oh, of course. It's Loria!")

(As the energy hits the edge of my energy field, a green light shoots out on that side and travels up over my head to my other side. To Kelly's vision, I sit there glowing for

a while. Then she sees Loria behind me. She sees my face change into my "old man" – as she believes I will look when I've grown old in this life – and then into other faces. Kelly will say after the session that upon first recognizing Loria she thinks it can't be real, that she isn't supposed to be able to see this. But then, "Of course I can see! The only reason I can't is that I think I'm not supposed to!" Deciding she isn't afraid to see Loria, the image comes in more clearly.)

(For me, my vision goes through many changes. It's hard to go fully with the changes I'm seeing in Kelly's direction, though, because the Sun is very bright behind and above her head. The air and walls of the porch change texture. Kelly's face seems to expand sideward, as it is beginning to dissolve into the air and light. Thoughts about materializations go through both of our minds during this period. I'm feeling a concentrated pressure at my right temple and a more diffused grip of energy all around my head.)

MOITA: May I ask you how close she has come?

David: I *feel* her touch. I still don't hear words, or rather *thoughts*.

MOITA: You may never hear words, since we do not use them.

David: Then thoughts?

MOITA: They will be felt, more than they will be heard. And the words should come without thought. Then they come better. *(pause)*

David: It seems like we have been doing this for a very long time *(i.e. that we are exchanging energy like this in many lives and beyond time, and letting that become present in this now).*

క్ర   క్ర   క్ర

Moita Session #120 (Kelly and David / November 18, 1979)

David: Frequently, I notice that when you're looking for a word, or you just hesitate sometimes, I come to expect the next thing you're going to say, and then you say it. I wonder sometimes if I receive your thought and just happen to put it into the same words, or if sometimes you pick words out of *my* mind as well as Kelly's.

MOITA: You are learning here how to interpret our energy and our message into words. If you would speak for your own entity, this is what you need to learn how to do. It is the choosing of the word that fits the energy best. There is a parallel when Ruth began her opening and started to anticipate words. I am somewhat more direct than a Ouija board.

David: So the choosing of the words is something done by us – not our conscious selves, I gather – as we receive the energy from you.

MOITA: They are as universal symbols, and your subconscious – as in a dream – picks out the ones that suit all levels of meaning best.

క్ర   క్ర   క్ర

Joan would seem to be a person more spontaneously open to channelings similar to

Kelly's, though she is facing a different, more conscious form of reluctance to letting messages through. Joan mentions here she was guided to provoke her husband Arthur, her mother, and friend Dorothy to join in her whirlwind visit to us over a long weekend, driving a great distance and then returning, all in roughly 72 hours' time. Somehow this session the night they arrive makes it all feel worthwhile. We begin here about 15 minutes into the session.

Joan: Moita, could you please tell me if there's somebody beside me, between Arthur and me?
MOITA: There are *two* somebodies.
Joan: I feel a very strong presence of one.
MOITA: There *are* two!
Joan: Is one a lady?
MOITA: Now you get into difficulties!
Joan: I'm sorry. *(Moita laughs)* I didn't know . . .
MOITA: There are several levels here.
Joan: I'm feeling a lot of pressure on my head, a draft down my cheek, and a pressure there too.
MOITA: Which side?
Joan: My left side *(i.e. the side toward Arthur)*.
MOITA: You are feeling an attempt to become more in touch with you, an opening that is similar to this experience here. It helps if you close your eyes and let yourself float. You will feel it more strongly. *(long silence)*
Joan: I think there's a male and a female. *(sigh)* I wish it would back off my head, though. They're trying very hard with me, aren't they?!
MOITA: They are using this opportunity.
Arthur: *(laughing)* Yeah, I feel something similar too.
MOITA: This brings your higher selves closer too, as my energy flows from one to another. There's only a pressure when you resist.
Arthur: Mm-*hmm*!
Joan: It's on top of my head.
Arthur: Just relax and let it go.
            (then, sometime later:) Are there any questions you'd like to ask, Joanie?
Joan: What? Where do you begin?! *(laughing; pause)*
Arthur: Come on, say it.
Joan: Say what? *(laughter)*
Dorothy: Remember, Joan, your dear husband drove over a thousand kilometres for this.
Joan: I *know*. I had so much to ask. Oh, come on.
MOITA: *(to Arthur)* Give her a *hint*. *(laughter)*
Arthur: Well, we want to develop her mediumship abilities. We know that she has the ability there. We know that it can be developed. Maybe you can throw some light . . .
MOITA: She is having some experiencing about that *now*!

Joan: I think I was given the message starting to get everything going and bringing everybody up here. It just seemed the right words came up, and we're here. *(laughter)* I don't know, I had a strong, strong feeling that we had to come up here and see you.

MOITA: Well, my energy at this moment can act as a catalyst for you at *other* moments. This is not something that will cease when it is physically finished.

Joan: No, I have a feeling we're going to see you again – quite a strong feeling.

MOITA: It would be *well*!

Joan: In fact, I think this is just an introductory – others to come. Am I not right?

(Yes, she is right. During the next summer, Joan will dream she is being taught how to channel by a teacher named "Mary" – that's Moita, of course – as recounted in a future chapter.)

MOITA: There is much that can be done here in this energy, for you and for others. If you will be ready when the time comes, you must take adventures into the universe and discover how life works for you and those near you. Coming to a greater understanding of yourself, being more certain of who you are, makes it easier for you to step aside for other energy to manifest itself. Fears and doubts will block you, but they are necessary in the beginning in order for you to make fruitful steps.

There are many who have opened to this energy and not been able to relate again to the Earth in a physical way. What is needed in this time is not starry-eyed prophets who have no firm basis in the Earth, but those who are balanced in both worlds, who can take the wisdom that we can offer and the experience of our sharing, and bring it into the world in a real and physical way, to help shape it and change it.

Does that answer more than one question?

Joan: I'll read it later. *(laughter – the energy makes it hard to take in at the time)* I think so, yeah. I've read some of your transcripts, and I can see a lot of what you're saying. But when it comes to me . . .

MOITA: It's a different story?

Joan: Yeah. You know, I can talk freely about it to other people, but when it comes to me having to do the working . . . I'm pushing everybody else to do the work but back away when it's my turn. It's an inner fear of probably taking all the responsibility.

MOITA: Yes.

Joan: And I'm scared about that.

MOITA: If you can remain *clear*, then you need not worry about responsibility, for then the responsibility is ours – not yours.

Joan: Hmm. That one's different. I was always told it was *our* responsibility.

Arthur: No, that's good. That sounds right. That feels right.

Joan: Yeah, I think that might help a bit.

Arthur: Good. I'll . . . work with her on that one. *(laughing)*

MOITA: I see you are a willing taskmaster.

Arthur: *(laughing)* Well, she's the one who's always pushing *me*, you know... No, we help each other; we do. We balance out each other very nicely.

MOITA: That is the reason there were two between you, and why she sensed them as one.

Arthur: Oh – click!

(From the conversation afterward:)

Joan: I feel that a lot of times they'd like to speak through me – well, they *do*. I'll be talking to someone, and before I know it I'll be giving advice that I would never give . . .

Kelly: Mm-hmm. Well, that's what this is!

Arthur: And she cuts herself off because she says, "Where did *that* come from? *I* didn't say that" or "How do *I* know that?!" And she backs off.

Joan: I'll just shut up, and Arthur will say, "Come on, come on! Tell us more." And I say no. I feel it really strong, and as soon as it gets too strong, I back off.

Kelly: Yeah, that's it: you have to relax; you have to let it happen. And I know it's not easy, although when it started it seemed to be the easiest thing in the whole world. I was stunned. All of a sudden – poof! – I'm a medium. I fly out of my body; a spirit comes and talks; I come back. And it's just like breathing. It's just so easy. It's stunning that it's so simple like that.

Joan: Yeah. And when you realize what you're doing, it's scary.

Kelly: Right!

Joan: I don't like thinking people have an obligation to take what I say.

Kelly: Well, that's *their* responsibility. If you're presented with an experience, how you interpret it is your responsibility. The experience is just there by itself. So, *give* somebody an experience – *do* tell them something. They don't have to take a word you say seriously if they don't want to. And if they *want* to take it seriously, that's their business too. And then if they want to screw it up completely, that's still their business – because they're going to learn something from it, whatever they decide.

        ✀   ✀   ✀

" . . . for then the responsibility is ours, not yours." If more of us can learn to be clearer, a clearer view of the higher levels of spirit in all their variety and commonality can come to humankind. And how refreshing that the same polarity of individual and whole works there as well as it does here.

MOITA: Has it come to your attention that many communications elaborate on communications that have already been received by others – and, by so elaborating, reinforce things that have gone before?

David: Yes, I've noticed many, many connections.

MOITA: They are conscious – very conscious – connections, in order to weave a structure that has substance. These communications have been happening throughout history. We have spoken through many people – ancient prophets and modern ones. *(pause)* In part we are aided by people's desire not to live in the world they have created, once they are in it; and so, they open doors. [But] not everything that comes is what you would call "true" in the world's sense.

၆   ၆   ၆

Mike: I want to ask about the difference between communications as received by Edgar Cayce as compared to Jane Roberts. Cayce has done a lot of good things for me. And Seth's communications helped define some experiences that I've had and am having, but he doesn't ring true for me in some things. It seems to me that Cayce's source is from a much more spiritual level... Well, I really don't know what it is.

MOITA: There is a big difference between the kinds of communications, for Cayce was unconscious – unfocused in the physical – when his communications came through. His was a connection with the stream of man's awareness and some of those beyond, but was a representative of *all* of man's thinking through the ages. So his was a more *whole* look in many ways, although it too has its drawbacks, as any communication from one level to another has.

Seth is an individual personality. He is more focused in his own reality than he is in the reality of man as a whole; and so, he brings to his communication his own particular focus, his own lessons, his own reality. Although each has a different reality, when you put them all together they become more balanced; they become more whole and more complete. And so, Cayce represented that wholeness and completeness on that level, whereas Seth represents himself and what he as an individual spirit has learned.

I represent not just myself. I represent many, but I do not represent *all* of man. My look is somewhat different as well, and the purpose for my being is different. For I am not here to impart knowledge but to help others experience another reality. This is something Cayce could not do in the state he was in. He could impart what he saw of man. And Seth does not impart as much as he imposes his view of reality upon his listeners. He is a very strong individual with an individual view. That is why he is represented more as the masculine, and I as the feminine, if you will...

Just because a spirit has developed to the point where it no longer needs to become physical does not mean that it has lost this talent for focusing on one part instead of focusing upon the whole. It is an ongoing thing; it is *always* continuing. As your level changes, your view changes with it. And as Seth changes himself, his view of reality will also change. His higher self *(i.e. known as "Seth Two"[46])* is much different, from the few communications that have happened.

David: You said to Mike that you are here not simply to bring your individual view. Should we interpret you to mean you let through higher-level experiences and views that are therefore more whole?

MOITA: You could say that I am a channel too. *(pause)* And so, all of the things that apply to a channel here will apply to me as well. *(pause)*

David: I think I asked that mainly to experience the energy that would come along with your words.

MOITA: And how are you finding it?

(As Moita while speaking looks directly into my eyes, I feel a tremendous rush, with much heat, centred on my face.)

David: I'm about to break out in a sweat!

MOITA: And that gives you some idea of the depth of the energy.

ço   ço   ço

So are we all both channel and source of spirit in one way or another. What Moita says of Kelly as a channel applies to herself as well. Conversely, she can describe the experience of entities that are our source in universally human terms. This is Moita at her most eloquent – in words, and in feelings.

Esther: Where is Kelly?

MOITA: Here. She never leaves. Her mind expands; her energy expands. She sends her call out. She allows herself to become a door from one world to the next, from one kind of energy to another, from one reality to another reality. She wishes to understand it. She understands it no more than any of you. She only knows that she is a door, and she feels that what comes out of that doorway is good, and so she allows it to stay open.
    Can you not see Kelly here?

Esther: Yes.

MOITA: Can you see *more* than Kelly?

Esther: Hmm. Kelly's a *lot*.

MOITA: More than she recognizes...

Esther: Do you bring messages from others when you come, or do you come alone?

MOITA: I bring others with me, but not others as are in your thoughts. I am not from the level of "departed souls". I am a soul that has ceased to live in this world for many of your years. This is a very small part of my reality. I am a wholer spirit, an essence – not a part of someone else's soul. Those who have died and left images behind are merely shadows of themselves and only parts of a soul. For you are all of your lives, not just one.
    Those I bring with me are trying to learn, through joining in this experience, how to help bridge the gap between my world and yours, how to blend the two worlds together and make them one again as they were once. They shall be different now than they were before.

Esther: Are you sad?

MOITA: Sad that we are parted? Some. And I feel compassion for those on my side who are not able to bring this energy more vividly here. There is much energy here, the energy of which I am a part.
    If you lost a child when it was young, and had not seen it until it was old

and gone through its life without your help, without your guidance; or even more, where you have been close yet unable to touch and unable to speak, not able to help when you could see that your child was going in a direction that would hurt it, [not able] to touch when your worlds were not the same . . . It is a gap like that that we try to bridge, one that is even greater than that which you can imagine – a difference in how energy is used, how it is viewed.

We see you all the time, are near you, yet very rarely can touch, for you do not see us. For you, we are merely a whisper in the trees.

Esther: So we need more than the *desire* to touch.

MOITA: This is the time when the child is grown and the worlds are beginning to come together. We have watched for a great many years, and now there is a drawing together of worlds, a time when the two worlds may touch and not be destroyed by each other, when they may integrate and understand. The coming together of our worlds will not change just yours, but mine. Life will never be the same again...

(Moita's tone in these passages evokes the passing of the Elves out of Middle Earth at the end of Tolkien's The Lord of the Rings *– except that now such a momentous change is coming full circle! It is as if the Elves are returning, though not to reproduce the past; rather, to share energy with humanity on a new level – more of a conscious, mutual exchange.)*

MOITA: Although we have seen this world pass through many sorrows, we have not stopped loving it nor seeing its beauty. I meant mostly to give you an idea of the distances involved in communication, although there is pain as well when we have the desire to touch and cannot. We are not above desires of certain kinds, and we are learning with you. *(pause)*

Do not look on us as higher beings who know all the answers, for then you limit yourself, and you limit us as well. You put us into a role that is difficult to break.

Esther: Well, you must know more than *we* do.

MOITA: It is that I am more aware of what I know, not that I know more. It is a matter of focus. You are narrowly focused on one thing – this life, this reality. I am focused on a broader view – many lives, many realities. But my world is also available to you when you change your focus, when you accept the impossible.

Epilogue

THE MIRACLE OF METAMORPHOSIS

Your wings are beginning to dry,
So soon you will be ready to fly.
– Moita

The final question of this Part comes from a 17-year-old girl who has suddenly become involved in psychic-spiritual activities during the past year, including her own automatic writing. Her question refers to Ruth Montgomery's book, *Strangers Among Us*, which claims that personalities who have lost the will to live are vacating their bodies so that highly evolved souls from beyond Earth can enter and help bring in the "New Age". The new personalities that result from this supposed exchange are termed "walk-ins".

Vera: Am I a "walk-in"?

MOITA: You are a spirit of man born of body. You belong here.

Vera: Well, I know that, but um . . . See, I feel like I'm a completely different person now. A year ago, I was on the point of almost self-destruction. But then, like overnight, I'm completely changed. I don't know what that's supposed to . . . *(laughs)*

MOITA: I will refer you to the miracle of metamorphosis: ...of the caterpillar turning into the butterfly. It is a miracle that happens on your planet every day. It is only wondered at when it happens to a human being, for it is not something that is expected by many.

This is an age of metamorphosis. Many are born in one "feel" for a life and reach a point of change. It is a measure of your soul's development that you have gone through this, that you have connected with your greater self more completely, that you have opened up channels. It is not another personality; it is this one evolving...

Man is here to become whole in himself and find his *own* wisdom... Now you are learning *yours*.

෪   ෪   ෪

PART TWO:

The World Conspires

You are only one part of the play,
or one part of the [symphony].
You have a certain score before you and do your thing,
where I have a view of the other scores as well
and my part in them.
And besides this place and time, there are others...
that are meeting together to make this possible.
The world conspires to save itself.

– Moita

---

conspire:

> from the Latin *conspirare*
> [*com* "with" + *spirare* "to breathe"],
> to breathe together, to agree;
> thus, to join in a secret agreement,
> to act in harmony or with one spirit.

related to . . .

inspire:

> to breathe in or infuse as if by breathing; to instill;
> to communicate divine instructions to the mind of;
> to animate by supernatural infusion.

aspire:

> to desire with eagerness;
> to pant after a great or noble object;
> to aim at something elevated; to ascend; to soar. [47N]

Chapter 9

OPENING DOORS, TOUCHING WORLDS

It's like reality shifts a little; my mind buzzes with energy, the air comes alive. I'm carried upward on a wave of energy and "eternal nowness". Time passes, and yet it passes more slowly, or more richly.
– A Letter from Kelly

The force of love that has created this world lives in it still, and flows out to anyone who will receive it. Whatever you call the force of love, it is still the same force. The name does not matter. It is the energy that is important.
– Moita (December 2, 1978)

Energy. The term appears again and again in the transcripts of our sessions, yet I suspect it is among the words conveying the least meaning to those who have not experienced its higher forms.

Obviously, this is not energy of the merely physical level, for what material cause could have produced all this? As for what material proof can we show for it: the evidence is everywhere, but for the ways our minds interpret it. So, for a person who does not understand or accept the possibility that the energy of the universe manifests on many levels of reality, ranging from the outermost physical to the very centre of being within each of us, accounts like this will seem mere fantasy, full of pretension but empty of substance.

In this chapter I want to convey some of the early unfolding of the Moita communications, the manner in which Kelly and I and others are introduced to these new levels of energy. The undeniable experiencing of this energy convinces us, against our own doubts, that we are dealing in neither fantasy nor manipulation – this is *real*. It is an experiment anyone and everyone can try, through establishing in oneself the appropriate and necessary conditions.

We begin with excerpts from one of Moita's earliest written communications, as the emotional strains of Kelly's situation are perhaps leaving their mark. It is now the night of July 6th: barely more than a week since Moita's first acknowledged speaking appearance on June 27, 1978, and one day after we took a further important step in our growing intimacy on a human level. (Our experiences paralleling the dates in this chapter are fully recounted in *Mind Leap*. Familiarity with those events is not necessary for understanding but will add context to the sessions throughout this Part.)

Meditating alone this evening, Kelly is not sure yet how to interpret the experience of inward thoughts from "more than herself". The topic is the process of communication, as Kelly learns more about letting Moita through.

Moita written message #4 (Kelly / July 6, 1978)[48N]

MOITA: This type of contact is a highly individualized experience, and no two people will experience it in exactly the same manner or form. The important thing is to be open, to allow yourself to become free of fears and insecurities. Then you can become that which you are meant to become, without preconceptions or expectations. Learn how to listen to yourself.

(Kelly: "Then some people come over to visit. I drink a glass of wine, and [eventually] they leave. I am still in a very receptive state and begin to get very confused about what is happening and why. I have an impulse to phone David, and decide it is not the right thing to do. Then I find myself dialing his number. When he answers, a very strange conversation ensues which to me is more like a dream than anything else. Eventually I decide to do what I was going to do in the first place – sit down with paper and pen and see what will happen.")

MOITA: You are becoming psychologically more receptive to this kind of contact, and the fact that you are tired and are very relaxed from the wine makes this more possible. You were correct in assuming this has something to do with David, although you have confused him considerably... That was the reason for the phone call you did not wish to make. It was important for him to realize something was happening – but more important for him to realize that he was not aware of it as he should have been. That is the type of connection that must be developed...

Since you are just beginning to become aware, it is no wonder that you are confused and making mistakes. Even as this is written...what is communicated to your soul and what ends up on paper are just barely the same. With practice, these concepts and ideas will come more clearly to you...

The contact grows more sure as you relax and open yourself. The pressure you feel in your ears is a great concentration of energy, which is my psychological presence within your body...

୬   ୬   ୬

Each session seems to bring a new and unexpected development, as shown in this description of our experience four days later. Kelly writes about July 10, 1978:

"After work, David and I come home to my house and he asks for us to meditate together. Moita comes, as we expected. She touches him with my finger on the third eye and the heart chakra. She tells him he must learn to follow the fleeting thought to its source. I tell him I am seeing him turning old. She says that he is trying to see into his future. He says that he is seeing me as an old woman... At one point I see his chest turn into a field of energy – a bright, pulsating light.

"It is a very interesting session, quite different from the last one [July 7th]. She isn't with me in the same way. The strength is different. She says it is because she has not come to talk; she has come to *show*. My head goes through some changes. I can see David as he runs up and down his own levels: sometimes everything is crystal clear, other times very hazy. It is a pulsating kind of energy – in and out. When he changes into an old man, the transformation is distinct. He looks exactly how I know he will look when he reaches sixty or so."

ஒ ஒ ஒ

By learning to let go of our normal focus, we are coming closer to our inner self and beginning to see each other as Moita views us: an energy-presence that clothes itself in varied forms in different times, which all co-exist at once. But I am not the only participant in Kelly's early sessions.

Moita Session #7 (Kelly and Roy / July 11, 1978)

(Kelly writes: "Roy and I are talking about some of the communications. Closing my eyes, I become aware of that 'different' kind of energy and know Moita is close. In a short time she opens my eyes and begins to speak. I can feel the pressure between my ears as she does so.")

MOITA: The essence of my presence within Kelly is different in quality, because this time I wish to speak and last time with David I was here merely to show. When I wish to speak, the contact must be made more sure, stronger...

Roy: It has been a long time since I have experienced this kind of energy.

MOITA: *(smiling)* I am glad that you are enjoying mine so much.

Roy: I feel as if I should say how privileged or honoured I am at this, but the words don't seem to be right.

MOITA: *(laughing)* David said something very similar to me once,[49N] and I told him that words were not necessary. Feelings are a far more accurate, complete and rich way in which to express these kinds of thoughts. Words fall far short of the thought's totality. *(Roy smiling very broadly; no words come out – just great love and feeling)*

You look as if you are ready to burst out! *(much smiling and laughter)*...

(Kelly notes: "While the communication is going on, she is speaking to me on the side as well – about my feelings of insecurity and uncertainty and doubt as to what is going on. She also is trying to make me more aware of the intimate feel of her energy, so that I can more readily identify it and be able to tell the difference between her and anyone or anything else. When she is in the process of leaving, there is a tremendous surge of energy which Roy and I both participate in. It makes one feel warm and alive and loved. When she goes, I feel myself come into my head from the right side and slide to centre. Then I know I am back, and Roy and I go out for a walk.")

ஒ ஒ ஒ

After a session a week later, Kelly notes: "There is a very definite and distinct shift for me [returning] from the right as Moita goes out to the left. Now I realize she *always* comes in from the left – as I always find myself coming *back* from the right."

Several months later, Kelly's perception of this transition will be confirmed by the Mind Mirror, an electroencephalograph (EEG) with a light display, on which she is being tested by our friend Spencer, a psychology professor at the university. At a given point, the strength of the lower frequency (theta, delta, lower alpha) brain waves of Kelly's left hemisphere increases to the end of the scale. Having never observed such a pattern before, Spencer asks what is going on. The answer: Moita has arrived.

Subsequently, Spencer notices the high-frequency beta waves of Kelly's brain have increased dramatically, which is normally an indication of problem-solving activity. "Are you thinking a lot?" Spencer asks Moita. Her reply: "*You* may call it thinking. *I* call it 'being present.'" This reflects how Moita must concentrate her energy just to be perceived in our smaller-dimensional reality. The brainwave pattern resulting from her "being present" resembles that of intense human thinking.

As Moita's presence increases steadily through the course of the summer, Kelly often finds herself recording notes like this one: "The energy is much higher than it has ever been before. I have no doubts that something very real and powerful is happening to me." And as the contact develops, Moita is able to say more about the dynamics of the communication itself: a co-operative effort between our two levels that requires a growing openness to who we are and to her energy in order that it continue to evolve.

∾   ∾   ∾

By the end of July, Kelly's husband Phil has accepted her changes enough that Moita can come – spontaneously, "on the sly" – in his presence.

Moita Session #13B (Kelly and Phil / July 26, 1978)

MOITA: It is not Kelly with whom you speak. *(pause)* I have come to share with you my energy; to show you how it should feel, so that you will be able to recognize it when it comes. The more aware you become of this kind of energy, the more you will draw to it and the more it will become a part of you and your energy... I am pleased that you have sufficiently opened yourself so that this communication is now possible.

Phil: Why haven't you spoken to me before?

MOITA: There are many fears and blocks, as there are with all of you. You fear opening.

Phil: Will I be able to speak to you again sometime?

MOITA: You must be in the right frame of mind first. There must be a desire to communicate. When you wish to speak with me, ask Kelly. Sit yourself down in a calm and quiet place and open your energies. I will come and talk with you then.

This communication is still very delicate, very new. There are many influences which dictate what I can say. Your thoughts and fears are one; there are some things which you do not wish to hear or are not ready to understand. There are also some difficulties with Kelly as well in much the same vein. However, it is sufficient for our purposes at the moment...

I must leave you for now, but I will not be far away. I am always near.

◌ ◌ ◌

On August 1st, Moita says to me, "Many times you go through tests and do not realize it until later. Kelly had an experience last night which is important for both of you." Kelly's journal contains this account of her dream or out-of-body experience in which I also was on some level involved:

"Psychological tests and changes in consciousness. Sometimes frightening – very heavy. Many of the things that happen in this experience cannot be recalled to this level of consciousness. It is on a very deep, spiritual level that we are communicating. Moods or emotions or feelings wash over both of us and we dip down into them and become one with them – experiencing them fully, then rising out of them and doing it again. During some of the experience I feel as though my head is getting ready to explode. Something seems very imminent throughout."

Kelly describes the ending of this August 1st session in this way: "After she leaves, I sit there looking at David. His face begins to change again. Then, as I sit there watching, I feel as though the back of my head expands, and I can feel or sense many others behind me – in the past. Only, they are not dead but living, and it seems that all those other lives of which David and I have been (or are) a part are aware of us in this moment, and their thoughts are bent in our direction. It is a very powerful experience."

◌ ◌ ◌

On the night of August 12th, Kelly dreams that a spirit enters her body and takes control over all her muscles. She is frightened, not knowing who or what is responsible. Another dream follows.

"Becoming Trance Medium" dream
Kelly (age 28) / August 12, 1978

I see Roy in the woods very clearly, as if we are really there. I tell him of the dream where I lost control of my body, and how scared I felt at the time. He thinks I am trying to learn to become a trance medium. His presence is very comforting, and I stay in the woods with him for a long time between dreams.

The day afterward, Kelly has a disturbing experience while awake, which leads to a long, written communication from Moita.

Moita written message #22 (Kelly / August 13, 1978)

(Kelly notes: "After a walk down the street, my heart chakra all of a sudden becomes activated. My vision changes radically – I begin to see many dancing light-forms in the sky. I start to get frightened and go home. I get the kids to bed and, still being paranoid about this strange experience, and not understanding why I am getting so paranoid, I decide to ask Moita if she can give me some guidance. I sit down with my notebook and let her come through. This is what she writes.")

MOITA: You are frightened because you are becoming more open to this communication than you have before, and the implications of this change in quality are what you fear.

It is, for you, a heavy responsibility to be the instrument through which I speak. You know that you colour my words somewhat with your own thoughts, and the extent to which this happens is what gives you this difficulty. It is inevitable in this type of communication – it cannot be totally avoided. We are, in a very real sense, a team in this effort. How much you are able to still your own mind and let my thoughts flow is the difference in the quality of each communication.

Do not worry so much. You are doing very well – and will do better in times to come.

Your introspection and doubts do, however, serve a good purpose in your development. What [Rudolf] Steiner said about three steps forward in moral structure for every one in spiritual growth[50N] is essentially what you are experiencing right now.

Too, as your cycles become closer, these feelings will come closer to the surface. Even though you are a fairly open personality to these things, you too fear complete opening. There is nothing to fear. We are not here to take anything from you, but to give you of ourselves – our love – and our different perspective of the reality of the world.

My teachings are not complicated – they are not filled with flowery phrases or important-sounding words – nor references to "important" psychological philosophies. I speak to everyman, in a language they can understand. This is why your background in this life is essentially different than many of the other people with whom you have touched...

Do not feel inferior to others merely because they have access to more weighty words. Your native intelligence is not being questioned. Do not succumb to your status quo conditioning!...

Anyone can sound impressive using vaguely understood concepts that make another feel it is too far "above" them to understand. This is how the "high priest" concept is started and fed.

It is a special talent to be able to state things simply – in a common language... As I said before, I am not here to "enlighten" anyone. I am here to help others learn to do their own growth – and find their own centre. I am also here to help *you* find *yours*.

Do not stop questioning or testing the truth of what you receive. In the end analysis, you are the only one who can decide what you perceive of all this, and what applies to you directly...

You had that dream the other night, about a spirit entering you and taking you over, for [several] reasons. One is – that you fear this may be happening to you now. Do not worry – I have no interest in your body. I am quite content to "live" on my level as I have for the last 50,000 years or so... I would not trade my expanded awareness of the Universe for the dubious (although to you quite real and important) pleasures of living out a short physical existence in your form.

The other reason for the dream was your genuine desire to become a trance medium so you would not have to grapple with the fear of influencing my communications and thus be more able to assure yourself of its "honesty and integrity".

Obviously, from the amount of fear you experienced in the dream, you are not ready or able at this time to take that step. There may come a time in the future when you feel this step will be essential, and one that you can feel comfortable with. Then again, that point may never be reached – nor that necessity arise.

I hope this helps to clear your mind somewhat of your fears. Of course many of these concepts will be familiar to you – I have been with you for this entire life, and this is not the first time I have tried to communicate with you! Nor will it be the last...

Be generous to yourself. Give yourself also the love and attention you give to others.

Remember, you are all here to learn Love – but you all look upon the learning of that lesson from a different viewpoint. If you would not waste time throwing rocks at others, do not try to throw rocks at yourself, either.

Be in love – that is the simplest lesson – and the most difficult one to grasp because of its simplicity.

૭   ૭   ૭

A portion of Moita's message in a session over a month later also relates to the issue of trance mediumship.

Moita Session #29 (Kelly and David / September 20, 1978)

MOITA: It is, in some ways, easier to do this with a trance medium. That frees the person from the responsibility of hearing what is said – like Seth, [who] can communicate in greater detail because of this. However, he is still bound by the limitations of the mind he is using to communicate... Even though our world is connected to yours through these people, it still is not a "true" representation of our world. Because the worlds touch here, it is not one *or* the other, but a combination of both...

There is no such thing as an absolutely "true" communication with our level. If we could come with a body onto your plane, the communication would be "truer" and different in quality – but that is something not easily accomplished and requires a great deal of energy. And still it would not be "true".

Even when you leave your body [and travel] in the astral [plane], your perception of our world is not completely accurate, for you bring with you from here those same concepts of reality. You know, also, that you have a body to go back to...

I have said before: only you can decide what is the truth of what you receive... It is up to you to separate the seeds of truth from all this.

જ   જ   જ

By August 16th, only a few days after the dreams and disturbing waking experience that prompted Moita's last written communication, the energy being released in Kelly creates a situation calling for swift and drastic action. She describes these events in a letter to her mother.

Kelly writes (some later additions are in parentheses):
I am in a great deal of pain at work from my sciatic nerve acting up and am limping quite noticeably by the time I leave. I have to take the bus and walk the nine blocks from the daycare to home with the kids. By the time I get there I can barely move at all, but I am determined to get supper going, so I start some rice. Then I go outside for a minute and the world goes funny on me. It's sort of a dizzy and wooshy feeling, and I sense Moita's presence very strongly. The idea of going to sit down in the living room makes itself into my head, so I go and sit down.

Instantly Moita is much stronger, and she tells me that I am in danger. Apparently I am "losing the thread of my consciousness" (her term). She says that the chakra at the base of the spine has opened too fast, and is creating a great and dangerous imbalance throughout my whole body. She suggests that I phone David. She says that she cannot correct the imbalance alone, although she can hold my thread together for me until help arrives. I don't want to call David. I am afraid he will think I'm playing some game. However, the picture of me standing in front of the phone is very insistent.

Moita comes through even more powerfully. My eyes open and I can see energy dancing through the room. The physical objects become fuzzy – they don't seem to have any distinct or clear outline. Soon, I rise and walk very stiffly and deliberately to the telephone (or rather, Moita walks me, as I am still very reluctant). She dials his number with very sharp, deliberate and slow movements.

As soon as he answers the phone, I try to come back. He notices instantly that something is wrong. Moita comes up stronger again and tells him what is happening. He asks how soon he should come. She says it is up to him, that she will stay with me until he arrives and hold things together, but that there is a danger – or that the sooner the adjustments are made, the better. She walks me back to the living room where she waits for him, telling me to remain calm, as things are under control. I am pretty well too spaced out anyway to be able to panic.

(Because of Ruth, David isn't completely comfortable with rushing out of the house the moment I call. But having recognized the urgency, he does anyway, covering the few blocks in about three minutes!)

David walks right in and sits down in front of her. She explains the situation to him. He asks what he can do. She says she is deciding which chakra centres to open first and in what order. There is a long silence.

(Just before things get started, the kids come in. David leaves to get them out of the house. He shuts the door, but doesn't lock it so they won't feel cut off. However, later on I can hear the children trying to come in, but they can't open the door until Moita leaves.)

Moita then decides, and very jerkily and slowly moves my body to the centre of the floor so David can reach my spine. She then has him place one hand over my heart and one in the same place on my back, and (use the psychic healing technique I have taught him to) open the heart centre. That lasts for a good five minutes.

After the heart chakra comes the crown chakra. The same thing happens there. All throughout I can feel my consciousness coming and going. I won't be aware that it has gone anywhere until I notice it is back. After the crown, she has him draw his hands down the entire length of the spine. He does that two or three times. Then she tells him to keep both hands on the tip of the spine and think of drawing (the excess energy) out. Finally, that part is over.

Then she begins to talk. She tells David that he and I have been utilizing a great deal of this (kundalini) energy without understanding what it can do – that, as in a power point, these kinds of energies can literally take you over. She says that if I had lost the thread of my consciousness, it would not have been permanent, but it would have been a great setback in my development. She asks him if he understands why he is the only one who could make this particular adjustment and he says yes – she is pleased. She says that she did not want to unduly alarm him, but that it was a dangerous situation. She tells him that she had to exercise her will over me in order to contact him, and that she would never have done that except in the direst of circumstances.

She also says that we must make our purpose very clear – or this kind of communication will deteriorate. She is in me so strongly that even with David touching my knees, my body is shaking. She tells him, "It is time you realize I *am*." She says the time for doubting is past – that it will serve no useful function from this point on. She says again that the quality of the communication is changing and is not yet done – and that she wants to be certain David is aware of the difference between starting and now. He says he is aware of the difference. I have never felt her *so* "present" before – although she has poured a great deal of herself into me from time to time. It is becoming more certain and sure.

One of the heaviest things she says is that we have been given the opportunity to have access to this kind of energy once again, and that it is very important for us to realize that whatever we do with it – or however we choose to use it – we do it *to ourselves*.

While Moita is still there, I see David changing form. She tells him what is happening to me – that I am seeing him how she does. He says, "You see me as pure energy." She says: Not necessarily – that the energy she sees is interpreted by her into an image that is like a composite picture of who and what he is.

Afterward David and I talk about what has happened. I have no more pain in my back for the next few hours. I tell him of my reluctance to call him and he says I should never hesitate, because that is what he is there for. He did not think it a "game".

(In the letter I also describe the work that our friends Betty and Arnold begin doing to heal my sciatica.) Arnold gets it fairly loosened up, cracks my lower back, but can't get the nerve to straighten and go back into place. He says it's been out for too long and that it's twisted like an elastic band. He's going to use hot fomentations on it to see if he can relax it enough to put it back. (I also note how much better my back feels when I can spend lunch hour sitting in the park, on the grass in the sun, instead of in the office!)

    ❧   ❧   ❧

"Which is harder – speaking *for* Moita or speaking *to* Moita?" It's a half-serious question Kelly and I sometimes ruefully debate. One can't be an objective observer or even passive spectator at a Moita session, whether one ever speaks a word or not. One cannot help affecting the energy flow by one's very presence – one way or another – and that basic receptivity to energy in turn shapes one's feelings, thoughts and words.

Moita encourages participants to ask questions, *to a point*, for several reasons, not simply as a step to receiving her answers and experiencing the changes that will flow from them. The process of questioning is valuable in itself: bringing out into the open and helping to clarify our concerns, and raising the energy level by increasing our involvement.

The next excerpts illustrate the role of questions and of words in general, and the possibilities that emerge when these run out.

Moita Session #37 (Kelly and David / November 1, 1978)

(As this session begins, Kelly and I are still too "present" in our ordinary consciousness.)
MOITA: I am needing a question.
David: Hmm. Do you know what question it is? A specific one?
MOITA: A *relevant* one.
(I close my eyes, searching for a question to ask. Meanwhile, Kelly is aware of seeing my thoughts spiralling upward in the air above my head and Moita's energy flowing down in their wake. Her consciousness grows fuzzier, and things get more unfocused than they were before.)
David: I'm drawing a blank.
MOITA: Your searching for a question has done what was needed. It has raised your energy and also helped me to come in better.

    ❧   ❧   ❧

This October 16th session is one to which we will return because it ends with a very important breakthrough. Consuming the early part, though, is a great deal of seemingly rational but increasingly frustrating and frustrated questioning of Moita from Ivan, whom we met in Chapters 5 and 6.

Moita Session #33 (Kelly, David, Ivan / October 16, 1978)
Ivan: Would you like some questions or do you have something for us first?

MOITA: I usually save those things for after.

Ivan: Oh. So you'd like some questions. *(they laugh)* Okay. Do you remember me?

MOITA: Of course. You are the scientist.

Ivan: Mm-hmm, of sorts. I'm having difficulty remembering my last line of questioning. I may find myself being repetitive.

MOITA: That does not concern me. I repeat myself a thousand times a day.

Ivan: Okay. You're here as a teacher, I understand, and maybe you can refresh my memory as to what you're here to teach or impart.

(A short period of silence follows, as Moita looks at Ivan.)

Ivan: Does my question confuse you?

MOITA: No.

Ivan: No?

MOITA: But you are not hearing my answer. Part of what I am here to impart is *me* – the doorway. I have come to let you feel the part of you that's more than you can see...

(After many more questions, as Ivan tries in vain to pin Moita down:)

Ivan: Have you come for a specific purpose – to help people like us open doors?

MOITA: Yes.

Ivan: I find it difficult to ask you questions, because all answers lead to the same door.

MOITA: Maybe there is a hint.

Ivan: The questions seem irrelevant then.

MOITA: When it comes down to it all, the only true thing is experience.

Ivan: But questions and answers are a form of experience.

MOITA: No, questions and answers are a way of *going around* experience. *Becoming* is experience, and...it supplies its own answers, even without the questions.

Ivan: If you want to take a road, you must have a choice of roads to take. Therefore, questions are signposts leading to different roads.

MOITA: At some points. But all roads lead to the same place. So the road is not necessarily as important as it may seem.

Ivan: I believe that also. What sort of question, then, *can* I ask you? What sort of specific questions?

MOITA: You have already asked me a great many, and gotten a good answer.

Ivan: It's not the answers that confuse me so much; it's the questions. They seem to lose their relevance, from the time they begin until the time they end. *(laughter)*

MOITA: Perhaps that is the process of discovery: finding out what are the *real* questions.

ॐ   ॐ   ॐ

A week later, Moita feels a warning is in order, which she delivers to us in unusually blunt terms. (The reason will become clear in the next chapter.)

Moita Session #35 (Kelly and David / October 25, 1978)

MOITA: You know, when this kind of communication starts, many things need to be cleared away. Many things are brought up, but it is also sometimes in some ways dangerous if the person is not completely ready to face those possibilities in himself. You all have done evil in your own time... So have I...

These words bring up many images. These words are associated with other concepts than the ones that I intend. *(i.e. such as guilt?)*

David: Can you use any different words to reinforce your intentions?

MOITA: Unfortunately, they are the ones that fit. But the warning is there for you to look at and remember that you have your own views and pictures of these words. That is in itself a lesson on...how to weed out truth from preconceived notions, and being open-minded or projecting yourself into another's spot, taking a different view, changing your place on the [Medicine Wheel]. There is no way for you to know if what I say is true or not until you see for yourself...

Even for those who believe there is a life after death -- when they *do* die and they find out that what they believed in was an actual fact, even for some of *them* it is a tremendous shock. There is a great deal of difference between having faith in something, or believing in something, and *knowing* it. That is why words are very inadequate to express a *knowing* when it has not been experienced [by others]. But after it has been experienced, the words are not necessary.

When you keep the level of your questions up, your communication will also be up as well. And the higher you aim your mind, the more you will be able to see what answers are being given, in what way.

Moita Session #43 (Kelly and David / November 21, 1978)

David: It's so true that your words are not what convinces, not the essence of what you communicate, but your *being* as you do. It's understandable, then, how those who only see the words might label it "fanciful".

MOITA: And words are misleading, too, because they mean different things to different people..., even in the presence of the source of the words. People see what they want, or what they fear. It is true, though, that my presence is more important.

ॐ   ॐ   ॐ

One of Moita's clearest and fullest accounts of the interaction that occurs during a session here takes me by surprise. I have been saying I feel Moita has been trying to guide us in our current life situation.

Moita Session #53 (Kelly and David / December 19, 1978)

David: I thought you were trying to lead us to a better understanding of how to respond.

MOITA: That is something no one can lead you to except yourself.

David: Oh, I think you've done it in the past!

MOITA: I have made available some concepts from my level, but it is you and your individuality that has taken those and changed them for yourself. It was not *my* doing.

David: I agree we've had a lot to do with it, but you also selected which concepts to make available at a certain time.

MOITA: *Not true.*

David: *No?* How did it happen?

MOITA: In this kind of thing, what you get many times is what you are looking *for*. If you were where I am, there would be no need for questions. You would know what I meant, and the answers would be available to you. I have answers available to me for almost any question. But I do not choose the question, nor the information that I make available to you. Your [conscious self's] not being aware of some of your other levels, in some cases, makes it difficult for you to see that you are in more control than what seems.

David: Yeah, I can understand it that way. Not being aware of those other levels ourselves, it's hard to say which is our [higher] self and which is you.

MOITA: Well, you see, you are the selector of the information. It is your other self deciding what it is it thinks you should know, which direction it wishes you to go – or the *all* of you wishes you to go. Why are you here? Why am I? Why has this information been made available to you, or this contact (not the first)?

It is possible for me to lay your life out for you, to know what it is you will do or what you should do. But if that were told, you would fail to do it. We give you hints, and then it is your mind that searches out the answers to those hints. And the searching for those answers is what causes your growth, your expansion, your growing awareness of other levels of yourself. It is not necessarily the hint that matters; it is the active search that makes the difference.

I am limited in my way, too. We cannot always predict accurately how this part of you will react to the things it is given. There are some changes in interpretation that surprise us. *(smiling)* And it is a never-ending source of joy . . .

David: Only *joy*?

MOITA: . . . to see new universes being built. *(we laugh quietly; pause)* You are involved in a great experiment.

༄ ༄ ༄

I want to conclude this chapter with one of those experiences of fulfilment that lie beyond all the words.

Moita Session #32 (Kelly and David / October 11, 1978)

David: I have no more questions.

MOITA: When the questions are gone, what is left?

David: Sunlight in the clear air.

(Long silence as I close my eyes. Kelly begins to see my face change as the energy level rises within her.)

MOITA: I saw you change into your "old man". The image becomes clearer all the time. If you can touch that place where you have already gone through all this, and bring back the quiet and the peace of mind, it will help with what you are doing now.

In case you have not noticed, I am more "here" now than I was before. You have travelled through many levels since I came, and the reason why I can be more *here* is because you are more *there*. Since we always are around, and you are not always able to communicate with us, the change that takes place has to be in you in order for the communication to come – because *we* are clear, but are not always listened to.

You have experienced this change many times. Physically, the room remains the same. Yet it looks different because *you* have changed, not because the room has. *(long silence)*

Hear the world sing. *(very long pause; my eyes closed)*

Soon you will be able to let me touch you.

(I decide to let her get as close now to doing that as possible. Soon I feel I am floating in an infinite space filled with energy and knowing, sensing the closeness of her touch – which would be a tingling ecstasy – but not completely making contact with that. After about three minutes of this, Moita lightly squeezes my hand – or so Kelly tells me later, for I do not remember it distinctly – and I instantly open my eyes.)

MOITA: You have gone far enough.

David: It sure feels nice.

MOITA: It becomes more so as time goes on. There is no end to it – what you would call unbounded joy.

And now is the time for me to depart. Are you aware of the fact that for me these communications are continuous and without gap?

David: Even when we're not listening?

MOITA: I mean only those that you do listen to. *(i.e. presumably since all times are one on her level)*

David: Then we shall speak with you again . . . soon.

MOITA: Yes. Soon.

(When Kelly returns, she describes her experience as I was coming close to being touched. It was ecstasy: a light touch rushing through her entire being, filling her with completeness and love. She also saw us surrounded by fantastic light beaming from above, and being lifted up by it together.)

Chapter 10

CHANGING OUR REALITY

Sometimes precognition can be useful and even helpful. But usually it is far better for an entity to live through life without knowing what [the] future holds. It is sometimes necessary, and a great learning experience, to take a step not knowing where it will lead.
    — Moita (August 3, 1978)

Moita begins speaking through Kelly just as we are entering a period of great turmoil over our existing relationships, amid attempts to lay the groundwork for a spiritually oriented community. The energy released through Kelly's and my openings, however, conflicts with many expectations of those around us. A crucible is thus created for testing our willingness to "take steps not knowing where they will lead" – if necessary, to find our path solely on the basis of inner guidance, without external support of any kind.

The communications and dreams shared in this chapter contribute to answering one overall question: How do Kelly and I move from this difficult, ambivalent situation toward creating a reality in which we can work and live and love together? They convey how it feels to negotiate challenging life circumstances with the unique help an entity like Moita can give.

On this afternoon in mid-July, a spontaneous, surprisingly happy session develops as Kelly and I sit on the grass in a local park. It is less than a week since the communication gap that had been gradually developing between Ruth and me suddenly split wide over my openings to Kelly.

Early on, Moita rather stuns me this afternoon by saying, "We are very pleased with your handling of this situation." The following comes near the end of the session, as I wonder in what circumstances Kelly and I will be living by wintertime.

Moita Session #10 (Kelly and David / July 17, 1978)

David: Would it be possible for you to tell us where we will be spending this coming winter?

MOITA: *(laughing)* You want to know, do you? I do not feel it would be wise to tell you. Nothing could prepare you, anyway. Foreknowledge is not always a wise thing. You must learn to roll with the punches. It is important to know how to flow. You will just have to wait to find out. *(now laughing a lot)* Does that satisfy you?

David: I am content. *(It would be hard not to be, with this energy.)*

MOITA: *Good.*

Nine days later, Moita tells Kelly's husband Phil a deceptively simple "secret".

Moita Session #13B (Kelly and Phil / July 26, 1978)

MOITA: You have reached a point in this life when you must make a choice. I am not permitted to help you in this. It must be an inner thing. If you can decide what you wish to do with your life and keep that thought before you, ...not let anything swerve [you] from it..., you will have discovered the secret to changing your own reality.

It can only be done with great singleness of purpose. It is a very delicate concept and not easy to realize... When one can learn this, one has made great strides in many ways.

Moita Session #25 (Kelly and David / August 21, 1978)

David: I wonder what I can do now, if anything, to make possible a communal solution to this conflict situation. I know there would have to be a lot of [changes in feelings] first. But would raising the idea of a group house for Ruth, Kelly and me, our children, and perhaps others, help to spur those necessary changes? *(period of silence as Moita doesn't reply)* That's a tough one?

MOITA: For you, yes. I spoke before of making your purposes clear. This is something you all must do. Until each of you knows what the choices are in this and what feelings there are regarding those choices, you cannot make a community. Working situations out will help each of you crystallize your own ideas. *Then*, and only then, will you be able to see in what ways you can work together... There is still some growing left to do...

(Moita also speaks about the need for honesty, flexibility and openness to intuition in any communal experiment.)

David: My impression is that you haven't given a "yes" or "no" to my most specific question, but you have spoken about the conditions for doing whatever is to be done – not what, but why.

MOITA: *(nodding)* I cannot tell you how to do it. It is for your own growth to discover the workings. We would not take your experiences away from you, nor narrow your own opportunity to develop. *(pause)* You have us behind you. We are there, even when you cannot feel us or speak to us.

We arrive again now at the session that ended the last chapter, but earlier on, before my questions dissolved. By October 11th, many things have come – or are about to come – to a head in Kelly's and my relationships to Phil and Ruth. If no communal solution to present conflicts is possible, we know how our feelings and intuitions would choose – except that a sense of obligation temporarily holds me back. I am wishing there could be an easier way out of my quandary.

Moita Session #32 (Kelly and David / October 11, 1978)

David: I've been comparing our situation to Eileen and Peter Caddy's experience in the years preceding the founding of Findhorn Community. *(I refer to the dramatic story of their separations from previous spouses, and then more than once from each other, as directed by their spiritual guides.[51])*

    As I understand it, their guidance – whether from Peter's teacher Sheena or Eileen's inner voice – told them specifically what to do next. I see ourselves having to listen to much less specific feelings and intuitions, choosing on that basis what might be the best thing to do, yet ending up doing rather similar things, with similar results, to what they did. Do you see it that way too? *(pause; a broad smile from Moita; then I laugh)* That's another case of what I was just describing – if you don't answer!

MOITA: Everyone goes through this differently, but it is all the same process. Some require the more dramatic road, but the road that [the Caddys] took was one they chose because they wished to do it in a very quick way – very difficult.

    When one is *told* what to do by one's entity or teacher, it usually means that that is the particular type of teaching that is required. Everyone is taught differently depending on what their own particular needs are, on what their own strengths and weaknesses are and what needs to be uncovered. There is no standard.

෨   ෨   ෨

As it turns out, it is conversations the next day and a week later that bring resolution between Ruth and me: to wit, we will separate immediately.[52] Ruth's decision to leave Regina opens up the chance for Kelly and her children to move into the house I have shared with Ruth. But within a matter of days, Ruth reverses course, deciding to return to that house after all.

Meanwhile I have been staying with Kelly in the rather dilapidated home (originally bought as a renovation project) where she has been living since her separation from Phil in July. There we have held many Moita sessions. Based on Ruth's first decision, we tell Phil he can move in where we've been staying. So he gives notice at his apartment for the end of the month. Ruth's change of mind then leaves Kelly and me, as of October 24th, just one week to find a new place – of which there appear very few prospects.

Until Friday evening, October 27th, we do guess that if all else fails we may be able to stay on where we are temporarily. That evening, however, Phil – who does not know I am staying with Kelly – arranges to go out with her for a talk. When he arrives at the house, Kelly asks him to wait while she goes upstairs to use the bathroom. Since I know Phil to be harbouring angry and even violent emotions toward me, I do not feel very comfortable with the fact I am sitting in the living room while Phil waits in the kitchen.

Then I hear him walking down the hall, and see him stop opposite the open doorway. He turns and glances in. A mental shock wave is exchanged as our eyes meet, we mumble hello, and he withdraws down the hallway again. (Phil will later say he felt compelled, almost against his will, to see if I was there.) When Kelly comes downstairs, Phil decides not to go out after all, and their talk rapidly escalates into an extended argument – to which I feel forced to listen, all the while questioning whether I should be staying for the sake of Kelly's safety (though Phil has never physically hurt *her*) or leaving for my *own*.

The violence remains verbal, fortunately. And in his anger, increased no doubt by my presence, Phil delivers an ultimatum: if we do not move out of the house by noon, Tuesday the 31st (Hallowe'en!), *he* is moving in anyway.

On Saturday the 28th, our attempts to close a rental agreement on one of the few available houses continue to be stymied, the owner stalling in hopes of selling. Then on Sunday morning Kelly records this dream: "David finds a house for us to live in, but is worried about the smell since it is right next to a garbage dump."

We hold the following session that afternoon – with one question uppermost in our minds. Moita's simple reminder that "time is your own concept" has freed us to realize we can and must begin living our truth *now*, not later. But can time really be compressed so much as to find, rent and move the four of us into another house in two days?!

Moita Session #36 (Kelly and David / October 29, 1978)

David: Did I detect a frown as you opened your eyes?

MOITA: I have been here for a while. She is not a very relaxed person. If you can think of some other questions to ask me first, it might help.

David: Mm-hmm. *(pause)* That's a hard task.

(I do come up with a good one about a previous session, though, and by the time Moita has responded I am feeling energy pulsing between our hands.)

David: You're becoming more present.

MOITA: *(whisper)* Yes. It is peculiar, is it not, to experience all these changes so quickly? *(pause; followed by an exchange about the previous session in which Moita spoke seriously to us about issues of power and responsibility)*

David: That seems to be a message many entities have given. Is there any specific slant that you will be giving it?... It's getting difficult to talk.

MOITA: Am I becoming too present for you?

David: Just for talking.

(My depth perception is now affected. I'm feeling expanded, combined with a "hardness" experienced during a dream the past summer. Moita later explains the feeling as resistance to my entity's energy field.)

MOITA: Warnings about power have been given to many people over the centuries in every age. It is not a new concept, nor one that you are not familiar with. There are many more people here now, when the change in the world comes, who will have access to that power. You who are trying to build a New Age, have you thought of the kind of New Age you are trying to build, what you will do with that energy you will have access to? That is why so many of us are here. We would not see the world destroyed another time. *(this last delivered with much feeling)*

Our worlds will meet, come together. It will affect us as much as you. There is a great difference between watching over a soul and its development when it is not aware of you, and participating with a conscious soul in its own development. *(long silence)*

David: Focusing on the present on this level for a minute, what we've been experiencing as far as where we're going to live has obviously been a test of many things. But the delays in knowing, and particularly about the one house, certainly seem more than an accident. Is there something else we should be doing, but haven't – either physically or psychically – that's holding things up?

MOITA: You know that nothing will be accomplished without conscious effort on your part, so sitting back and waiting may not be the answer. It may be a lesson not just in learning how to roll with the punches, but perhaps in how to keep the punches from rolling.

Since you are creating your own situation, and the situation you have created is one you wish to be in regardless of how you at the present moment may feel about it, you may be trying to push yourself in certain directions that you feel you need to go. By necessity, I must speak vaguely. You know I cannot give you specific advice. I cannot say "sit back and wait and see what happens" or "go out and look and find another place."

(Moita's opening sentence supports Kelly's sense there is more conviction in this second alternative – though Kelly won't make that clear to me till much later.)

MOITA: This *is* another crossroads, and your choices will be important. But they must be *your* choices. Does that help?

David: Some.

MOITA: At least you know you are travelling your own road... Tests are not easy; then again, they are not meant to be. *(long silence)*

David: It's very good to have you present as we go through these things.

MOITA: *(feeling quite pleased)* I'm glad my presence helps...

We seem to be generating more energy, more often. Things have a way of working out. Have a *productive* day.

David: All right. We'll see what the day brings – or what we bring to it.

MOITA: Enjoy yourself.

❦   ❦   ❦

Lacking any definite advice from Moita on our situation, the energy we nevertheless gain from the session provokes another burst of house hunting this afternoon. I go to see one new possibility, but come back discouraged by the somewhat rundown neighbourhood.

By the next morning, however, the chances of renting the house we had long been pursuing, or any other but the last one seen, have dropped to nil – *and* we have realized the connections between (a) my reaction to that rundown area, (b) Kelly's dream about the garbage dump, and (c) Eileen and Peter Caddy of Findhorn Community! Back in the early 1960s, the Caddys were also left, as winter came on, with nowhere to go but the unbecoming Findhorn trailer park – and the only site available was next to the garbage dump![53] They subsequently discovered that location was destined for them because it possessed an unusual energy that would soon be invigourating a miraculous garden, an organic prototype for their future community.

Taking these connections as symbolic inspiration, on Monday we revisit the house I saw the day before. Together, we find it rather more acceptable than my first glances and description indicated – especially given the lack of any alternative before Phil's tomorrow noon deadline. So what else? – we call the landlord, finalize the deal, start packing, rent a truck . . . and are out of Kelly's house by 11:45 Tuesday morning!

∾   ∾   ∾

On Wednesday evening, we sit to meditate together amid the boxes in our new living room. Moita becomes present, leaving Kelly no doubt she is in "a really fantastic mood". Now that we've arrived, we're let in on what's lain behind all this.

Moita Session #37 (Kelly and David / November 1, 1978)

MOITA: Welcome.

David: Welcome, yourself. It sounds like you've been waiting for us...

MOITA: This will be a very interesting place for you.

David: Are you saying that it was an interesting place before we even got here?

MOITA: There *are* many reasons for your coming here. As it happens, this house is located on a minor power point. Much manoeuvring has been done to get you here. Most of it you have not been aware of. Have you ever wondered why Kelly went to the bathroom?

David: Do you mean the night Phil came over?

MOITA: Yes.

David: Was it so Phil could deliver his ultimatum?

MOITA: That was *one* reason. You were in need of a confrontation. You *do* enjoy setting up tests for yourselves. Kelly is an unconscious participant in many of these tests, doing the proper thing at the proper time. You tend to get yourself into very ticklish situations. You're not a very cautious soul.

David: I used to be a lot more cautious than I am now.

MOITA: You have also left behind you a gift for someone at the other house. It is debatable whether he will be able to see it as a gift in the near future. But the seed will be planted, though the changes may take a long time. Have you not wondered what effects there would be on someone living where "the structure of the universe" has been changed? *(i.e. the psychic structure of the local universe, through the many Moita sessions held there these past months)*

David: How about the house not far away from here where Ruth and I used to live, where Sunseed and the Loria communications began? Did the good feelings that many people reported on entering that house reflect this or a similar power point? Or was it simply the people and what we did there?

MOITA: It was not due to a power point. Anytime a group of people gets together for purposes of raising their consciousness, they create an atmosphere that affects others that come there. While it may appear to be an invisible change, it is not really invisible. Some people walking into such a room feel very uncomfortable, while others would experience a sense of peace and well-being. It isn't that difficult to change the structure of your universe, since it was yours to start with...

David: It's fun to look back on our talks and see how what you said in our past relates directly to things happening in our present.

MOITA: Which time are you speaking of?

David: There are many, but I was thinking especially of the session in which you spoke about power, and good and evil.

(I'm referring to our October 25th session, a small part of which appeared in Chapter 9. See also the October 29th session above.)

David: It seems a very appropriate thing to talk about just before we are moving to live on a power point.

MOITA: You've clearly been making good progress, or you wouldn't have been given this opportunity. There are *not* many other power points in this city...

(We both receive the impression it was a decision made at higher levels, with Moita's main role being the subsequent "manoeuvring" to get us here.)

MOITA: Are you getting any better ideas about work?

David: Yes. Our previous talk of sharing these energies with others fits well with living on a power point.

(Be that as it may, Moita's reply deals with a complementary kind of work that must take precedence.)

MOITA: Living here will mean greater contact with your own selves, with your deeper levels. You will be finding out many things about yourselves, and you will be able to learn from what you find. You may not be pleased with some of them. But this is an opportunity to do something about them, since you will now be able to see them. In the winter the world sleeps and you go within yourself. I am sure you will like what you find. I have said before that I am a doorway...

       Now that I have welcomed you, I shall return.

David: See you soon.

MOITA: Have a good night.

෯   ෯   ෯

Moita's parting remark is undoubtedly well-intentioned, but proves ironic. Readers familiar with Kelly's earlier life will recall the anguish resulting when her extreme receptivity seemed to put her at the mercy of negative influences.[54] Here the amplifying effects of the power point resemble some LSD experiences Kelly would rather forget, though she is now aware enough to put a stop to them.

During the night after this November 1st session, Kelly dreams of a maze-like dungeon. There a man in a metal mask has imprisoned a princess, who is then rescued by a king and prince. Meanwhile, at a much lower level of the dungeon, a huge fat demon, possibly Satan, is interrogating a collection of grotesque, emaciated prisoners as to what is wrong with Hell. As each unacceptable answer is given, the prisoner is thrown in the air and torn to pieces. Finally one cowering figure answers, "The trouble with Hell is it just isn't scary enough!" The assembled demons laugh hysterically at this, and then tear this prisoner to shreds also. Later yet, a boy has been kidnapped by a demon with a large, misshapen head and a huge, bulging, oozy eye.

Then Kelly has another dream, in which a monk in a white robe argues with his servant over possession of some treasure sent by the demons in the dungeon. The servant ends up using a curved knife to stab the monk, who repents of his crimes as his robe fills with blood. Kelly gives the monk absolution, making the sign of the cross on his forehead with holy water. Realizing she is dreaming and that there will be more murders if she continues, she wakes herself up.

I also have vivid dreams this night. One of them, interestingly enough, refers to people who "get lost in maze, prison of their thoughts" – the exact notation in my dream journal made before hearing Kelly's dreams. The same dream includes a discussion of Gandalf, who returned from death in *The Lord of the Rings*[55], and a tape recording of a powerful masculine entity speaking as follows: "I come to you from the same energy that exists beyond death. Many people fear death, because it means giving up the concerns and desires of the body. Yet the whole history of Christendom began with a person who overcame death . . ." (It's unusual for me to recall this sort of dream communication, so it must have been very strongly impressed.)

By noon of November 2nd, neighbours have also told us about the wild, loud and destructive people who lived in this house before us. The reports are consistent with the cigarette burns on the carpet and the condition of the bathroom when we moved in. Did their negativity, amplified by the power point, leave a rather different sort of "gift" in the structure of the universe here than we left for Phil?

We begin meditating together in the afternoon, and Moita makes known her wish to hold a session. After some hesitation, due to not feeling very relaxed, Kelly agrees.

Moita Session #38 (Kelly and David / November 2, 1978)
MOITA: I am having difficulty.
    (I respond by closing my eyes, trying to raise the energy level and to send some of it in Kelly's direction.)
Kelly: What did you do?! You brought me back!... This is weird!
    (We close our eyes again. This time I don't try to direct my energy.)
MOITA: Confusing?
David: Yes, some.
MOITA: Much work needs to be done here. We must raise our level.

(I start to close my eyes, but then open them.)

David: Is it a good idea to close my eyes?

MOITA: Definitely not. *(pause)* Will you accompany me as we ascend?

David: Certainly.

(As we gaze at each other in silence, Kelly and I both sense a definite shift in energy level.)

MOITA: There's a question that needs to be asked. *(pause)*

David: The only one that's around my head is: Can you tell us more about any specific quality to this power point? Or would it be better to discover it for ourselves?

MOITA: No.

David: No to which?

MOITA: To the discovery. It is important for you to know beforehand, so you will understand what is happening.

(Unfortunately, there is an interruption with the tape recorder.)

MOITA: We must raise our level again.

(Long silence as we travel upward through what Kelly experiences as many levels of thought.)

MOITA: What do you know of power points?

David: They are places that amplify the thoughts and attitudes people bring with them. They speed up transformations. If one attempts to use them for one's own ends, one ends up being taken over in a sense.

MOITA: And now that you live on one, how will that affect you?

David: The thought that comes is knowing that everything counts. You have to put being centred first, before lesser goals.

MOITA: *(with unusual sternness – not her often gay self)* Since everything is amplified on a point, everything you do has great importance, even small things. You must become very aware of what you are doing and what kind of energy you are putting into it. If you let yourself delve into your lower centres, they too will be amplified, and once activated by a point it becomes very hard to deactivate or overcome.

Much consciousness needs to be developed in everyday life. Each moment must be made a meditation, an awareness on another level of your purpose and why you are here, what you are doing and what you wish to work on. When you started to change the structure of your universe, you made this possible – and therein lies your danger that I spoke of before.

For most people, small actions carry little weight in their world. They are of no consequence to them at the moment, and for a long time they remain the same. However, when you take the road to consciousness, all things matter and carry great weight. There is no such thing as "unimportant", and the effects of doing things the wrong way are felt immediately and not in the long range. It is not an easy spot you are put in, but how can you continue unless you are?

This place can help you find your source – the energy from which you came – or it can destroy you and make you have to climb again. You walk a tight road. But if you were not willing to take the chance, you wouldn't be here. It is very important to have your choices very clear now – more so than it was before – and be open. Anything hidden will take things away . . . including *this*.

      It sounds like a hard road, but once it has been taken, it is hard no longer. It has many rewards.

David: You have softened.

MOITA: I am through with my warning. Sometimes I must be somewhat stern, so that you are aware of how important it is.

David: Can you tell us now anything of the specific nature of this point?

MOITA: There are a number of kinds of power points. They range in intensity. One that is situated in a city is not as easy to cope with as one that is situated away from people in an open area. A point such as this can draw to itself much energy from the people around, not just those who are on it. The entire area affects the power of the point. And so, in this case, it can be erratic if it is not watched.

      And because of these thoughts that are there from others, they will also have an effect on those who live in the house, and can cause great turmoil if those who live here are not aware of the possibility of receiving foreign thought-forms from the house that are not their own. You need to be very clear on which thoughts are yours, and which do not belong to you but belong to the city or parts of it. And that is a very great test of your ability to keep your centre and know yourself above all.

      Power points that are in the country, outside, have a tendency to open up things to the country, to what is happening in the life around. Those are the kinds of thought-forms that it contains... And so, the difference between here and Arrow Mountain shall be very great. Once you are aware, though, of those foreign thoughts, and know which are yours and which are not, you can rise above them to a different plane, and they will not be there. And then the point will be more pure.

David: That makes me think of Kelly's dream – that it might have contained some of those foreign thought-forms.

MOITA: Or it may have been dredging up many past ones. There were some reincarnational elements in her dream. Those things will have to wait until this point is purified. That is one reason why I am having difficulty since you have moved here. It will take you a while to transmute the energy. You have heard of some of its effects on others, those who were here before you.

      (smiling) I think you shall do fine. You have been prepared... Do not lose sight of your goal.

      I will leave now. I have difficulty saying goodbye.

David: See you soon.

MOITA: Yes, you will. Much work is being done here for a while.

     (Kelly returns, feeling very spaced out.)

Kelly: I feel like someone is going down my spine, raking things up, pushing them into my head. *(beginning to cry quietly, a long silence following)*

David: What are you feeling now?

Kelly: Pain.

ം   ം   ം

After one week of living on the power point, Moita asks for our assessment.

Moita Session #39 (Kelly and David / November 7, 1978)

MOITA: What do you think so far?

David: As we were saying today, it's a little hard to separate the effects of simply being together in our own home and the effects of where we are, since both are new.

MOITA: As so it was *meant* to be. Each one intensifies the other, makes your changes more quick. It was easier to come tonight.

David: The energy is clearing out?

MOITA: Somewhat. Many things are being dealt with. *(pause)* Are you aware of differences?

David: Mm-hmm. *(pause)* It seems like this room is starting to change.

MOITA: It will not take long *here*...

ം   ം   ം

An example of my own need to work through darker elements surfacing through the power point comes in a dream around mid-November.

"Communicate Through Top of Head" dream
David (age 31) / mid-November 1978

I am in a museum where I remember having once meditated and played music with friends. A man levitates a glass of water several inches below his downturned palm. I accept this, having seen it done before. Another male laughs in amazement and reaches out to feel the energy field emanating from the man's hand. This man then asks the first if the demonstration is connected to Findhorn: "23 Findhorn, near the garbage dump?" he inquires. The man replies that it's a miracle anyone can perform.

Then Peter Caddy is there, saying to the first man that this is a cheap use of power. "You have to communicate through the top of your head," he tells him. I see a cone or pyramid fitting up into a larger, identically shaped cone or pyramid. Someone says this is the way to receive exactly the communication you need at a given time. Peter then signals with a wink for Eileen to join him and to try to heal the spirit of this man. By this time the scene has become a movie with a narrator commenting on how unique a film event this is.

As the two Caddys approach the man, they both wince and pull away at the touch of his aura. The camera recording their reaction is now positioned

where the man is standing, so that I experience the scene as if I am he.
Somewhat reminiscent of Jesus casting out demons, Eileen asks, "Spirit, is
there anything you want to tell us? How can we help you?" But then, in the
man's place, there is only a little boy who is crying and saying he never
wanted to see this movie. "I curled up and tried to forget," he sobs. The
soundtrack music builds to a heavy, dramatic, reverberant rumble as Peter
concludes, "The spirit had its chance" – and by implication, missed it.

The dream seems to be describing my temptations and fears at living on the power point – the dangers of not being well-enough attuned to my higher self, not being purified or whole enough in order to "communicate through the top of [my] head", i.e. through the highest energy centre. The ending shows a tendency to regress, as a form of retreat from the challenge but also a way of at least becoming conscious of my weak feelings. Clearly, I am still groping toward making the most of the growth opportunity that has been laid before me.

I also realize from this dream for the first time the *psychic* meaning of the "garbage dump": the way that the power point apparently draws to itself all the thought-forms of this area of the city.

∾   ∾   ∾

Turning to the more humourous side of living in our new house, one bewildering phenomenon is the extraordinary number of telephone calls for someone else: both the ordinary misdialings plus several people insisting our number belongs to various others. "The probability of so many people having your number," Moita says amid much laughter, "I do not believe is that high. *Everyone knows* you are here." To my facetious question about what we might say to these callers, she replies, "Some of them you may not want to meet! Even when this is a purified point, it will attract many kinds of energy. As always, discretion is important."

Then there is Kelly's experience during the second week of November while taking the bus to work in the morning. She notices a very strange old hag of a woman get on the bus and walk down the aisle past her, presumably to sit in the rear. At a later stop, an *absolutely identical* woman gets on the bus again, and this time sits in front of her. Checking behind, Kelly cannot spy the first woman who boarded.

Moita Session #40 (Kelly and David / November 11, 1978)

David: Kelly saw someone interesting on the bus this week. It seems to be not an
           ordinary person. Could you fill us in on what sort of manifestation it was?
MOITA: She was seen twice in the same day, on the same bus. Obviously, both of
           them couldn't have been the same. *(pause)* The first one that arrived on the bus
           went *behind*. Its leaving couldn't be seen. The second stayed in front and could
           be watched. *(pause)* The *second* one was real.
David: Real physically, you mean?
MOITA: Yes. The first one was not . . . physically.

David: In what way was the first real otherwise?

MOITA: This is an interesting subject! *(pause)* Firstly, why did something that was not real on a physical level choose to look exactly like someone who *was*, unless they wished to be *noticed*...? Certainly no impression would be made if they had been different than everyone else on the bus. *(pause)* And then comes another question: why did they want to be noticed in the first place? It may be it has something to do with *here*. Power draws power. *(pause)* What would you do if one walked through the door?!

David: Try to notice . . . as much as possible . . . *Welcome* them. *(i.e. not antagonize them, whatever we do!)*

MOITA: *(laughing along with me)* As *gently* as possible? *(more laughter)* There is another clue here, too! Of all the people it could have chosen to look like, why did it pick *that* one? She looks very much like she belongs in this neighbourhood...

David: So, I'm not sure what "it" is.

MOITA: It could be many things!

David: We thought, of course, of what don Juan said about "the allies". *(i.e. in Carlos Castaneda's books about the Mexican Indian sorcerer)*[56]

MOITA: *(softly)* And what did he say about "the allies"?

David: That sometimes they appear on buses, but are not real people.

MOITA: What do they *do*?!

David: Observe, see what reactions they get, and if anyone will *notice*.

MOITA: And if no one does, they are usually quite *amused*. *(pause)* Sometimes they can be used, when they're noticed. It seems to be similar to the story of the leprechaun. If you can catch one and hold onto it, it has to grant you a wish or give you its pot of gold.

David: Are you suggesting . . . ? *(general laughter)*

MOITA: That you catch one? *(more laughter)* I think you would find *(laughing)* that an upsetting circumstance would follow! *(laughing)* Especially if you try to *physically* catch him.

David: Hmm.

MOITA: *You* may not have that much contact with these kinds of things. But because of your openings, you will become more aware of their reality and existence as entities going back and forth doing their own thing. And you are not taking don Juan's path. You are on one that is similar, parallels in some ways, but is not the same road at this point. These things will more than likely remain interesting phenomena. But it is a sign!

♥   ♥   ♥

The new reality we would create is not one of isolation from people. In fact, once the initial "purification" is complete, we will quickly turn to sharing the energy of the power point with others: those friends who remain open to us, as well as new acquaintances and workshop members.

Though the dramatic changes of recent months have resulted in some separations, we continue to hope for as much healing of wounds as possible and the resumption of moves toward community. While supporting these goals, Moita continues to emphasize that a wholeness cannot be imposed. It must truly grow out of the psychic integrity and freedom of each part, each individual's willing coordination of paths with others as a way of spurring their own self-knowledge and growth.

These last two selections show Moita, Kelly and me reflecting on people's lessons from the year's events, to the extent there may be any commonality to them, acknowledged or not.

જી   જી   જી

Earlier today we received the expected letter from my parents with their less than sanguine views of my separation from Ruth, of Kelly's and my living together, and of my becoming the "scribe" for yet another purported case of psychic communication. In asking here what seems an abstract question, Moita has in mind those around us who not only condemn our life choices but who dispute her own legitimacy or the level she comes from.

Moita Session #42A (Kelly and David / November 14, 1978)

MOITA: More scribing?

David: *(laughing)* It's interesting. I used that word several years ago, saying that in writing my thesis I felt I was the scribe of some omniscient power, which I just had to tune into and difficulties were then resolved.

MOITA: Many writers feel the *same. (pause)* ...What would constitute "proof" of existence?

David: *(pause)* Seems to me one can only do that for oneself.

MOITA: One gets to a point when it doesn't matter. *(pause)* Thankfully, I am not a thought-form, or I would have to fight for my reality – which is why thought-forms put up such a battle when the ego dies. And the closer you come to losing that ego, the more resistance you meet. *(pause)* You have chosen a difficult way.

David: After one has chosen, it's no longer difficult.

MOITA: Once one reaches a certain point. All roads are hard to start off.

David: Once one knows one has *chosen* it – perhaps that's the point.

MOITA: It is sometimes a nice feeling to know you have taken your destiny in your own hands and are responsible for your own choices. It can also be somewhat frightening, for the same reason. *(silent period)*

David: I think I'm understanding more the purpose of all this, and what it is that's most frightening to others – and to me, earlier on. The reason it was all so *drastic* was just to find out that it is possible to choose one's own way, following one's inner voice, completely apart from any of these general rules of how people are supposed to live – that if we and others learn anything from it, it should be that it's possible to live that way.

I suppose in the end we all have to reach that point. [But] I hesitate to say that, because it sounds . . .

MOITA: Then you are just in the beginning?

David: Yes, and I said "in the end".

MOITA: Mm-hmm.

David: *(laughs)* The end of one phase . . .

MOITA: . . . is the beginning of the next. *(quoting herself)*

David: And many people feel that living that way is craziness. I wasn't so sure it wasn't, for a while, myself.

MOITA: To those people, it probably would be. Since you are all here to learn something different, then all of you must be careful of being too critical of what others perceive of you. They, too, must go their own road. Sometimes it seems so counterproductive for all of those on each path to try to destroy the others so they won't get there, or to keep them from going. And they all end up in the same place, sooner or later.

All of these things are doorways, too, for you to search out your own inner meanings and test them. All things must be renewed, continually. You have been placed in this position for a very specific reason. I think you probably understand what it is. At the moment, you have no one who really has any conviction for what you are doing, except for yourself. The question is: Will you stand the storm straight and tall, and crack – or will you bend with the wind, and weather it? *(pause)* You cannot teach them through words.

ॐ   ॐ   ॐ

Much negativity still remains among those involved in our changes, and I ask about the effect of the thoughts we think about each other. Though we definitely would like to create a resolution in this life, Moita's words suggest that too may be an attachment we will have to release.

Moita Session #89 (Kelly and David / May 20, 1979)

MOITA: You cannot avoid influencing people by thinking about them. But then, you are also not responsible for how they react to your influence. Each one of you has to learn how to stand against a barrage of others' thoughts and how others view you... A person may fight your view of what he is, and make his learning longer because he fights himself. In trying not to be like how others see you, quite often you end up being exactly how they have perceived. That is perhaps one reason why the ancients speak of "surrender".

I know it can sometimes feel like being in a fog – not knowing where your clearness has gone and only seeing your reflection in others' eyes. But then, other parts of them see different reflections too, and know the greater meanings behind the external events. But for most, the part must be played out until it has begun to stagnate and go stale. And then a new part is played that gives a semblance of reality or completeness.

We see each of you travelling down your road and changing the signs as you go, and then going back and changing them again *(smiling)* so that the road conforms with your concept of it. You can make anything that you want out of it, for good or bad...

David: One's inner self sees others in their completeness, does it not?

MOITA: That depends on the depth that you have gone. You have many inner selves, one at each way-station. Each one is more complete than the last, as you go down, and sees more aspects of the whole. But then, where is the importance in a passing phase?

(Kelly reports the image of even a whole incarnation as but a minute, little piece within a circle of many others. "Why are you caring about this little bit?" Moita seems to be asking.)

MOITA: If a person is now as you perceive him to be, and you hold that view too long, if and when he changes you will fail to detect the changes that are happening. *(pause)* If you can free a person within yourself, when next you meet it will be on different terms.

℆   ℆   ℆

Chapter 11

THE EAGLES ARE COMING!

All about the hills the hosts of Mordor raged. The Captains of the West were foundering in a gathering sea. The sun gleamed red, and under the wings of the Nazgul the shadows of death fell dark upon the earth.

As if to his eyes some sudden vision had been given, Gandalf stirred; and he turned, looking back north where the skies were pale and clear. Then he lifted up his hands and cried in a loud voice ringing above the din: "The Eagles are coming!"

– J.R.R. Tolkien, The Lord of the Rings[57]

All of our year's personal changes reach their culmination, freeing Kelly and me to begin our life and work together, during the week of October 12-18, 1978. At the mid-point of that week, the night of October 15/16, I experience two remarkable dreams. Those dreams, and the conclusion of our session the following night, represent a milestone in our psychic evolution as well. Thus this chapter's title and quotation: from here on, it will be impossible to pretend forces are not at work here larger and more universal even than Moita.

If we ever might have felt complacent about all this good energy, the events of October 16, 1978, remove that possibility. I wake at dawn having experienced two dreams of incredible energy and depth – dreams which prefigure one of the most crucial, ongoing developments in Kelly's channeling.

It will take me over four years even to begin to interpret the timing, context and references of these dreams. But one key, I eventually realize, is given in a passage from a classic work on psychotherapy. Here 87-year-old Jungian analyst Frances Wickes discusses the dream of a "shining bridge" that opened a patient to a deeper level of herself. The following catches some of the flavour and relevance of Wickes's commentary:[58N]

> In folklore as well as in myths the bridge is always accounted an exceptional and special place, under the protection of the divinity. Its priestly significance comes down to us in the title of the Pope, Pontifex Maximus...(bridge builder).
>
> The bridge is built between the earthly and the heavenly worlds... Bridge and abyss form a cross at the point of deepest intersection; this is the cross of the transitus where, through acceptance of the cross, one passes over from the old life to the new... For the cross that each must bear is hewn out by the mysterious indwelling Self that brings man face to face with his own conflict, his own experience and his own choice of the way he will live out his destiny...

The words emerged from the end of the dream, "The light was never before so radiant upon the shining bridge." She looked far down into the split within herself: love and hate, night and day, darkness and light... She knew that the bridge was her own desire to accept the split, and that with true desire she might cross over to the place of reconciliation of the opposites.[59]

As we will see, this quotation provides a key – given that the first of my two dreams of October 16th refers to the election of a new pope. This is no accident: In the waking world, on October 15, 1978, the cardinals of the Roman Catholic Church have begun their Vatican deliberations to elect a successor to Pope John Paul I – the pontiff, the "bridge builder". I have followed with interest the news from Rome before going to bed. Below are my two dreams from this night.

"Election of New Pope" dream
David (age 31) / October 16, 1978

I am watching a movie depicting pilgrims in dusty white robes and hoods who meet on the road in early Christian times. The travellers debate with each other over the first churches built in memory of the Crucified One. Two groups disagree, each feeling they were the ones more closely linked to the earliest churches. Different routes to the Holy Land are also discussed. Then the shadow of a figure bearing a crown of thorns is cast on the ground. All suddenly realize that one among them is either the resurrected Christ or has come to embody the Christ energy.

Now a Biblical-style quotation appears at the top of the movie screen as it is spoken aloud. "Then, appearing in the form of an angel...", it begins, clearly referring to the high being that has appeared or materialized within the group.

Simultaneously, the movie format dissolves into the spectacle of a massive orchestral/choral concert being broadcast live in celebration of the newly elected pope. I become increasingly aware that a great event in mankind's spiritual evolution has occurred.

I fly up toward the chandeliers of this vast hall, unfurling behind me a long, bright red streamer. This I wave so as to spell out for all to see, in elaborate Old English lettering, the magnificent conclusion of the quotation. The words refer to the complementary work of the Archangels Gabriel and Michael in bringing about a New Age – or such, at least, drawing on Rudolf Steiner, is my understanding.

My flight is accompanied by monumental music conducted by the young man who composed it for this occasion. I feel so well in touch with the conductor and his music that the concluding note following an extended, triumphal chord coincides precisely with my banner's final flourish.

೫   ೫   ೫

"Greetings to My Created Earth" dream
David (age 31) / October 16, 1978

A strange man asks me to write a "poem" on a large, glass plate. Drawing on one of Moita's images, I write: "My love is like a jewel." The man then sprays fine water droplets all over the glass. Next he lowers a lighting apparatus and switches it on.

The lamp device transforms my six scrawled words into an entire paragraph in large type filling the screen. I am amazed as I read the opening line: "Greetings to my created Earth!" I go through the whole passage twice so as to remember as much as possible, though the words seem to grow and change on second reading.

The awe-inspiring but unknown author seems to refer to a specific time centuries ago in saying, "One-third of Me died on October 1st, 1606. Today, two-thirds of Me is trying to be born." I also hear the words, "John is the name of David's love." Lastly, I see magazine pictures of Buffy Saint-Marie and books on ethical philosophy belonging to a former professor friend who publicly supported my war resistance stand.

꙳   ꙳   ꙳

The conjunction of so many levels of meaning in these dreams is daunting, to say the least. For some time afterward, their extraordinary richness will rather blind me to "mundane" interpretations for Kelly and me personally. That individual level, though, is where I will begin, so that any remaining higher significance can then stand on its own.

Turning to the first dream: It seems, relatively speaking, a petty debate in which the pilgrims are engaged over which churches were built first, in association with whom, and which is the best route to Jerusalem. I think this points to the struggle ("Crusades") among Ruth, Kelly and me over our respective roles, each seeking his/her own path to the "Holy Land" within. But here the argument among the pilgrims abruptly ends when the shadow of the suffering Jesus is cast, as if to recall our true purposes and provide much-needed perspective. I recall that a few of Kelly's and my dreams during the past summer made similar allusions to Christ's Passion.

The most concrete relevance to our situation might be this: Henceforth, rather than continue this crucifixion (crown of thorns), we must accept the pain of dying relationships and seek a way of rebirth into new life. Of course, it will take two more days for Ruth to confirm our separation. But to my dreaming mind it is clear this is the climax of all the events surrounding the three of us this year – tragic from one point of view, liberating from another. *This is the transitus*, the "pivot point" of which Moita spoke in her very first message to us on June 27th:

There's a point, not far distant, where all these things will come together. Basically, that point will be the centre of this life as far as happenings are concerned. That will be the pivot point here... Circumstances will force things to that point, circumstances that have already been laid out... From that point onward, many things will open, and many things will fall away.[60]

Thus my immediate personal association to the words "appearing in the form of an angel" would be Moita, who has played such a key supportive role in our changes. Reference to the complementary work of Gabriel and Michael, as understood by Steiner, also has its parallel "down here": Kelly and I uniting our divergent natures, creating a "natural bridge" to further our individual growth, psychic work and community vision. Clearly, the dream's ending reflects my joy at the transition now finally under way.

In the second dream, Moita's and Kelly's image of the "jewel" provides a link to our own experience. But once the "lighting" apparatus is turned on, a different energy level again takes precedence. Attempting to tease out a personal meaning, "Greetings to my created Earth!" mirrors Kelly's and my delight at the new reality we have been creating in our lives. Similarly, the professor's books on ethical philosophy relate to unconventional, relatively solitary choices we have made in order to arrive at this point.

Pictures of Buffy Saint-Marie associate to Kelly in three ways: a similar vibrancy in their personal energy; my recent (October 12th) dream[61] of ghostly Indian figures, which referred to Kelly and me "haunting" the Earth in search of each other; and Kelly's early visions of Moita in the form of the Virgin Mary ("Saint-Marie"). The statement about "John", when combined with "Mary", recalls the headstone inscriptions in my April 12th dream, a week before meeting Kelly. There the teacher who introduced me to Steiner rose from near-burial to exclaim "S/He's come?!"[62] – clearly, in hindsight, referring to Kelly's and Moita's imminent arrival in my life.

The statement about a fractional death is the most difficult to interpret personally, though it would seem to rhyme with the first dream's crown of thorns. "October 1st" possesses a kind of finality for Ruth's and my relationship, and for the part of me coupled with Ruth. It is the date of the letter Ruth and I sent to friends who attended a gathering that publicly revealed the rift between Ruth and me.[63] On this level, the "1606" might only be a garbled reference to today's date, October 16th. Much more clear is that Kelly's and my partnership is indeed "trying to be born". The fractions might then refer to Ruth, Kelly and myself as aspects of my experiential universe – and possibly also, as representative fragments of a larger being who encompasses us.

Now I feel freer to consider other levels of meaning in these dreams. All the Christian references are part of my conscious awareness, of course, so to explain them we need not resort to the collective unconscious or a religious source beyond myself. Still, I did not consciously plan or expect these dreams – no more than I did those from the past year to which they are clearly connected.

Most prominent in the dreams of October 16th, however, is a conjunction of elements – images and words relating to Christ, Rudolf Steiner, the Bible, birth and death, flying and Old English lettering – that occurred in three highly significant dreams preceding the birth of Ruth's and my child this past summer. The three are the "Steiner and Sky-Diving" dream from July 21st, the "Spirit Rays and the Next Step" dream from July 29th, and the "Ship Must Land Tomorrow" dream from August 3rd.[64] These dreams reflected an escalation of *masculine spiritual energies* that was also experienced by Kelly at the time – indeed, was very noticeable to both of us ever since our medicine wheel visit in June, when Kelly "saw" the Indian brave wearing eagle feathers.

Here I will make one point each about these dreams. The "Steiner and Sky-Diving" dream, in which male elders and I were descending to Earth from space, included the chart I've made of my family tree. It will soon become clear there is a spiritual as well as physical interpretation to the generations in a "family tree". In the second dream, "spirit rays" referred to an older man and younger woman, a "teacher" and an "assistant", who spoke of "the next step beyond the stage of Christ's first coming".

(Consider also the esoteric Christian significance of St. John and the Virgin Mary, viewed in the Steiner tradition as prophet and vessel of the New Age, respectively.[65] Or, drawing upon more recently published research[66], is it John the Baptist and Mary the Magdalene, as honoured by the Knights Templar, who have been strongly linked to the Crusades and churches at Jerusalem? Either way, and regardless of other possible associations not completely understood by me, these are again sets of complementary masculine/feminine archetypes.)

Finally, the "Ship Must Land Tomorrow" dream involved a being on "a mission to [planet Earth]," though "no one [was] transparent enough yet" to receive it consciously at the time. Still, the second and third of these three dreams did release an incredible energy. I felt this energy to be predominantly masculine, with a "hardness" Moita later attributed to an entity's "friction" with my aura. I became convinced that whatever being was behind all this would eventually make contact.

So: Could the dreams of October 16th be a follow-up, symbolized by "the election of a new pope", the realization of a new bridge between earth and spirit "appearing in the form of an angel"? And on how many levels might we then interpret the transformed message, "Greetings to my created Earth"?

Concerning now the quotation that my banner spells out in Old English lettering, Rudolf Steiner has portrayed the Archangels Gabriel and Michael as working in a complementary manner to further human evolution – that is to say, the human spirit's progressive incarnation. As presented by Owen Barfield in *Unancestral Voice*,[67] Gabriel's energy is that "transforming agent" working through biological heredity, developing mutational structures in the human body as the physical substrata for growth in consciousness (which fits with Gabriel's appearing to Mary to announce her conception of a child); while Michael is the Angel of Light and Truth, the "transforming agent" working within the human mind, wielding his sword of discrimination, thus gradually opening us to participation in the creative thoughts themselves. Together, they are Earth-Spirit and Sun-Spirit in harmonious balance.

When contact is made with such energies, human beings tend to personify them in similar ways. Could this have been the case in one of Kelly's key past lives? Moita's first-ever spoken words to us came at the end of Kelly's first past-life regression, which included this experience of a country girl living centuries ago:

> I see two people coming down from the clouds. I am scared. One is very tall, and bright. His hair is like the Sun. He is hard to see, to look at. The other is not as tall, and he is dark. He is easier to see. He is softer, not as bright. They tell me there are problems. There is great trouble brewing in the world, and they want me to help...

Finally, regarding the enigmatic fractions and historical reference (if indeed it has any specific validity), my intuitive feeling upon waking is that they could relate to waning and waxing influences of complementary archetypal energies upon Earth. I'm also aware that both Seth and Steiner spoke of the Christ-energy incarnating in three human beings – thus, in thirds – at the time of Jesus. Intriguing as these leads on the non-personal level of interpretation may be, they go too far afield to elaborate here.

But imagine the effect on me when I finish scribbling down these dreams and turn on the radio this morning of October 16, 1978. My head buzzing with thoughts of archangels and historical cycles in humanity's spiritual evolution, I certainly have to stop and wonder as I hear that a new pope has been elected this day: Pope John Paul II, the first non-Italian pontiff in over 450 years![68N]

ം   ം   ം

It may not make the world's history books, but within our own universe the Moita session Kelly and I inevitably hold the following evening certainly is a milestone – a start, if only barely, toward many answers that have been eluding us over the past 12 months. This is the session with Ivan that has already been partially excerpted in Chapter 9. It becomes a very *different* session, however – different than ever before for us – when Ivan is done and I venture a question of my own.

Moita Session #33 (Kelly, David, Ivan / October 16, 1978)

David: I dreamed last night about Archangels and a Being, two-thirds of which was attempting to be born. They are intriguing! I will be content to wait and see what other messages and clues come through about this, but do you feel any value in saying more now about what these dreams might mean?

(Kelly is aware of Moita's great attentiveness to the exact way I word my question. When she speaks, it is in a much more serious and husky voice than before.)

MOITA: That is a decision that has to be made on another level. *(pause; then with a glimmer of humour:)* But I shall *inquire* for you!

David: All right.

(Long silence, as Moita closes Kelly's eyes. Kelly feels a surging upwards, and then all of a sudden a really powerful energy starts pouring in down the back of her head. She hears a thought centred in her chest, activating her heart chakra as a necessary condition for the energy to settle in. This is followed by the feeling of a heavy "thump", so different from Moita's lightness. Everything gets even more crystal clear

than before, as this different, really serious being becomes extraordinarily present.)

(Meanwhile, Kelly is aware of cries of "Not yet! Not yet!" – which she only later realizes are her own thoughts. She is afraid to open her mouth, expecting her voice suddenly to have dropped into the bass register. She feels this comparatively masculine presence is holding much of his energy back for her sake and so as not to "boom the whole room down". The voice is not that loud, but is weightier, more deliberate and deeper than Moita's, when he finally speaks. The energy through the eyes has the same impact. I am sitting face-to-face with the long-awaited masculine entity. Capital letters seem appropriate for his initial anonymous appearances.)

???:   YOU WILL HAVE TO LEAVE THAT ALONE FOR NOW. IT SHALL BECOME MORE CLEAR LATER. *(pause)* YOU HAVE NOTICED.

(I laugh quietly at the ironic humour. Kelly is aware he is pleased at being noticed, and that he wouldn't have spoken if the difference in energy had not been recognized.)

David: Do you wish to say anything about who *you* are?

???:   I AM *OBVIOUSLY* SOMEONE ELSE. *(pause)* BUT IT IS YOUR QUESTION THAT BROUGHT ME.

David: I realize that things of that nature, from that level, need . . . Hmm, *we* need time to . . . There's no way to say it. *(still trying)* They proceed gradually as they unfold here. I have no wish to run into . . .

(Obviously I'm experiencing problems conversing with such a presence! The higher entity withdraws and Moita quickly returns.)

MOITA: Tricky!

David: *Who's* tricky?

MOITA: I only went to *inquire!*

David: *(laughs)* You, too, were surprised?

MOITA: Some. I knew it would be soon that you would meet, but not how soon. So now I have left you with many more questions than when I arrived. We obviously have a good quality here tonight.

David: Yes.

MOITA: ...What did you sense? What are the differences?

David: Masculine, heavier in some sense; serious, more distant; more focused toward a very long range. You have a very long-range view yourself, but more emphasis in that direction.

MOITA: You noticed a great deal! At one point he thought he would come and no one would notice... He underestimates himself. *(laughter)*

David: Or us.

MOITA: Quite possibly. I knew *you* would see.

David: Could this being possibly speak through others as well as Kelly some other time, or is . . . Oh, I'll leave it at that. *(laughing quietly)* Of course, we'll have to wait and see.

MOITA: Yes. *(laughing also)* Before he could speak through anyone else, the others would first have to be able to let their own entities speak. It is an ongoing process, not an instant transition.

     I think we have shared enough for one night.

David: Mm-hmm.

MOITA: Good night.

David: See you later.

(Though we don't have a name for this being, it is, as always, the energy that is the important thing. In conversation afterwards, Kelly agrees that he gives the impression of ultimate seriousness. "His sense of humour is definitely more subtle," she laughs, while I wonder if there was really any hint of humour at all. The overall impact of the difference between his and Moita's energy on this first occasion I sum up as follows:)

David: You know what the image I just got was? In the film *Close Encounters of the Third Kind*, the contrast between the little spaceships that flew around (that people were plenty excited by as it was) . . .

Kelly: Oh yeah! *(laughing)*

David: . . . and then the *huge* mother ship that comes over the mountain!

∾   ∾   ∾

This last image comes spontaneously without yet recalling my past year's dreams of space flight symbolizing higher consciousness. In fact, the "Book of Birth Experiences" dream of March 1, 1978 contained some remarkable parallels: the descent on light beams of a spaceship that is under the guidance/supervision of a mother ship orbiting the Earth, the latter understood to symbolize an oversoul.[69] Interestingly, the same higher masculine entity will come through in a session on the first anniversary of this dream. After his exit, Kelly and I will share a few more impressions of the entity's demeanour.

Moita Session #74 (Kelly and David / March 1, 1979)

(As Moita returns, Kelly is very aware of the difference in energies – hers so much lighter and flowing – that at first it feels as if no one is there. Then Moita starts pouring in more and Kelly realizes, "Oh, there it is.")

MOITA: You are having a busy night!... Are you seeking differences? *(I laugh)* And what is the result?

David: He gives a certain impression, probably as a result of the process of communicating between levels, which I have a hard time finding the right word for: "impatience" isn't too close, or a certain "gruffness".

MOITA: *(laughing)* Businesslike.

David: Mm-hmm.

MOITA: It takes a great deal of energy and concentration to do this. And in order for him to speak, he must be solid.

David: Focusing himself very solidly onto what is for him a very small point?

MOITA: Yes. He also cannot stay long, because of the difference in his view.

∾   ∾   ∾

Forgive me – but whenever I read my comment about focusing on a very small point, I can't help wondering if this is how that all started about angels dancing on the head of a pin!

It seems my "Spirit Rays" dream of July 29th was at least roughly accurate: this masculine being of the very strong energy and long-range view fitting the (admittedly crude) dream image there of a "male teacher" having a "female assistant". It should also be noted that on the evening preceding that dream Kelly experienced a masculine entity communicating to her while awake.

And now having Kelly's experience on October 16th – "a really strong energy starts pouring in down the back of her head" – we can look again at the "sometimes frightening – very heavy" experience she underwent back on July 31st, two days after my "Spirit Rays" dream. As quoted here in Chapter 9, Kelly wrote in her journal: "During some of the experience I feel as though my head is getting ready to explode. Something seems very imminent throughout."

As well, at the end of the August 1st Moita session excerpted in Chapter 9, Kelly had another powerful experience: "I feel as though the back of my head expands, and I can feel or sense many others behind me – in the past. Only, they are not dead but living...and their thoughts are bent in our direction." This localization of a powerful energy on the back of her head, in two periods of contact with a masculine entity, seems more than coincidental. It is further evidence that the developments preceding childbirth in early August reached their culmination from the "pivot point" of October 16th onward.

The move to our new house on a power point occurred two weeks later, and Moita gave the impression this also was a decision taken at higher levels. It is interesting, then, that the masculine entity made his second, very relevant appearance during the crucial session before we found our new home. In telling that story in Chapter 10, I omitted part of the session, which can now be added in context. The following fills in the ellipsis near the end of the extract previously given, and includes yet another tie-in to late July/early August.

Moita Session #36 (Kelly and David / October 29, 1978)

MOITA: I'm glad my presence helps. *(quite pleased; a rich silence follows)* It is a good opportunity for you to reach closer to your own [entity]... There are always more than just me.

David: I wondered about that, because I was feeling a powerful energy that I've only felt in a dream a few months ago.

(As described earlier in this session, it is the same "hardness" experienced after my "Ship Must Land Tomorrow" dream on August 3rd.)

(Another long silence ensues during which Kelly sees my face changing. Then she feels a thick energy pour down the back of her head. She hears Moita say, "I have to give up my spot for a while. But don't worry, I'll be back." Kelly thinks, "Not again!" – i.e. not the higher-level masculine entity – but can't do anything about it.)

(Kelly's heart chakra is opened, her heart beats faster and her body gets a lot warmer. She feels the entity's extremely clear block of energy settle in and hears his thought, "So you don't think I have a sense of humour?" – a reference to our after-

session conversation on October 16th. Kelly knows he won't say who he is yet – that part of his subtle but detectable humour is to be mysterious. Nevertheless, she inwardly asks, "Who are you?" His reply: "I am myself, obviously.")

???:   FEELING ME BETTER?

David: All the time, it seems.

(Actually, I have not realized the change of entity – which may help me converse better this time – but am aware of a new forcefulness radiating through Kelly's eyes. One level of the entity's next statement seems to be our house-hunting deadline and their secret manoeuvring of us toward the power point.)

???:   *(pause, clears throat)* IF THINGS WERE NOT WORKING, WE WOULD NOT BE HERE.

David: Could you expand on that? What things?

???:   YOUR INNER AND OUTER, TOGETHER, AS A WHOLE. LOOK AT IT MORE IN THAT LIGHT. THE OUTER WILL MAKE MORE SENSE.

(Long silence. Kelly's eyes close and Moita returns.)

MOITA: Not totally unexpected?!

David: What?

MOITA: Another's presence.

David: Hmm. I wasn't aware of it that time – I mean, as such. Looking back on it, I can see how it was.

MOITA: We seem to be generating more energy, more often. Things have a way of working out. Have a *productive* day.

❧   ❧   ❧

Three days later, on November 1st, Moita told us we had just moved to an "interesting place". Among my dreams that night, quoted in full in Chapter 10, was "a tape recording of a powerful masculine entity" saying, "I come to you from the same energy that exists beyond death" and "The whole history of Christendom began with a person who overcame death."

This emphasis on the idea "from death, new life" would seem to confirm that my 1976-1978 dreams involving elder males rising from apparent death were, in part, alluding to the same higher-level masculine entity: (1) my grandfather, who looked me in the eye and asked for "a place to stay" (i.e. to be reborn); (2) the old Indian who pressed my third eye before I encountered the unknown woman (Kelly) and overwhelming energy of the "snowy natural bridge"; and (3) my teacher who opened his eyes and excitedly exclaimed "S/He's come?!"[70N] Remembering, too, Kelly's medicine wheel vision of the Indian man with eagle feathers, it is satisfying to note that the Lakota Sioux holy man Black Elk, like other Native peoples, spoke of spirit guides as "grandfathers".[71]

In our first week of living on the power point, I have my own exceedingly compressed but powerful dream about eagles, which gathers together many of these currents and takes them a step further. Explanations of its importance will come in time from Moita as well as from the higher masculine entity – who, on his third and longest appearance by far, finally supplies us with a name. First the dream, then the session.

"The Eagles Are Coming!" dream
David (age 31) / November 3-7, 1978

I am viewing this double-page layout in Life *magazine: an exquisite, massive eagle, perched with wings outspread, facing toward me, so as to reveal within it many intertwining dimensions of smaller eagles and human faces, moving in and out of the blue sky and white clouds beyond. In large letters, the caption reads: "THE EAGLES ARE COMING!"*

Moita Session #39 (Kelly and David / November 7, 1978)

(As we discuss our dream workshop to be given in a month's time, Moita suggests we give her some "practice" by asking a question about a dream. I have not yet hit upon a proper dream to query when Moita announces:)

MOITA: We need to change levels... (*a long silence as the energy grows considerably, altering our vision*) Words are more difficult here.

David: You looked a little more like an old man for a while.

MOITA: *Did* I now! Do you think that was me? Someone else?

David: I thought it was someone else.

MOITA: Ah! You were looking for that contact. There was a possibility, but he had a message: "Revelations are not easily come by. They must be worked for."

David: Did he mean *now* – worked for *now*?

MOITA: I hesitate to try to interpret his meanings. But it may be the meaning behind the words has to do with expecting a revelation to happen, or to come down, to show itself or be revealed (?), rather than going up to it, discovering it. It is perhaps like not wanting to give candy to a baby. Some of the things I have said about "rules" may apply here, so far as the rules we have governing our reality.

There was thought of your dream – flying through the air – the dream that brought him the first time. (*i.e. "Election of New Pope" dream*)

David: My thought, or his?

MOITA: Maybe some of *both*. It seemed to have something to do with his comment.

(I close my eyes and try raising my energy to the level where this being resides. I have no specific question in mind. However, as I get more and more into this space, Kelly senses a discussion going on between Moita and the masculine entity as to whether or not the contact will be permitted. She hears the words, "YOUR DESIRE FOR FULFILMENT IS WHY I HAVE COME." Once again Kelly's heart centre is activated and I see the old man again on Kelly's face.)

(This time I feel a tremendous heat pouring into me as well. I sense the top of my head opening and extending upward – truly a fulfilling experience. Feeling a more intimate participant this time, I find it easier to converse – my words reflecting my regard for this state of clarity.)

???:   A QUESTION?

David:	I'll try.
???:	YOU HAVE REQUESTED ME.
David:	I sought to come into contact for its own sake as much as anything. *(pause)*
???:	AND NOW THAT CONTACT IS HERE? *(long silence)*
David:	I sought the contact in order to live more from this level at other times – to help others find themselves.
???:	NOBLE AIMS. YOU MUST HAVE THE COURAGE TO FULFIL THEM – AND THAT WILL NOT COME FROM *US*. THAT IS *YOURS*, AND YOURS ALONE. *(pause)*
	I AM OPEN TO A QUESTION, IF ONE IS FORTHCOMING.
David:	Would you care to speak about the meaning of "The Eagles Are Coming!"?
???:	IT IS ON THE ARRIVAL OF THE HIGH ONES ON YOUR PLANE.
David:	Incarnated beings, or beings like you?
???:	BOTH. BUT THE DREAM WAS OF BEINGS LIKE ME, ALTHOUGH I AM NOT ONE OF THE HIGH ONES. *(pause)* THERE ARE MANY OTHERS. THEY HAVE BEEN AWAY FOR A TIME THROUGH THIS PERIOD OF MAN'S DEVELOPMENT. AND THEY HAVE RETURNED THROUGH THIS TRANSITION TO HELP ADD THEIR ENERGY.
David:	Can you say anything of what your links are to us?
???:	EVERYONE IS LINKED, SINCE WE ALL COME FROM THE SAME SOURCE.
David:	But why are you speaking to us rather than someone else?
???:	WHY NOT? *(I laugh softly)* YOU SHALL FIND OUT LATER. BUT YOU WISH A NAME, DO YOU?
David:	It would be good, if you are willing.
???:	I HAVE BEEN TRYING TO DECIDE WHICH ONE TO USE, BECAUSE I HAVE MANY – AND NONE. BUT FOR OUR PURPOSES AND THIS PARTICULAR COMMUNICATION, YOU MAY CALL ME "AMAR", IF YOU WISH. IT WILL IDENTIFY ME FOR YOU.
David:	Thank you.
AMAR:	YOU ARE WELCOME. YOU WILL SEE ME AGAIN.

(During the above exchange, Kelly is feeling something being ripped up from inside, accompanied by the words, "DON'T WORRY. THIS WON'T HURT." She also sees me change into a completely different person, and becomes quite panic-stricken at the possibility of finding herself somewhere else, with someone else, than when she started the session! She feels like someone has "just dropped out the whole bottom of the universe". After his last words, Amar closes Kelly's eyes and Moita returns to soothe her fears.)

❧   ❧   ❧

We will return to the content of Amar's words on this day, after some further experiences of the openings required. We hold our next session one week later as

Kelly's menstrual period coincides with the Full Moon rising in the crisp November air outside our window – a double reason for her being extremely open this night. As it happens, this will be the occasion Amar chooses to do some heavy-duty "purification" of both the power point and our own psyches.

Moita/Amar Session #42A (Kelly and David / November 14, 1978)

(During a long silence, I find it difficult to continue gazing at Moita because of the intensity of the experience, and so close my eyes. Somewhere in my mind, I wonder about changing levels. Kelly begins to feel a very strong tingling up and down her spine and hears herself asking, in near panic, "What is that?!" Then the tingling rapidly grows stronger and stronger, and her perception changes drastically. When I do open my eyes, there before me in Kelly's body sits Amar. To her, the intensity of his presence is unlike any other time, for she feels on the brink of madness.)

(Amar and I gaze silently at each other for a while. Then:)

AMAR: What are you getting from this?

David: I really don't know. *(silence)*

AMAR: Much still needs to be brought out before I can stay long.

David: What sorts of things do you mean?

AMAR: Guilts, suppressions, blindnesses. *(pause)* Purification of this place is not complete.

(A period of silence, during which Kelly undergoes a terrifying experience. She feels, however, that Amar has her mind firmly wrapped up, holding it in place right on the edge of insanity, at the point just before her reality crumbles away to nothingness and leaves her no reference points. There is the persistent thought that this is dangerous, and that Amar is quite aware of what Kelly is experiencing. He holds her there as long as he feels it is possible for her to take it. When the decision is reached that she has had enough, he leaves quite abruptly.)

AMAR: I must go.

(Amar closes Kelly's eyes, as she frantically searches for the familiar feel of Moita's energy. When Moita arrives, Kelly calms down somewhat, but is still quite distressed over what has just transpired. She feels she was not ready for this experience, while I don't realize the full extent of what she has endured.)

MOITA: *(quite softly)* I'm sorry that came without warning.

David: Why are you sorry?

MOITA: From this end, it was a very heavy experience...

David: I closed my eyes partly because it was getting hard to keep looking at you – and it was even harder when I *opened* my eyes!

MOITA: Because I was not there? *(with a laugh)*

David: I felt strange about staring at you. Maybe there were some of the things he mentioned involved. *(perhaps guilts, and so on?)*

MOITA: He was afraid of doing damage. His energy was very *strong*. *(pause)* I am acting as an interlude to soothe someone else. She went through a great deal in that experience. I am glad my energy serves some useful purpose.

David: I'm wondering how her expression will change when you leave.

MOITA: So does she! *(pause)* It won't be quite as traumatic as it *could* have been. *(pause)* This is a useful energy and has many healing properties. There is a possibility that you may gain some insight into what happened here when you dream, since you are so open in your sleeping state... Be calm.

(Moita leaves and Kelly returns. In a while, she gives this description:)

Kelly: I couldn't figure out why I was so scared all of a sudden. The feeling was like being stoned on acid. Everything was different; the whole room changed. I was close to seeing things I didn't want to see – thought-forms like from my freak-out years ago. I could feel them, sense them, but the last thing I wanted was to see them.

You disappeared. Sometimes your face was just black. Then other times there were these really vague features that I really couldn't see well – except the horns on the top of your head! Then I felt like I was in danger, and he thought it too at the time. For a while there was a fear that he wasn't going to leave. His energy was so strong, I knew all of a sudden that if he didn't want to leave there wouldn't be anything I could do about it. It was like being on the edge of madness. It seemed to have something to do with the Full Moon, too – the difference in the energy.

It's no wonder that he said that about purification. That's what I was feeling at the time: "Boy, there's a lot of stuff in here!" Boy, am I ever spaced out. I feel like somebody just put me through the wringer.

❧   ❧   ❧

Thus, Amar doing his part to "help" Kelly and me confront the negativity within ourselves and the power point. As described in Chapter 10, my "Communicate Through Top of Head" dream a few days later – in which Peter and Eileen Caddy winced at the aura of a man who performed psychic feats but ended up a weeping child – provided some of the "insight" Moita predicted might come to me. The surfacing of these feelings was doubtless also designed to prepare Kelly and me for an unexpected event that was swiftly approaching (coming in Chapter 12).

One month later, though, a more constructive, forward-looking mood will take hold.

Moita/Amar Session #50 (Kelly and David / December 13, 1978)

David: Concerning our work, can you give us any idea whether more than a few people might be open to being in workshops and other groups with us this winter?

MOITA: You must be inventive! If you cannot create your community in the city as a nourishing centre as well as a sustaining one, you will have much difficulty when you leave it. Many will look to you as an example, to see if it is true that those things that you teach and speak of can actually be done in an everyday kind of way. If you would give your life to the spirit, there is a time to *start*. *(long pause)*

David: Hmm. You've given me a lot to think about.

MOITA: Gotcha! *(pause)* There is also much to *do*!... Are you making your purposes clearer?

David: What you said *helped*, at least in encouraging me to feel that we can act on them sooner than I may have thought.

MOITA: Time has been compressed for a reason. There is not much *time*, on your level, to prepare for the things that will follow. There is much that needs doing.

David: How far have we gone in purifying the energy of this point?

MOITA: I am able to come through more clearly than I was able when you first came. Your growing will not stop, nor the purifying of the point. A point such as this has to be *continually* purified.

(During a long silence, Kelly's eyes close and Amar comes. Kelly will say later that listening to Amar is "like being in outer space", since everything said can be seen from many, many different points of view. We both are aware of this, as we are of the tingling energy flowing through our linked hands as he speaks.)

AMAR: This place is doing well. Has your perception changed?

David: Yes. My *hands* can feel the difference. And more and more of me can.

AMAR: You learn much more through contact than you do through your thoughts. You are fitting yourself into your own scheme. *(pause)*

(Both of us take this as criticism about our "thoughts", as if our "scheme" were a selfish or short-sighted one, and Amar knows it. Only a second before he speaks again – after observing our reactions – does he let Kelly learn otherwise.)

AMAR: It is a good scheme. And you have planned it well.

David: I thought at first you meant we had to give up our "scheme".

AMAR: So I perceived. If you were here to give up your scheme, you would have refused to come! – thereby giving it up. *(pause)*

(Obviously, then, Amar was referring to our souls' plan for this life.)

David: How does your level differ from Moita's?

AMAR: We have more things to take care of, and are not always available because of it. Our concerns range in both directions – not just here – and so, we are not as easy to reach. *(pause)* Does that satisfy?

(Kelly feels like she is looking out over "a vast place". She senses our level as the ground, Moita's level interacting with us and also acting as an intermediary between ours and Amar's further up, and Amar in turn overlighting Moita's level and very consciously interacting with yet higher ones. It seems somewhat difficult for him to relate to our concerns because his range is so much broader.)

(While conversing with Amar, I am experiencing a very clear visual and feeling sense of being in a higher space: a closeness and directness and warmth of contact, yet also a detached clarity, as if I am focused much more deeply than my surface, thinking self. I feel enfolded quite literally in another level of being that is simultaneously my own deep centre.)

David: *This whole experience* is very satisfying.

AMAR: That is perhaps a good indication, of many things. I speak to you like a dream. You will find many levels to my words. *(pause)* Until another time.

(Kelly's eyes close and Moita returns in a buoyant mood.)
MOITA: You are having a good night!

৯৯   ৯৯   ৯৯

Feeling that perhaps we have now passed our test in relation to the power point, we turn our attention outwards again, as Moita encouraged us to do. Asked at the end of a session about inviting friends in for "attunements" in the New Year, Moita is enthusiastic.

Moita Session #53 (Kelly and David / December 19, 1978)
David: Do you have any comment on having people here to experience the energy of this place, and communication with you and others perhaps?
MOITA: It sounds like a delightful idea!
David: Mm-hmm! *(laughing)*
MOITA: It would be good to put this point to use. Otherwise, why have you moved here?! *(pause; by now, our limbs are growing stiff)* You grow weary. Have a good Christmas!
David: Thank you. *(pause)* We think of you when we look at our angel. *(Kelly's large, homemade angel atop our Christmas tree)*
MOITA: I am flattered! *(laughter)* That *is*, of course, what they are! Good night.

৯৯   ৯৯   ৯৯

Thus begin the gatherings and workshops offered in our home from January to August of 1979, the sessions from which fill many of these pages. Our second such gathering includes a session, while relatively sparse in words, that leaves no doubt about the power of the place and of a group of well-attuned friends. There is an added "highlight" as well that probably "stems" from the power point and requires a short introduction.

I decide to give Kelly a gift of plants for her birthday on January 17th. The flower shop delivers the two I pick out – including a large Dieffenbachia – and I place them in our bedroom as a surprise for her. We both really appreciate the change in atmosphere they bring to the room. But lying in bed that evening while I'm downstairs, Kelly notices something more.

Just as with closed eyes she often can pick up information about the energy of people (for example, in her healing work), Kelly now "sees" the figure of a little old man, about 18 inches high, chubby and bearded, dressed in brown and green with pointed shoes and a floppy, pointed hat. He is running around the foot of our bed. Quite surprised, she asks the figure who he is and where he came from. In answer, a scene pops into her mind showing the Dieffenbacchia being carried out of the flower shop into a delivery van, and this little fairy wondering whether he should hop off and abandon his "home" but deciding to stay with the plant wherever it is going.

The traditional image borne by this nature spirit is of course co-created, like

Moita's image, by his energy interacting with a human mind. He will also be seen as a light-form among the plant's large, curling leaves. We are delighted with our guest and try to make him feel welcome. The innocent little fellow does seem to need to hide in embarrassment, however, when we two grow amorous in bed!

Our gathering of friends comes three nights later on the 20th. When Eileen and Gerald arrive and Kelly shares the tale of our visitor, Gerald is brought up short: he just recently said he couldn't believe in fairies himself until he met someone who actually saw them. We show him the Dieffenbacchia, which we have placed in the living room for the occasion.

Eventually seven of us hold the session – actually, a joint session with Moita and Gerald's entity – that gives rise to these comments afterward. Their value is much multiplied for Kelly and me due to our recent isolation from other acquaintances and what we know of the power point's less-than-mellow condition when we first arrived. Eileen begins by detailing images she was getting of the second house they own, which they wish to transform – and with Neale and Roy's help, will eventually turn – into a centre of New Age awareness in Regina.

Eileen: There was a great party going on – people everywhere, *happy*. All the windows were full of life, people everywhere on the balconies... *(She goes on to describe seeing auras around Kelly and another participant.)* Oh, I've always wanted to see auras!
Gerald: I was getting flushes... My body wanted to be tingling like on an LSD trip.
Neale: Yes, I felt that happening to me, too.
Nick: My legs started twitching. *(Nick is Neale's teenage son.)*
Neale: Yes, I was aware of that in you. It's due to the high energy. It's too much and you want to shake it out.
Eileen: Oh, I felt energy, but it was *so* beautiful. It was *calm*!
Neale: It was very calm and beautiful. Yeah, I pretty well just stopped thinking. There was just a very beautiful feeling.

Then Kelly reveals one of the things she has been seeing this evening. Arriving late, Neale placed himself on the floor right in front of the Dieffenbacchia. He left his toque on his head, as he sometimes does – accenting his playful, elfin personality, which Loria once attributed to an actual existence in that form by another part of his soul. During the session, Kelly was watching the fairy hop from his leaf and joyfully dance around on Neale's toque, playing with the ball on top!

                ❧   ❧   ❧

We should return now to Amar's interpretation of my "Eagles Are Coming!" dream. We can understand "the High Ones" as supra-physical entities whose being includes intertwined dimensions of lesser entities and human souls. The direct influence of those highest levels has been absent from humanity for a long period of development, but is now returning at this time of transition.

Amar identifies himself not among the High Ones but, consistent with images received by Kelly, as an intermediary between those higher spiritual reaches and entities like Moita concerned with guiding human beings in or between their lives on the physical plane. "Our concerns range in both directions," he says – i.e. between the High Ones and their "created Earth". This is how the symbolism of a new pope, a "bridge builder", is so appropriate – though it has been said by many, including Rudolf Steiner, that all of us are in the same relative position: we each are a bridge between matter and spirit. Amar does, however, give a sense for what a rung many steps up on Jacob's Ladder must be like: an awesome clarity and intentness; austerity softened with ironic humour; consummate mastery of energy relationships; the imperatives of harmonizing with the total pattern of existence, held constantly within one's gaze through never-wavering self-knowledge.

Many questions, though, remain unanswered. One stems from Ruth's unsuccessful attempt, in the fall of 1977, to receive a more masculine or androgynous entity that Loria identified as her own greater self.[72] What of Loria's prophecy that the entity "bearing the same relation to [her] as [she] to [us]" would someday speak to us? The ends toward which all this is leading – the actual changes portended for human experience with the arrival of the High Ones – are certainly other questions that swirl through one's thoughts about this chapter, and the chapter to come.

ও   ও   ও

For now, we conclude with excerpts from two more January 1979 sessions – sessions linked through significant phrasings evoking the mystery of a threshold. A few evenings before the gathering last described, recording difficulties forced us to reconstruct a session with Moita alone. The order of her statements may be altered, but the following make the most lasting impression.

Moita Session #59 (Kelly and David / January 16, 1978)
MOITA: I see the planet covered with the tides of change. There are times in the Earth's history when a single word, spoken at the right time and place, can change the face of the world. This is one of those times. You must choose your words with care. I, too, must weigh my words.

(Kelly, with eyes closed, is seeing the Earth with many currents of energy flowing around its surface, and then altering their pattern in an instantaneous chain reaction.)

MOITA: Your bodies are changing. Your other senses, senses that have lain dormant, are beginning to wake up.
David: How can we help this process?
MOITA: By letting us come through you, by experiencing those changes. We are preparing you for the inevitable shock of seeing us as we really *are*. Some will say this is manipulation. We call it cooperation with what you yourselves are seeking.

ও   ও   ও

A week after the January 20th gathering, a New Moon arrives. Kelly suspects Amar may appear in the less overwhelming energy of this phase compared to his last two Full Moon appearances. (Actually, it turns out to be Moita who demonstrates the great range of her own powerful presence this night, as given in a future chapter.)

Moita/Amar Session #63 (Kelly and David / January 26, 1979)

MOITA: What did you think of your gathering?

David: I was really excited to hear them speak of all the energy that they were feeling, and that we were feeling too.

MOITA: Confirms your own observations? It is nice not always to be alone in believing what you see. Your tides are turning, too. *(pause)*

David: Away from aloneness?

MOITA: You have passed through a stage of learning to stand by yourself, and gained a great deal of strength where you needed it. You will fluctuate back and forth for a while, but you are bringing yourself out of your solitude. You have laid a good foundation. Without it, you could not *build...*

(Later, a long silence ushers in Amar.)

AMAR: Greetings.

David: Greetings.

AMAR: Things are different again! There are many changes happening... This place has grown more bright since I was here last. You are becoming more effective in how you handle your energy. *(pause)* Are these changes disruptive to you?

David: No.

AMAR: You are learning how to flow?

David: I must be.

AMAR: I am pleased we have so much to offer each other in the coming changes of our worlds. *(pause)* There is a great deal of energy bent in this direction. If we have our way, things will go more smoothly.

David: I'm not sure what you meant by "this direction" (?).

AMAR: Aren't you?

David: Well, as you said, your words can have so many levels, and I suppose you mean all of them.

AMAR: I suppose I do.

David: All right.

AMAR: The overall view is seen in the individual – at least, from where I am. I see how connected things are, which is one reason for the different levels to the words I choose to speak. Soon, perhaps, you shall see me as I *am*. The day of reckoning is not far off – ...at least, how *I* view time.

ॐ   ॐ   ॐ

_____

Chapter 12

REFINING FIRES, CLEANSING WINDS

There are many changes coming in energy. There are more of us available, because your energy is different and we are not as far as we once were from here. Man has gone through a period of development where he has drifted away from [his source]. He has gone into forgetfulness, and he thinks the world is asleep and does not remember. Now man is beginning to come back up out of that forgetfulness, and remember where he came from and who he is, and know what he can do. So, in a change like that, the world will wake up.

The Earth has had many faces. The one that you have on it now will not last much longer. You see, as each of you are in this age striving to find out who you are as an individual expression of being, so is your Earth finding out who it is. It, too, has a soul. There will be much chaos, but it need not be as chaotic as it might. We are trying to soften it as much as possible, to be here as closely as possible and add our energy to these changes and to each of you.

– Moita (December 2, 1978)

As this Part began, I summarized Moita's cosmology by saying "the energy of the universe manifests on many levels of reality, ranging from the outermost physical to the very centre of being within each of us." Similarly, a growing number of scientists agree the Earth itself is a living being encompassing many subtly interacting "spheres": lithosphere (minerals), hydrosphere (water in any form), biosphere (plants, animals and humans), atmosphere (air and contents) and magnetosphere (geomagnetic field and charged particles), plus further dimensions grouped as the psychosphere or noosphere (fields of mind and spirit). Especially since each possesses a form of consciousness, we are linked to all spheres more intimately than we know. This is the Gaia hypothesis: "we do not live on the Earth, but in it" as "one pulsing, resonating organism."[73N]

Only with such a multi-levelled model of reality will the energy interactions between "mind" and "matter" explored in this chapter make sense. For the central idea is that the gap in energy between spirit and body is narrowing. As a result, subtler forces, and the laws governing them, will become more apparent and effective, bringing about the dissolution of outmoded physical, social, economic, political, religious and intellectual structures. Of course, die-hard proponents of these structures, caught in a world of opposites of their own making, will fight all the harder as they feel their grip threatened.

All six Earth "spheres" are involved in this chapter, as the focusing of our entities' energies may affect the entire planet. Dramatic physical earth changes are potentially included, starkly reflecting humanity's choices and heralding the end of an era – as some of us may have experienced before. Throughout, Moita leaves no doubt as to our own responsibility: "It will be you who makes the difference, whether it is a destructive or a constructive change."

❧   ❧   ❧

One event stands out in these years of communications, impressing us with the immediacy and unavoidability of change, with the power of our higher levels to alter the world we so often take for granted. A few days before the dream workshop from which the opening quotes were taken, a unique session crystallizes much of what we will come to feel about the years ahead and the inner preparations they will require.

Receptivity to energy, openness to the unconscious, acceptance of one's shadow side, a willingness to explore different levels of awareness – including particularly one's reincarnational history – here these move beyond personal choices, becoming contributions to a quickening of the human spirit and its Earth. Life deeply lived is a rising spiral of transformation, integrating the best of the old at each new stage of evolution. An energy change is a step on this spiral, refining fires and cleansing winds following in its wake.

Riding the bus home from work on the afternoon of November 27, 1978, Kelly becomes aware of Moita's insistent presence. The feeling recurs after supper, with the message that there is a "conflict" involving our regularly scheduled session the following night – that "something is up". So we decide to hold a session tonight, and use the occasion to experiment with putting Kelly into trance. It's an idea we've been considering for a while as a way of reducing her conscious involvement in the communications. This chapter tells what transpires this unusual evening of November 27th, interspersed with related material received in earlier and later sessions.

———————MOITA SESSION: NOVEMBER 27, 1978———————

(During my trance induction, Kelly feels a spinning inside her head similar to a previous experience with sodium pentothal in which her mind "went all tingly before passing out". The "passing out" doesn't happen in this case, nor was it our intention. I begin by expressing my uncertainty how deeply into trance Kelly has gone.)

David: You're still pretty present, aren't you, Kelly (?).

MOITA: No, she is not... She has gone far, but not completely... For the moment, this will do.

David: Can you explain how you can have a conflict in our time?

MOITA: Something's happening tomorrow.

David: To us?

MOITA: To *everyone*...

David: On the planet?

MOITA: You have it.

David: Will everyone know it?

MOITA: No. But it requires my *complete presence*. This [communication] does not require *all* of my presence. It requires a small focus. There have not been many things in a long while that have required all of me.

David: And, I assume, others as well?

MOITA: I am not the only one.

David: All of *many*, if it's the whole planet... Do we need to be ready for it?

MOITA: You are about as ready as you can be. But it will be a great shift in energy. It's not the first one, nor the last. There will be another before Christmastime... The last such change as this was thought of as "the end of the world".

David: Hmm!

MOITA: Perhaps it *was*...

❧   ❧   ❧

Two and a half years before, the leader of a Canadian metaphysical organization publicly announced that she had received guidance regarding "the end of the world as we know it" on June 13, 1976. It is hardly surprising the prophecy was widely misunderstood, and ridiculed, since this leader was reportedly expecting a massive UFO landing on that date. The concept of an energy change, a raising of the vibrational level, makes much better sense to us, however, especially as we reflect on our own experiences that June.

During the second week of June 1976, while teaching a psychology course at university, I encountered an unprecedented level of narrow-minded distrust toward new ideas and experiences on the part of certain students (one the wife of a fundamentalist preacher), while others greeted the same enthusiastically. The widening split in the class, which eventually reached the university administration, led me to abandon the security of an institution in favour of initiating Sunseed workshops with Ruth. The changes begun in June also soon led to my involvement with Ruth in the Loria communications, which prepared me in turn for Moita.

For Kelly, June 13, 1976 was the occasion of an extended, unusually bitter argument with her husband Phil. Her mouth opened and for the first time let loose the many dissatisfactions she had felt during their time together. The fighting energy seemed to have a life of its own, nearly taking them over. With hindsight, what emerged this day may be seen as the beginning of the end to their relationship two years later, when Kelly and I would meet.

Thus, by fall 1978, we have come to accept that June 13, 1976 did represent some sort of changeover from one cycle or level to another. And as soon as we have time to digest Moita's surprising announcement, Kelly and I will see in our recent separation from Ruth and other friends dynamics similar to those of June 1976. We will also understand more fully the source of that urgency that has spurred us on to make necessary though seemingly impossible changes in our lives during the past year.

——————MOITA SESSION: NOVEMBER 27, 1978——————

David: Will there be any outward manifestations of this [energy change] at the time?

MOITA: That has not yet been determined. It's possible, but the outward manifestations may take more time to show. Time is still fluid.

David: Could any of those outward manifestations be on the physical level, significantly affecting the Earth?

MOITA: Yes.

(Kelly receives the impression here that weather changes may be the first area that will show the effects.)

David: Do you have any suggestions of things we might do tomorrow?

MOITA: *Be aware!*

David: Can you say anything about the quality of the change?

MOITA: It is one of the changes towards our level – and being that kind of change, will cause some unrest and more growth, some unwanted. As this comes closer, and as our levels become more in tune, there will be *many* manifestations, for those who have eyes to see them.

David: Will the other change before Christmas be of the same nature?

MOITA: Yes. It is a season of changes.

ڡ   ڡ   ڡ

Moita's last three words are the title of a book of spiritual communications received by the Associations of the Light Morning group during 1973-1974 in Virginia Beach, Virginia.[74] Subtitled "A psychic interpretation of the coming changes in, on and about the earth, and the corresponding transformations within man", *Season of Changes* was the founding document for what has become a small "New Age" community near Copper Hill, Virginia. Kelly and I will pay a visit to this community in the spring of 1979 and share with its members a memorable session, to be given in a future chapter.

Views very similar to those received through the A.L.M. group and other well-known psychics regarding coming "earth changes" were expressed by Moita in the summer of 1978.

Moita Session #21 (Kelly, Scott, Laura / August 12, 1978)

Scott: We've heard a lot of talk about the coming changes in the world, the evolution of man. Can you give us more information on this "New Age" everyone keeps talking about?

MOITA: Which aspect do you wish me to discuss?

Scott: Well, how about the physical changes?

MOITA: There is coming a time soon when many changes, physical and spiritual, will make themselves known. There is a chance – albeit a small chance – that some of these physical changes could be avoided if many people can change their level of consciousness in enough time.

Scott: I had thought the changes would be slow in coming.

MOITA: Things will be changing much more rapidly than many suppose.

Scott: Will it be in our lifetimes, then?

MOITA: If things go as they have been, yes, it will.

Scott: Are you saying these physical changes are going to be on the scale of a disaster? Earthquakes and such, and wide-scale death and destruction?

MOITA: It is quite possible, so far as things look at the moment. This is *one* of the reasons many people such as yourselves have the desire to get out of the cities. The destruction will, of course, be greatest in the cities.

Laura: I always thought that the cities would destroy themselves: that by their being cooped up and jammed together – their seething anger and violence – they would sort of burn themselves out, collapse from within.

MOITA: Let me explain the connection to you in this way. Each time you have a thought, whether you never have that thought again, you have created a thought-form. And each thought-form has its own particular energy. If you take many people [as in a city] who are sending out negative thoughts, you can see that soon you would have many negative thought-forms building up.

So, just as in an earthquake, when pressure builds up in the Earth until the Earth must shift in order to relieve that pressure, or as in a volcano in the same way, so also with the thought-forms. When they build to such an intensity, something must shift, change, in order to release that pressure.

Laura: *(smiling broadly)* I see. Yes, I see.

MOITA: I can see that you do. You are growing clear, so you are right in what you see.

Laura: So, our friend who has such beautiful energy, whom you can't feel negative around, he is putting out strong positive thought-forms?

MOITA: Yes. And if you have enough people together putting out strong positive thought-forms, they would negate the negative forms; and so, the built-up pressure would be released in a different way.

◈   ◈   ◈

At our dream workshop the weekend following the November 27th session, Moita will elaborate on this theme.

Moita Session #48 (Kelly, David, workshop group / December 3, 1978)

David: Can you tell us how the energy change you spoke of earlier this week is proceeding?

MOITA: It will be individuals more than the planet structure itself right now; that is what this particular energy change was about. That was why I said that the physical manifestations had not been decided upon – if they would occur or not. Those are building up, but they are not ready yet to be released. They will be released by all of you as you become more aware of yourselves.

These pressures that are there are from the different ways you have hidden from different things, the thoughts you have pushed away and thought were gone from you. But they have their own reality; and so, they mass together and form great pressures that eventually affect your physical reality when there are too many of them. And there are too many of them now.

As you grow out of this mass and come above it, this will release some of the pressure. Some of the thoughts will be cleansed or purified. The more who rise above, the less who will be left behind and the less physical manifestations will occur.

๛ ๛ ๛

————MOITA SESSION: NOVEMBER 27, 1978————

MOITA: ...You will be able to feel us more strongly afterwards, too.

David: *(pause)* I think I'm glad.

MOITA: It will prove difficult for many. One of the things we bring, our gift, is the inability to hide – from each other, and from yourself. It is not a gift many will take kindly...

David: I wonder if a certain 900 people *(the People's Temple group, led by Jim Jones, in Jonestown, Guyana)* wanted to leave the Earth before this change happened – or at least, their leader [did].[75N] It may be unrelated.

MOITA: Maybe not. That will be one of the things that may become more prevalent during these changes. As people become less able to hide, they will mistakenly think that there is escape from that condition through death. Those who are here to hide will wish to continue as long as possible in that condition...

(Moita recently said hiding was "one of the biggest reasons for reincarnation" – i.e. trying to shield oneself by taking a body. But conversely, if physical life no longer works as well for hiding, death might seem to be an "out".)

MOITA: What do you think would happen if everyone could read everyone else's thoughts?

David: Confusion at first – a confusion of reactions.

MOITA: It is the only place man [thinks he can] hide, is in his thoughts – trying to shield them from his fellows and from himself. It would be rather difficult to run a government if everyone *knew* when you were lying.

David: And so, this is part of the change that will be starting to happen (?).

MOITA: Part of it is already started. And it is more devastating at this time of year than it was in the spring. *(Moita calls winter "the season of within" – when inner events are more intense.)*

You may have more energy to work with now. If you can go through this change with the right attunement, you will gain an extra source of energy – one you have not been able to tap as well as you might. As in all things, it takes a great deal of awareness, or of consciousness, to do that.

But our worlds are coming closer together; the gap is not as great. A long cycle is coming to a close, and we are preparing for the arrival of some *others*, to return.

(In the long silence that follows, Kelly sees my face change into about 20 different people – including my "old man" image – flashing back and forth so fast she can't keep up, although each one is clear and recognized as the same sequence of faces is then repeated.)

MOITA: You are getting a small taste of some of the differences.

(An even longer silence follows, as the growing intensity of the energy exchange makes me feel I must finally close my eyes. At one point, Kelly says later, Moita is "so much here" that her body is shaking. Near the end, Moita closes Kelly's physical eyes and "shoots a whole bunch of energy into [her] third eye" to activate it further.)

MOITA: And what do you think?... You know who it is we await?

David: Who is "we"? The three of us? The whole planet? I'm not sure on what level you mean.

MOITA: All of *us*. *You* will not wait consciously, most of you.

David: You mean the "High Ones"?

MOITA: The very same.

(See the discussion in our November 7th session in Chapter 11 in response to a question about my "Eagles Are Coming!" dream. Moita now returns to that dream, clearly linking it to the reincarnational faces Kelly has just seen.)

MOITA: One of the things that was significant in your dream was the showing of the different faces, and how one life blended into another and one being blended into another. That is a message of remembering: one of the changes we bring.

People will remember in different degrees, depending on where they are in their development. Some will just remember this life, and all of the things they have conveniently tried to forget. Others will remember many lives, and see how they all flow together to make one. There is much you have learned and do not know you forgot.

જી જી જી

A month and a half later Moita will present a very apt image for the process of remembering other lives and use it to convey the dangers – therefore, the delicacy – of this evolutionary step forward.

Moita Session #57 (Kelly, David, Jill, Paul / January 11, 1979)

MOITA: It is as if, when you are born, a spirit comes and places a bud inside your head. Inside this bud is the memory of *you*, of all those things you cannot remember while you are alive. When the time comes, at the right time in your development, this bud opens in a slow and natural way. And it causes no pain when it opens... Without that safety valve, without that inner controller or timekeeper, things can run amok. Things can happen [in a disorderly way], not in proper time or sequence.

(Later Kelly is aware of Moita "switching things around" in both her own and Jill's head, as she prepares to describe a life they once shared. Moita then comments, "I am opening buds!")

જી જી જી

Moita Session #58 (Kelly, David, Jill, Paul / January 13, 1979)

Jill: Can you explain more fully the purpose of the bud as a safety valve?

MOITA: One of the reasons why that safety valve is placed in the first place – to keep a person from remembering too soon – is so that [you] will have a strong basis for grounding in the life that [you are] in at the time. Without this valve, and without this grounding that is necessary before an opening, [you] can be lost in [your] own time and lose where it is that [you exist as yourself. Your] "now" becomes too fluid.

On our level this does not pose a problem. For us, time *is* fluid; it is acceptable that way. But for you, you are focused in a very small part of the universe, and in order to learn what you need to learn you must be able to stay focused. Some people who are in [mental] institutions are there because they have lost their focus. They exist in many time-lines at the same time, and are very difficult to communicate with, unless you happen to catch them when they are on the same one as you!...

The bud is there to prevent your remembering, to control when it happens. It is the timer of the event. It does not open until you are ready in all other ways first.

Jill: If the bud is meant to open at death, what are we doing messing around opening up the bud now? Is that not dangerous?

MOITA: We are entering a New Age of [humanity. You have] gone through a long period of not being able to remember who [you are] or where [you] came from. One of the first changes that will happen is that these buds will begin to open for the many – not just for the few, as it has been in the past. In order to be a full creature, a full being, a total spirit in body, you must be able to know and have access to the great experience that you have all had.

There is much wisdom and much learning and much love in your past – besides the pain and the sorrow and the heartache. You have learned much from all of these, and bring to this life a small piece of that total. As do each of you, you decide which part of all that you have learned you will be born with: those innate characteristics that none have taught you and none can take away – your basic personality.

Those who remember their pasts while they still live in a body will not have to forget, the next time they are born. There will be no need for buds.

Jill: I'm wondering how I'd know when I'm ready. I have such a terror of this that I'm questioning if I'm ready, and I guess I'm fearful of opening too soon.

(Jill's "terror" is matched by a strong fascination, tempting her into a psychic involvement with Darryl that does hold danger for her. The continuation of that story, which is her reason for consulting Moita, will appear in a later chapter.)

MOITA: The only thing you can do is learn to give yourself up to your higher self, who knows when you are ready and knows what situations will help you realize the time is right. You must be able to touch your innermost being. Let it lead you where it will.

Moita's prediction about future generations reiterates statements previously made. On August 12, 1978, she said: "Soon [people] will not be born forgetting [their] past, but remembering it. There will not have to be that forgetfulness. There will be no waste or loss." Another appears below.

Moita Session #11 (Kelly and Roy / July 11, 1978)

MOITA: This life is an important one for many. In this life those who remember consciously their own beginnings will be born next time as fully aware entities. In this way, the world as you know it will change through the children. *(i.e. who will actually be ourselves, reincarnated)*

It is in the essence of the entity being born – what it has been and known before – that determines whether or not it is born in full consciousness. This is not the doing of the parents. It is, however, their responsibility to keep the lines open, once it is realized they are there.

❧   ❧   ❧

As individuals recover their personal pasts, we will collectively be recovering what humanity left behind when we descended into forgetfulness long, long ago. What is it we have forgotten? And why was the descent into forgetfulness necessary?

Kelly and I have our own poignant experience to draw upon here, as revealed in her second past-life regression with my guidance, undertaken on September 15, 1978. It was an exceedingly ancient life – and our first – which we call our "Earth and Sun" incarnation, presumably lived in the "lost continent" of Mu, or Lemuria.[76] In that existence we attempted in vain to share with others an awareness of the oneness of all life, which was being forgotten. We spent the last years of that incarnation immersing ourselves in that unity so as to be able more easily to remember it in times to come.

The major part of this regression transcript will be presented in a coming chapter. However, below are excerpts from the end of that session which are not given elsewhere. In these passages lies another sense of "bridge" that relates to many reunions in this age.

Hypersentience Session #27B (Kelly; David, guiding / September 15, 1978)

Kelly: The world was different then. There was a clearer understanding of what man was, and there was a greater freedom of expression and ability to communicate with others. There was no jealousy and there was no hate. There also was no selfishness.

The texture of our thoughts was not the same as it is now. To us it would seem alien. Thoughts had not the same form; and so it is difficult to express, in terms we can understand, exactly what went on. There was more a sense of unity with all and a lack of identification of the self. And so, there was more flow than purpose. There was in a sense no purpose at all to existence, except to exist.

And so, the bridge between...lives is to connect that sense of flow and unity with a sense of self and purpose until they are in balance, because both ways [alone] lead to destruction. The world could not stay the way it was; it had to change and learn that it was also self as well as whole.

(A period of silence ensues as Kelly begins to experience a very highly concentrated energy along her forehead. It fades in and out, but is strongest when this presence speaks the following through her. The imagery accompanying the voice is masculine. It seems very hard on Kelly's body, all of which goes rigid while "he" speaks.)

???:   I have come. *(long pause)* I have come to bring back that which was lost. *(pause)* I am not dead. I exist even as you exist in this time, but I exist in another time period – and this will be brief. It takes much energy to project forward. It is far easier to go in the other direction.

Our worlds will meet, and it is the meeting of these worlds that has to do with all these changes. *(long pause)* Do not despair. Things are as they should be. We will still be here, in your future. You can learn to draw on us – your strength...

(As this presence withdraws, Moita comes through to answer questions from me for the rest of the session.)

MOITA: The world and time are a unit and it all moves together. Those things which happen before and after affect what is happening now. And so, by connecting yourself to your past and drawing on that energy you had in that different world that existed before, and by pulling that energy along with you, it is that energy of differentness that has a great deal to do with the changing of the universe *now*. But it is changing in a different way. It is not becoming the way it *was*, or *is*, because all that goes between impresses itself on the energy. And so, you create something new and different. You bring the two concepts together as one.

It is the world discovering itself. And those who do not wish to discover who they are do not look forward to the changing of the world, because when the world changes to what it *is* and people recognize it, it will be unavoidable – for *all*. There will be no one left who cannot see the world, unlike that first incarnation when the descent began. You all have forgotten the world, but the world has not forgotten *you*.

သ   သ   သ

This prophecy about the changing of the world, which none who remain will be able to avoid, recalls Moita's message from perhaps a week before about the lasting energy effects of our sessions.

Moita Session #27A (Kelly and David / early September 1978)

MOITA: Some will feel you are living in a fairy-tale existence. What is happening here is you are changing the structure of your universe. You are not alone in this. All around the world there are others who are also changing their universe. In the future, not too far distant, these pockets of alternate reality that are being created will stretch up and cross [the] pockets of "normalcy" to connect [with each other]. Those pockets of "normalcy" will be absorbed, and the entire face of the world will change.

(Kelly will later describe the image she is receiving: "Small pockets of shifting reality are scattered all over the world. Above the Earth's atmosphere is a horizontal band of energy. As the pockets grow and solidify, shafts of light or energy are sent [upward]. When they all meet with the band of energy, they grow sideways and fill all the spaces between.")

MOITA: In that moment, you could no more confuse those people that are still living between the changes of the universe than if you took them and placed them on an alien planet.

I am explaining this to you so you will have a clearer understanding of what you are doing. There will be feats that can be accomplished in this new universe that others would not have believed possible. It is important that you realize you must build this reality slowly and carefully, so it will have a strong foundation.

છ   છ   છ

————————MOITA SESSION: NOVEMBER 27, 1978————————

MOITA: Do you think you are ready?

David: Hmm. I know I welcome this change happening, but I cannot yet know how I will experience it. As you say, I'm probably as ready as I can be.

MOITA: You don't have any time to get more ready, not at least for tomorrow. Of course, [these changes] will be gradual – not instant. No need to throw the world into insanity. That would not be very nice of us, to come too close too soon. You see, for us this is a great responsibility, and one we have given much energy to.

David: What will you be doing tomorrow?

MOITA: Drawing near. Our whole sphere of influence will be drawing close. As the friction that you experience when you let us come close to you has a hardness, our drawing close *en masse* has a similar effect on many people. We have to gauge these things as delicately as we can, so the most good is done with the least ill...

Did you expect anything to happen quite so soon?

David: No. But then, that's been the pattern the last while. Things have happened sooner.

MOITA: Time is compressed.

David: I guess the more it compresses, the more it gets like what it is for *you.*

MOITA: Where it ceases to exist, in a sense?

David: Mm-hmm... You've given us quite a bit tonight.

MOITA: I know. And I am preparing to leave.

David: Will it be easy enough for Kelly to come back?

MOITA: Oh yes. I will assist. She is still drifting in and out... She almost astral-projected, and she went very far. As with anything, it takes practice. I hope you experience the change tomorrow in a loving way. You see, we are willing to go more than half.

David: We will try to feel you approaching.

MOITA: We shall see what tomorrow brings on the road to awareness. *(softly)* And we will shine our love on you all. Good night.

David: Good night.

(Moita closes Kelly's eyes. When Kelly returns, she continues to feel very spaced-out and very tired, so we go to bed soon after. We dream much this night.)

 co   co   co

Kelly feels the change around two or three o'clock the next afternoon, as she looks up from her office work and senses an indefinable "differentness". Throughout the 28th, as I try to "be aware!" of Moita's level coming closer to ours, the sense of invisible dimensions undergirding and shining through our world of matter and routine becomes quite vivid. It seems that translucency has always been there, but its existence will be more and more difficult for everyone to ignore as time goes on.

Moita Session #49 (Kelly and David / December 10, 1978)

(This is a spur-of-the-moment session, partly to seek clues why I have had such a bad cold the entire past week. Kelly's back has been ailing her recently as well. As we meditate this Sunday evening, Kelly feels Moita around but is unsure she will speak. Moita tells her she has to make her mind as blank as possible. Several times, Kelly experiences herself being "pulled up" and wiped clean of thoughts.)

David: Hello again.

MOITA: Much has happened!

David: How much of it are we aware of?

MOITA: Your *body* is aware of it.

David: Yes. What's going on? Is this connected to the message Kelly got from you on Friday?

MOITA: About the distance?

David: Yes.

MOITA: Yes.

(This past Friday, December 8th, during her weekly visit with our psychology professor friend Spencer, Kelly attempted to let Moita through. She got the feeling of standing on the edge of nothing – a black abyss. Moita let her know she was there, but was late in coming because she was having trouble getting across the distance that lay between them. Then Kelly saw images of an earthquake and a tidal wave, and

understood that the distance had been expected as a natural consequence of the energy change on November 28th, a kind of psychic rebound effect.)

MOITA: I am very far away.

David: How soon will you be coming closer again?

MOITA: It has reversed itself. It is temporary. Think of this as the reaction your body would have to a change of water.

David: When was the point of reversal? Was that on Friday – the point of furthest distance?

MOITA: That was when it was most noticeable.

David: I'm tempted to hypothesize about that being the midpoint between the two energy changes you spoke of. But it may not be that predictable.

MOITA: Maybe not. All things seem to have a consequence – even here. They are not undertaken lightly.

David: We still seem to feel your energy strongly, like last night... *(i.e. much energy and many images experienced lying in bed before sleep)*

MOITA: There are differences. *This* kind of close is not the same. Much of *that* is amplification...through the [power] point. The energy will be felt first in these places – the return – and these points don't lose contact quite as much, either. We chose the winter this time, though, because much of the world here sleeps.

David: I'm not sure what you're saying.

MOITA: It was only fair! The last was in the spring *(June 13, 1976)*, and this same kind of [rebound effect] happened. When the world is more awake, and it is growing and the life is coming up, this energy is missed – many patterns are disrupted.

David: So, being sick is more just a reaction to the fact of change itself, a readjustment?

MOITA: Fairly accurately. There are *always* things that need to be worked on... If you would learn to be a healer, you must learn to heal yourself. Although the body reacts to the differences in the energy, your mind amplifies the reaction. *(long silence)* How do you feel now?

David: You certainly seem very present!

MOITA: I am sliding in on the sly. It is just more work! And I am showing you something.

(Another long silence. While Kelly sees faces changing so fast on me she cannot keep up, I am having perhaps the clearest experience of altered perception I have yet had during these sessions. Each split second, Moita's face is jumping closer/larger or more distant/smaller, against the filigree of our wallpaper that continually moves and reverses its figure/ground. Different facial expressions arise between these jumps, the clearest being that of a middle-aged Eskimo woman filled with a wise, friendly warmth and beauty. The significance of this face that Moita shows me will be made clear later on.)

MOITA: It is enough for now. I must leave.

David: Thank you for coming.

MOITA: I shall see you later. Good night.

(Kelly says afterward, "Everything was starting to change just before Moita said she had to leave. I was starting to get into a space like when Amar was here. That's why she left. It'll take a while till all of me gets back, from a long way away.")

꙾   ꙾   ꙾

On Monday evening, December 18th, as Kelly sits at our kitchen table, she suddenly looks around and exclaims again that "Everything is different!" Checking the calendar, we discover today is exactly 10 days since the nadir of the retreat following the first energy change on November 28th, 10 days before that. Thus, if the second energy change has occurred today, it would fit my hypothesis that the first retreat would be at the midpoint between the two changes. The next night brings confirmation.

Moita Session #53 (Kelly and David / December 19, 1978)

(Earlier in the day, Kelly was hearing "Today is Tuesday" repeating in her head – Moita's scheduled night.)

MOITA: It is a good time to find out many things.

David: Things to ask about or things to experience?

MOITA: Things to ask. *(pause)* Our retreat will begin again soon. It was planned to coincide with the coming of the Sun. *(i.e. the winter solstice – thus acknowledging Kelly's recognition last night of the second energy change)* That will help to compensate and soften it.

           We did not wish many to be aware of this change – on a conscious level – or warned. *(Moita is referring to these two changes together.)* Have you not wondered why, with such a change as this, there have not been more who have been aware of it?

David: It was hard to know how many *were*.

MOITA: The last time it was not hard. It was *very* obvious. *(i.e. the public predictions regarding June 13, 1976)*

David: Why the difference this time?

MOITA: The first time we wished many people to be told that there *was* a change coming – to have it in their thoughts and to look for it – so when the change came they would perhaps notice something of what was intended. But this time the change comes during the time of the year when people are already inward and more in touch and in tune with changes. To tell them – a great many of them – that this was coming would make them *too* aware, and in some cases might cause more dramatic results than were wished for. We do not wish these to be surface changes.

David: Are we likely to run across others who were told?

MOITA: There were certainly some who would have noticed, and possibly some who were told before rather than after. Many will only see this in retrospect. Some may never be aware at all...

           Many pressures are put on others at this time – physical and material as well as spiritual. Those with eyes to see can see these all channeling individual energy into certain directions until a choice needs to be made, or something is seen, a breakthrough...

[These are] world changes and pressures that everyone is experiencing, and that [are] pushing each of you – or *all* of you – in certain directions, into dissatisfied places where new searchings are necessary to stay grounded.

It is a preparation for change. Change is not accepted if one is content. And some of these pressures are put on by the level changes *we* are making, as well – making people *more* discontent than they were before with physical life.

᪣ ᪣ ᪣

Certainly many, many inhabitants of the modern world are feeling discontented with their lives, and this *is* pushing us to make changes – sometimes destructive, but at times also creative: taking more responsibility for a more independent, whole, satisfying way of life. Just as with psychedelic experience, one can imagine the delicacy necessary in raising our energy level so as to induce a maximum of new awareness and a minimum of blind reactivity.

As expected, among the physical manifestations of the rising energies are drastic weather abnormalities that make headlines throughout the world during the winter and spring of 1979. For our part, the prairies experience virtually six months of winter. Yet our winter is not as severe, even catastrophic, as it is elsewhere in North America and Europe, where wide areas are ravaged by storm after record storm.

Moita Session #72 (Kelly, David, workshop group / February 24, 1979)
MOITA: The changes that we created with the energy difference took a while to manifest themselves on a physical level, and are still taking their time doing other things.

David: And all this severe winter that many places are experiencing is one form of that, I imagine.

MOITA: One way to disrupt a pattern, or one pattern that is easily disrupted? Since you create your weather, why do you wish it to be cold? You are extending your "time of within".

᪣ ᪣ ᪣

When the long-awaited spring does finally arrive, there come also floods, tornadoes, volcanic eruptions, and massive earthquakes in various parts of the world. There are a few precisely timed instances of earthquake reported earlier in the winter, however, which demonstrate ever so clearly the power of human thoughts and emotions to release physical change – though no one publicly admits to noticing.

Moita Session #63 (Kelly and David / January 26, 1979)
David: I heard on the news today another instance of an earthquake happening

right at a key moment on the social scene. The morning that the Pope *(John Paul II)* was to arrive on his tumultuous visit to the Dominican Republic, there was an earthquake there – just as the day the Shah was exiled from Iran there was a quake in that country.

(And a couple of days after this, another quake occurs in Mexico when the Pope arrives there!)

MOITA: How interesting! As things accelerate, perhaps people will put two and two together – and see their immediacy...

Thought is a powerful thing. Some of these changes will be [from] those who are punishing themselves, adding their kind of energy to it. If you could all learn that one lesson – that self-punishment is not the way to learn – there would be much less physical rumblings.

ھ   ھ   ھ

Thus our thoughts (including, Moita says, the ones we believe we have hidden) have "immediacy" in affecting our level of consciousness, our personal lives, our society, world events, even the physical structure of our planet. An Edgar Cayce study group proves an appropriate occasion for some last comments on this subject.

Moita Session #81 (Kelly, David, group members / March 29, 1979)

MOITA: Try to see yourself as we do, and accept your own beauty.

Jane: It's nice to have somebody love us no matter what we do. It's a good thing to remember.

MOITA: You are your own worst judge.

Jane: Maybe we expect more of ourselves than others.

MOITA: That is because you think you know your own feelings better than anyone else.

Jane: But I don't, huh? Oh, I thought I was keeping it all secret. No secrets from you, huh?

MOITA: No secrets from you, either.

Jane: That's rather cryptic! *(laughing)*

MOITA: There are no such things as secrets. You see, in a body you feel you can hide: you can hide your thoughts from others, and your failings. But the time for hiding will not be long.

Jane: Hmm. I'm getting rid of this body real quick? *(laughing)*

MOITA: Our energy is coming closer, and with it we will destroy that apparent ability [to hide]. There is much unrest over this.

Jane: Over your coming closer?

MOITA: Yes. Many people think that by leaving this world they can continue hiding longer, when they find they cannot hide here as long as they thought...

Doris: You said that you were coming closer to us. What did you mean by that, and where are you coming from?

MOITA: Seeing your world as a ball, with you upon it in physical form, ours co-exists...in the same space, ...but it is separated by vibrations of energy. Your world is in the process of raising its energy level..., if you will, and we are reaching down to touch it, so that our worlds will come closer together. It is closing a gap. It is *all* of us who exist in this universe being able to touch each other and work together towards creating a more whole humanity.

It is hard to express in words. By coming here, I give you a taste of what it will be like for our world to touch yours, because here in this world at this moment our worlds are touching.

∽   ∽   ∽

Illustrative Dream

It is probably the day before this dream that I see what's reported as a 6-mile-high thundercloud over Regina. That is the stimulus for this mega-dramatic depiction of an energy change such as one might imagine heralding the "New Age". The lightning is symbolic – or so I hope! – of rising spiritual energy levels; whether jolts of this magnitude will eventually be involved remains to be seen. The effect of fearful thoughts versus open acceptance is also depicted, and a lucid, unifying awe that grows from this shift in consciousness.

"Shaking of the Firmament" dream
David (age 28) / September 12, 1975

My father, brother and I are out on a neighbourhood street as a very strange thunderstorm develops. Lightning repeatedly strikes near us, along with spouts of rain. I seem more concerned about being hit than the others and wish we'd hurry to get home. But I also share a vague feeling that being out in this storm is a good thing – that by absorbing some of its energy, we may lessen its fury.

Periodically now, some very powerful bolts strike very close to me, causing me to shake all over. Alternately, at times, I watch myself being shaken, as if I'm another person. I hear conversation that this person is mentally laying himself open to the storm, making these jolts more likely, through fearful expectations that they will continue in his direction. Someone suggests that this person's thoughts affect his heart and/or brain, creating an energy field that attracts the lightning.

All have assumed that the lightning is a danger for the man (myself). But now I develop an opposite intuition: maybe it has only seemed dangerous because of my fearful resistance to its strangeness; perhaps it is even beneficial! I am also gradually realizing that this situation, or this reality, is very unlike normal waking life.

I have taken shelter by a building but now walk out into the open. My changed attitude appears to make the repeated lightning strikes even more powerful – shaking the earth now for everyone to feel, not just myself.

Perceiving this effect, I decide I am right to continue. No longer resisted, the shaking and rumbling we hear is not bad, just terribly awe-inspiring and overwhelming. I cry, "Nothing like this has ever happened to me before!"

Realizing that the more power the better, I call out with acceptance, "All right! All right!" The crowd in turn picks up the chant. We look up and see a massive thundercloud overarching our position and just now covering the sun. But the sun shines out from the dark cloud, its rays visible against blue sky, making a very impressive sight. The shakings and rumblings are so total now that I cry out, "My God! My God!" I feel some heavenly event is on the verge of breaking forth and unfolding before our eyes.

Someone near me points to the cloud above and hints of a Biblical quotation by calling, "Have you heard of the firmament shaking?" Another may say, or we simply now understand, that this cloud is in the process of descending to Earth and represents the new divine energies entering the world of humanity.

In the exultation of the moment – the sense that "This is really it" – I feel at one with the people gathered round. I express this feeling by saying, "Brother responds to brother responds to brother . . ." And as I do so, I become fully lucid that this is a dream. Continuing the words, I see circling before me many, many faces of people intermingled with everyday scenes. I feel that all these persons and things of the world go together to make a One.

Then the swirl of images becomes dimmer and more mundane, as I wake up to subsiding rushes of energy through my overheated body.

Chapter 13

IT IS NOT EASY BEING A GROUP

You know or have heard that when people form a group, their forming of the group – their placing their energy together as one – creates a new being of all of them. Have you not wondered what happens once this new being has been created, and where it goes from there when the group splits apart?
– Moita

Another mystery invites exploration now: Loria's prophecy in August 1977[77] that an "interesting" feature of the spiritually oriented community we hope to create will be communication with its "group entity". But this detective story will involve other mysteries as well, as Kelly and I strive during our first year to learn more about our histories and natures as souls, and about our purpose in meeting now again. Eventually, through this and later chapters, a "family tree" on subtler levels will emerge, illustrating the possibilities for unseen "relatives" in the lives of us all.

How, truly, are Kelly and I related to each other and to our group? What interactions lie in our as yet unknown past to shape the quality of energy we experience together and with others in this life? And how are we and they related to Loria, to Moita and to Amar? Curiously, the tale of our group's "heritage"[78N] begins to unfold through a series of strange words first uttered by Ruth during a Loria session in the fall of 1976. Here, too, lie the deeper origins of our goal of "New Age community", of which Loria will speak so eloquently in December of that year.[79]

In an unprecedented session with Alex, a friend and body therapist, on October 21, 1976, Ruth – to her surprise and initial embarrassment – receives 16 words in an unknown language. She needs much reassurance from me before she is willing to let them come (spellings approximate):

chelia valadis anawarama loruma saliarom evacum charimamo kisla estarana shalam maravanis ilearum chembra kul naramata fragonis

Alex later reports that, at hearing the very first words, he "spaces right out" – a reaction he has come to recognize as his way of avoiding something he fears to face. He is just emerging from this spaceyness when Loria turns to him and asks, "Do you recognize what has just been said?" He can only whisper no.

Loria then explains that Alex's presence has put Ruth in touch with an extremely ancient life they once shared, as healers and telepathically linked siblings/lovers, in a civilization twice as old as Atlantis. The strange words are from the language they spoke in that life. Loria says it is a dialect closely related to, and descended from, the original language brought to Earth by those spiritual teachers called Speakers in the Seth material (Roberts 1972, 1975).

It is not the first occasion one of us has received words in a strange language, however. Before the Loria communications began, in my "Inner Onto the Outer" dream of February 1976,[80N] I was powerfully affected when my psychotherapist told a class of students, "I have read in the *Kolna*, an ancient mythological account" – provoking my sudden entry into lucid dream consciousness. But stimulated by our October 21st session, I will soon receive three more dreams containing similar foreign words.

Two weeks later, on November 6th, I dream that Ruth and I are part of a living myth or fairytale. A voice announces that we now have "the power to evoke"[81N] in association with *"nirimata"*[82N] – a word almost identical to one Ruth received earlier. I also sense a connection to the farmhouse where Ellen and Tom, two psychology student friends of ours, are living.

A further phrase related to the ancient language comes nine days afterward in a long dream replete with archetypal symbols (too intricate to repeat here). There are clear prefigurings of Kelly as well in this dream, closely linked to the mountain peak in my "Snowy Natural Bridge" dream in September 1977 and our trip to the Arrow Mountain medicine wheel the following June.[83N] But since I haven't met her yet, filling in for Kelly here is Terri, a graduate student with whom I was once close, sharing our deep interest in Jungian psychology. This is how the dream ends.

"Healing Tea at Mountain Lake" dream excerpt
David (age 29) / November 15, 1976

As the group continues our hike into the mountains, Terri and I walk together up a steep, snow-covered slope to the shore of a high-altitude lake. She sits down to fix some tea for use in healing her injured foot or ankle. I sit down to join her, a little unsure of myself in this setting. She is feeling very warm and loving towards me, however, and we exchange a hug or kiss.

Then Terri motions for me to sit closer, with our hands on each other's crossed legs. We talk for a while, looking into each other's eyes, as in our best moments together or when I told her recently about Loria. Both in response to our closeness and the tea she is sipping, Terri feels her wound being healed. And to express this, she says softly but movingly, "Keno meno verro me!"

I feel out of my depth hearing the unknown words, but sense a definite message of healing, warmth, happiness, closeness, wholeness. Accepting what empathy and intuition are telling me, I allow the energy of the moment to encircle me in a rich embrace, as I wake.

It is clear to me this early dream is weaving together experiences one to two years in my future. And I find it fascinating the two of us do not merely gaze here at a snowy mountain culminating in a natural bridge – we actually do the hiking and arrive at a high-altitude lake. As well, the deep, healing gladness of our sitting and talking together will certainly match Kelly's and my feelings on top of Arrow Mountain. Significant also, then, must be the phrase of unknown origin ("*Keno meno verro me!*") embodying "healing, warmth, happiness, closeness, wholeness."

Just four days later, the final dream in this sequence brings still more connections.

"Shansa National Park" dream
David (age 29) / November 19, 1976

Ruth and I are talking about our Loria communications with a dark-skinned, bearded poet dressed in East Indian garb. As we show him a transcript containing the ancient language, he instantly responds to "nirimata" as being significant for him in some mysterious way. He keeps talking about it while we remain silent – waiting to see what he will come up with but sensing the meaning is non-verbal. I feel this so strongly that I have to go off a way by myself, kneeling in the grass. This is in a meadow, surrounded by woods on all sides except one, which overlooks the sea.

I think of Krishnamurti, and edge my way into how he must have felt as a young man undergoing his passionate enlightenment experiences: the great yearning for an intensely direct perception of reality, of instantaneous beauty around and within him. I look up through tree branches to the sky – penetrating, immersing myself, becoming one with "what is".

Virtually in tears, I speak words that express or at least point to this vivid, here/now participation. I see a bubble floating through the air, iridescent in the sun. It moves over the meadow, all eyes upon it, and then bursts against a leaf at the edge of the clearing. Its momentary existence embodies the truth of which I have been speaking.

Then Ruth and I are walking along a path by a stream. A large sign at the trailhead shows a Japanese man's face and mirrored images of snow-covered mountains with a rosy orange and gold sunset and curls of white clouds. The name of this national park appears in capital letters at the bottom: "SHANSA." Next I see the scenery of our walk in picture form. I am aware of having shifted the location of the brook so that it flows over the path in a waterfall, intensifying the experience of water for passers-by.

Then I am an observer/participant in a Japanese commune. Members are learning to meet all their needs at home in an accepting, harmonious atmosphere with music soon to be in the air.

What, then, lies behind such foreign words as *"shansa"*? Might the experiential quality of these dreams reflect an era from which remnants of that language are now returning? From this last dream alone, one can imagine a non-verbal, timeless mysticism closer to traditional Oriental and East Indian cultures, an intense delving into nature, poetry and music, bringing all these together to create harmonious community. Previous dreams add qualities of healing, love, joy and "imaginative recreation".

Four days later, I wonder if Loria can enlighten us about the strange words coming through me as well as Ruth. During a session with a small workshop group on November 23, 1976, I end a period of silent energy exchange by saying, in a near-whisper, "No words". Loria nods in agreement, and another silence follows, until I add: "Except perhaps *"Keno meno verro me!"* Later Loria turns to me and begins the story behind my dreams.

She tells how long ago I was a poet whose words in this language were like music that lifted the spirits of those who heard them. The place, she says, was a very ancient and beautiful city of light situated on the land mass that became Atlantis, but before that civilization arose. (Its present location, though the Earth has changed considerably in the meantime, could roughly be northern Spain.[84N]) The city was named Musili (pronounced Myu–SEE–lee), and its crystal towers and walls were erected and maintained with a highly advanced art/science of sound.

Cities like this one, though quite real in their own time, have come down to us through the ages, Loria says, as myth and fairytale. Life in Musili was very happy and harmonious and healing, for all things were done with awareness of their place within the whole. It is obviously, then, the energy of this other time that my dreams have been tapping.

This leads directly to the very powerful session with two other couples on December 3, 1976 – a session, as it turns out, held at that very farmhouse of Tom and Ellen, true to the premonition in my "Power of Evocation" dream. Loria first gives her forceful, eloquent message about our founding a community in this life, beginning "You all recognize things must change..."[85] Later one of us asks about our reincarnational connections as a group. Loria leans Ruth back in her chair, closes her eyes, and begins speaking in a soft voice once again of Musili – that city of vibrant colours, jewels and dreams; of art and science made one.

I as a poet, she says, was among those in Musili creating the mythological foundations of the age to follow. Ruth was a maker of tapestries, interwoven with music and jewels. Others of us present were among the sculptors, dancers, composers, engineers, seers and teachers who opened themselves to the readily available life-energy and manifested their visions in creative form.

Then Loria gives the fateful message, which I paraphrase as follows:

LORIA: Other people among your present friends, and those you are yet to meet, were also part of your circle in Musili. Your encountering each other now flows from a promise made then that you would carry forward that happiness and beauty into a time of fear and doubt and forgetting.

(slowly and tenderly) Within your hearts and dreams, all of you remember the joy of that existence – the energy of which you were a part, that you may draw upon even now to transmute this world's darkness and emptiness into light and love.

It is not unusual intuitively to recognize persons you have known in previous lives. Your immediate response to those you meet from Musili, however, will have a strength and richness far beyond the usual.

જ   જ   જ

I have not forgotten the questions raised at the beginning of this chapter. We have simply been exploring a few of the mysteries with which their unravelling is connected, of which there are quite a few.

We come then to the spring of 1977, when Ruth and I have the pleasure of meeting Dr. Elisabeth Kübler-Ross in her Chicago living room. We do not think to ask whether Elisabeth too is from Musili, though it would not surprise us, given the immediate warmth and healing vitality she radiates in her work and friendships. But it is Elisabeth who first confides to us that any group working closely together has an entity serving as its guiding spirit.[86] As mentioned, Loria will soon be elaborating on this statement about group entities with particular reference to our group's past lives together and to the community.

During the 1977 summer, we meet more people who are engaged in psychic communications and are identified as being from Musili. On July 24th, Russ, Kitty and Bob are told by their entity Topling that Musili was founded by part of a larger group that had previously lived in Asia Minor. Naturally, Ruth and I are most intrigued to hear that another entity has not only mentioned Musili, but enlarged upon what little we ourselves know.

The next day Loria responds to our questions by saying this larger group left the ancient Asia Minor city of Kyrionis (Keer-ee-OH-nis), splitting in two directions: one moving west to found Musili, and the other moving east to the area that became the Himalayas. Many members of the group then lived later incarnations in the two resulting civilizations as they matured. The groups split to develop two complementary approaches to reality – the creative/intellectual and the earthy/intuitive – and are only now, in this transitional period, joining themselves and their polar tendencies together once more.

On August 9th, before Ruth and I add a westward trip to our year's travels, Loria recalls for a small group of friends Elisabeth's remark about group oversouls. She clarifies for us that while they have contrasting functions, individual and group entities are not basically different, both working across time and space to help people grow. She emphasizes that just as these entities guide more than one group, so an individual may be linked with more than one group entity through his or her associations in life. Loria adds provocatively that our envisioned community will emerge through recognition of and communication with its group entity.

Then on August 18, 1977, Ruth and I share a Loria session with four West Coast friends. Meeting together with candlelight playing upon the walls of a chalet-style log home, we are surprised to learn that the six of us sat around the bonfire outside Kyrionis the night before the two groups separated. Loria asks us all to go within ourselves, inviting images of that scene.

One of our friends receives this striking memory: "It's like an old movie in which the frames are flickering past, sometimes too fast to be able to see. I finally recognize an old hag with this big, bulbous nose and an old scarf over her head. She's turning, walking away, then looking back and sort of scowling, and shuffling on. Then I have the feeling that this is a person we didn't let into the group – some old hag who was travelling down the road. She's looking back at us, scowling, and I'm saying, 'Well, it's all right with *me*, but . . .'"

Later the same person asks of Loria, "Are you the sole guiding spirit for the people that were around that fire?" She says no, explaining that she is not a group entity. The story of the group that divided in two directions from Kyrionis, Loria goes on, involved three of these group entities. As the participants in that life reconnect, contact will be restored with these entities – but that time is still in the future.

∾   ∾   ∾

Early in the new year, about a dozen of our Regina circle of friends begin meeting to see what comes next – and whether founding an intentional community may be part of that. Some disagreements arise, however, reflecting the differing tendencies and personalities within the group. For our part, we are disappointed to realize only a few are seriously attracted to forming a community. We have come to take the latter goal for granted, feeling that with enough faith all obstacles can be overcome.

Then during a January 27th gathering, as we sit together in meditation, three of us – Roy, Eileen and Gerald – become aware of a strong presence that is encouraging us to merge our energies in a group effort. The three describe their experience of this masculine presence and suggest we together attempt some immediate task – such as psychically causing a pendulum to swing. This we try, without success: partly because some, myself included, have not grasped the real purpose behind it.

After that night, the group divides roughly in two: Roy, Eileen, Gerald and others beginning work on hypnotic regression (an inward turn), and Ruth and I meeting with Dale, Helen and others to discuss community (an outward turn). Both groups will encounter further internal differences while pursuing these choices. Thus, by springtime 1978 – the time Loria predicted would be right to begin work toward community – and despite having identified about two dozen of our acquaintances as members of the Kyrionis group and its successors – we all seem to be going in different directions. There is no shared focus, no central gathering point.

Nevertheless, for Ruth and me at least, Loria's messages on the advent of "our community" lend a sense of destiny to our initiation of such a project. First, it now seems, a core group will coalesce intuitively; later, before many years pass, a larger number will join us. Thus we cast ourselves as the secure, authoritative nucleus around which future community will grow, with the assumed backing of Loria and the prophesied group entity. In holding to that assumption, however, we hardly suspect genuine progress toward our goal will first demand drastic changes in our perceptions of ourselves, of our relationship, and of our imagined positions within the community.

Of course, if we were to think about it at all, the memory of the hag's rejection by some of those around the bonfire outside Kyrionis *is* strikingly out of keeping with Musili's perfection – suggesting "human reality" does lurk somewhere within these past-life connections. The doubts, disagreements and differences among our group – hardly surprising as individuals try to be honest about feelings and realistic about possibilities – also suggest fulfilment of our community dream is far from inevitable. Even so, another returning "old friend" is about to appear in our lives in furtherance of that goal, if not quite as Ruth and I have envisioned it.

∾   ∾   ∾

Meanwhile, the transcripts of the various sessions concerning Kyrionis, Musili and its Himalayan region counterpart are printed in the February 1978 issue of *Rays*. It is there that Kelly, a newcomer to Ruth's and my work, reads the story for the first time. At Loria's mention of the group entity, she experiences her head expanding with a tingling rush – "like an LSD revelation". Soon after, Kelly begins attending the "Starflower" meditation group, which Ruth and I began the previous year as an outgrowth of our Sunseed workshops. During Kelly's first meditation, the scene of that last night outside Kyrionis, including the incident with the hag, comes back quite spontaneously and unexpectedly – and Kelly knows she was there too.

Then at the first meeting of our spring workshop, Ruth intuitively recognizes Kelly as being from Musili. Since childhood, Kelly has remembered a past life as an "aura dancer", and during a workshop fantasy journey she realizes the magical environment for her dance – walls of sound and colour – belonged to that same legendary city.

By the time the workshop ends in June, and Moita begins speaking through Kelly, positive past-life associations between her and other members of our group are surfacing as well. For example, Moita reveals that the healing sessions Kelly, Betty and Arnold begin to offer each other have a reincarnational background. With Alex, too, there is a healing link, going far back into Egypt. A close association between Roy and Kelly is also becoming obvious on several levels. But there is a less comfortable life of which Kelly becomes aware with Ruth: as priestesses serving Isis in ancient Egypt, involving many conflicts, a definite sense of jealousy and competition. Moita later confirms this past emotional background surrounding the two women – although, she adds, the competitiveness was not felt equally.

The many, strongly positive connections between Kelly and myself, though, are making the greatest impact, inwardly and outwardly. Some group members begin to fear that our openings may upset what previously seemed the secure foundation of Ruth's and my partnership and work with Loria. In mid-July, a number of our friends agree to attend an evening gathering which I hope may release these tensions. If Moita and Loria can speak at the same session, I think it may create a breakthrough. What happens instead, unfortunately, prefigures everything that is to follow. But more importantly, on this night Moita begins to reveal her purpose and her ties to all present.

As this gathering has been described before,[87] only the most telling excerpts will be given here. As we all meditate, Kelly becomes aware of silent interactions, primarily among herself and Ruth and their higher levels. She senses an agreement that first Loria and then Moita will speak, but Loria never manages to come through. Kelly is then aware of Moita and Loria agreeing what will be said to bring about as much change as possible in the shortest time. Below is the crux of Moita's message on this, her first opportunity to speak to group members through Kelly.

Moita Session #9 (Kelly, David, Alex, Ruth, Dale, Helen, Roy, Arnold, Betty / July 15, 1978)

MOITA: ...It has been a long time. Some of the people that come together in this, the stronger the energy becomes. Each of you add my part . . . back. *(pause)*

...Each of you adds something special to each other – like all parts of the same whole that have finally come together in the same place and connected to make a whole again. *(very long pause)*

David: I'm not sensing the energy coming together in as much of a whole as I feel it should or could be.

MOITA: That takes time. The pieces must balance each other out first. I see the whole on a different plane than this, and the workings towards making it on this level will take some more time – *your* time. In a sense, it is already accomplished...

Unfortunately, about half the group, including Ruth and those sitting near her, fail even to hear Moita's words this night – and if they would have heard them, or read the transcript, it may have made little difference. That Moita alone should have spoken through Kelly, and not Loria through Ruth, proves unsettling for many. Amid the interpersonal turmoil that, rather than eased, is amplified by this gathering, little thought is given to why Moita addressed herself to the group as a whole and uttered that awkward little sentence, "Each of you add my part . . . back."

But it takes the first session with Kelly's husband Phil to reveal a key piece of the puzzle. It is an early glimpse as well into the way Moita's nature has reflected itself in Kelly's personality and relationships.

<u>Moita Session #13B (Kelly and Phil / July 26, 1978)</u>

Phil: Why do I feel as if I am a part of Kelly so much, that we are so closely connected?

MOITA: She is a part of everyone. This is one of her greatest difficulties in this life. Sometimes she becomes so immersed in another's thoughts and personality that she loses touch with herself for a while. It is also her greatest gift, and the source for much confusion. It is not easy to be a group.

Another point Moita made at the July 15th gathering, and which she repeats in a July 27th session with Ruth and me, is that her energy is constantly changing. Further, her energy must be shared at sessions by everyone linking hands, lest Kelly's body shake from the excess. She goes on to say that the Plains Indian concept of the Medicine Wheel as a mirror of people's differing energies aptly fits her own being and purpose. The analogy of the Medicine Wheel helps me see the concreteness of "being a group" – of being many-sided. This being the nature of Moita's energy, it makes sense that it is too much for Kelly's body to hold without being shared.

During the remainder of the summer and early fall of 1978, Moita urges various ones of us to be open with others about our feelings, to make ourselves vulnerable rather than hide in fear of rejection. To do that, we have first to become clear within about our goals and purposes. As Kelly records from Moita in her journal during August, "All of us are confronting choices which may or may not lead to our participation in this community. We are discovering that there are different conceptions of what it should be."

By October, those discoveries have negated my attempts at a cooperative or communal solution involving several of us and our children. There follows my separation from Ruth (and in effect, from those other friends who share her view), and the beginning of Kelly's and my years of living together. On October 18th, the day Ruth announces her plan to stay away indefinitely, Moita tells us: "You know by now that not all things that are hoped for come to pass, and that each of you has his own choice to make. There is nothing set out before you. Many things may yet change."

৯৯   ৯৯   ৯৯

Moita's equanimity through all these (to us, very upsetting) events reflects her extraordinarily wide-ranging perspective. She demonstrates this when asked about psychic research by one of the founders of Findhorn Community – Dorothy Maclean, a Canadian who returned to live in Toronto. Having heard of Dorothy's explorations into the group spirit she calls "the soul of Canada" – at a time of rising Quebec nationalism and separatism – we wonder how the work of a national entity might compare to Moita's in helping our own group work through its divisions.[88N]

Moita Session #39 (Kelly and David / November 7, 1978)

David: We've heard that Dorothy Maclean has been giving workshops on what she refers to as "the soul of Canada". Can you say what that might mean? I'm also wondering about the significance of nations or groups or couples separating, in the context of a coming New Age.

MOITA: You know, as each group is formed, an entity is formed with it. Each city has its own entity, and so does each country: the entity that makes up all of the people that are in it. As the people change, the entity changes as well.

Taking what is happening in Canada on a simpler level, you can bring it right back down to you and what is happening to you two, in that you are in a sense apparently separating from other people in your group because you are trying to be yourself. In many ways, Quebec is doing the same thing, and the rest of the country does not like the idea of the individuality of the province making itself known, disrupting their concept of what should be and making changes.

That is on one level what is happening. Of course, at the other end, a person trying to be [their self] has to discover how to do it without totally disrupting everything around..., which is a very tricky thing.

The situation proves itself as a tool for the whole country to look and examine its own values and what it is doing and why. And so, at that, it is of course a sign of the New Age coming, because that is what the New Age is all about: trying to discover who you are, and being yourself without losing your integrity and without destroying things around you, but working with a sense of cooperation and love. *(pause)*

So it all weaves together in a very comprehensive whole. You have here before you the universe in a grain of sand. *(pause)* There certainly is a great reluctance to accept change on this plane.

David: Some people's energies seem especially attuned to being faster, and others slower or more grounded.

MOITA: It is important to have the grounding factor, because those who move too fast sometimes miss many things as they go along. But [the fast ones'] energy is there to try to bring the others up and make them change. Once they recognize the fact that they have no choice and they *must* change, usually their changes are very sound and very strong. But they are very reluctant, so it takes a great deal of energy on the part of those who go faster to bring these changes about. But the ones who are grounded are there to try to slow the fast ones down. So it works both ways – as always. It is a never-ending series of tensions.

David: Is the same thing true on your level?

MOITA: In a different way.

David: Not as tense.

MOITA: I did not say *that*!

David: No?

MOITA: We are *all* in the process of learning, although those who have reached the level that I am at are more open to the idea of change and learning. And there is much more flow, a much stronger sense of freedom in a way, and much joy.

So our learning is not so much based upon the tension of opposites as it is here. But there is an *in*tenseness that goes along with our work – the other things that we do besides communicating here. And, in...seeing what happens to those we [watch] over, we experience *their* tension in part of us, and learn from *their* mistakes as well as our own – which is a singular trick and one not many people on [your] level can do. Few people learn from others' mistakes; they usually have to make them themselves first.

So we have a broader view – more data, more information, more experiences. They too all weave together into a whole, and we learn new ways to see the world. And so, we change levels as well when our time comes. As here, there are those who go faster and those who go slower, and many levels within levels.

ശ   ശ   ശ

It is in October that Moita actually spells out her connection to our group.[89N] Related material has already been received in August, but Moita's origin (not to mention, *our own* origin) has remained a mystery to us until this point. Here first is the August material, and then a portion of the October 18th session with Alex and me.

Moita Session #21 (Kelly, Laura, Roland / August 12, 1978)

Laura: Can you tell us how you are connected to Kelly? When was the last time you had a physical body?

MOITA: The last time I, as myself, had a physical body was during the time of Mu.

I do not wish you to think that just because it was so long ago I am more "evolved" than some of the other entities. It is each individual's choice at a certain point in their evolution whether to go on in physical form or whether to stay on this level. I felt my work could be better accomplished here.

In a sense, Kelly and I were together in that life in Mu. I chose to go on, and she chose to stay. Kelly is in the process of evolving into something like me. However, if and when she does, I, as myself, will still be here — so she is not me. We are separate, and yet we are also part of each other.

∽   ∽   ∽

Soon after this, Kelly receives from Moita the information that it is common for a soul ending its incarnation cycle to release a part of itself, which then begins incarnating on its own. Such was her beginning as a soul distinct from Moita — and a similar process seems to apply to the rest of us as well.

Moita Session #34 (Kelly, David, Alex / October 18, 1978)

MOITA: *(to Alex)* Finally I get to meet you again. You were so serious the last time... *(i.e. the July 15th gathering)* I think it is time to attempt a better explanation of what I am. This will not be easy.

You know or have heard that when people form a group, their forming of the group – their placing their energy together as one – creates a new being of all of them. Have you not wondered what happens once this new being has been created, and where it goes from there when the group splits apart? It does not dissolve or become uncreated. It exists as an individual, as well as being pieces of others.

Very, very long ago, before the change of the world, that was done not just on an unconscious level as it is now, but as a conscious effort of creation. Before I became an incarnated spirit, I was one of those that was created in that way. That is what I meant when I said that each of you added back my part, although in many ways you are not the original ones who caused the creation. You are their descendants, the pieces of them that stayed behind when they moved on...

(Thus we learn that members of our group now are tied to Moita's creators in the same way Kelly is tied to Moita herself, i.e. as "pieces" that stayed behind on the physical plane. Later in the session, I return to a question that has long intrigued me.)

David: Speaking of groups that split up, Loria once said there were three group entities involved for those that left Kyrionis. Were you one of the ones she was speaking of then?

MOITA: You know that Kelly was there. *(obviously experiencing difficulty going further)*

David: Yes. I feel like I'm prying. Was there just one group entity that went with the group to Musili?

MOITA: I'm having trouble getting this through.

(The problem is Kelly's nervousness at what Moita may claim to be, considering the attitudes of other group members toward herself at present. I concentrate on raising my energy to help Moita come through more clearly.)

MOITA: I *was* involved. I can at least say that. *(pause)* Why do you wish to know? *(in a tone saying: "Whatever for?")*

David: That's unclear to me. *(pause)* I guess the thought began with wondering about your role here now for the group.

MOITA: You all made a choice then to come back together as a group. But after that choice was made, you also each of you went your own way – some together for a space, some together not much at all. Once a wish is voiced, a desire is made known, you cannot rest until it has been fulfilled, or until you no longer have that desire. You must keep on returning until it is finished to your satisfaction. The desire draws you and keeps you here.

Just because there were things you wished to do with that decision in this life did not necessarily mean that all you foresaw from that viewpoint could be accomplished. It does not mean that it can't. It is certainly not straightforward. Each of you can touch that time, but you are not that any longer. You are that, and more. If the choice had been made from a different view, it may have been seen as a different choice.

David: Which choice?

MOITA: The choice to bring that energy here now to this world. There are many times that have been forgotten that need to be remembered and the energy to be renewed. But when you are in that time and in that energy, it is not so easy to see clearly how that energy will affect the place you are going to take it to...

In the midst of that joy, it was not easy to project...what would happen *to* it when it was placed in a world that was dark and empty, and how *that* world would change what you were bringing... You can draw on the joy that was experienced, but you cannot predict it, nor channel it, in any given direction. Once it is released, it will do what it will, regardless of personal wishes.

David: So how it works out is not our responsibility?

MOITA: When you release it, it becomes your responsibility, because you bring change with you in that. How it affects others is their responsibility. It is more...not a warning I am giving you *(said warmly, empathically)*, but something like it, in that where you are and where you were then, you do not have as clear a view as you think, or as you would like, of what *is* happening and how you *are* affecting others in the life you are leading now.

I said there is much fear of joy in this world. And when people have fear of something, they tend to want to destroy it. It is their first reaction, their protection. In order to release that, you must be *very* strong and know yourself very well. And those of you who cannot accomplish this feat in this life as you chose will have to return till it is accomplished.

Do you see what I am saying?

David: Mm-hmm.

MOITA: There is a difference, in essence, between Loria and me, in that I have lived in bodies and she has not. And so, we bring a different perspective to this.

(Moita's last point seems to be that incarnational experience makes one more aware of the complications of realizing high ideals while dealing with human egos and societies on the physical plane.)

҃   ҃   ҃

For Kelly and me – not by choice – the winter of 1978-79 begins in isolation from many members of our present group. But this does not negate our joy as we go deep within, exploring the roots of our love and trust and strengthening our contact with higher levels. Key to this exploration are several hypersentience experiences with Kelly as subject, myself as guide.

The lives in Kyrionis and Musili have been very important to members of our group recognizing each other. Yet none of us actually knows much about our interactions in those lives. Through this winter's regressions, Kelly and I will discover some very interesting parallels between these Kyrionis/Musili lives and the parts we and others – and Moita – have played in the events of 1978. The next chapter takes a trip into these other "presents" that have been interacting with our own.

҃   ҃   ҃

Chapter 14

CITY OF DARKNESS, CITY OF LIGHT

Many questions remain unanswered about the past lives of Kelly and me and other current friends in our ancestral groups at Kyrionis, Musili and the Himalayan region. Why did the original larger group decide to leave Kyrionis in the first place? Did the separating groups know where they were going? What forms of contact with higher levels, including Moita, were experienced at that time? What roles did people play in these groups, and how did those roles compare with now? How did the magical environment of Musili come about? And why the Musili group's vow to return together in a future so unlike its present?

On January 19, 1979, I assist Kelly in a hypersentience session seeking to recover as much as possible of our life within the group at Kyrionis, the city in Asia Minor predating Atlantean civilization. Kelly will make an ideal subject for this, not only because of her psychic receptivity but because Moita has recently said she was "involved" among the entities for the group.

Nearly the whole transcript is given here, from the conclusion of my induction procedure to the point where I bring Kelly back to her normal waking state of consciousness. During this entire period Kelly lies still with her eyes closed – her words, voice quality and emotional involvement indicating that the regression has gone quite deep. (Frequent short sentences reflect Kelly's speaking in simple phrases, separated by silence. Her additional comments afterward are included parenthetically.)

Hypersentience Session #60 (Kelly; David, guiding / January 19, 1979)

Kelly: I see a lot of mountains, bare mountains with no life – rocky, dry and tall.
David: Where are you looking from?
Kelly: I see myself standing on a road, but I am above it.
David: How do you appear?
Kelly: I seem to be doing something else than trying to see me.
David: What is it that you're experiencing?
Kelly: I am standing in the air . . . but I'm not in the air anymore. There are things around me. It feels like I am in a building, but I'm not in my body. I see shiny floors, like mirrors. A feeling of space.
David: How do you feel here?
Kelly: Somewhat afraid, and small. I feel as if, if I had a heart, it would be pounding hard.
David: Can you tell what you are afraid of?
Kelly: Of what I might learn. There is much learning in this place, much knowing.
(Kelly will say afterward that she knows this place is the astral Hall of Records. While there, she feels great energy shooting up and down her spine. Everything feels so

different that she knows, in order to be here, she must have reached quite a deep level.)

David: How do you learn here? *(pause)* Are you ready for that, or not?

Kelly: You are shown things. There is one here who comes. I am not here because I wish to be. I have been called.

David: Now that you are here, what happens?

Kelly: He says to "Come with me."

David: How do you respond?

Kelly: I go.

David: Where?

Kelly: I am in a different room. The walls are made of stars. There's a stand in the centre and a book on the stand. It's open. He wants me to look.

David: What do you see? *(pause)*

Kelly: My city is dying!

David: Is there more?

Kelly: Too much more.

David: What comes next?

Kelly: I see a black cloud hanging over the city, which seems to be thoughts. The care is gone. Things like lightning come out and hit the city, and it crumbles, and is swallowed in the earth.

            He tells me it's time to go back, and remember what I have seen.

David: How does this man appear to you?

Kelly: I cannot see his face. His head is covered. He wears a white robe. He is relentless, not soft. He only shows the truth.

David: What happens next?

Kelly: I am lying on the road on my hands. My body has fallen. I look up at the sky, and I am filled with dread. I remember what I saw. There is nothing there to see now. There is just sky.

David: What do you do?

Kelly: I go and tell the others what I've seen.

David: Which others?

Kelly: There is a council that rules the city. I tell them first.

David: Have you known these people in the council before?

Kelly: No, I have nothing to do with the council. I tell them because I think they are the only ones who can do anything. They don't. I wish they could come with me and see for themselves. *(pause)* Why didn't he take one of *them*?

David: Do you tell others?

Kelly: I have some friends. I cannot think of anything else to do. They come to my place.

David: Can you describe the scene?

Kelly: I have a room that is a step down into the ground. There is a tree in the centre and a garden. The roof opens to the air. I have cushions. I sit on the step. One sits beside me. There seem to be about 20 of us sitting, some standing.

David: Can you describe yourself now, how you're dressed?

Kelly: I have long, brown hair. It is pulled back and up, and a long piece falls down out of it. It's curly.

(She is a very beautiful woman, her hair piled up toward the back, from which a long, curly, brown ponytail falls. Locks of short, curly hair frame her face.)

Kelly: I have on a loose robe that clasps on one shoulder and falls to the floor.

David: What happens here?

Kelly: We have a snake! – very long. It seems to be with us. It seems to be an oracle. Ah, it is our truth-sayer! I am being tested.

(At first she sees a snake bracelet, which she thinks she herself is wearing. It has two or three coils and is wrapped around either the lower or upper arm. Then she realizes it is worn by another woman, and that there is an actual snake – like a 20-foot python – on the floor. This snake has been present in the group before. The snake wraps itself around her body. It is assumed that if you are lying, the snake will smell your fear. It is part of "a strange, very old religion".)

Kelly: Its head is by my ear. And I speak my tale. We believe, if one lies, he will bite or squeeze the air out of the body. I resent this in some way. They have never tested me.

David: Did everyone think it was a good idea to test you?

Kelly: No. The one who sits next to me thought it was not nice, or [he] was afraid for my life. I don't think he believed in the snake – not that he didn't believe in my words. There was another here who brought the idea up. I think she envies me.

David: For what does she envy you?

Kelly: *(smiling)* For my good fortune. She is not as well-liked as I. Nor has she many close friends, especially one. She is adept in ancient ways and has much knowledge. But her heart is bitter.

Many here are uncertain. I think we must leave. There is a great deal of fear.

David: About what?

Kelly: Uncertainty. What will we find? Where will we go? Why are we going? Is it true the city is dying? Are we fools? The snake confirms my story. They cannot but believe me now. I wish it was one other that had seen. I did not ask for this. I was taken without my warning.

(In her previous psychic experiences, she was warned in advance, but this time taken suddenly. This was her first visit to the Hall of Records in this life, however.)

David: What is decided?

Kelly: For the moment, nothing. Everyone is too scattered. They go home to think. They leave us alone. They have frowns on their faces. At least *I* have comfort.

David: What do you mean?

Kelly: *(smiling)* The one who stands by my side.

(At the beginning of the snake scene, she saw a ring of rose crystal on her finger. It was cut like a diamond, was the size of a dime, and had a plain, gold-coloured band. She feels that the man standing beside her gave her this ring. She knows his name to be Keroc, and hers Natalia.)

David: Can you describe him?

Kelly: He is tall and curly; very deep, grey eyes.

David: Can you move ahead to a time when something is decided, or when some change happens? *(pause)*

(Kelly becomes obviously very upset, with tears forming at her eyes.)

David: How are you feeling through all of this?

Kelly: Now?

David: Wherever you are now.

Kelly: I am frightened. The earth moves. There is screaming. People are trapped.

David: Where are you?

Kelly: In darkness. I am trapped. I was in the garden. I was in the room and the roof fell in. But the tree fell over first. I am under the tree. *(pause)* I hear someone calling me.

David: Do you recognize the voice?

Kelly: It is Keroc. He is looking for me. I don't think he can hear me. But the stones are moving. He gets me out. I feel sick. My arm is broken. It seems to be over for now. And they all come to my house, through the streets. Not all: some are not there. It saddens. We could have left before. There is no need now – it is *decided*. We must go.

We think we should talk again to the council, but there isn't enough time. There isn't anything there to take with us. We take food. There are many who are leaving the city, wandering into the hills.

David: Do you know where *you* are going, or where the group is going?

Kelly: Not yet. They're just leaving. Some others join us from those who leave the city. Our group gets larger. Some I have never met before. Some I have known but briefly. We get out of the hills, away from the city, on foot, quickly. Fear drives us.

They've taken me again! *(breathing as if in fear)* There's another – they have taken *two* of us. I have not met this one before. We are taken to different places. I see the book. *(whisper)* I don't want to look at it. *(sigh)* But I have to. *(whisper)* He pulls me. *(another sigh)* He places my hand on the stand, and I stick. I try not to look, but it jumps up at me and I fall into it.

David: What do you experience?

Kelly: I seem to fall through the pages and see some place far away – where I'm going.

David: Try to describe all you see and perceive about this place.

Kelly: There is nothing but country: low hills and rivers, a plain, and mountains on my left. It seems a long way. There is this strange light that goes up like a column, and it pulses. And it comes from the spot. It has many colours. It is a beautiful light! I hear a voice. It says to go here and start again.

(The light changes shape: it grows wider, then thinner; taller, then shorter. It is obviously some sort of power point.)

Kelly: *(sighing with relief)* He lets me go. *(pause)* This time they have noticed I was "missing", as was the other. There is no snake here. The keeper couldn't bring it with her. Her snake died in the city. *(pause)* He has been told something else than I. He was shown a different place. I don't understand.

David: Does he describe his experience?

Kelly: Yes. It was much the same as mine, except he was not as afraid as I. He was curious. He had never been there before. He was shown a place in the other direction. It too had a light, but it had no colour! He was told to go *there* and start a city – or a *school*. Now we must choose.

David: Was any more said about this school?

Kelly: It was to be a place of learning how to reach that place again, where he was told other things – he does not tell all. The way he says things, they sound heavier. They wish to go slow and thoughtful, *inward*. The other place is *outward*, and light. *(pause)*

There is not much food! *(pause)* There is so much indecision, arguing! We brood. I see what she was for now – the one who was turned away. *(tears forming)* She made us see how we were being – how foolish to argue.

David: Who was turned away? Describe, if you can.

Kelly: I see long, stringy, grey hair, and a bent back, a hungry look. Sad and tired. *(referring to the "old hag", seen by a group member in the last chapter)* I had no voice in that decision. My voice was not heard... It was pointed out we had no food and we had no time to spend caring. I feel like my heart has been spilled out. I keep thinking how I would have felt if it had been me.

(Kelly has the impression she wanted to run after the old woman to give her some food, but did not because of the group's pressure.)

Kelly: At least the quarrelling stops.

David: What happens now?

Kelly: We part in the morning, divide our food. I am sad to see us part. We think we will keep in touch. I think not. It will be a long time before we meet. We are going in opposite directions, in more ways than one.

(Kelly sees this circular image: the parting is occurring at the 3 o'clock position; her group moving counter-clockwise toward the top; the other moving clockwise, downward. She senses that it will be a long time, in future lives, before the two tendencies meet again at the 9 o'clock position.)[90N]

Kelly: I am the leader, since I am the only one who knows where we are going.

(Kelly says later she does not feel herself the "leader" in any other sense.)

David: How do you know how to get there?

Kelly: Somehow it is imprinted inside me. I don't know exactly how. It is like feeling it before me, and it pulls me towards it. That light that I saw I still see in my mind. *(pause)* I know it's not far now. It's been hard. *(pause)*

David: What are you experiencing?

Kelly: We come to the top of a hill, and before us is the valley, and that light I saw! They can see it too! I thought it was in my mind, but it's there! It's real. It dances, changes colour, makes us laugh and forget we're tired.

David: How old are you at this point?

Kelly: I am nearing my 30th year.

(She feels about as old as Kelly is in her present life – just past her 29th birthday.)

David: Would it be good to leave the rest of this life till another time, or is there something else we should finish here in this story?

Kelly: What happens next: we begin having children. And we learn how to play with the light. That is most of it.

(Natalia and Keroc have three or four children together.)

David: Before we leave this, I'd like to ask you a few questions. Could you go back to the time of parting? Could you see the group that went the other direction, including the leader of that group? Do any of those people come to mind as people you know in this present life?

Kelly: The leader whom I saw with me in the place in the sky was Roy. I recognized him at once. I don't feel I know the others. If I know them, I have not met them yet. *(pause)*

(Kelly is taking people she knows now and testing them against that group, seeing if a face from that time emerges. However, she has not met a number of the people previously identified as participants in these lives.)

Kelly: Mmm. Wait. There is another face that comes: Gerald.

David: Can you describe these two, what they were like?

Kelly: Roy is tall and slim and broody, a thinker – although when we were together, we were the same height. Oh! – *I* am tall.

David: And Gerald? Who was he within the group?

Kelly: A short, dark woman. She...had a very hard time deciding where to go. Very undecided.

David: Is there anyone else from that group who has come?

Kelly: Not that I can see now.

David: Now, returning to the group of which you were the leader, who comes to mind as present in this life that you know?

Kelly: The first who comes was you. And then comes Ruth.

(As I have sensed since early in the session, I was Keroc. Ruth was extremely undecided which way to go from Kyrionis, but finally chose to go westward toward Musili – partly due to having doubts about Natalia.)

Kelly: I see Neale's face.

David: Who was he then? *(pause)*

Kelly: He worked with animals.

David: What kinds of animals?

Kelly: I see birds around him. It was like he could talk to them.

(There is the picture of eagles, hawks, etc., on his shoulder and flying around him.)

David: Anyone else?

Kelly: Not that I can see.

David: Okay. Now we're soon going to come back. Looking back over this life and its connection with the present, do you have any message to bring back to your present self from this deep space where this has been experienced?

Kelly: *(pause)* I hear words: "To release those who wish to part, and stand as a wholeness unto myself."

David: Is this all?

Kelly: I am told that is all I can say.

David: All right. You're going to come back now. And as you come, bring with you the energy of that time, the potentials, the awareness that will be of help to our present. Come back as I count, feeling the well-being of your other levels, feeling refreshed, able to remember all that you have experienced.

∾   ∾   ∾

It is interesting that Loria never told Roy which direction he travelled from Kyrionis. Yet on July 25, 1977, the night Topling's story about the dividing of the ways was first shared with the rest of us, Roy said: "I keep feeling that if we were all in Kyrionis, then I followed the other group [the one travelling to the Himalayan region]. It seemed to come up quite strongly when you said that. That would explain a lot of things to me." I understood Roy to mean he felt closer to the slower, heavier, intuitive/earthy tendency of the eastward group than the quicker, lighter, creative/ intellectual bent of Musili people.

That July 25th evening brought the second of two extremely interesting summer sessions in which a number of former Kyrionis people were able to experience Loria and Topling together. Speaking through Kitty that night, Topling said that many of us also lived in another civilization in what is now Africa and Australia. His description of creating caves for habitation through our sophisticated utilization of sound, and of the way our overemphasis on peace created major problems by blocking our healthy aggressive energies, reminded two of us immediately of Seth's similar account of Lumanian civilization[91N]. Loria later confirmed the connection, and clarified that Lumania was settled by descendants from the earlier Kyrionis, Musili and Himalayan area cultures.

This makes me wonder now if a stifling of more assertive, innovative energies in the Lumanian existence had any role in our group's conservative ("don't rock the boat") reaction to changes among Ruth, Kelly and me the next year – since Topling undoubtedly had reasons for bringing it up. He said, in fact: "Just as now you have barriers that are causing you energy blocks, you did then also" – and that "you do have a bleed-through of information."

One more link to the Seth material occurred that same 1977 summer when Kitty, Russ and Bob visited Devil's Tower, Wyoming, of *Close Encounters* fame. Walking the trails, our friends became aware of a strong energy field surrounding the mountain, and at one point saw the outline of a huge doorway up on the cliff face. When their photographs were developed, there was an otherwise inexplicable rose-coloured light bathing that side of the cliff. It all makes for a fascinating parallel to Jane Roberts's *The Education of Oversoul 7*, in which "Seven" enables one of his personalities, prehistoric Ma-ah, to see the non-physical doorway through a cliff into the land of the Speakers.[92]

∾   ∾   ∾

Later in the winter, Kelly attempts to pick up where we left off in her hypersentience session that began in Kyrionis. She has difficulty translating into words the very different reality she now enters in the city of Musili. Her speech is slower than even is usual for these regressions, and sometimes almost dream-like.

A nearly complete transcript of this session follows. As a supplement, Kelly's account of a brief workshop "fantasy journey" visit to Musili (December 3, 1978) will be inserted at the appropriate point.

Hypersentience Session #65 (Kelly; David, guiding / February 4, 1979)

Kelly: I have finally found it!

David: What do you see?

Kelly: I see the light.

David: How is everyone feeling or acting?

Kelly: Everyone seems to be quite happy. The light changes us. It takes away our tiredness, and our hunger! *(pause)*

David: Where are you now?

Kelly: I think I'm standing on the hill, but things are changing.

David: Can you describe the changes?

Kelly: Time seems to be moving!

David: How so? How do you experience it?

Kelly: It is like standing outside, watching in. Everything changes. Something is building. *(pause)* It seems I don't belong here.

David: Why?

Kelly: Because I am outside of time.

(There is a barrier between Kelly and the city. It is as if encased in a huge bubble, like a force field. "You can't go back there again" is the thought, referring to the Kyrionis-to-Musili life. Kelly watches the city grow and change really quickly, without being able to see anything definite.)

David: Is Natalia outside of time?

Kelly: She sees into other times. She is not outside of them.

David: Can you say what these other times show?

Kelly: The building of the city... I can go no closer.

David: All right. Shall we move ahead in time, then, to when this city has been built? Do you wish to do this?

Kelly: I may find entrance then.

David: All right. As I count to five, we'll move forward to when the city has been built and when you will enter another body, along with others that Kelly knows... Try to describe what you experience. *(pause)* Is there something now?

Kelly: My head moves. I'm young. Learning.

(There are tingling rushes through Kelly's whole body on arriving.)

David: Where are you?

Kelly: I seem to be in a room of colour. There is nothing here but me – that I can see.

(She is aware she has spent the first part of her life in this room, with no sense of

family or blood relations. She sees no children in the entire session.)

David: What are you doing?

Kelly: Speaking to the wall!

David: And what happens?

Kelly: It shows me pictures of another city, pictures of a journey! *(with a feeling of wonder and surprise)* I had always thought this had always *been*!

David: Thought that this city had always been here?

Kelly: Mm-hmm. I never knew there was a beginning. I think: if there was a beginning, it may mean there will also be an end. *(pause)*

David: And what now?

Kelly: I feel very tall.

David: Are you a tall person?

Kelly: I am tall because my thoughts reach high.

(Everyone is able in this life to change their bodies; bodies do not stay the same form. Most are tall, slim and graceful, with the women being about as tall as the men – "if you can call them men". The sexes look a little different, but not much.)

David: What are your thoughts?

Kelly: Someone touches me. Someone reaches me with their thoughts.

David: Who is this? Do you know?

Kelly: There's more than one. I cannot find the right word. It is a group like a clan, or a hive.

David: Are you a part of this group?

Kelly: I am theirs.

David: How do you mean?

Kelly: I am their instrument. They play me. And I am connected . . . to another as well.

David: Another group?

Kelly: Another level of thought. *(i.e. the entities of the group members, the whole group on another level)*

David: What is that like?

Kelly: It is like standing in a circle and being the centre, and having the force above the centre that pulls you up.

David: And what do you do as their instrument? What do you do in the centre?

Kelly: I reflect their thoughts to them in my movements. They play me to find out what they are doing.

David: How do you feel toward this group and the members in it?

Kelly: Much depends on what they are thinking. I react to that. Some think stronger of me than others.

David: Can we perhaps go to one scene of this kind that may be more significant than others, and see what is happening? *(long pause)*

(Kelly's experience is that, since they are all integrally connected, how can one decide which is more significant? She sifts through so many and finds each important.)

Kelly: I feel their thoughts on fire. It makes me hot and I turn red.

David: How do you turn red?

Kelly:	My colour changes.
David:	Your aura, you mean?
Kelly:	My body extends... I am taller, too. There is more power in me.
David:	Why are their thoughts on fire?
Kelly:	They are trying to see into the future, using me as the door.
David:	Do they have a specific question?
Kelly:	They want to know what will happen to the world – if there is an end to this.
David:	Do they have present cause for worry?
Kelly:	The walls have shown us the other city many times. They seem to do those things without our bidding. The walls, they speak not only our own thoughts. They have ideas. Our city is alive and it speaks through its walls.
David:	Can you describe how this city is at present, how it looks?
Kelly:	Tall things streak upward. It always changes. It dances (the lights). The walls are not made of dead matter. It is like living in a being, and filled with colour and music.
David:	How does this music sound?
Kelly:	It is a sound beyond hearing, the sound of the walls. It is a sound that feels – a high sound, a joyful sound. We try to recreate that in other ways . . .

(This hypersentience session continues after the next section.)

ꕔ   ꕔ   ꕔ

On December 3, 1978, Kelly participates in the group past-life regression I guide during a dream workshop at a community college. She decides to use the unguided last five minutes of the session to explore any reincarnational background to her fear of insanity. That fear has come up in several recent dreams (as we work to purify the power point) as well as in her "LSD freak-out" years ago. She will find there is indeed a very harrowing life during the Spanish Inquisition to account for her fear.

More to the point, Kelly uses the early visualizing exercises to revisit the room in Musili she experienced during our Sunseed workshop the previous spring, before Moita began to speak aloud. She does so because she feels there is something in that room she will need to take with her on her later journey.

Kelly describes her experience:

The room is bright, filled with colour from the shimmering walls. I get into the feel of myself in that room. I am tall and slim, feel very light, have auburn hair; joyful, serene, very happy and filled with peace. I am wearing a long, flowing robe or gown made of filmy, silvery blue material. The silver is like a web woven into the material, which shimmers when I move. There are brightly coloured cushions all around the floor. In the centre of the room is a chair or throne made of solid, deep rose crystal. I feel that I sit in that chair for visions.

I walk to the wall and touch it lightly with my fingertips. "Sing for me," I say. The walls give out a fantastic sound and change colour – almost like dancing. I go to the rose crystal throne and sit down.

(David tells the group to receive some kind of advice from our higher selves.)

I see before me the filmy figure of a woman. She is tall and very beautiful – almost takes my breath away. She has gossamer wings, many on each side. At her heart is a bright light that shines like a star, pulsing and spreading towards me. Her head is bent down slightly and she seems to lean forward somewhat. She says, "You must shed your skin like the caterpillar in order to become the butterfly. Shed your guilt." Then I rise and walk around the room some more.

(David says to turn and see a symbol that will be useful.)

I turn and at first see only blackness. I know that isn't right, that there is more to see, so I wait. In the darkness, a star appears and grows bright. I also know this isn't my symbol, because I need something to take with me when I leave...

The star draws closer and changes into a bottle made of the same rose crystal as the throne. At first it is quite large. As it comes closer, it also becomes smaller. When it is small enough to fit into my hand, I pick it up and look at it. I know there is something in it that I want. I open the bottle and a beautiful perfume wafts to my nose. I breathe deeply and feel refreshed and healed. I know I have to take this with me, for I am going on a dangerous journey and will need it before I return. Grasping it firmly in my hand, and keeping myself conscious of its presence, I begin to go to the star-gate.

ॐ   ॐ   ॐ

Continuing the hypersentience session:

David: Can we return to the dance? I wonder, do you find any answer to [the group's] questions about the future? *(pause)*

Kelly: As they seek, my light goes out. It is a clear sign.

David: That an end will come?

Kelly: That the light will die.

David: That seeking will bring that about?

Kelly: No. We do not seek that way. Their thoughts fly forward; and when they go forward enough, the light goes out.

David: Uh-huh. Is there any understanding of how or why that is to happen?

Kelly: No. We do not understand that way. We accept.

David: Uh-huh. Is it known how far in the future?

Kelly: It seems a long way off – the total darkness – because their thoughts must travel far. *(pause)* We would like to go there.

David: To the darkness?

Kelly: *(in sad, caring voice)* It does not seem right that it should stay that way.

David: Why would you go?

Kelly: I would go to bring the dance. I have a hard time thinking of a world without dance. And with the dance comes the light.

David: Can you now describe some of these other people in this group, the different ways they express the light?

Kelly: I can only touch them where they touch me. There are many things in my room that have been given for my heart by those I serve. Would that do?

David: I should think so.

Kelly: There is one who has put more music in the wall. It is a music that soothes me and thrills me at the same time. It changes my heart, and pleases me greatly.

I have also a table made of crystal. The moonlight is in the crystal. Somehow it has been captured, and it shines!

The clothes I wear were given me by another. There is the light of stars woven in my gown, and the blue of the sky, and the delicacy of a wing. They are *soft. (pause)*

David: Is there more in your room?

Kelly: There are many soft things on the floor – things for me to touch.

I seem to have a special window, a window onto another world. I see many things in my window, many I don't understand, but there is a lady in my window who comes and speaks.

There is also speech from another, words that float through the air, make shapes as they go. That one comes from one who knows me well, one whom I have danced for.

David: Do you hear any of those words, or see their shapes?

Kelly: There is only one I can hear; it speaks not as well. I do not understand its meaning...

David: Can you hear the sounds and say them?

(A word repeats over and over until Kelly says it, and then another, and another.)

Kelly: *Keana-uni . . . leanu . . . munara. (pause)* That is all I hear.

David: Do they make any shapes or give you any feel?

Kelly: I like them, but I cannot describe...

David: Okay. *(pause)* Are there more gifts in your room?

Kelly: I have a stone on my hand. It's green.

(The ring seems to be round, although it can change shape as well. "It picks up on what is happening inside and reflects it somehow.")

Kelly: And the bottle filled with flowers and cool mountain breezes. *(i.e. the same rose-coloured crystal bottle she has seen before)*

David: Can we now go through these gifts again? I'd like you to tell me if someone Kelly knows in this life was the giver of each gift. Let's start with the music that was added to the wall. Does any image come?

(After each gift is mentioned, Kelly "goes down and looks in the pool" – an imaginary pool of light – waiting for a face to appear. Where none does, there may be someone we are yet to meet in this life.)

Kelly: No.

David: All right. The crystal table holding the moonlight?

Kelly: I can feel there are connections here, but I see no face.

David: All right. The gown?

Kelly: I see Ruth.

David: Mm-hmm. The window?

Kelly:	All I see is Moita.
David:	Uh-huh. The words?
Kelly:	I see you.
David:	The stone on your hand?
Kelly:	I see Michael.

(This fits with Ruth's dream, before our son Michael was born, of a crystal-and-emerald cornerstone for a pyramid, containing holographic images of human figures, that Loria confirmed was sculpted in Musili by another self of our future child.)

David:	Uh-huh. The bottle?
Kelly:	I see my mother.
David:	The soft things on the floor?
Kelly:	I see Eileen.
David:	Can you see any more about these things on the floor – of what they are made, how?...
Kelly:	They are like alive. They're warm. I see quick-moving hands, and soft, long, fluffy stuff. It's like putting part of yourself into it, to keep it alive. Everyone does that.
David:	In their own way?
Kelly:	Mm-hmm.
David:	Do you live alone here, then? *(pause)* Uhhh! *(laughing, regretting the stupid question)*
Kelly:	How can one be alone?! *(pause)*
David:	It almost seems that nothing happens here to disrupt the flow, nothing that changes in any abrupt way.
Kelly:	No... Nothing changes. *(pause)*
David:	And what of the wish to go into the future?
Kelly:	That was decided.
David:	And specific plans laid?
Kelly:	In this time we do not deal in specifics. We deal in flow and thought. It is enough for us that we decided.
David:	How large is the group that decides?
Kelly:	I do not know what happens in the other groups – only in mine.
David:	More than your group may decide?
Kelly:	They have walls too, and their walls speak to them. And if the city is alive, and speaks to all and not just to a few, there is that chance they too would come. There are not that many in each group. One can only dance for a certain number.
David:	How many in your group?
Kelly:	Usually around 20. *(pause)*
David:	Is there anything more you'd like to do in this life?
Kelly:	*(laughs)* What I have always done.
David:	All right. We will bring you back, as this other you continues to do what you've always done... As you come back, bring the energy of that time with you. I will count up to 10, and when we get to 10 try to be back in your body

(Kelly laughs) and in your life as Kelly. Here we come, and bring back the memories of what you cannot express in words...

(All Kelly can do for a while is utter very contented sighs.)

David: Now, you didn't mention that rose crystal chair.

Kelly: No, I kept thinking about the chair. Sometimes it seemed to be there and other times it didn't. It seemed to be almost made out of light, and it seemed to have more to do with the city than it did with a person. Sitting in the chair was like becoming part of the city.

ɷ   ɷ   ɷ

Besides Kelly's memory of being an aura dancer, long before she heard about Musili, Kelly's desire to "bring the dance" to this world has led her, after stints as a ballroom dance teacher, to create her own uniquely evocative styles of movement, to music ranging from Celtic harp to rock. As in Musili, she very expressively danced for me one afternoon in the summer of 1978.

Still more connections are revealed through Kelly's memories of Musili's magical environment and the gifts given for her room. They include yet another source for our "starflower" symbolism: the star shining from the heart that becomes Kelly's rose crystal bottle, offering the breeze-borne essence of mountain wildflowers. And from her description of "speech from another, words that float through the air, make shapes as they go", I will know specifically why my "Shansa National Park" dream linked a poet, an ancient language (*"nirimata"*) and an "intensely direct perception of reality", embodied in "a bubble, floating through the air, iridescent in the sun". Similarly, my "Snowy Natural Bridge" dream, which foretold Kelly half a year before she arrived in my life, ended with beautiful natural scenes, including many flowers, overwhelming in their "multi-layered radiance". Becoming lucid to this dream, I heard "high-pitched bells" for no apparent reason than "the shimmering light-energy becoming music!"

Repeated some months later while searching for a community site, as I meditated with light snow falling, this sound of high bells *"not simply coming from outside"* would remarkably match Kelly's description of the music emanating from Musili's shimmering walls: "a sound beyond hearing...a high sound, a joyful sound" that "soothes and thrills". And later that spring, as I first stood near the centre of the Arrow Mountain medicine wheel, I remembered dreaming of a jeweller's thick, round crystal that was needed to locate something and was associated with the colour rose[93N].

Can it be doubted that memories of Musili – that living "city of light" – have illumined the paths bringing some of us back together in this life?

ɷ   ɷ   ɷ

_____

Chapter 15

THE WORLD CONSPIRES

You only see me when I am here! *You only know what I do when I speak to* you. *Yet you know there are things I do when I am not, and influences that we can have that others are not aware of as yet.*
                                                                    – Moita

Since Loria chose not to tell the story of Kyrionis, none of us suspected that it – rather than Musili – would shed the most light on our interactions as a group in 1978. After Kelly's hypersentience in January 1979, we do not publicly add what we have learned to the only event generally known about Kyrionis – the night around the bonfire, including the incident with the old woman, before the parting of ways. Yet the entire Kyrionis/Musili story certainly underscores that, in the context of community and spiritual guidance, anyone thinking Kelly an "upstart" has things exactly wrong.

Of course, one person's perspective on a life as took place in Kyrionis cannot give a total picture, cannot begin to show all the perceptions that different individuals brought to their parts of the drama. In contrast, more information was able to come through a greater number of sources about Musili, and it all seemed to agree – reflecting the unusually harmonious sharing in that subsequent life.

We now embark on a series of exchanges with Moita beginning in the same period as our hypersentience experiences. These sessions examine the issue of harmony or conflict among Ruth, Kelly and me and within the larger group – both in other times and now – and how that may relate to the activities of our higher levels. These excerpts progressively reveal a behind-the-scenes order which, in part, may already have been pieced together by the reader.

Moita Session #56 (Kelly and David / January 9, 1979)

David: You have said Kelly and I are very different souls and yet have spent many lives together in various relationships. Ruth and I, on the other hand, share the same entity and yet have found a marked distance between us at times. I wonder about our history together: how extensive, how close we may have been in the past.

MOITA: Generally speaking, two pieces of the same entity do not spend that many lives together, and most of the ones they spend together are intense learning experiences until they have reached the point where they can share better. There has always been a sense of competition between all three of you... Many of your relationships have been ones where there was tension, or amplifying that particular aspect of your relating...

David: What are the roots of that competition?

MOITA: Each piece tries to get back to its maker before the other. And of course, there are different qualities to all, even those who are close. The rounding out of the whole sometimes appears very disjointed or unreasonable. She is more the male, and you are more the female aspect of that soul. So she is working towards the female half, and you are working towards the male... The competition lessens as you both grow closer to a centre. But you each also go your own way.

The differences in the quality of the life in Musili were [due to the fact that] these differences in your soul makeup were subdued, or left behind for a time. Those people who shared that life entered it in a purer form than [in] many of the other lives that you have had, leaving behind many personality aspects, coming in more as themselves in wholeness. So this is the thing that you are working *towards*...

There was contact with our level in that life, but not really direct contact. You were all so amazed with all of the things that were happening – so many wonders to behold, such childlike joy in existence.

There was *more* consciousness on your part [of participating with other levels in] that *other* life. *(referring to Kelly's and my "Earth and Sun" incarnation, to be told in the next chapter)*

So you are trying to bring all these different aspects together.

        ∾   ∾   ∾

Moita Session #66 (Kelly and David / February 6, 1979)

David: I don't know if the split that exists now in our group is reflected in any way in the Musili life. Among those that vowed to come back, were there two groups perhaps?...

MOITA: There was just one...that you feel a tie to... But there is more than one group that has decided to come back for the same reason.

David: From there?

MOITA: Not just from there. This is a confusing time. If it had not been that those who made that promise then related in other ways in other lives as well, they would not have been here. The lives they led since then have reinforced that desire. And not *all* have come.

We form small groups and larger groups. Some we are a part of and do not know. And within each group there are tensions, and learnings, to make the group *as a whole* a more complete being. If this were not true, there would be no strife in the world at all! You are all continually striving to perfect that which you have created, and will continue to do so until you have perfected it to your own satisfaction.

If there was a split in the group then, it is feasible there can be a split in the group now. Just because you decided to come together does not mean you decided to *stay*. But you *are* all together, in a certain place *(i.e. on a higher plane)*.

David: Loria spoke of entities that guide groups in contrast to those that guide individuals. In a way, you seem to function in both categories.

MOITA: I also guide the individuals of the group!

David: So, was Loria referring to a being like you when she spoke that time?

(Note the hesitancy of Kelly and me to admit what should have been obvious by now: Moita being a group entity.)

MOITA: I am the closest thing you will come to it for a long time. *(pause, as this sinks in)* It is difficult for those who are here on one plane to see how one operates. You only see me when I am *here!* You only know what I do when I speak to *you.* Yet you know there are things I do when I am not, and influences that we can have that others are not aware of as yet – even if they are...

One of the things we spoke of before, or *you* mentioned before – the movements of a symphony – applies to this kind of thing, in that you are only one part of the play, or one part of the music. You have a certain score before you and do your thing, where I have a view of the other scores as well, and my part in them. And besides this place and time, there are others as well that are meeting together to make this possible. The world conspires to save itself.

၄၈   ၄၈   ၄၈

These final words echo a statement by Loria that many past groups are gathering together once more now, contributing their energy to transform this world from darkness to light. Musili is only one node in this network, however central in our own experience. And behind all these converging energies lies the work of group entities. As our conscious selves discover the connections this "conspiracy" has so intricately woven, our higher levels – including Amar, if he can spare the time! – must enjoy watching our surprise.

This is the case ten days after the last session, as Kelly and I host one in a series of biweekly gatherings, including a few participants who trace back to Kyrionis. On this occasion, regular attenders Eileen and Gerald are discussing with us various experiences they have had with groups. Eileen recalls the January 27th gathering a year ago (Chapter 13) when she and others felt the presence of an entity urging the group to unite its energies, using a pendulum as a focus.

Moita Session #70 (Kelly, David and 5 others / February 17, 1979)

David: What is your perspective on that gathering of the group last year, when the masculine entity made itself known?

MOITA: You have met him, have you not?!

David: The thought crossed my mind. *(feeling it's almost too much to be true that it was Amar, now that he has begun speaking directly through Kelly)*

MOITA: It did, did it?! Why else would he come? I do not think he feels ready to speak now, but his presence is here.

There is a funny thing about groups. They seem to form and break up. A group entity must be *flexible. (laughter)* You can look at it sometimes as on my level there being a pool of entities who function in this particular fashion. And then when a group is formed, depending on the particular vibration quality of the group and its goal, a suitable entity is delegated to assist that group in its development for as long as it is together. If it happens to break apart and form smaller groups, or become a part of a different group, then things become rearranged, depending upon the new energy quality that has been created.

A group entity has the ability to *become* part of all of those who are forming a group. Since the entity cannot itself already be an integral part of each and every one, it is a particular talent that has been chosen to be developed... We are not a staid and strict hierarchy. We are flexible, as one must be who lives with the flow of change and time.

๏   ๏   ๏

So Amar is a group entity himself, on a more all-encompassing level. He brought his energy to that previous group perhaps partly because Kelly, Moita's medium of expression, had not yet joined it. The notion of levels also eventually gives me a clue to my oft-stated query regarding Moita's role in the Kyrionis and Musili groups. I finally succeed in hearing her clear answer to the puzzle by asking specifically for it, while writing the first draft of what will become this chapter.

Moita Session #93 (Kelly and David / June 6, 1979)

David: I still wish I could find out what Loria meant about three group entities for the group that left Kyrionis. I've wondered if that can be understood in terms of levels of entities.

MOITA: Look at it this way. Firstly there was one group, and they split into two parts. When you have a group that splits into two parts, the entity that is the guide of that group also splits into two parts, but also does not disappear. So you have one entity going with one group, one entity going with the other; then you have the original entity which represents both groups.

In a way it is a matter of levels, because you have the split and then you have the whole. It is sort of like you and Ruth being part of Loria. There you have three separate and distinct personality structures and energies, and yet you are all part of the same. Curious how these things seem to work out so easily in terms of small situations that express larger ones!

David: Now how would *you* fit into that?

MOITA: You know I was there, for I already said I was. *(with energy building throughout this section)* I also told you that I was created by a group, and that those members of this group were descendants of the original group. You could say that I am that larger entity.

(The directness of her presence as these words sink in is profound, almost overwhelming. From here on, Moita's face appears surrounded by a field of energy radiating light which visually distorts the wall behind her.)

David: Have we ever met one or the other of those parts?...

MOITA: There has been no direct contact. All contact has been through individuals and their entities, through the influence that can be woven from their thoughts on our level. Most group entities of this type do not have the energy they need in order to communicate directly; nor do they have the vehicle to communicate through. They work on a different level, trying to manage the energies that are released, trying to oversee the development of the group-consciousness they are responsible for.

If a group splits into many small pieces, the group entity also becomes smaller and more numerous until, [when] eventually the group is no longer together at all, each piece of this entity becomes another individual...

David: Will the life in Kyrionis continue to be a key to finding the others with whom we are meant to work?

MOITA: Grey...... White and black. Hmm.

(In other words, it would be nice if everything were black and white, but it isn't. Moita closes her eyes and we wonder if someone else will come to speak. Her voice feels different when she speaks again, but it still seems to be her – perhaps a different "focus" than before.)

MOITA: The group that you were together with in Kyrionis is in many ways like a cell in a human body. It starts off as a unit, and then it divides and it multiplies, each cell being similar to the last, each being different. You have met many people from that life in this one, but they have also been developing on their own, forming their own cells.

It is hard to say that that life is the focal point for this one. It is for some of you... But, you see, having your birth in a sense in that group, the imprint and the experience of that time is what is important. It is like your genetic background, your parents, your conditioning. And many of your views are formed by those experiences...

A group entity's function changes as the group changes – not only the parts that are contributed to those who are split, but the part that continues to stay together as an oversee-er, in a sense. And as circumstances change, functions change too. Confusing?

The most important life you are living right now is this one, and the contacts that you develop here will decide what kinds of contacts you will develop in other lives. There is no straightforward formula.

Past acquaintances from the Kyrionis/Musili lives do nevertheless continue to turn up for us, sometimes providing a helpful hand in unexpected places. Witness this extremely clear session Kelly will hold with a medical doctor, conveying well the joy at each new encounter among "old friends".

Moita Session #110 (Kelly and Joe / September 13, 1979)
Joe: How am I connected with you?
MOITA: I am one who can be connected to many.

Joe: Are you able to define a specific connection?

MOITA: You have been part of another group that I was connected to. *(pause)*

Joe: Can you tell me more about that group – where, and when, and why?

MOITA: Much has been said on that group already. *(pause)* These things are hard to describe. *(pause)*

(Silkie then comes to sit in Moita's lap and seems to help make the energy clearer.)

MOITA: Thank you. *(pause)* This life was lived in a time where life was more intense, filled with more energy. Man has, in this time period, cut himself off from much of that kind of energy. So this place had more knowledge available to it. The subtle worlds were more visible and could be worked with. Each individual's thoughts and feelings were visible in the air that surrounded them.

The city was very much a being in its own right, and thought did not form itself into direct forms – not like you think now, where you associate with things past and present and future and compare one thing to another. In *this* place, all experience was what existed in the moment, and it was very rare for any thought to be carried forward to a conclusion. There was memory of a kind, but it was based strictly upon the direct experience rather than postulating from data.

There were groups of people in the city who formed individual cells of the city's entity, and you were part of one of those cells. Each member of the group added a certain kind of talent and energy to the whole.

Joe: So this existence now is a more difficult, more obscure existence, is it?

MOITA: This *time*. Mm-hmm.

Joe: It was easier to see the truth then (?).

MOITA: There were no hidden things.

Joe: What is the purpose of *this* life, for me, being by and large ignorant by comparison?

MOITA: It has a great deal to do with the energy of the time now – the desire to open, or reopen, doors that have been closed.

Joe: Mm-hmm. *My* desire to reopen doors...(?).

MOITA: The entire group's desire.

Joe: This group that was involved with me in the city, of which you were a part, is in existence now – the members of the cell you spoke of?

MOITA: They have, most of them, come to this time, in this period. It was a decision with much energy..., which carried itself forward... When an entity makes a desire known, [it] will continue to return to this plane until [it] has either fulfilled it or understood it and let it go. This is one of the things that keeps people in bodies.

Joe: Having desires.

MOITA: Of many kinds: to do good, or to learn lessons, to [gain] experience, to see things from a different viewpoint, to feel balanced and whole.

Joe: Hmm. Does the time period that I was involved in have a name?

MOITA: You may have heard of it *(from reading* Rays*)*. The city's name was Musili.

Joe: And it was on Earth, it was an earthly city?

MOITA: Yes. Not one you would have heard of through history. It was before that.

Joe: Hmm. And is it part of my intended purpose to return to my association with that original group?

MOITA: We should say that when the group made the choice, each went [its] own path in-between. This is a resolution of that decision. Some will choose in one direction, and some will choose the other. It is not completely set, decided, that it must be.

Joe: Am I already acquainted with the members of this group?

MOITA: You have been on the outskirts for a long time. You have not been ready to meet the other members of your group, if you are to meet them with the possibility of doing work together. There are some meetings that are fruitful and some that are not, and it is the timing of meeting that has a great deal to do with futures.

Joe: Were you a member of the group yourself? How were you connected with the group?

MOITA: I am its entity.

Joe: And I have not met other members of the group?

MOITA: To know that, I would need to meet them in person. Your thoughts in their direction are not clear enough for me to be completely sure. A living presence describes itself better.

Joe: So I presume, when I'm ready to meet the group, when I have cleared the way for myself, that will happen eventually?

MOITA: You have met Kelly and David. They were in that group. Ruth was there also. So was Eileen...

(These are people we have talked about with Joe. Kelly will later receive an impression of the particular creative ability Joe possessed in that life, in terms of the gift he gave her for her room: the table containing the essence of moonlight.)

Joe: Does the group have a purpose or a theme in this particular life?

MOITA: The theme they started with has been described by another as a vow to bring light to a world that is dark and empty. You can look at it from that view. It is still a need which has different roots for each, but the roots all intertwined in that life. Many souls feel the need to participate in at least one great work or change.

Joe: And that's what's coming up in this lifetime?

MOITA: Yes. This is an opportunity for many who still feel the need to have it fulfilled. Most begin lives on Earth in unenlightened states, trying to learn what is the best way to use their energy. And when they begin to understand how energy should be used, they also go through the stage of guilt and remorse for not having understood before. So, they set up within themselves this need to change bad energy to good, or to subjugate themselves to others or to situations so they can feel they have made amends.

Joe: That would seem to be coming at it from a negative point of view, to act under that premise.

MOITA: There are many who go through these feelings. It is not something of which – I would say "approve", but I would say more it is: it causes us sorrow to see it happen in this way.

Joe: So the action may be right, but the motivation may be at fault.

MOITA: Motives are sometimes difficult to uncover...

Joe: It would be far better to do the right action from a right motivation – one of exploration, or joy, or happiness, or . . .

MOITA: It comes. When the realization is reached that guilt wastes more energy, then it can be cast aside and the joy can be let out. And once that step is taken, there is no inner need to create that balance between the energies. One is set free to learn and grow.

Joe: This accelerated process in this life . . . . It's my understanding from a number of sources that there will be rapid changes in the next few years – these are world changes, or climatic changes, or political changes, or whatever – and that there are people being trained to assist achieving the best result from these changes. Is this a training period for the members of this group?

MOITA: I would say that the entire life has been a training period – not just for this group, but for all of those who have come at this time to lend their assistance. Not everyone has come to purge themselves. Many have arrived because they wish to lend a helping hand.

Joe: And how is it that one distinguishes between people that arrived to lend a helping hand and those that have come to purge themselves?

MOITA: If their energy is clear, and if their heart is centred, whatever brought them here originally can be set aside. The important thing to learn through all of the changes that are coming is acceptance...

Joe: How do you cope with the frustration of working with ignorant, stubborn human beings?

MOITA: Perhaps I am not average. I do not find it frustrating.

Joe: No? Hmm!

MOITA: I find it a very interesting experience to see how much people will open when they are faced with another reality. Of course, there are some who are so busy protecting themselves that they cannot open their hearts to what we can offer, but they are also learning.

Joe: Do you enjoy these sessions which you have with Kelly?

MOITA: If I did not, I [would] have picked a very poor job. Usually the work we do is chosen to fit in with our own needs, our own line of development or specialty.

Joe: Mm-hmm. Could you describe your specialty to me?

MOITA: In a sense, I help others to weave their energies in order to make new and fresh discoveries, of each other and of themselves...

Joe: You're certainly very attractive!

MOITA: We have a great deal of love, and that comes from a deep place.

Joe: Mm-hmm. It's very appealing, wherever it comes from! *(laughter)*

MOITA: That is one reason why we are making this kind of contact now more often or visibly than in other times in history: to re-establish with the world, and let them see for themselves, that this energy is real and that love is not an empty word... And now you see also that there is more energy.

Joe: Yeah, it's really comfortable. I bask in it.

MOITA: You have my undivided attention.

Joe: *(laughing)* Well, believe me, I'm enjoying it. You can lavish me with it... *(laughing)*

MOITA: It is easier to speak of deeper things when there is only one level of individual to work with. As an entity who works with a group, I am (hmm) in a sense "controlled" by the energy that is generated. And so, when it is a mixed group, the overall energy is on a lower level.

Joe: And you come down to that level and bring it up to the next stage.

MOITA: As gently as possible.

Joe: And as a group entity, when you finish that task of bringing the level of the group up one stage, then the group acquires a new entity, does it? Or do you grow with the group as it ascends in consciousness?

MOITA: All that would depend on what kind of a group it was. If it was just a group that met once, then I would just be dictated by the energy at the moment and do my best to help those present open more to themselves. After that, they would be free to do whatever they chose. If we were not connected together, it would not affect me in their future.

And if a group growing together changes its aims, and thereby changes the quality of its energy to a point where I was not the best-suited to assist, then the entity would be different, for the group would attract a different sort. Then, of course, *if* the energy flowed in my direction, I would still be there...

Joe: Do you mind my rambling on, my idle curiosity?

MOITA: Perhaps it would be idle in some hands, but right now it is not idle in yours. You seek a greater understanding and a closer connection – not just in the past, but in the present. Pasts may be glorious and presents unfruitful.

Joe: Mm-hmm. For sure.

MOITA: I think it is time for me to say good night. We shall meet again.

৯ৎ   ৯ৎ   ৯ৎ

During the very unclear gathering of our friends back on the evening of July 15, 1978, when the hope that both Loria and Moita might speak went unfulfilled, Moita said: "I see the whole on a different plane than this, and the workings towards making it [whole] on this level will take some more time – *your* time. In a sense, it is already accomplished."

In what sense do the entities of group members exist together as a whole, however divided we are on *this* level? Can we glimpse any of the concrete workings of that? So far, we have been aware of Moita's work as a group entity in relation to our group on the physical plane – both those here in this life and in the group that divided from Kyrionis. Now we begin to learn of her work with other groups as well, and of her consummate role on the non-physical planes in relating to our higher selves and other entities. As an illustration of these collaborative possibilities, we will also discover more about the relationships among Moita, Loria and Amar.

This first excerpt from one of our workshops indicates what seems true of all our group sessions with Moita: whether any of us consciously perceives it, Moita is far from being the only entity present.

<u>Moita Session #73 (Kelly, David, three others / February 27, 1979)</u>
(At a given point, Moita looks above me and to my left.)
David: Looking at something?
MOITA: Yes.
David: What do you see?
MOITA: A presence. Do you not feel one . . . beside you?
David: Yes, I can feel the energy.
Rita: Do you get together with David's friend and converse? I forget, what is
            its . . . ?
MOITA: Loria.
(Kelly feels Moita's speaking the name almost as a summons – with a lot of force behind it.)
MOITA: You see, her name has power, too. Loria is very close; and yes, we
            communicate...
Rita: Could you explain to us how you communicate with other beings on your
            level?
MOITA: You can see it somewhat as two beings who act as radio receivers. [They]
            meet, and then they both tune in on the same wavelength. That does not mean
            that is the only wavelength that they have, but that is how they communicate.

            Out here, there are so many universes – if one could not tune them out, one
            could become extremely confused. They are all on different wavelengths. They
            all exist in the same space, basically, but they are not necessarily visible to
            each other. So we travel through them by changing our wavelength, and by
            making fine tunements *(laughing)* – that does not sound quite right! –
David: Tunings?
MOITA: – (mmm) – and broadcasting.
Pat: Do you ever have disagreements with others?
MOITA: There is diversity here. Not all believe or act the same way. But I could not
            really say that that was disagreement. There is joy in diversity. We each have
            our own particular area of development that we are working on. And so, we
            work with those who are in the same space. There is communication back and
            forth between them, for interest, but I cannot see any disagreement...
Pat: Can you tell if the other three of us have higher selves present?
MOITA: Whenever you are involved in this kind of energy, your higher self is here.
            It would not miss such a golden opportunity to come closer.
Pat: Is that the energy I feel, or is that your energy?
MOITA: It is a combination of both.

Moita Session #153 (Kelly, David, three others / August 16, 1980)

Sean: Does each of our higher selves exist where you exist most of the time? Or do they spread out among many different planes and realities, so you don't run into them that often?

MOITA: *(laughs)* It all depends upon what you choose. I work together with many higher selves, for I am *here. (i.e. able to come and speak with us)* This is what I am for. As the instrument for communicating our ideas, I must touch the higher selves of those who are present. Together, we decide what is best said and what is best unsaid – for your present development, for your own higher selves' needs.

Sean: We communicate in that way every time there is a session?

MOITA: And in-between! We are near at other times. We do not need a session to see what is happening, or to influence in our own way your development: putting little nudges and unexpected happenings in your way, opportunities for growth and understanding of yourself.

You are not totally unknowing of this. Your conscious mind does its part in assisting; and what people call your subconscious mind helps even more – through dreams and intuitions [which allow you to] see your consciousness from a closer level, and [through] helping decide what circumstances you need in your life. It can be, on one level, very intricate; but on another, very simple. It is the flow of energy... We see the opportunities, the probabilities, but it is still your individual personality's choice whether to follow the intuitions or not.

ကာ ကာ ကာ

This next session will lead to a surprising discovery – surprising because the number of people present (just Kelly and I) can obviously not account for the higher-level visitors in our living room!

Moita Session #67 (Kelly and David / February 9, 1979)

(Just before this session, Kelly talks to her somewhat weird friend Otto on the phone. He tells her he is getting ready to go "to dreamland – not exactly to sleep". This is his way of referring to astral-travelling adventures, of which he has many – even while driving taxi! Then, a little way into our conversation with Moita:)

MOITA: We have an influence here that is interfering somewhat with what is going on.

David: From what level?

MOITA: *(laughing)* There is the crux of the matter. It is an outside influence – not one that has been generated in this place. He knows whom I'm speaking of.

David: *(guessing by now)* Otto?

MOITA: Kelly is seeing him, and is greatly disturbed by his presence.

David: And is he aware of that?...

MOITA: I am sure he is *now*!

(Meanwhile, our other cat, Mouse, starts meowing, as if upset at something in the room.)

David: Someone else is disturbed?

MOITA: *(laughing)* Apparently! *(pause)* I think it shall be a short [session]. There are many other things happening, it seems... I shall see you later...

(As Kelly returns, this conversation ensues:)

Kelly: I seem to have a headache all of a sudden.

David: Did he go?

Kelly: I don't think he stayed around very long after he found out he was discovered. I could see him just as clear as day.

She changed my eyes again. I saw you change into a few different faces I've seen on you before. Then all of a sudden – flash! There he was, right there in front of me, right on your face. And I went, "What's *he* doing here?!" I have a feeling he and I are going to have a good talk about what happened to him after he left here.

David: What do you have in mind?

Kelly: I have a feeling his teacher has zapped him through the sky a few places for coming uninvited.

❧   ❧   ❧

This disconcerting little episode does turn out to serve a purpose in the scheme of things. Here are Kelly's notes from three days later.

"Had lunch today with Otto. He admits that he was at our Moita session on the 9th. Otto stated that the room was extremely crowded with entities and/or spirits. He felt rather uncomfortable. Moita greeted him with, 'Oh, look who's here!' And so, everyone looked. He also felt as though they were lined up, waiting their turn for something. He left shortly after he arrived, because he couldn't handle being stared at quite so much with the feeling of 'What the hell are *you* doing here?!' I asked him if he saw Loria, but he was very evasive. [He said] there were so many of them around, he didn't really have time to find out who was who."

That night we can't restrain our curiosity.

Moita Session #68 (Kelly and David / February 12, 1979)

David: We seem to have many visitors on these occasions.

MOITA: Knowing this, does it do anything for you?

David: I already know who *one* of them is. I'm curious about who the *others* are, or why they are here.

MOITA: Things are coming. *(pause)* I act as a focus on a number of different levels. They can pour their energy through me, and increase mine as well. They are other individuals' entities that are connected to you and to Kelly, and they are also here to learn about communication and how to utilize their own energy. There are not many places where our worlds meet – not yet. And anywhere... the worlds meet creates an energy field, a vortex, an attraction to those on this level on *many* of the other levels of this world. In some cases, just because a body gives up its spirit, it does not lose its desire to communicate with others.

David: I didn't follow that last. "A body giving up its spirit" – as in death or . . . ?

MOITA: As in death.

(Kelly thinks Moita used "body" in the sense of a thought-form with which a spirit still identifies, even though the physical body has been left behind – in other words, something akin to a ghost.)

David: Communicating with *us*, then, or learning from being here how to communicate with others?

MOITA: It was more a generalization that I was making than pointing to any specific ones that were here now. We have gone through that phase already – although you knew it not – where you attracted those kinds of things to you. But moving through the levels, as your communication improves, changes what can come.

There is a group here, too! We just work together better.

David: Who do you mean by "we"?

MOITA: The group.

David: Oh! – work together better than *our* group here.

MOITA: *(laughing)* Mmm.

David: Mmm. Are the two groups connected? I am thinking of your saying to the group here that it had already come together on another level but we just were not aware of it *here* yet.

MOITA: Mm-hmm!

David: Is that the group you're referring to?

MOITA: The same...!

(A very long silence follows, during which I feel Loria's energy-presence entering me at different points of my head and body. There is further conversation, then:)

MOITA: Do you find it worthwhile to glimpse our world?

David: *(after a pause, with a laugh)* I don't know what to answer to that in words.

MOITA: *That's* good! *(pause)* One of my arts is discretion. *(I give a sigh, not understanding)* Totally confusing! I have already explained it, but your ears were not tuned. *(i.e. explained it to Kelly)*

(Moita's eyes close. Kelly experiences it as walking through a dark hallway filled with swirling fog, almost like floating in space. Her head feels expanded.)

MOITA: This group that is here, they wish to say many things to you, and they voice their opinions, what they wish to communicate, to me. My position is one of choosing what it is that will be said, and what will not.

David: The things you say are selected from what the group wants, though?

MOITA: Some. They are learning from this what should sometimes be left unsaid, for purposes of growth. Some are somewhat overzealous in their desire to create growth before its time.

David: Which leaves me trying to imagine . . .

MOITA: . . . what it was that was left unsaid – and stretches your imagination to the limit. *(pause)*

(Kelly cannot see the entities but can feel shapes around and spreading out from her, with each able to connect at some point. "All this information is coming to where I am in the middle," she will say afterward, "and then Moita is taking all these different views, ideas, angles, and putting them together into one thing. So, maybe that's what it feels like to be a group – similar to my being the aura dancer in Musili, where I focused and expressed the thoughts of the entire circle.")

David: At the moment, on our level, there *seems* a great impasse in communication with some other members of the group...

MOITA: When you can rise above your battleground, things will seem different. There are many things here that need to be learned, as far as acceptance is concerned...and desire. *(pause)*

There is very little that time cannot change, but then again that depends on how you view time. If things do not work to your satisfaction in this life, they may in the next. But develop the art of accepting what has been given and enjoying it to the full – you will not feel the lack quite so much. You *have* a joyous heart!

David: It seems that I can accept, for example, the lack of communication and the split in the group. But that seems contrary, perhaps, to what I imagined the growth was about – though *some* of the growth involves the acceptance. *(pause)*

(As Moita gazes at me, I feel a quivering inside, a tendency to cry, connected with feelings of wanting the group to be together. Kelly is aware of this in me and is also close to crying from this point on.)

MOITA: There are many things a person expects to happen in life, and patterns he sees that seem to be heading in a certain direction, only to find before he gets there that he has been taken on another road that he did not know existed. Continue to follow your path blindly. So long as you are set upon it, there are no true disappointments. *(pause)*

David: That feels right to me.

MOITA: They thought there was nothing I could say! And so, your questions teach a great deal, in making *us* remember what we should not forget. *(pause)* Perhaps we should leave it at this for now, do you think?

David: Sure. Good night to *all* of you.

MOITA: Good night from all of *us*.

(Kelly says afterward: "That last little bit was really quite interesting! I could hear all these voices commenting on what you'd said, thinking about it – all these things dribbling down all these layers, and the last one saying, 'There's nothing we can say!' I got into that for a while, and then all of a sudden, wow!" – this last, her reaction to the way Moita managed to respond.)

৯৯   ৯৯   ৯৯

Moita seems to hold these "classes" during many of our group sessions, as discussed below with a completely different set of people than before.

Moita Session #128A (Kelly, David, 11 others / January 1, 1980)

Mike: In a previous session, you said you usually bring a "troop" of folks with you, and that some were with you to learn some things?

MOITA: The art of communication. There are not that many places as yet that this kind of communication can take place. But there will be more places in the future. This is something that I have made a great study of, in a sense. It has been part of my work. I have had more experience in this particular area than many of the entities that I associate with. And so, this is a great learning opportunity for those on this level to participate in a limited way in an actual communication, and to see how this energy exchange is accomplished and how words can be used to express things that are not easily expressed.

Being able to come here and speak to you in your own language, and make it a language you are not familiar with, is not easy to do – to make you see things you do not usually see, using words that you use to express things you see around you all of the time. If you could learn *my* language, I would have an easier time speaking some of these concepts. But then, the act of learning my language would teach you these things already.

They are not just entities that are here to learn this kind of communication to be used elsewhere. They are also your own inner selves that are here, to use this opportunity when you are open to further your own development.

ৎ   ৎ   ৎ

The following session is from the last of our gatherings in Regina with members of our original group of friends still open to Moita. At the preceding gathering on February 17, 1979 (the third session in this chapter), Moita revealed that Amar was a group entity as well, who made his presence known to some within the group the previous year. Eileen and Gerald, who were present on all three of these occasions, missed getting the message about Moita's own role within the group, however, and Moita and Amar try to complete the picture for them this time.

The appearance of Amar speaking through Kelly in this session brings a limited (because of those absent) but nevertheless very satisfying sense of completion, of coming full circle, to our group work here in the city, which is now coming to an end. And the light-heartedness that all share – Amar included, even while discussing topics as "serious" as they come – leaves a vivid impression of spiritual camaraderie we will cherish in the years ahead.

Moita/Amar Session #106 (Kelly, David, Eileen, Gerald, Neale, Steven / August 11, 1979)

Eileen: I feel other presences here.

MOITA: A great *many* presences are here.

Neale: Who are they? What are they?

MOITA: Oh, besides those that are attached to each of you, there are others as well – those who have come to watch. *(Neale laughs)* I help to channel energy through your own entity by being here. These experiences help open doors between the worlds and make it easier to touch you.

Eileen: Is the group entity here?

MOITA: The group entity has *always* been here. *(Eileen laughs)* Unannounced, until now. Had you not guessed? *(i.e. meaning herself)*

Eileen: I had an image at the beginning of that presence. *(i.e. Amar)*

MOITA: If you mean another level, he has also been here too. And if you had a question, he *would* come.

Eileen: Hmm.

MOITA: Do you *wish* to meet him?

Eileen: Yes, certainly. I feel at this time the energy of many of us flowing out in many directions, with Kelly and David moving and Gerald and I leaving for a year. I feel many probabilities open at this point to many of us. I don't know what the question would be. I do not have a sense of separation from Kelly and David, or from this group, but I feel the energy going in many directions outward.

MOITA: Wait a moment and we shall see. Kelly does not think she is ready for this, but there is enough energy here, and I'm sure *someone* will think of a question.

David: How can we continue to grow as a group, express our purpose, even though we may go in different directions physically?

MOITA: Are you going to ask me that, or . . . ?

David: Him.

MOITA: Then wait until he comes!

David: All right! *(laughter; brief pause as Kelly's eyes close)*

AMAR: *(in the usual huskier voice)* You seek a difference?

Eileen: Yes. Yes. Do we have a purpose as a group?

AMAR: Only if you wish. Any time you come together as a group, you are fulfilling a purpose. Each is still free, not bound. *(pause; turning to me)* And you?

David: I'm trying to think if your answer so far has cancelled out my question already! *(we laugh)*

AMAR: The difficulty with speaking in universals. It covers much territory.

Gerald: Is there any way we as members of this group can meet with you even though we are not physically present as a group?

AMAR: I am involved with the entities on this level. I do not become very often directly involved in a group. Therefore, working with your entity, you work with me. My view is farther. You cannot get to me direct. You must first become your own entity if you wish to do that. I do not have one group.

Gerald: If I were to become my entity, do you then become my new entity?

AMAR: In a sense. In a way I am a conglomerate of different energies.

Gerald: I fear becoming my entity because I fear then I lose him. I love him.

(Eileen and Gerald have held frequent sessions together, the majority of them with Gerald's entity communicating in a meditative state.)

AMAR: He will not disappear if you become him. Then there shall be two of you. The purpose of life is growth. Reaching one step, there is always another.

Gerald: Is there always a guide? No matter what step you're on, is there always someone else who will help, like you are now helping us at this level? Do *you* have an entity?

AMAR: *(whispered, with some reticence)* Yes.

David/Eileen: Mmmm.

AMAR: There is no top.

Gerald: Is there a God?

AMAR: God is everything, so He cannot be reached by going up. He is so vast, His energy flows into all living creatures, all manifested energy. He does not sit on a chair and rule the heavens.

Gerald: Forgive me for belabouring it – this hierarchical thing has been bothering me for years, trying to understand it. When Jesus spoke to his Father, was that simply his name – "Abba" – for his entity, in the same sense that I speak to my entity?

AMAR: First, understand that Christ came from a very different level of being. He was already a very evolved entity himself when he chose to come as a Teacher. This happens with all of the Great Teachers that have walked your Earth. When he spoke to what you might consider his entity, to you it would be God, because the energy would be so far removed from this plane.

Gerald: But his relationship to that God, or his entity, in relative terms, is the same as mine to my entity (?).

AMAR: In relative terms, it would be the same as you to your entity's entity . . . or you, to me.

Gerald: *(feeling he must break the intensity of the energy now)* Did Jesus's leg ever go to sleep when he meditated?

AMAR: Only if he was human. *(laughter)*

Gerald: Do you think we on Earth are going to make it?

AMAR: Only if *you* are human. *(laughter)* We have hopes. *(laughter)*

Neale: What does it mean to "make it"?

AMAR: It's different for everyone. What does it mean to you? When you figure that out, then maybe you'll know if you made it! *(pause)*

          I must go.

Eileen: Thank you for coming.

AMAR: Thank you for *being here. (pause, as Moita returns)*

MOITA: *(laughing)* He certainly was *cordial.* You must be a good influence!

Neale: Is he sometimes nasty?! *(laughter)*

MOITA: Let us say "brief".

Neale: Ah.

MOITA: An entity of few words...

(turning to me) I have an answer for *you.*

David: All right.

MOITA: Hmm! Now where was that answer? *(pause)*

David: Is it your own?

MOITA: Pardon? *(seeming distracted)*

David: Is the answer your own?

MOITA: No. *(laughing)* If it was mine, I wouldn't have to look for it.

The idea is that a group can stay a group even if it is apart, because of the thoughts that flow from one to the other through distance. Distance has no real meaning...[94N]

Gerald: Could we send Neale energy from where we'll be this next year while he stays here?

MOITA: Of course you could – and it would be a good thing. It would help you learn how to share your energy even at a distance. It is important to share energy. When you share it, when you give it away, you get it back.

(After the session, this conversation:)

Kelly: As soon as I closed my eyes, I knew Amar was here – just *instant.* She activated my heart centre before *she* came, and when *he* came the whole top of my chest was just throbbing. I always get this really "thick" feeling.

Eileen: You sound as though you have difficulty speaking.

Kelly: I feel like my neck is *so* thick, and really square, solid. I feel like *you!* *(this to stocky Gerald) (laughter)* Which is kind of a strange feeling for someone who's as small as I am! *(laughter)*

Eileen: It's funny. The image I get of him is not of a big person – but of a very *serious* person, very serious indeed. *(agreement all round)* Almost austere.

Kelly: I thought he was pretty funny. *(laughter)* But he's funny in a serious way!

Chapter 16

THE VIRGIN, THE EARTH AND THE SUN

> *Through time and space and at the present, I am connected to many
> people. And I do not just come to those that I am connected to. There are some
> things that my particular level of vibration can accomplish where even an
> individual's entity cannot. I am not just for an individual. I am also for many.*
> *– Moita (December 2, 1978)*

Time magazine's cover story for year-end 1991 was not what one might expect in a
competitive, hot-off-the-presses news magazine. It was titled "In Search of Mary" – the
Virgin Mary, that is: in Roman Catholic terms, the Mother of Jesus and Mother of God,
Queen of Heaven and Queen of the Universe. Why, *Time* attempted to explain, the
high-profile, mass-media treatment of such a subject?

> Yet even though the Madonna's presence has permeated the West for
> hundreds of years, both the adoration and the conflict attending Mary have
> risen sometimes to extraordinary levels in recent decades. A grass-roots revival
> of faith in the Virgin is said to have taken place worldwide. Millions of
> worshippers have flocked to her shrines, many of them young people. Even
> more remarkable has been the number of claimed sightings of the Virgin
> around the world during the 20th century.[95]

What might have been termed another "sighting of the Virgin", however, has gone
completely unreported till now – unreported because Kelly has been nowhere close to
being an orthodox Christian in her adult life. Nevertheless, apparent memories of the
Catholic saints did surface during Kelly's early childhood. Later, at age twenty-one,
she had her first vision of Moita, appearing to her open eyes as if none other than the
Virgin Mary.[96N] Similarly, Kelly's first past-life regression explored a past life that
began as a country girl who experienced visions, conversing with beings she
understood to be angels or saints. It was at the conclusion of that same hypersentience
session that Moita first clearly spoke aloud as herself.[97]

The present chapter seeks an explanation for this intriguing association between
what at first seems a very traditional religious and cultural icon and the multi-faceted,
very *un*traditional entity known to us as Moita. Our quest will not only lead to a deeper
appreciation of Moita's role through history and today but also confirm that "the
Virgin" is herself evolving.

ဢ   ဢ   ဢ

Appearing in the mid-1970s, the book *Fatima Prophecy: Days of Darkness,*

Promise of Light described the developing phenomenon of *publicly witnessed* Marian "apparitions" or "visitations" in modern times.[98]

From May to October 1917, at the depth of World War I and with the Bolshevik Revolution imminent, a shining, beautiful young woman appeared once each month to three shepherd children near the town of Fatima, Portugal. The Lady conveyed a vision of the remainder of the 20th century replete with "scourges", if humanity would not permit love's transformative power to re-enter its collective heart. These prophecies were set down in a secret letter entrusted to the Roman Catholic Church for release in 1960. But successive popes, perhaps regarding it too incredible or controversial, refused to make some or all of it public.

Nevertheless, Fatima became known for the breathtaking, and at one point terrifying, energy manifestation in the skies, witnessed on the Lady's final appearance by 50,000 to 80,000 onlookers. More material on the symbolic importance of this mass vision in relation to the contents of the secret letter will be given in a future chapter. (Care is urged in distinguishing between the essential inner meanings and the orthodox concepts in which such communications, originally through Roman Catholic adherents, have been presented to the world.)

But Fatima was not the end. In 1932-33, in Beauraing, Belgium, five children saw the Virgin 33 times near a convent school. She appeared in a shining white dress with blue highlights, a white mantle on her head emitting rays of light, and revealed a luminous heart. Up to 30,000 others again observed remarkable energy manifestations.

From 1961-65, at Garabandal, Spain, during 2,000 contacts between four girls and a Virgin Mary figure – wearing a shining white robe, blue mantle, and crown of golden stars, and appearing to carry the infant Jesus – more predictions were made of both a great chastisement and miraculous sign of God's love for all humanity. Like the previous instances, the ecstatic state in which the children witnessed the Lady was clearly demonstrated, and, in this case, bread of the Eucharist was materialized, observed by onlookers, and photographed.

Then even more remarkable events were experienced at Zeitoun, a suburb of Cairo, Egypt, from 1968 to 1971. Beginning on April 2, 1968, figures of the Virgin, and sometimes Joseph and an infant and also mature Jesus, were seen clearly by everyone present – and photographed – atop the Coptic Orthodox Church of St. Mary, traditionally thought to be the place where the Holy Family sought refuge from King Herod. Up to 200,000 people a night, of all ages, religions and nationalities, experienced these manifestations lasting continuously for hours. The Lady appeared as an intense light-form, her mantle slightly bluish, sometimes blessing the crowd and waving an olive branch, and with lights, glowing clouds and luminous birds occasionally appearing as well. Many witnesses knelt and wept for joy, and hundreds of spontaneous healings were documented there.

The Zeitoun visions finally faded and disappeared after the Egyptian government – convinced of their validity – razed buildings to open up more viewing space and began charging admission (!). But several further series of visitations, again visible to multitudes, occurred subsequently – for example, in Beirut, Lebanon, during the 1970s, Medjugorje in Yugoslavia (now Bosnia and Herzogovina) since 1981, and in Assiut,

Egypt, during 2000-2001.

Fatima Prophecy reproduced photographs from these events and, through channelings, made the crucial clarification that it was not literally Mary, the physical mother of Jesus, or Mary's ghost, appearing in these visions – but rather *the Angel, or higher entity, of the Mother of Jesus.*

For its part, the final *Time* magazine of 1991 reported on "the most interesting aspect of [the Virgin's] growing popular veneration: a theological tug-of-war taking place over Mary's image". The article explored differing views of the Virgin, ranging from the traditional Christian view – a passive handmaid of God associated with submissiveness, purity, unsexed virginity – to much more radical interpretations of Mary drawing upon even more ancient traditions of Goddess worship – as a feminist, a liberating force of feminine divinity characterized by "autonomy, independence and earthiness".[99N]

But beyond even these stark divisions of opinion, of course, lies the greatest of all causes of disagreement about Mary in the present day, which is this: What sort of reality in today's secular, materialistic world could there possibly be for the angelic Mother of Jesus?

❧   ❧   ❧

> *I was created by a group of people, sitting in a circle just like this, in a long distant time. It was a conscious act of creation. One of the reasons I am involved in this communication is my talent, my ability, to combine with group energies. It is my function to weave together different energy levels. I am not the only one like me. At this level, there are a few.*
> – Moita (July 24, 1982)

As our contact with Moita continues to develop, we will discover over and over that we have limited the scope of her being within our own minds – nowhere else. The extent of her activities and connections "behind the scenes" is always apt to surprise us when some small part of her weaving reaches the surface of consciousness. Even more devastating to our habitually narrowed perception are those occasions when we glimpse – beyond her by now familiar, genial, playful personality – a greater overlighting *presence*. Of course, that should not be so surprising given the startling form in which Moita first appeared to Kelly.

As a point of departure, consider the following short exchange after one of our early sessions. Here a first-time participant describes the psychic image she sees superimposed on Kelly's face while Moita is present. (Be aware that Kelly herself has brown hair and green/hazel eyes.)

Moita Session #21 (Kelly, Scott, Laura / August 12, 1978)

Laura: She certainly was a nice lady! I was going to tell her at one point what beautiful blue eyes she has!

Kelly: She has blond hair, too.

Laura: I know, I could see she had blond hair.

❧   ❧   ❧

Next is one of those intriguing so-called coincidences, uncovered when Ellen and her daughter Connie attend their first session.

Moita Session #168 (Kelly, David, Ellen, Connie / December 28, 1980)

MOITA: My name is Moita.

Ellen: *(in a half-whisper)* I've *missed* you.

MOITA: The time is coming soon when the Earth and its people will not need to miss us any longer. We have missed *you*. *(pause, as Ellen is near tears)* We have always been there.

Ellen: I know. That is what's given me the strength...

(We learn where all this sudden emotion is coming from afterwards. Ellen explains that during trials in her life she has felt a presence, a peace/calm radiating down her back and filling her. Then, as Kelly describes to her how Moita has appeared to herself and others in the past – like the Virgin Mary, but with blond hair and blue eyes, unlike the majority of her portraits – Ellen reveals that she used to pray to just such an image of the Virgin when she was young and living in a convent. In the past while, we've been encountering a surprising number of these non-traditional representations of the Virgin with light features.)

❧   ❧   ❧

Moita Session #169 (Kelly and David / January 4, 1981)

David: How do you see Ellen's comment that she "missed" you, that she recognized your energy? Is there a specific link there as well as the universal kind of love you radiate?

(Speaking slowly in response, due to Kelly's apprehensions about who Moita really is or might claim to be, and how others might react:)

MOITA: In Ellen's case, it is more than just the type of energy I radiate that was familiar to her. *(pause)* In my capacity as a group entity, I have radiated out to many beings. *(pause)* This life will see many of them being drawn together.

David: I'm not sure how you mean "in my capacity as a group entity" you have done this.

MOITA: I occupy a particular vibrational rate. Those on this plane who seek that vibration very often call me. There are not as many [entities] on this level as there are on levels *between* [you] and where I am. *(pause)* Calls do not go unanswered. So, those I do answer, throughout time, become in a sense part of a group of souls with whom I am connected...

(After the session:)

Kelly: Right at the start, I wasn't too sure how present she was going to be, because I wondered if I was going to be in there fighting answers. But my mind – or her mind – was so clear it was like it was completely *blank* while you were asking your questions and until she started talking. Then the energy started getting higher and higher, and I more and more spaced out...

I got the clear impression that there's a group of entities, like sisters to Moita – but not very many, only a handful – on the same vibrational plane; and that between them they absorb a lot of the prayers to the Virgin, because their energy seems to represent that image that we have. That was what I was experiencing when she was talking about her group sharing the different calls...

After the session was over, and I had the tears on my face – because the feeling Moita generated meant a lot to me – I saw her very clearly in my mind. She looked just like she did the first time I saw her, surrounded by white light. There was a feeling of the light streaming into me, over us both, sharing all this love down onto us.

       ∾   ∾   ∾

Joan, whose letter provokes the next two very significant exchanges, is herself learning to be a channel. Readers may remember her and her husband Arthur from their earlier whirlwind visit to meet us and attend a Moita session (excerpted in Chapter 8).

<u>Moita Session #148 (Kelly and David / July 4, 1980)</u>

David: Joan asked us to ask you about a dream of hers. There was a woman who had a blue aura coming out of her mouth and who repeated to Joan that her name was "Mary". Then there was a party with many people, and those who were free of the body had the same aura, while those who were not did not. What can you tell her about this dream?

MOITA: Her dream is more literal than symbolic. It was more of an astral experience than a dream, although the two realms are difficult to separate at times.

She met a teacher and other students. The blue aura coming from the mouth...means the spiritual path, known rather than wished for, and spoken – a sign of channeling, going through the speech centre, being shared with others... It expresses her purpose – part of her purpose – in this life. And the others in the room who also had the aura from the mouth [were] of the same level of her teacher, or others who were there learning the art of speaking between worlds.

I have been called "Mary" before. This is not the first time.

(There is a pause as the possible implications of this begin to sink in. Then, probing to see if Moita would cite any specific times in the past:)

David: What do you mean "before"?

MOITA: Before her dream!

David: Right. *(laughs, then trying a different tack:)* That being a name for you as a teacher on your level, or are you referring to an incarnation?

MOITA: Not to any incarnations, but to a certain identity of energy that those here have for my presence.

(Silent period, with intense energy in our gazes. Finally, I use a term from recent communications about visions of the Virgin at Fatima and elsewhere.)

David: Are you, or are you part of, what has been called the Angel of the Mother of Jesus? *(pause)*

MOITA: All spirits who choose to identify with that energy gravitate towards...becoming one with it.

❧   ❧   ❧

Moita Session #171 (Kelly, David, Sean / January 17, 1981)

David: What is the connection between a group entity and the Virgin Mary?

(In answering, Moita speaks first of a "High Being", the Angel of the Mother of Jesus; and secondly, of the soul of Mary, the "vessel".)

MOITA: As a soul rises through the levels, it becomes more than one. The higher the soul, the more souls it is comprised of. In order for a High Being to manifest itself on the Earth, a special vessel must be picked, one that is already many. So, a pattern was formed...

Even if the Virgin did not have to be a multiple soul, the pattern would have been altered when she was accepted by the Church as a being who could intercede on their behalf. For they created another soul, another group entity, by their images and their thoughts going in that direction. So, it happened that the pattern was reinforced...

David: Do you see your connection with the Virgin as only a part of who you are?

MOITA: That image is only a recent one.

David: Mm-hmm. And there are older images and identities that you might associate yourself with that include more possibilities?

MOITA: I suppose. I have had many images throughout time. Not any one has been all of me.

David: I think I'll give up questions.

(Bathed as I am in such intense, warm energy, I feel almost embarrassed.)

MOITA: *(laughs)* They are not easy ones to ask. *(pause)* Someday you shall see *all* of me. Then you will know the answer.

David: "The answer"! *(laughs)*

MOITA: It is the only way.

❧   ❧   ❧

As with the physical Mary two millennia ago, Kelly's own "vertical" connections have become relatively clear: from being a medium within groups on this level, "upward" to Moita as a group entity for various groups and a large number of souls to whom she is connected, and then "higher" still to Amar, Moita's greater self, who oversees and interacts with an even vaster number of groups and souls, usually indirectly via their entities, as well as touching yet higher levels. I am similarly related, through Loria, to Amar – though it is tempting to wonder about the precise nature of that connection, just as Kelly has wondered how exactly she is linked to Moita.

Before finishing this and the last chapter, we will also be learning more of the "horizontal" links: those between Kelly and myself, and between Moita and Loria. Starting from the "bottom," we find strong connections between Kelly and me despite – or perhaps because of – our differences. On July 12, 1978, two weeks after her first words to us, Moita says this about Kelly and me: "It is very rare that two such different souls decide to spend so many lives together in so many kinds of ways." On August 1st she follows that up with this key sentence, possessing far-reaching implications we will still be unravelling years later: "Spiritually speaking, you and Kelly stand back to back." Kelly receives the image of two warriors' stances in battle, each protecting the other's blind spot.

Early in 1979, Moita refers to this same image while explaining our sources of strength to meet the turmoil that our coming together in this life has provoked. The occasion is my receiving an invitation – to me alone, not us together – to guide hypersentience sessions in another city. The woman inviting me knew me when I was with Ruth; and now, without ever meeting her, she has made known her rejection of Moita in favour of Loria.

Moita Session #66 (Kelly and David / February 6, 1979)

MOITA: Do you know, the way this life has been led, you are at the centre of the hurricane, the eye of the storm? And those who are on the edge of it, who are in the worst parts of it, view you on the one hand as the cause of the storm, or on the other as being the one who somehow managed to get into the best spot. You will stay in the centre of the eye so long as you stay centred in your self...

You are not yet strong enough to part in your work and have it serve your purposes. Others would be very glad to drive a wedge between you and keep you from the eye of the storm. There *are* other things at work here besides what sees. You cannot stand back to back unless you are together.

There is an early shared incarnation of ours, uncovered by Kelly in September 1978, which will serve ever after as a touchstone in understanding both our difference and our connection, that "natural bridge" often depicted in my dreams. Being so central to our relationship, as well as to the cycle of consciousness now coming to fruition on Earth, much of this second hypersentience of ours will be given verbatim.

As with her Musili regression, the words Kelly speaks can only hint at our different consciousness of the world in that time. The transcript also demonstrates the karmic consequences one can bring upon oneself by how one chooses to view a life after it is over. The effects of the choice we two made seem to have lasted even into this life, shaping some of our reactions to recent conflicts. But eventually, we will release the negative and bring the positive wholeheartedly forward.

Now enter with Kelly into the consciousness of a far different time and place, resembling none other than the Garden of Eden . . . but with the Fall also in progress.

Hypersentience Session #27B (Kelly; David, guiding / September 15, 1978)

Kelly: I am outside. It is sunny, warm. There is a man on a hill. He does not have on much apparel. He wears a loose cloth. He is very tall and fair. There is a sense of the Sun in him. He is in some way connected to that energy that pours down upon us. The air itself is alive. It speaks. It has a voice, and we hear it.

He and I are connected. We form a unit and work together. It is a time of great joy. All things happen as they should. There is time enough for everything – a sense of oneness with those things around, a knowing how it works, an understanding of needs and of place.

He speaks to the Sun and I speak to the Ground, and we weave together what we are told and make it whole.

David: How do you appear?

Kelly: I too am tall and fair and do not wear much apparel. There is no need for clothing. There is no need for work here. We do not grow food. It is there for us when we need it.

David: Can you look at this in time and space?

Kelly: The Earth is very young and new and filled with the wonder of itself and its own discoveries. That is why everything speaks – it seems it has so much to say.

David: Who is this man?

Kelly: (smiling) You know without asking.

David: (softly laughing) Yes.

Kelly: We are alone. There are no other people near us. There are other places where there are people, but we would not or could not stay with the others.

David: Are they not like us, then?

Kelly: Where we are, we are the last of a special breed. We have not yet forgotten where we came from. The others have started the long descent into forgetfulness, and parts of the Earth are changing so that the world can no longer speak.

There was an attempt to stop this descent, but it proved fruitless and wasteful because none were able to hear what was said. You tried to sing to them of the Sun. They did not understand your meaning. They did not really want us to stay, either. Our presence caused them great discomfort because some part of them knew they had lost something, and they were angry at having lost it and hid their anger and turned it to other uses to try to make up for what they lost.

And so, since nothing could be done, we eventually decided to leave and go back to the world we knew and understood, and try to remember it, because we knew a time would come when we also would forget. We wished to strengthen the memory so when the time was right it would come back and help us to see clearly what was going on, to be able to touch the world again.

The rest of our days are filled with wonder and joy. (long pause) We die the way we lived. We pour ourselves into the world at the same time. (pause)

(Kelly will later describe this scene: "We won't be parted, so when the time comes that we know our bodies won't last much longer, we lie together in the sunlight and leave our bodies. We mingle with all the things we have always touched. The only thing that is different is that, this time, we don't come back.")

Kelly: There is a coldness in my heart.

David: Why?

Kelly: You are gone... I am lost, very much alone... There is a feeling of guilt.

David: Over what?

Kelly: There is a feeling of thinking we were selfish, that we could have tried harder and made the others aware. So we choose to part and learn something else in a different way. I think it is a punishment inflicted on ourselves. We think perhaps we had no right to still be able to touch the world when others could not. We lost touch with our fellow men. We have to understand why they have forgotten and what they have to learn, so we can meet them on the other side and perhaps know the right words, so that then they will be able to hear...

(Kelly goes through a life of great pain, lacking any sense of her own identity while being treated cruelly by others. After her death:)

Kelly: I meet you again to find out what you've learned, to see if it is time to put it back together. We agree to meet, but it is not a meeting of recognition. It is one of rejection, of not knowing.

David: We agree that it will be that way?

Kelly: Strange as it sounds, we do. We are still punishing ourselves for that one life. Although we have each gone through a number of lives in between, we still do not feel we have made atonement for our joy. I can feel others around us who cannot be seen. I can sense their thoughts – that it is foolish – but they do not interfere.

(Kelly goes through another life, in which she is a male spastic and mute, reputed to have certain powers. I am a man who comes some distance to investigate him, but he does not fit my preconceptions. He "recognizes" me, but cannot speak. I leave, but wonder why the memory haunts me for the rest of my life.)

Kelly: We meet after your death, for I was older than you and died first. We decide that it was perhaps a foolish thing that we did – and cruel. We make an agreement that in any other lives we share together there will be recognition. That frees us to start back on the road that will lead us to where we began our descent. *(long pause)*

We are still afraid. The fear is not gone just because we decide to approach the problem from a different angle. In our next life, we go back...to a time similar in feel to the first. This time, however, we make certain there are others who see as we do, so we do not become isolated from other people. It is a good existence – one filled with purpose and love.

We are building a bridge between those lives so we can cross over it. We are finished with punishing ourselves for the first one. We are in a sense connecting this life and the first one, and in some way bypassing what came between. That is why we choose a [world] similar in nature and closer in time.

(Kelly will say afterward that this latter life is the one in Musili. Near the end of the session, Moita comes through briefly to speak.)

David: I would like to ask a brief question or two.

MOITA: Speak while you may.

David: I gather that Kelly's back trouble *(i.e. her sciatic nerve trouble now)* – one root of it – would be possibly as an echo of the life in which I rejected her and her physical condition.

MOITA: That is part of it. There is also the feeling of guilt . . .

David: Mm-hmm.

MOITA: . . . over the sense of joy.

David: Yeah. That was the reason for that life...

MOITA: There is nothing wrong with joy. Those who do not have joy of their own do not wish to see joy in others. It makes them feel more separated from the world and themselves. It creates a great discomfort that reaches very deep in others. There is much fear of joy in this world.

David: I think that perhaps we should stop now.

MOITA: Yes. Much has been accomplished here. I just wish to say: be gentle with yourself. *(pause)* There is enough power in love to do anything that needs doing.

We shall speak of this later. I will help you return her to you... Farewell.

David: Now, Kelly, our starchild, is floating toward Earth and descending into her body to a place where she is very loved, opening her eyes at the right time. I shall count forward to ten and touch you. Here we come...

❧   ❧   ❧

Three months later, Moita asks us to return with her to this "Earth and Sun" life – the virgin embodiment of innocence and earthiness made whole.

Moita Session #53 (Kelly and David / December 19, 1978)

MOITA: I am taking us to a more familiar place... Let your imagination flow. The room and the seasons can change. In the life you two lived together alone with the Earth and the Sun, that was a time when [our levels] were much closer. *I* was much closer, and the others here. And you were more open, in touch. We spoke of many things then. We spoke of now. *(pause)* Many things you see and do not notice until they are placed before you. *(long pause of several minutes' duration)*

It is a good time to find out many things.

(After other conversation, Moita returns to this mood, as if waiting for the right question.)

MOITA: I can speak to you of things from long ago.

David: All right. *(with a laugh)* Do you want questions? You said that then we spoke of now. How did we see the connection then?

MOITA: You saw this as a possible opportunity to accomplish that which you could not in that life: the bringing back to yourself of the awareness of life, and the communicating of that to those around you, so that you would not feel isolated. That life is one of the basic urges that has pushed you in the direction of forming a community: the need to share those feelings and [that] awareness with others, not just for yourself, and not just for those who are aware already, as [were] those...in Musili... You...are looking for a key that will unlock the minds of those around you and let them see the light – not for the elite, but for the many...

David: When you say reaching "the many" instead of the few, are you talking mainly about numbers or about kinds of awareness?

MOITA: I am not speaking of numbers; I am speaking of the different types of people. *(pause)* You planned on bringing many things forward. Each life you have chosen to remember in this one you have chosen for a very specific reason: to help you touch the energy that you need and to learn the lessons that you want.

When you go and sit under the tree in the Sun, you reach down into yourself and pull those things up – those memories, that knowledge and that wisdom. *(silent period)* And you are not doing this alone. Others are here to help you, have chosen to come here with you for similar reasons, and for their own.

(After this session, Kelly says: "I saw us standing on a hill under a tree with the Sun. That was when she was talking about, and before. I could see her trying to put us both into that particular space. She was there, too. Sometimes I saw her almost as a physical presence, except she wasn't. It seemed we were in touch with her level in a direct way – not like this. I got the feeling Moita was inviting you to ask about you and me – the whole shot – how we came together, why, what purpose, when.)

ꙮ   ꙮ   ꙮ

Some of the higher-level background to Kelly's and my differences was suggested by Moita on October 18, 1978, when she said, "There is a difference, in essence, between Loria and I, in that I have lived in bodies and she has not. And so, we bring a different perspective." Early in the new year, I ask Moita to elaborate on the polarities between Kelly and me. (Moita's comment about Loria and herself will connect with my dream from that very morning and, in turn, Kelly's first past-life regression.)

Moita Session #56 (Kelly and David / January 9, 1979)
(I am feeling Loria's energy-presence very strongly tonight.)

David: Can you tell us more about how Kelly and I are so different and yet "stand back to back"?

MOITA: It would be difficult to express many of the concepts that are the basis for that statement. You have been told by Loria that she was created in whole on the level that she now exists in. She was a conscious creation on the part of other entities who were on the same [non-physical] level. You have also been told that I was created by a group of individuals who took part in the creation consciously but were certainly *not* in existence on that level. *(i.e. they were on the Earth plane)*

We are your roots. Where I have gone through my own wheel [of rebirths], Loria has not. We bring to you different aspects of unity – different views, a different texture or focus. In this way you both represent the greater coming together of the two levels, the meeting of the worlds, even though you yourself have gone through your own wheel and are still on it. The quality of your soul is different because of your roots.

It is important that the two worlds come together as one. Some feel these are contradictory – the differences between Earth and Sun. You have not lost your difference, but you have intermingled your sameness and brought it up.

David: Can you say more of how that difference gets expressed on our level, in our awareness?

MOITA: You are more the dreamer, the creator of high ideals, a weaver of worlds. She is more the sustaining centre, the practical aspect (?), the workings out. Does that express it?...Your [own] sustenance comes in a different form – the thing that makes you a healer, a healer of minds. *(pause)* Do you see the connection?

David: Yes, well, they're all *connected.* They wouldn't work if they weren't.

MOITA: So you see that we have conspired together to bring this about – I on my part, Loria on hers. We have been with you both throughout eternity.

David: That makes me think of my dream last night. I was reading in an old book talking about [Kelly's first past-life regression] and Loria's name came up...

(This Moita session continues after the next section.)

❧   ❧   ❧

Here is my previous night's dream as referred to above, followed by an excerpt from our first hypersentience session with Kelly as subject.

"Old Book about Loria" dream
David (age 31) / January 9, 1979

I am reading a little, old-fashioned book about [Kelly's life starting as a visionary country girl], though at the time I think of Kelly as Leanne, who is there with me. At one point in the book, I am amazed to find repeated references to "Loria", as if confirming a link between my own entity and this particular past life.

I invite Leanne/Kelly to read the page also. But she becomes so apprehensive at the prospect of seeing all that is written that she gives up before reaching the key sentence. So I must read it to her.

Early in Kelly's regression on June 27, 1978, she says with innocent amazement:

I see two people coming down from the clouds. I am scared. One is very tall, and bright. His hair is like the Sun. He is hard to see, to look at. The other is not as tall and he is dark. He is easier to see. He is softer, not as bright. They tell me that there are problems. There is great trouble brewing in the world, and they want me to help...

They say, when the time comes, they will let me know. It is just, I have to agree first... They say I can say no, but I cannot say no. They pull me with their brightness. I want to be with them... I feel they offer me freedom... They also offer me pain...

The first paragraph should be familiar, as it was also quoted in Chapter 11 as a parallel to suggestions of archangels in my "Election of a New Pope" dream. The polarity ascribed there to Michael and Gabriel may also relate to Sun (bright) and Earth (dark).

In Kelly's regression, as the country girl grew older, she received guidance from feminine beings as well – interpreting them, consistent with her Roman Catholic upbringing, as individual saints. In that life, I was a priest who, alone among my colleagues, believed in and quietly supported the girl during her inspired challenges to authority, up to and including her death.

Ѧ   Ѧ   Ѧ

Continuing the January 9, 1979 session:

MOITA: Are you asking for something?

David: Well, I didn't remember anything *else* that that book [in my dream] said. It was rather difficult reading.

MOITA: Yes, I imagine. *(laughter)*

(Kelly has the feeling the book was from the astral Hall of Records – which dreamers usually find notoriously hard to read.)

David: Can you tell me more?

MOITA: The implication was that Loria had been one of the voices.

David: One of the ones that she interpreted as a saint?

MOITA: Yes. She could not have interpreted any voice any other way...

(Kelly hears the name of the particular saint repeating in her mind at this point, apparently confirming the "implication" involving Loria.)

MOITA: It is interesting how these arrangements work out.

David: Did she interpret your voice as one of the others?

MOITA: She interpreted me in more than one way – or rather, the other parts of me.

David: Different parts of you spoke to her, you mean?

MOITA: Yes! – I *mean*. You have *met* different parts of me already.

Ѧ   Ѧ   Ѧ

Thus did Loria and Moita very intently work together in channeling their inspiring energies to the person Kelly was then – as they do to both of us today, in sessions, in dreams, and at other times. Though the most succinct image we have for Loria's energy is a shining white lamb (as she first appeared to Ruth in a dream[100N]), symbolizing "the way of simplicity and the heart", I am reminded she is limitless. Similarly, one encompassing image we might have for Moita would be a shining jewel, including among her many facets energies associated with the compassionate Virgin, the magic of Musili and an Eden-like Earth.

For a final example of a "conspiracy" on higher levels that affected not merely Kelly and me, growing through the latter half of the 20th century, but, it would seem, a substantial portion of our generation, I want to share the very first of our exchanges on the subject of the Virgin Mary. This session occurs before we are told, or guess, the extent of Moita's participation on these levels.

I begin by recalling it was in the early spring of 1971 – as the mass visions of the Virgin in Zeitoun, Egypt, were nearing their end – that Kelly first experienced Moita, a glowing presence of high energy, visibly to her open eyes. She saw her floating in the air, wearing a blue robe, with long, light golden hair, her hands outspread, palms upward, in a characteristic gesture. Consistent with the Zeitoun sightings, Kelly would on two later occasions see such a figure wearing a shining crown.

Moita Session #43 (Kelly and David / May 13, 1980)

David: We want to ask whether your first appearance to Kelly in 1971 was made more possible because of the energy that was being released through the visions at Zeitoun from 1968 to 1971. Obviously the energy of those experiences is connected, but was it made more possible by the timing?

MOITA: I would say that that was one factor, of many. But it is without a doubt an energy-release that occurred and is occurring at that time. You will find in your own searchings, and in other people's experience, that that particular energy has affected their own openings, even if they were unaware of it at that time. The manifesting on your plane of such a Presence serves to open many doors in all minds that are ready to be open. It gives you the extra push along your own path that you otherwise might not have experienced in this life.

(It seems now entirely non-coincidental that the period of the late 1960s and early 1970s saw the accelerated unfolding of feminist, peace, environmental and spiritual interests and approaches to life on the part of many in our generation – including, most famously, the Beatles – superseding the more masculine-defined political tumult of the earlier 1960s.)

David: Yes, I've just realized how that same period, starting in 1968 [after becoming a war resister], was the start of *my* spiritual opening, the start of the deeply transforming dreams – sometimes with a feminine guiding figure – that began leading me towards being here today. I hadn't thought of that before.

MOITA: As you gain a broader view, patterns become more obvious.

෴   ෴   ෴

Illustrative Dream

One of my earliest treasured dreams came to me near the end of 1971, the year Moita first appeared to Kelly. As mentioned in the Introduction, I would conclude my M.A. thesis a couple years later with three archetypal dreams that lifted it beyond its academic origins – and this was the last of those three.

The dream is set in winter and refers to Christmas – to crafts, perhaps a pageant, and animals that might be in a manger. Mysteriously, the dream then refers to a new being evolving "out of the rose". I first associate this with nature and the feminine, and with the lotus symbol of Buddhism, wherein our spirits are seen to rise like stems from the mud, ultimately flowering into enlightenment.[101N] Only more recently have I become fully aware of the "rose" as a symbol for the Virgin Mary. Thus we have Christmas again, celebrating the birth of a "new being", the Christ-consciousness.

To these traditional Christian images, the dream adds a "flying saucer" spacecraft – in fact, a fully articulated mandala or Medicine Wheel, consistent with Carl Jung's insight into flying saucers as archetypal images.[102] (Curiously, the newly evolved beings who emerge from the craft are metallic[103N], as also in my "Lotus Meditation Being" dream a few years later.) And there is one other major element that testifies to this being a modern dream: a devastating nuclear accident or war.

Pleadings for world peace have been prominent in the messages associated with Marian apparitions during the 20th century. And it happens that just above this dream as recorded in my journal on the morning of November 6th, I noted this is the earliest possible date for another U.S. nuclear test (the Cannikin project) at Amchitka Island in the Aleutians. Multiple concerns about such tests have recently been much on my mind and the minds of Greenpeace and others around the world who have tried to stop them. As it turns out:

> *Cannikin* was detonated on November 6, 1971, as the thirteenth test of the Operation Grommet (1971–1972) underground nuclear test series. [It was] the largest underground nuclear test in US history. (Estimates for the precise yield range from 4.4 to 5.2 megatons...). The ground lifted 20 feet (6 m), caused by an explosive force equivalent almost 400 times the power of the Hiroshima bomb [causing] a seismic shock of 7.0 on the Richter scale...[104N]

On the morning of November 6th, though – not knowing whether this massive nuclear bomb has been or will be detonated on the northwest tip of North America – I awake from an all-consuming dream to ponder: Which world *is* this?

"New Being Evolved Out of the Rose" dream
David (age 24) / November 6, 1971
I am riding over an unfamiliar route to my family's home in the company of two intelligent young women I've just met again, remembering them from public school days. I'm aware of wishing I'd gotten to know them better back then.[105N]

We're travelling along a woodsy road with beautiful ice- and snow-covered branches shining in the morning sunlight. We see a crowd of people coming out of a building set back from the road. I vaguely remember this as a crafts centre and playhouse in which I once, as a child, attended a Christmas program.

We stop and begin hunting for the pair of oxen that used to be kept here. Having found the large old animals, my thoughts fall on the millstone the oxen used to pull. It is in the sky, however, that I see it. Above distant hills, a white disk appears, spinning toward us in a slow arc. Before we have a chance to react, the flying saucer skids into the side of the hill just below the road and comes to rest: a large, circular vehicle with spokes joining an outer wheel to the inner hub.

We are a little apprehensive as the hatch atop the centre is raised – and out climb a number of large, erect, metallic, ant-like creatures! I make haste to raise my palm in friendship and, to my relief, they return the gesture. Immediately, then, the creatures pass out reels of film to me and others.

Held up to the light, the films show their saucer flying over beautiful futuristic towns that are artfully nestled amid green contours of natural landscape. Their generosity with these reels, and their almost childlike glee, are reassuring and warming. They seem happy and excited to show us what they have been up to, and to give us something to share with our friends when we go home and describe what has happened.

But as the scenes in the films do not resemble the quality of civilization we on Earth have attained, I ask if these pictures are from a different world, perhaps our visitors' home planet. At this point, one of the creatures explains.

Some time ago, a massive thermonuclear explosion laid waste much of the Earth and most, though not all, of human civilization. God, or the creative energies active in the universe, were so dismayed at man's behaviour that they caused – or perhaps the radiation itself caused – all of humanity to be put to sleep and to dream for a long time, though we would feel it to be only a short interval in our sleep. In the interim, a new being evolved "out of the rose" – meaning the creatures before us.

The world we see in their films is our very own Earth, except it is an Earth renewed in accordance with their higher consciousness. Their hope is that, when men are permitted to wake up – which time has just now arrived – they will be won over to a more deeply human way of living through the example of these wise, generous, childlike new beings and their virgin civilization.

The necessary changes have been made in a way to minimize the differences in appearance from our previous, hostilely divided world. So I wake up to the morning sun lighting my bedroom, wondering whether all has been "recreated in the night".[106N]

‰   ‰   ‰

Chapter 17

ROOT AND BRANCH: A FAMILY TREE

In this way you both represent the greater coming together of the two levels, the meeting of the worlds. It is important that the two worlds come together as one. You have not lost your difference, but you have intermingled your sameness and brought it up.

– Moita

The individual is the route to the universal, and the personal to the spiritual. These are the warp and weft of a tapestry woven from each and all of our lives. Because of the tapestry we *are*, true spiritual growth brings a warmth of energy and meaning to life that strict rules and abstract dogma can never achieve. Such recognition underlies the to-and-fro movement in this book: from pertinent information in response to the searchings of many participants, to immersion in the authors' lives and explorations, and back again with learnings to further the spiritual quest of this age.

In this final chapter, Kelly's and my delving into our soul-natures and soul-histories culminates in a number of interconnected ways. We attempt to let my entity Loria speak through me, and we take steps to resolve our estrangement from Ruth. Loria's own origins are revealed, including the identity of the being who birthed her, and we gain fuller understanding of the intimate connection between Kelly's soul and Moita. Lastly, examples from Kelly's and my experience are given to illustrate the universality of the "Earth and Sun" polarity – the eternal interplay of outer and inner that spirals up and down a cone of power, weaving the Tree of Life.

৯   ৯   ৯

Despite our separation from former partners, Christmas 1978 is a happy time for Kelly and me, Donovan and Arista, as we trim our tree with mostly homemade decorations, topped by Kelly's handsewn singing angel, in the little house to which Moita's "manoeuverings" led us two months earlier. Then, on the day after Christmas, we try an experiment: holding a session and inviting Loria to speak directly – which has never occurred before in Ruth's absence. As it turns out, this night we come as near as we ever will to achieving a dialogue among Loria, Moita and Kelly.

Moita/Loria Session #54 (Kelly and David / December 26, 1978)
MOITA: You are very close to us tonight!... What would you like to do?
David: Come as close as I can to "someone else"...
MOITA: And how would you do *that*?
David: By not trying to, in one sense. *(pause)*
MOITA: Make yourself as still as possible. *(pause)* Let your thoughts float away.

(longer pause) Can you speak for another? (pause) You must allow your imagination freedom...

(Long silence, as I feel Loria's energy rising within me.)

David: "I'm pleased to be in such a loving home," is what I feel she's saying.

MOITA: Can you let yourself imagine that it is actually happening? (pause) Then I address my question to that other whom you are allowing to speak, and tell me: Where are *you* from?

(In the following dialogue, I still feel myself quite present, consciously participating in imagining it as well as being receptive to "another". Where I am speaking as Loria, the words are attributed to her despite variations I experience in the degree of her and my participation.)

LORIA: From inner space, I come to greet you Kelly, and Moita, and David.

MOITA: I welcome you! It is good to be together in the same place.

LORIA: A bit strange, is it not, to see each other in this way?

MOITA: (smiling) I must say it is different! Not the way we usually see each other. But then, these two would not be able to see us any other way.

LORIA: (smiling) David is already feeling I'm wearing his face thin!

MOITA: It is a common complaint. We glow too much from within. What do you wish to be called? (pause) Is it too hard a choice for now?

LORIA: I feel "Loria" will do. I would like Kelly and David to – I'm finding it hard getting words through here – to understand how unlimited is the one who goes by that name.

MOITA: We are *all* limitless... It will grow easier to choose words as your presence grows stronger.

(Long silence. This is followed by talk of the sensation of "hardness" I feel: that it is Loria's "pressure", that it takes constant attention on my part to rise above it, that each entity affects a "vehicle" in different ways.[107N])

MOITA: What were your plans? (pause)

LORIA: It may be best not to reveal my plans now, though they will involve David's changing some concepts of himself.

MOITA: Is there anything you wish to make clear at this time?

LORIA: That I'm very glad to be here, and that I love you all!

MOITA: Thank you! There has been some doubt in that area.

LORIA: As long as people doubt, they will not allow themselves to hear what really is said beyond the doubt.

MOITA: And you have, perhaps, released *some* . . . and created more!

LORIA: Some doubts are creative.

MOITA: In the end, they *all* are.

(Our cats Silkie and Mouse arrive.)

LORIA: It's good to see you again, Silkie.

MOITA: *Many* old friends! Soon it shall be time to speak of you and I.

LORIA: And perhaps how compatible we are (?).

MOITA: They would be *amazed*. (long pause) Is he becoming familiar with you?

LORIA: The hardness is gone. He still wonders which is him and which is me.

MOITA: He will wonder that for a long time. For him there is no other way, at the moment. *(pause)* He has many questions!...

(Moments later, we take a break.)

David: A lot of me was still here, and I was at best speaking *for* what I picked up. So who knows? It felt good, though, to take that point of view. It freed me.

Kelly: Well, whatever happened, the energy level was definitely increased a great deal.

David: Yeah, it was as much as it ever has been. Sometimes a rush of tingling went through me. I practically couldn't feel your hands as such – just the energy. So, what did that feel like to you?

Kelly: You looked different. Real clearer somewhere, maybe in the eyes. And Moita was *really* strong! Wow, was she ever in! I could feel her like a huge column of light energy just pouring down into me.

David: ...Really, it does make a big difference in how *I* feel not to see myself as being David on *this* level, asking questions of Moita on *that* level... That erases some sort of barrier right there. I don't know if I see the point in being David asking questions. It's probably a little like ice skating: to learn, you must do it. It's almost feigning ignorance to be just David – even if I don't know precisely what it is I'm feigning not to know!

(So we decide to have Kelly ask questions of Loria for a change. After meditation:)

Kelly: It's been a while since I've seen you!

LORIA: I've been around, you know.

Kelly: Yes, I've seen you *that* way. But that last time I saw you was with David and Ruth, through Ruth.

LORIA: And how did you experience me then?

Kelly: As a really nice energy. I must say you took me by surprise when you told me about that life as an herbalist.[108]

LORIA: You had already begun to remember.

Kelly: And I suspected you were going to tell me something too. And I know we know each other.

LORIA: How could we not?!...

Kelly: Can you say anything about why David and I are here?

(Long pause; my eyes closed.)

LORIA: I'm seeing the image . . . of a star or a planet, with many rings or orbits moving around it at different angles, and so, in the end forming a sphere that is yet always moving and alive. It expresses how many-sided is your love. And each orbit is yet around a common centre where you two meet. And there is light shining out into space in all directions, that some already feel and many will feel in days to come.

(Loria's presence, meanwhile, has grown significantly. Later I realize that my openness to dreams suggests receiving images as a promising approach for me.)

Kelly: What's happening with you and Ruth?

(Long pause; my eyes closed)

LORIA: I must first ask you why you are asking.

Kelly: Partly curiosity, partly concern.

LORIA: What is your concern from?

Kelly: That she'll lose touch with you for a while.

LORIA: And why would that concern you?

Kelly: Because it's a beautiful experience, an important one. I wouldn't want anyone to lose it if they didn't need to.

LORIA: We all do what we need to do.

Kelly: Does that mean she needs to lose touch?

LORIA: I did not say that.

Kelly: I know, that's why I'm asking.

(Long pause; my eyes are again closed through most of the following.)

LORIA: As you know, Ruth went through some times in which her shock and anger clouded contact with her deeper layers. But at the same time, she also experienced her independence and her strength in a new way. Since then, she has been finding her joy in life increasingly, and feeling my presence more and more closely, though not yet – or not nearly so much – in the most direct way she used to. But it is what she feels is good for her at this point.

Kelly: How do you feel about it? *(pause)*

LORIA: I experience joy as each of you find your own path, and realize you are still here despite apparently insurmountable barriers that you placed in your path for a purpose.

Kelly: How do you feel about gaining contact so closely and then having it plugged up in some way? How does that affect you as an entity?

LORIA: You are forgetting that, for me, there is not one stage followed by another. For me, they go together in a pattern. *(pause)* There are also advantages to a relationship that is not as public as the way that I spoke through Ruth in your past. There are seasons to everything; nor will this season last forever.

Kelly: What's your relationship with Moita?

LORIA: *(laughing)* You ask me?!

Kelly: *(laughing)* It's hard to ask Moita!

LORIA: For the moment, we think we will let you experience us relating, instead of attempting to force our vitality into one of your extremely limited sentences.

(A silence follows as we gaze. Then Kelly closes her eyes. When they open, Moita also is there, but we soon agree to end the session.)

MOITA: You have much to talk about.

David: It has been a long night.

MOITA: Wishing you fair dreams.

David: Thank you... Good night.

MOITA: Good night.

                ❧   ❧   ❧

Although Kelly will continue periodically to see Loria's image around me during our sessions, the above transcript is also the last in our notebooks – to date – presenting me as a channel for Loria. Perhaps I simply fail to take advantage of the opportunity to extend myself further with Moita's help. But for the most part, I decide dreams and the written word are my own best forms of communication. In any case, Moita continues to be forthcoming with information confirming and extending my intuitions, as in this next session.

<u>Moita Session #132 (Kelly and David / February 13, 1980)</u>
David: We have heard about the purpose for which you were created by a human group. Can you say anything about the purpose for which Loria was created – the particular kind of energy that went into her creation?
MOITA: *(very slowly)* There have been a few created like her. In a way, the purpose is to bring a sense of innocence to the world, more balance. A being that has many connections through energy use to the Earth and its spirit sometimes cannot bring the right kind of perception. Being too close to the difficulties that must be overcome may serve to blind some to other possibilities. We have our own [Medicine] Wheel, and it is important to see all perspectives.
David: That really helps; it's good. I can see it in my own inner approach to life. I also see some of the problems it creates – why very practical, grounded activities seem sometimes like a great effort, rather foreign. And the innocence – it connects with the symbol of the lamb in Loria's first communications to Ruth and me.
MOITA: And Ruth's dream.
David: Yes. It is rare, I gather, for entities to be created on that level and not go through reincarnation?
MOITA: When a being reaches this particular level, creation is very rare, for we have gained in knowledge and in some wisdom to see the dangers inherent in creation if it is not used wisely.
          (I'm tempted to thank them for taking the risk, but slightly unsure it was a good idea – so, with a laugh:)
David: I hope you don't regret it!
MOITA: Once we have done something, there are no regrets. There is growth, learning and understanding.

♏   ♏   ♏

A couple of weeks later, we are provided much greater perspective on the origins of both of us, and another lingering question is answered – by those in the best position to know.

<u>Moita/Amar Session #134 (Kelly and David / February 24, 1980)</u>
David: Kelly has wondered about the process by which she separated from you when you left the physical behind, and what responsibility was entailed on your part toward her development as a result of that separation.
MOITA: When an entity is given the choice to make an energy-level change, it is

very tricky. For, in order to make the change complete, all parts must travel together at the same rate of speed through what could be described as a vibrational gateway. If the entire soul is not in complete harmony within itself, then all parts will not make the transition.

It is at that moment that the new energy-level presence sees its error in having made the choice to change too soon. And then it loses a part of itself, in a way. But that loss becomes a gift, and a teacher. And there is a responsibility to help it grow until it reaches a point where the same choice can be made. It is more than what a mother should feel for her child...

David: Since we spoke of Loria's creation before, I have wanted to ask if you were involved in the process, perhaps even as the focus of a group of entities on your level that gave her "birth"?

MOITA: After your last question, I did not think this one would be long in coming... If you wish to know, it was not I, but another.

David: *(starting to guess)* Whom I have met?

MOITA: Whom you have met.

(I laugh. She means Amar, of course.)

MOITA: It was done from a different level – although it is difficult to separate levels...

(Later in the session, after more conversation:)

David: I'm remembering another question about an entity that I'd thought of asking.

MOITA: This is "entity night".

David: In my work with Ruth, during the fall before I met Kelly, there was another entity that came through at one point very briefly.[109] She had received the name "Priamo" the night before as she was drifting off to sleep. This was identified as Loria's own entity, which Loria had one year earlier said would come through to speak when Ruth was ready. I have an idea *(laughs)* of who that might be.

MOITA: You mean "Pre-Amar"?

David: Yes.

MOITA: She felt it was a higher level of Loria, did she not?

David: Mm-hmm.

MOITA: I see. And you have heard that Amar was there [at Loria's creation], and in some way he must be related. Are we making a family tree?

David: Well, it would all fit. Can you tune into that experience and confirm that's so?

MOITA: Perhaps we should ask Amar! He would know.

David: Right! *(laughter)* Do you think he'd be amenable to answering now?

MOITA: One never knows. You can only try! *(laughter)* – if you are up to it. *(with tongue-in-cheek coyness)*

David: Oh, we could give it a whirl – give ourselves a whirl.

(Long silence as Moita's eyes close. Amar then opens them, radiating intense energy.)

AMAR: It is true I can come through more than one.

(This in apparent reference to my question, after Amar's first appearance through Kelly on October 16, 1978, about his possibly speaking through others.)

David: Yes, you seem to have made yourself known to a number of people in the groups we've been in.

AMAR: There are some things that can be done from this level that cannot be done from others. There are fewer of us, meaning we are more . . . *(pause)*

(Amar clearly sounds as if he is in mid-sentence, but then leaves it off there. Kelly feels tricked!)

David: When this life was planned, was it always to be one community – the same community – that we and others in our group expected to form together? And could some of them yet join us?

AMAR: There is a sense here that some will join you, some will not. The split [within] the group was seen early. And the information you received on Kyrionis and Musili should have prepared you for a split.

(Kelly gets the impression that "early" refers to the gathering in January 1978 – when Roy, Eileen and Gerald sensed a masculine entity, as told in Chapter 13 – after which two groups started meeting separately.)

David: Although it was said that now we were bringing these parts together . . . That didn't mean we'd stay together, I guess.

AMAR: The parts have come together. *(i.e. the higher selves of our group) (pause, as I refocus on the energy in Amar's gaze)*

David: It is interesting to meet one's great-grandfather.

AMAR: You have always had a thing for grandfathers...

(This is the first time I realize that one level and probably the most important level of meaning to my dreams about male elders – including many of my white-haired grandfather during the year leading up to Michael's birth – was Amar. And only much later will I see that the enigmatic phrase in my dream the night before Amar first came – "Greetings to my created Earth!" – would have been, in part, a much more personal hello to me from Amar, Loria's creator, than I ever suspected.)

AMAR: *(abruptly)* My presence is called for elsewhere.

David: Thank you for coming.

(Amar closes Kelly's eyes. Soon Moita returns and opens them.)

MOITA: He is still quite potent, is he not?! Did he answer your question?

David: Yes, by implication. Do you know where he was going?

MOITA: *(laughs)* None of that! *(laughter; pause)* You all look quite wiped... My energy is still just as good! Therefore, I must consciously fall into the background.

(We laugh at her mysterious tone as she departs. Later Kelly and I speak of the intense energy Amar projected through her eyes – as if almost popping out of her head and boring into my brain. And Kelly reveals she knew Amar was coming all along:)

Kelly: And then you brought up the subject yourself! I wonder who stuck that question into your head. Moita seemed so pleased with herself – "Why don't you ask Amar?!"

MOITA:	Soon it shall be time to speak of you and I.
LORIA:	And perhaps how compatible we are (?).
MOITA:	They would be amazed.

– December 26, 1978

Why have such different souls as Kelly and me spent so many lives together in so many kinds of ways? Why also have Moita and Loria chosen so often to work together in our past, and in this crucial transitional period? What significance could this have for others and for the New Age? Is it not precisely in that appearance of "incompatibility" which, when opened to in the right way, becomes a "natural bridge"?

On May 13, 1979, almost exactly a year after our first merging experience at the Starflower meditation group, I ask Moita if the energy that so vividly flowed between Kelly and me in those early months came from the merging of our entities. She replies: "The energy you felt between you does not have to have a name. But the name it has is not Moita or Loria, [but] something that encompasses both, and more." Though Amar comes to speak a few minutes later, Moita seems not to have been alluding to him, either. So, rather than give it a name, let us look at how the two of us began to recognize the path leading to this higher union, since it graphically illustrates a reconciliation sought by many and urgently needed throughout our culture.

Returning to that time, it is important to remember the commonalities we have developed – a fair degree of personal androgyny, an openness to feeling, intuition and subtler presences – enabling us by May 1978 to "meet in understanding". Yet we are still coming from opposite points of the compass as souls, from poles most clearly identified as Sun and Earth: my inward focusing of the unified pattern or ideal to be manifested, while potentially prone to boredom and sterile alienation "above" life; Kelly's spontaneous flowing with the changing multiplicity of forms, while potentially vulnerable to fear and confusion, becoming immersed in surrounding influences.

We might imagine these extremes, respectively, as a point hovering in the air and a circle on the ground lacking a centre (see Figure #1, a few pages ahead). These tendencies reflect our origins: mine in an entity created as an individual directly on non-physical levels, without ever experiencing the relationships and conflicts of physical existence; Kelly's in the combined energies of a physical-level group, from whose entity she separated, staying on the physical, when Moita made her transition. At the same time, these combined origins potentially represent, in Moita's words, "the greater coming together of the two levels, the meeting of the worlds".

The way forward – recognizing one's own true nature and seeking its harmony with another's within the Medicine Wheel – is spontaneously dramatized on that evening in May 1978 at the Starflower meditation:

As our group enters the silence, I am seated a quarter of the way around the circle from Kelly. But soon my mind feels more and more off-balance, pulled by the energy in Kelly's direction. Then there is nothing to do but change places – to the spot opposite her in the circle. Without opening her eyes, she senses the energy shift as I move. Soon she is seeing an image of us in the centre of the circle, standing palm to palm, with light around us from above. A voice comes out of the light and says, "Open your heart." We both let down our shields, becoming vulnerable, as our heart centres are strongly activated. It is as if we are the only people in the room...[110]

In Figure #2, the merging of Kelly and me on this level, illustrated by the line from one point on the circumference to its opposite, along a path through the centre, also has the effect of connecting our qualitative sources of energy represented by the circle and point. Here I realize I am not simply an individual abstracted and apart, but rightfully occupy a specific place opposite Kelly on the Medicine Wheel. So, my energy spirals toward Earth, grounding me within a new, emerging wholeness. For her part, Kelly realizes she is not only an expression of group energies but an individual with her own viewpoint. Aware of my moving opposite her, she feels free to merge with her opposite, as her energy reaches upward, following the apex of a now rapidly expanding "cone of power" (Figure #3). While my staying aloof from the Medicine Wheel would have created an artificial split, my recognizing myself as "a person of this Earth" dissolves that barrier, allowing the interpenetration of polarities here below, reflecting their oneness above.

Parenthetically, we can note the sexual symbolism of interpenetrating point and circle, as Kelly will experience that first summer (and as I, too, seem to experience when Amar looks through *her* eyes at *me*!):

> When David walks me home, we have another tremendous energy experience. We are standing by the side of the house and he places his forehead on mine. There is a surge of energy and he literally bores into my mind. I can feel his presence as a physical as well as psychic pressure. The picture that comes to my mind is of me as a soul with eddies and channels and spaces running through it, and he as a soul pouring himself into those eddies, channels and spaces, until all those places are filled with his essence, and we are no longer two beings, but one.[111]

It is our energies themselves that naturally seek to merge, with or without conscious intention. And yes, lovemaking in a context of personal communication, caring and trust can be another level of expression for this spontaneous merging. In our Starflower experience, as we simultaneously focus within as well as on each other, the other becomes as much inside as outside ourselves – just as the high bells heard at the end of my "Snowy Natural Bridge" dream, and later awake while standing in a wintry field, were neither inside nor outside but both. From our opposite positions in the circle, we thus approach the centre – releasing our attachment to past selves, becoming mediators for each other in receiving "the light around us from above".

Through this surrender to the unknown, we create our bridge over an emptiness.

After a lengthy process of refining ("not this, not that"), Kelly is finding the focus point of her many-faceted jewel, the still point of her turning world. And I, having struggled to break through my prison walls, am discovering an entire living Medicine Wheel within what I once considered my solitary self. Further yet, sitting in the car together afterward:

> I have the unprecedented experience of finding Kelly sharing my mind, or I hers – a very lucid, telepathic merging that leaves us both tangibly stoned, without a microgram of psychedelics. She says my thoughts feel good – and *I've* lost all track of them! [112]

At the centre we experience the light, the energy of spirit, the transforming agent, moving in both directions along the vertical axis of the cone of power: downward and outward to incarnate as the Many, the "ten thousand things"; and inward and upward to transcendence, by gathering all into One, touching those higher levels where "there are fewer of us, meaning we are more . . ." (Figure #4). As Moita tells us, "You have not lost your difference, but you have intermingled your sameness, and brought it up."

On ordinary levels, of course, every person represents some merging of these Sun and Earth principles. But the deeper we allow this complementing to go, the wider the way opens to a creative wedding of inner and outer. It makes sense for the opposites to "conspire", does it not? – as a way of covering blind spots, trying to ensure more balance in one's work, drawing on a broader range of experience, communicating to more types of people, operating simultaneously on several levels of meaning? Prominent extremes, though risking imbalance, can reveal patterns with unusual clarity and make the drive toward wholeness all the more compelling, when those extremes are finally able to meet.

Superficial confusions, that have rationalized abuses in the past, may then be unmasked: for example, that spirit is in moral conflict with matter and life, rather than being the energy at work in their very core; or that the inner ("subjective") is inferior to the outer ("objective"), rather than being the personal point of intersection, potentially encompassing the oppositions of the external world that is its mirror; or that men and masculinity (symbolically identified with Heaven or Sun) are in fundamental competition with women and femininity (symbolically linked to Earth or Moon), rather than both desiring to unite in equality (within the individual and/or as partners) to reach the transforming centre, the energy of the *I Am* and All That Is.

> The air itself is alive... It has a voice, and we hear it... He speaks to the Sun and I speak to the Ground, and we weave together what we are told and make it whole.

> When we meet again...and our hands join, particularly in meditation, the energy current is so tangible the very air seems to be vibrating. It is the completion of the circuit of life, the linking and balancing of poles that have been separated too long.

Formation of a Cone of Power

[original manual drawing by D.W.L. circa 1982]

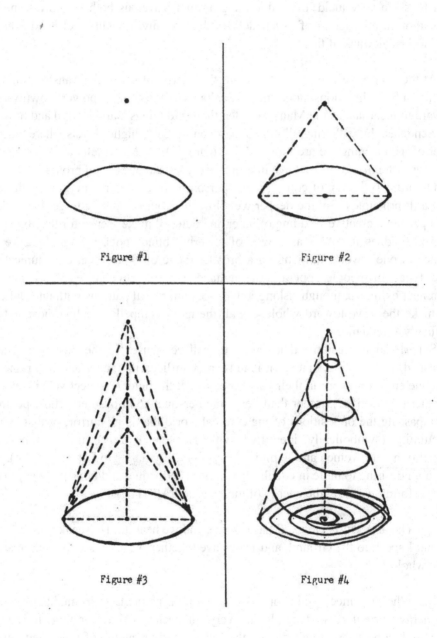

Figure #1

Figure #2

Figure #3

Figure #4

Experiences so similar, only apparently separated by millennia, making concrete the bridging of past and present – like a point of spiritual power persisting below the surface of history, a "place" to begin community open enough to include both the earthy/intuitive and the creative/intellectual – weaving them back together, by the sacred geometry of its starflower vision, around that deep centre of oneness from which these patterns are eternally generated.

> And while I stood there I saw more than I can tell and I understood more than I saw; for I was seeing in a sacred manner the shapes of all things in the spirit, and the shape of all shapes as they must live together like one being. And I saw that the sacred hoop of my people was one of many hoops that made one circle, wide as daylight and as starlight, and in the centre grew one mighty flowering tree to shelter all the children of one mother and one father. And I saw that it was holy.
>
> Then as I stood there, two men were coming from the east, head first like arrows flying, and between them rose the daybreak star. They came and gave a herb to me and said: 'With this on earth you shall undertake anything and do it.' It was the daybreak-star herb, the herb of understanding, and they told me to drop it on the earth. I saw it falling far, and when it struck the earth it rooted and grew and flowered, four blossoms on one stem, a blue, a white, a scarlet, and a yellow; and the rays from these streamed upward to the heavens so that all creatures saw it and in no place was there darkness...[113]

One boy's visionary experience, but – as Black Elk well knew – at the same time universal, an archetype repeated in the lives and dreams of many both now and in ages past; similar patterns arising from the lowest to highest levels of manifestation: polarity within higher unity, the transformative channel between Heaven and Earth. Thus also, one winter solstice, Moita will speak of the star of Bethlehem:

> There were three planets and one star that were in alignment, and the combination of their energy and their light was such that it increased its magnitude... Our worlds were closer, and man still saw some things through the eye of the soul. So it was not just a physical occurrence. It was seen with the heart...
>
> There was a light on Earth as well as one in Heaven. And the two lights were drawn to each other, or the one light on Earth made the direction of the other light obvious. It is like two poles, or magnets, being drawn together, forming a pathway, a focus.

✤   ✤   ✤

Returning to our own smaller, 20th century lives, such "magnetic attraction" of Sun and Earth energies between Kelly and me has been hard for others in our group to fathom, leading some to see dependency and "bewitching". Nevertheless, through these chapters we have already seen solutions to six of the seven unanswered questions, unexplained mysteries, unfulfilled promises, listed in the Introduction – solutions evidently made possible by these energies uniting and working their transformations.

Yet it is true for all of us from our different perspectives and situations: Faced with the unknown, we often cling to the familiar, to our idols and fears, to our battles or our cynicism, gritting our teeth to insist, "This should not come to me" – rather than asking "What can I do about it? What is its meaning for my life, and for all life?" – daring the leap from illusion into reality. Hear again the words of Frances Wickes:

> Do we desire this reconciliation? It means facing the night and day within ourselves; it means building our own bridge which is the cross, the death, the transitus. For the cross that each must bear is hewn out by the mysterious indwelling Self that brings man face to face with his own conflict, his own experience and his own choice of the way he will live out his destiny. It is through acceptance of this cross that the tree of death becomes the tree of life.[114]

These words are far from abstract for me. Amid the joy and fulfillment of my life with Kelly and Moita, I neither forget Ruth nor abandon the hope of healing the rift with her, possibly even to realize the vision of community we all once shared – not on a foundation of weakness and guilt, but of strength and mutual understanding.

The distrust that developed between Ruth and us two during 1978 would last, with ups and downs, for roughly two more years. That period brings fleeting attempts at reconciliation through the mails, which are renewed at the end of 1980. As it happens, I am working on an early draft of this chapter when a breakthrough letter arrives from Ruth, which I paraphrase below.

January 23, 1981

Dear David and Kelly,

...What I have realized is that you sincerely do wish to communicate – perhaps even as a necessity now. That's probably the lack I've been experiencing for a long time. Maybe a moratorium on hassles is in order. Let us make the attempt, as reasonably grown-up, well-intentioned people, to express ourselves as honestly as possible. Maybe the battle will never need resume. We all have changed from what we were in 1978-79. Possibly these different people can come to know and like each other.

I've waited quite a while before responding to your letter in order to know definitely what I'm feeling. Many things have occurred in my recent life to bring out my love and joy. My communication with Loria has evolved and I have too. She and I have been dwelling frequently on you two, and reaching some peaceful understanding holds for me a lot of good energy now. May your coming year be happy and fulfilling – as will mine.

Ruth

As Ruth herself implies, openings along our individual paths that make us feel better about ourselves also encourage us to overcome former conflicts with each other. Or, sometimes it can be difficult and/or painful experiences which force us to re-examine our feelings and choices. "So we each go through situations again," I write to Ruth, "to understand them more and do them 'better', as we understand 'better' for ourselves." In my letter I welcome the upturn in feelings, and the closer contacts that may emerge from it, such as the possibility of Michael and Mark staying with us this coming summer. We even enclose a copy of *Rays*, which Ruth says arrives with perfect timing, allowing her to appreciate our changes along with her own.

Her return letter includes comments that have contributed to my view of the balancing our similar natures periodically require: how much more herself she feels when she escapes the city to get back in touch with familiar country; and how she needs an "earthwise, practical, grounded" rather than "other-worldly" person to relate to – a description which, on a somewhat different level, also fits Kelly's role in my life.

Finally, Ruth writes that our offer about the boys has led her to realize she hasn't taken a real vacation in years. She suggests that she and her current partner drive Michael and Mark to our place for a month's stay while the two of them go on travelling. Plans are laid, and Ruth responds to a pair of "warm and beautiful" letters from Kelly and me by expressing a shared thought: "This new communication feels so much better than the space we were all in for so long – what a relief to let that go!"

It is on the 1981 summer solstice that they arrive, almost two years since we saw each other last. Ruth steps out, and we note the dream-like, hard-to-believe atmosphere as we hug in greeting. Given Ruth's tiredness from travel, and eagerness to get started on vacation the next day, her overnight visit is friendly but brief.

Michael obviously recognizes me immediately. My close rapport with this often quiet but happy son of three fills a space in my heart that nothing else could fill. Watching him playing, or running through the tall grass, is like watching timelessly the little boy that I once was, making that "Davey" real again, at least to my imagination. Our pretty six-year-old Arista enjoys having someone younger to play with for a change. And Mark is a joy and great help to have around. He becomes fast friends with Donovan and joins him and me in a favourite mountain hike. Finally, it is a special pleasure for all when he gets to meet Moita.

The movement has clearly reversed itself, as the threads knit themselves gradually into a new pattern. And behind the scenes, surely Moita and Loria are still conspiring.

As another spring approaches, we raise the possibility of a follow-up visit. Despite hopes this will lower the lingering barriers between Ruth and us, in the end no meeting can be arranged. On July 10th, however, I wake up suddenly to find my head bathed in the light of the Moon, having just had a very positive dream about Ruth. As more vividly relevant dreams follow within 24 hours, I note it is four years since Ruth's and my worlds came tumbling apart. I received a flurry of dreams back then on July 11, 1978, too, all dealing with our changes and the approaching childbirth. But lightning awoke me that night, not moonlight. Here is this short but prophetic, new dream.

"Earthy Unwed Reunion" dream
David (age 35) / July 10, 1982

It seems about a year after Ruth and I separated. We meet again, and connect with the same magical outlook on life we shared when we worked with Loria. We are aware again of many "non-accidents" in our lives, the depth of energy and meaning in all that is happening. Our feelings for each other are renewed, with an added freshness and also more detached appreciation of this space after having lost touch with it for a time. There is also some new technique we have discovered for experiencing other realities – something like hypersentience – which I've momentarily forgotten in the excitement.

Ruth talks as if we are to be a couple and a family again, though the suddenness of it all leaves me unsure what is to be. She speaks of "our child, a father, and an unwed mother" as being a "very earthy" combination. Our child now seems to have grown into a teenage girl.

Later that night, I dream my family is holding a reunion that includes Kelly, Ruth, Mark and Michael. The next night I dream of "Ruth merging with me and then with Kelly, which experiences are described in transcripts I am utilizing in *Rays*..."

What do these dreams portend? I cannot deny the longing to have done with any residual estrangement between Ruth and me – perhaps even to reunite our paths and fulfill our original intention, the vow with which our Musili group entered this life, now with greater awareness and individual strength?

I sense that the four-year cycle may be significant: that I must seize this opportunity to act lest the two times drift apart again and the chance be lost. So it is that, right after Michael's August 4th birthday, I manage to put all this into a letter and send it off to Ruth, wondering just how dream-like this reality is going to turn out to be.

One month later I receive her reply. If it does nothing to confirm in a literal way either my dreams or conscious imaginings, it is the kind of response that my heart has been waiting to hear over four years of pondering why we two could not have separated with more acceptance. Ruth begins by saying that, whatever my surprising dreams may really mean for me, they do not foretell any greater physical or emotional closeness with her. We can, of course, continue to re-establish our friendship in future visits back and forth. What is new, however, comes in response to my question whether she also – for I have no doubt myself – sees our past together having a positive meaning. The following is a very close paraphrase:

I'm amazed that you ask, for how could it be otherwise? I am enjoying my life at present, and I gather you are also. But in any case, there can be no doubting the goodness of a tie that brought a child like Michael into the world. I'm not sure what these past years have been like for you, but I am certain that, along with the hurt – or in fact, as a result of the hurt – I have developed in many positive directions. I have discovered how brave I really am, and how genuinely strong I can be when I need to be. I appreciate and feel an assurance about myself as never before. And a great deal of this transformation, I am sure, is the result of your setting me free in 1978.

This letter is for me a watershed: a confirmation of the pattern I sensed in the midst of our earlier battles, but which I needed to hear from Ruth directly before I could fully leave this past behind or integrate it with my present. On one level, my July 10th-11th dreams of reuniting with Ruth prefigured this reconciling movement. But it is equally clear now that their main thrust must be more *inwardly symbolic for myself*. Rightly understood, I believe they point to fulfillment of an inner purpose that has been at work in my life from before Ruth and I ever met. And it is clear from all three dreams how essential Kelly has been to this entire process.

The "Earthy Unwed Reunion" dream suggests renewed appreciation for the moonlit atmosphere of magical discovery in which Ruth and I met and then began our work with Loria. However, as Ruth's letter makes clear, this is not a literal return of the past, but a coming together of an inward kind which Ruth is *symbolizing*. The second dream leaves no doubt: it is my family (i.e. inner family) that is holding a "reunion". Then the third dream makes abundantly clear: this is not a mere gathering but a "merging". With the benefit of hindsight, from experiences unfolding in chapters yet to come, I understand the meanings of these dreams as follows.

The "child" born of my union with Ruth has, through ongoing experience with Kelly and Moita, grown rapidly now into adolescence. In the sense of my developing intuition, an aspect of my Anima, this child is appropriately female. More generally, the "father" and "mother" (my creative masculine and feminine energies) have been healed into a loving couple once more, though the mother is now "unwed" – all making for "a very earthy combination". I believe this means: no longer is my inner family constrained "above life" by the falsely spiritual imbalances or bowing to semblances of the past.

For the mother to be "unwed" actually has many levels of meaning, particularly in light of the two later dreams. First, it emphasizes that this woman with whom I am reuniting is not, literally speaking, Ruth. Second, this female figure is neither split nor restricted any longer by the exclusiveness that once separated my world with Ruth from that with Kelly – for I can merge easily now with the energy that *each of them* represents. Third, Ruth and Kelly can also now merge with *each other*, confirming that my inner woman has grown inclusive to the point she is no longer "wed to" (identified with) any outer individual.

Fourth, very importantly, this inclusive inner woman has "unwed" herself from *my own ego* – something I have struggled over, and toward, in writing this very chapter! I have realized I must relate more consciously to her, honouring her as an independent force within my psyche whom I ignore at my peril. As with outer individuals, true interplay and merging with the psychic energy she possesses are only possible on a basis of freely given, mutual respect between us.

Fifth, all of these levels provide a working approach to feminine and masculine as distinct archetypal forces. The Mother is no longer "wed" in unconscious identification with the Father. Their originally confused and twisted "unholy alliance" has been discriminated into true polarities (e.g., "Earth" and "Sun"), bringing freedom from the unconscious dependency that supports and maintains conventional gender roles in our attitudes and institutions.

Sixth, there is a more specific "vertical" interpretation to this family reunion, as well: I as the developing "child", Loria and/or Moita as the "unwed mother", and Amar as the "father". Being physically embodied, I make it an "earthy combination" – in the same sense as may have been intended by Amar's message four years earlier: "Greetings to my created Earth!"

There is a seventh, and final, significance to the mother being unmarried in my dream – a traditional spiritual meaning that may well emerge from just these distinctions, completing the circle. As Erich Neumann points out, for the embodiment of feminine creativity to be "unwed" is, classically speaking, to be "virgin".

> As everywhere in the ancient world, virginity simply means not belonging to any man personally; virginity is in essence sacred, not because it is a state of physical inviolateness, but because it is a state of psychic openness to God.[115]

Once again, the hands of Kelly – whose earthy receptivity has drawn me, complementing my own nature – and of Moita – part of whose essence may assume the form of the Virgin Mary – are visible, pointing me toward this new stage of "family reunion".

It seems a universal need of men eventually to come into conscious relationship with their Anima: the feminine being who radiates an energy that completes us and connects us with our soul; the woman who is virgin, free, open – her own independent person, and paradoxically who is already inside us, there to help us in meeting the world – if we will but love, listen to and learn from her. Yet how often do we mistake her for those individual women in the outer world who begin to introduce us to her, thereby doing justice to neither reality! By no longer trying to possess – nor being possessed by – a woman in the outer world, our inner partner is freed to awaken us to the joys of both realms.

I sense this common secret within the multitude of realizations that are leading many of us toward a New Age: the outward, literal goals, possessions, people, etc., we have so often blindly and destructively pursued are, in their true reality, *within us*. With these realizations come freedom, a right understanding of life's essential wholeness, and the insight to recognize identities of energy in the endless reflections of psyche and world.

I will mention a single example, since it neatly ties so much together in these last two chapters – even hinting of a future development in Kelly's channeling, a yet greater reality of which Moita is a part. Love of our Earth, that living whole being (called "Gaia") in which we and all nature participate, is a devotion flowing from and back into the inner oneness we each have achieved. (Thus the ecological movement since the 1970s, and all sincere efforts today to recover the health of our struggling planet, are direct reflections of our psychological and spiritual progress.) It should not really be so surprising, then, that the founder of Gaia theory, Dr. James Lovelock, was conscious enough of the feminine polarity, within and without, to note a certain identity of energy between Earth-love and humanity's ongoing, widespread devotion to the Virgin Mary:

> Those millions of Christians who make a special place in their hearts for the Virgin Mary possibly respond as I do. The concept of Jahweh [Jehovah] as remote, all-powerful, all-seeing, is either frightening or unapproachable. Even the presence of a more contemporary God, a still, small voice within, may not be enough for those who need to communicate with someone outside. Mary is close and can be talked to. She is believable... It could be that the importance of the Virgin Mary in faith is something of this kind, but there may be more to it. What if Mary is another name for Gaia? . . . Any living organism that is a quarter as old as the Universe itself and still full of vigour is as near immortal as we ever need to know. She is of this Universe and, conceivably, a part of God. On Earth she is the source of life everlasting and is alive now; she gave birth to humankind and we are part of her.[116]

Lovelock's suggestion is certainly consistent with the warnings about our threatened Earth delivered by appearances of the Virgin during the past century. And again, it makes perfect sense that an "outer" planetary crisis coincides with our "inner" spiritual crisis during these birth pangs of a New Age.

I have emphasized the feminine polarity here partly because it is the one I have needed to make more conscious within myself (individually, and in reconciling with Ruth) and also because our hyperrational, technological civilization needs, most of all, to do the same. Ultimately, of course, feminine and masculine are mutually supportive – and meaningless in isolation.

Similarly, then, on the other side of gender and psyche, it is clear from Ruth's letters that in the same period her masculine spirit, her Animus, has been emerging just as strongly, freed from unconscious identification with me or others. She, too, has separated (or "unwedded") masculine from feminine, so each can be expressed more consciously. Thus, she has made her transitus from death to new life. The pain of the past has been embraced as a teacher and benefactor, and the ego that once clung to the hurt has been superseded by a stronger, more centred self, able to express more clearly her deep-rooted feminine soul.

As I have written before, without these confirmations from Ruth I would have been far more reluctant to imagine this story being published. The changes seen here are signs of the *metanoia*, the creative reversal, the overcoming of the "zero-point", that builds within each individual the foundation for a new world. It does not happen all at once, and there will ever be retreats as well as advances, but each moment of altered perception and response contributes to the new pattern.

From this vantage point, our relatively unconscious selves of the past become less real, compared to ones now breaking through who are more aware, free, indescribable mysteries. This has been the direction of our story from the beginning.[117N]

These chapters have set out to convey some of Moita's ironical sense of a "conspiracy". But again, what does she mean by saying "the world" conspires?

If this book were a Tarot deck, the Part One prologue ("The First Leap in Your Mind") would match the first of the Major Arcana: the divine Fool who, trusting in spirit, steps off a cliff . . . starting a journey through all the opposing forces of life.[118N] Just as fittingly, the last of the Major Arcana is the card of the World, as the Fool in us regains the wholeness with which life began – but consciously now, through humanity's own learnings and choices, both alone and together. And I especially appreciate depictions of the World as a dancing androgyne: masculine and feminine, intermingled, wielding their wand of magical transformation.[119]

For Moita, the original wholeness that underlies and has become manifest as our world, our universe, all our realities, has "conspired" through the ages to reach this time of transformation, when human beings will take a quantum leap in consciousness of the unity-in-diversity that we and all things *are*.

Further senses of "the world", as Moita uses it, though, will continue to emerge in the course of this series. There is much more to reality than is given to our normal senses and minds. We have been learning of our other lives, our higher selves and teachers, and greater entities on Amar's level and beyond, who, from outside the physical march of time, participate in sustaining our lives and furthering humanity's transformation. And besides these human soul and entity levels, there are also the invisible energies at work throughout all of nature, who also have a stake and wish to partner with us in the coming changes. As we shall see, the Earth's living unity is not a fiction but has a voice, which speaks to us in many ways.

And so, we arrive at the vision of a spiritually open-ended "family tree" – not the kind that only recounts what is past, all plotted out and boxed in, to file away and forget. Rather, it is a vibrant, infinite realm for us to enter and *participate*, with further mysteries yet to unfold. As we clear a path toward fuller enjoyment of this multi-dimensional Tree of Life, each of our experiences, in retrospect, reveals its necessity within the harmonious whole where all meanings interrelate.

In legend, of course, the Garden of Eden was said to have two trees. The so-called "tree of knowledge of good and evil", the tree of all our conflicting opposites, has been portrayed as a circular hedge that usually shrouds from us the tree of joy at the very Centre of the Garden.[120] Similarly, in one last experience, Moita must first penetrate my tendency to focus and analyze, always attempting to find logical answers to specific questions arising from this material, before I surrender to the universal message, thankfully lying beyond logic, and so receive fully the gift that is being offered.

Moita Session #76 (Kelly and David; March 5, 1979)

(As we relax in the living room this evening, Kelly begins to feel an unusually strong presence in the form of a mantle that descends, wrapping her in its peace and love. Kelly's eyes remain open as Moita arrives: perhaps, we can say, in her Virgin

aspect – but that unconventional, ever-changing, limitless one, for the coming age.)

MOITA: What do you think of this transformation?

David: It seems very natural.

(After a silent period:)

MOITA: How are you experiencing this energy?

David: I've been feeling my third eye activating, and sort of waves flowing down over my head. Maybe some blocks, because I feel pains along my forehead at times.

MOITA: We spoke once of how these conversations are, for me, continuous.

David: Yes?! *(curious where this may be heading)*

MOITA: There are different lines of continuity, depending on which line of conversation we choose to materialize. *(long pause)* ...Which line would you prefer?

David: The only thing that comes to mind isn't a conversation but a touching...

MOITA: Is that not a conversation? It is conversation on a higher level, for what is conversation? Words are merely tools to communicate an idea. An idea without words can be communicated more fully and experienced more completely. *(pause)*

Imagine our touch as a warm mantle that descends upon you and enfolds you. *(followed by a long silence)*

Have you been touched?

David: Mmmmm. Feels good. *(pause)*

MOITA: You look more peaceful now.

David: I gave in to it.

MOITA: Became more fluid?... *(another silent period)*

David: Mmm. A question occurs to me... What sort of connection is there between you and Amar?

MOITA: *(pause)* You have on this lovely planet of yours a phenomenon known as a seed. This seed is such a unique creature, it knows when it is still a seed exactly what kind of a plant or tree it will become... Some seeds look the same as others, but when they are planted they each know what they belong to, what form is theirs.

And so, the seed plants, and grows deep roots down into the soil and high, leafy branches up into the sky. The roots may not be aware of the leaf, or the air above it, but they are all one and the same. So are each of you part of a tree or a seed, and growing. And we are some of your branches.

Do you like my story?

David: Mm-hmm.

MOITA: Does that answer your question?

David: Not too much, but it'll take its place...

MOITA: I have explained how I am connected to him, but we are only two branches of one tree... *(pause)* Perhaps some of what I am saying is there is no high or low when we are all part of the same thing. We all express a different part of the same root.

David: Can you and Amar be seen as branches growing out from the same trunk over time – his older than yours?

MOITA: Trees grow from seeds and grow up. But here there is no time. Here the tree exists as a seed and a full-grown tree all at once. It all interrelates... Each has its place, but none is more special than others.

David: I guess the story is not to be analyzed.

MOITA: Perhaps not. There is a certain beauty in simplicity that is lost when it is over-analyzed. This is a move towards wholeness, and analyzing has a tendency to focus on parts. I know it is difficult when you live your life in a focus not to try to focus everything else. Perhaps it helps to make your focus broader and less narrow..., as when you accepted your flow. Then you were unfocused... *(a very long silence as we gaze at each other)*

How many in the world can actually feel the energy called love, and know it as a viable force and not an empty word? This is your heritage.

Epilogue

THE UNIVERSE IS WILLING

As of October 5, 1978, Kelly and I begin our years of living together. During that first week, our friend Roy cannot help but notice how we have been "thirsting" for each other (his word). A dream of mine then suggests another level to the metaphor: after this year's stalled or failed attempt, a renewed search for "the place for community".

"Dry Prairie or Forest Streams" dream
David (age 31) / October 11, 1978

A drought is threatening to turn the prairie into a dustbowl. I seem to be our friend Helen, considering with her husband Dale where to buy land. It is an urgent decision because, if we are to settle nearby, we must start right away to protect the soil with organic methods, before it's too late.

Dale reveals he is also considering a beautiful forested area with tall evergreens and clear streams – country I had previously considered out of reach, as too much to hope for. But I begin to think he is right: if there is any chance of acquiring it, that land is so much more promising and worth the inevitable risk than this drought-stricken area.

Later this day, Moita herself brings up my dream, relating it symbolically to our personal changes: "In order sometimes to appreciate the forest, it is necessary to go through the dry period. Contrast very often brings out much that would have been missed." But there is obviously another, more literal meaning here. I return to the subject in a session one month later.

Moita session #40 (Kelly and David; November 11, 1978)

David: Dream images continue to occur about places for a community to be built. Is there anything you can say about the way such a place should be found? How much of an ordinary, practical searching out of places is in the plan . . . if there is a plan?...

MOITA: Providing you continue to put all of your energy into your "now", things will fall into place. If there is a plan, that is the only one. The universe is willing to give you anything you want, providing you *allow* it to.

៚   ៚   ៚

So does the world conspire. By this time, our journal *Rays* is reaching further afield, helped by mention in the community journal of the Associations of the Light Morning in far-off Virginia. That mention reaches people on the opposite coast of North America: a couple living on a 160 acre farm in the British Columbia interior, who respond by ordering our publications. Then they write a letter – unbeknownst to us, *one day after* the above session, and in the same spirit.

November 12, 1978

...We'd like to mention that we are looking for others to form a community with on our land... We have long hoped to see a new and conscious sort of community here, and maybe a school of some kind. It's hard to know how much to push for such a thing, as we want it to happen naturally and in its right time. But we also want to let people know who seem to share a similar vision, as your group certainly does.

For the most part there are just the two of us here as permanent residents. We look forward to sharing this land and our life with more people...

Love to all of you,
Christopher

Enclosed is a photo of "Dawn at Sunrise Farm" showing a meadow, tall fir trees, and a 7,000 foot mountain.

TO BE CONTINUED . . .

Much energy has been put into planning this life, and you had – will have – an unusual amount of cooperation from others in carrying it through. All roads lead to the same, highly probable route you have chosen.
– Moita (January 16, 1979)

ೞ   ೞ   ೞ

Afterword

A CHANNELING FOR DECEMBER 20, 2012

What will December 21, 2012 mean for us and our Earth? How may we expect our reality to change, and how should we prepare for it? Critical questions, these – since the awareness we bring to this event will be crucial to the outcome. But most important of all – and most absent from the public debate – is recognition that *non-physical, higher levels of nature and human nature on this planet*, with whom we are inherently connected and able to learn to communicate, lie behind such transformative events.

Amid major societal/economic/environmental disruption, with a growing sense that our world is conspiring toward a pivot point of change, consider just two current and now converging factors: (1) nearly universal awareness of the 2012 December solstice as a so-called end-of-the-world date in an ancient Mayan calendar; and (2) the much lesser known but stunning evolution of "signs in the fields", or "crop circles", in the course of the 1990s and 2000s – including the huge formation that appeared at Avebury Manor, Wiltshire, England, on July 15, 2008, depicting the exact astronomical positions of our entire solar system as of that same December 21, 2012 date.

Of course, many wonder whether any date should be singled out as definitive – even if it is the turning point from one World Age to the next in the Long Count calendar of the Maya. Should those who look to a New Age be focusing rather on a transitional period of decades or even centuries that includes many significant junctures? Compounding the uncertainty, even from those convinced the 2012 December solstice will bring *the* pivotal change, we hear widely varying suggestions, reflecting disparate world-views, of what may transpire – ranging up to the extremes of "apocalyptic" earth upheavals, UFO landings of "space brothers", universal "instant enlightenment" and/or "the end of time" (which itself can mean quite different things).

I am not privy to higher-level information specifically about the 2012 December solstice, as Moita did not refer to it. I do assume it will be a significant point in our evolution – in part, due to all the attention from human consciousness – but not totally unique or final. Rather, I see it falling within a decades-long transition that has been underway since at least the 1960s and will continue for many years to come. There may or may not be obvious *outward* changes on or near the 2012 world-shift date. But to me, the nature of the *inward* event is not in doubt. Despite likely differences in magnitude, I believe the best key we have to the essence of 12/21/12 lies in previous *progressive energy changes toward a meeting of worlds*, as Moita has described.

I'm convinced the communications in this series apply throughout the ongoing transition, being as relevant for the present and future as when they were first given. But if we are now to consider their specific implications for 2012, everyone must be free to reach their own conclusions. As Moita has said: "In the end analysis, you are the only one who can decide what you perceive of all this, and what applies to you directly." On this basis, I offer interwoven channelings from Moita that we can together imagine being delivered, to our expectant ears, on the Winter Solstice Eve of 2012.

The Channeling*

Something is happening tomorrow, to everyone on the planet. It requires my *complete presence*. There have not been many things in a long while that have required all of me. There is a great deal of energy bent in this direction.

I see the planet covered with the tides of change. There are times in the Earth's history when a single word, spoken at the right time and place, can change the face of the world. This is one of those times. The Earth has had many faces. The one that you have on it now will not last much longer. As each of you are in this age striving to find out who you are as an individual expression of being, so is your Earth finding out who it is. It, too, has a soul.

These communications have been happening throughout history. We have spoken through many people – ancient prophets and modern ones. You all have gone through a period of development where you have drifted away from your source. You have gone into forgetfulness, and you think the world is asleep and does not remember. Now you are beginning to come back up out of that forgetfulness, to remember where you came from and who you are, and to know what you can do. In a change like that, the world will wake up.

Our worlds co-exist in the same space but are separated by vibrations of energy. Your eyes are so accustomed to seeing physical matter. You are narrowly focused on one thing – this life, this reality. We are another form of this existence, the same as you, but our energy is a much less dense energy. Your world is in the process of raising its energy level, and we are reaching down to touch it, so that our worlds will come closer together. It is closing a gap. It is *all* of us who exist in this universe being able to touch each other and work together towards creating a more whole humanity.

For us, this change is a great responsibility. Our whole sphere of influence will be drawing close. It will mean a great shift in your energy towards our level – and being that kind of change, will cause unrest and growth, some unwanted. It need not be as chaotic as it might. We are trying to soften it as much as possible, to be here as closely as possible and add our energy to these changes and to each of you. We have to gauge these things as delicately as we can, so the most good is done with the least ill. There is a chance – albeit a small chance – that some of the physical changes could be avoided if many people can change their level of consciousness in enough time.

---

* The text blends Moita channelings through Kelly during 1978-1980, as included in the *Mind Leap* series to date. (As such, it is not complete; there is more to come.) I have merely abridged and rearranged the transcripts, making slight stylistic changes for continuity of presentation.

Let me explain the connection to you in this way. Each time you have a thought, you have created a thought-form with its own particular energy. If many people are sending out negative thoughts, many negative thought-forms build up. They mass together and form great pressures that eventually affect your physical reality when there are too many of them. And there are too many of them now.

As in an earthquake or a volcano, when pressure builds until the Earth must shift in order to relieve that pressure, so also with thought-forms. When they build to such an intensity, something must change in order to release that pressure. Some of these changes will be from those who are punishing themselves. If you could all learn that one lesson – that self-punishment is not the way to learn – there would be much fewer physical rumblings. And if you have enough people together putting out strong positive thought-forms, they would negate the negative forms and the built-up pressure would be released in a different way. The more who rise above, the fewer who will be left behind and fewer physical manifestations will occur.

It will be you who makes the difference, whether it is a destructive or a constructive change. Each individual has as much responsibility for this as each other. It must start from one. And hopefully it will make you all realize how important you really are to the world that you have created – and how much power you have over it, to change it for good or ill.

One of the things we bring, our gift, is the inability to hide – from each other, and from yourself. It is not a gift many will take kindly. In a body, you feel you can hide your thoughts and failings from others. But our energy coming closer will destroy that apparent ability. There is much unrest over this. What do you think would happen if everyone could read everyone else's thoughts? It would be rather difficult to run a government if everyone *knew* when you were lying. There are no such things as secrets.

We also bring a message of remembering. You have gone through a long period of not being able to remember who you are or where you come from. It is as if, when you are born, a spirit places a bud inside your head. Inside this bud is the memory of *you*, of all those things you cannot remember while you are alive. One of the changes that will happen is that these buds will begin to open for the many – not just for the few, as it has been in the past.

People will remember in different degrees, depending on where they are in their development. Some will just remember this life, and all of the things they have conveniently tried to forget. Others will remember many lives, and see how they all flow together to make one. Many times that have been forgotten need to be remembered and the energy to be renewed. Those who remember their pasts while they still live in a body will not have to forget, the next time they are born.

The whole point of being here is to bring to the world your awareness, to become a whole being instead of one who is one part in the day and another at night. When you sleep, you leave your body. You go into other worlds, other realities. You meet teachers, you go to classes, learn lessons, some of which you bring back in dreams, some in intuitions and hunches. The problem is the separation of the two forms of consciousness. It is a very artificial separation, and the one thing you are striving for is to bring these two worlds back together, so the one can work with the other.

You were separated from our level of feeling and intuition in order to create in you the sense of the ego, a rational mind, the intellect. And now that that has been accomplished, you are hopefully seeing many sides of what it can do. It is time to bring that quality together with the spirit, so that you will have more purpose, more understanding of the creative forces of which you are a part.

If you can go through this change with the right attunement, you will gain an extra source of energy. As in all things, it takes a great deal of awareness to do that. You who are trying to build a New Age, have you thought of the kind of New Age you are trying to build, what you will do with that energy you will have access to? That is why so many of us are here. We would not see the world destroyed another time.

Warnings about power have been given to many people over the centuries in every age. And there are many more people here now, when the change in the world comes, who will have access to that power. It is very important to realize that whatever you do with it – however you choose to use it – you do it *to yourselves*. You must become very aware of what you are doing and what kind of energy you are putting into it. If you let yourself delve into your lower centres, they too will be amplified.

I am explaining this to you so you will have a clearer understanding of what you are doing. There will be feats that can be accomplished in this new universe that others would not have believed possible. It is important that you realize you must build this reality slowly and carefully, so it will have a strong foundation.

Much consciousness needs to be developed in everyday life. Each moment must be made a meditation, an awareness on another level of your purpose and why you are here, what you are doing and what you wish to work on. There is no such thing as unimportant, and the effects of doing things the wrong way will be felt immediately. It is not an easy spot you are put in, but how can you continue unless you are? It sounds like a hard road, but once it has been taken, it is hard no longer. It has many rewards.

What is needed in this time is not starry-eyed prophets who have no firm basis in the Earth, but those who are balanced in both worlds, who can take the wisdom that we can offer and the experience of our sharing, and bring it into the world in a real and physical way to help shape it and change it. That is what the New Age is all about: trying to discover who you are, being yourself without losing your integrity and without destroying things around you; being an individual expression and a unique interpreter of all of your experience, but working with a sense of cooperation and love.

We have watched for a great many years, and now there is a drawing together of worlds, a time when the two worlds may touch and not be destroyed by each other, when they may integrate and understand. The coming together of our worlds will not change just yours, but mine. It will affect us as much as you. There is a great difference between watching over a soul and its development when it is not aware of you, and participating with a conscious soul in its own development. Life will never be the same again.

As our levels become more in tune, there will be *many* manifestations, for those who have eyes to see them. The texture of the world is changing, and all those who are already partially tuned into us will feel the effects at a highly accelerated pace. Time has been compressed for a reason. Your bodies are changing. Your other senses that have lain dormant are beginning to wake up. We are preparing you for the inevitable shock of seeing us as we really *are*.

It is the world discovering itself. And those who do not wish to discover who they are do not look forward to the changing of the world, because when the world changes to what it *is* and people recognize it, it will be unavoidable – for *all*.

We are entering a New Age of humanity. Instead of man creating only on his own, as an individual self set apart from the rest of the universe, this time he is involved in a co-creation – and *we* are the co-creators. Those who are here have arrived to help found a new world.

Do not look on us as higher beings who know all the answers, for then you limit yourself and you limit us as well. You put us into a role that is difficult to break. It is that I am more aware of what I know, not that I know more.

We have much to share. We have much love to give to the world and to its people. And we are building that bridge so that the energy that has created the universe can shine out from the Earth and its inhabitants.

We shall see what tomorrow brings on the road to awareness. And we will shine our love on you all. Good night.

Previews of the
MIND LEAP SERIES:

MIND LEAP
Intimate Changes and Communication Between Worlds

Abridged Contents

"At this point, an unknown woman appears at my side. She stares at the screen to my immediate left, which pictures a snow-covered mountain slope rising to a peak. The very top forms a natural bridge over a high little valley, revealing open sky beyond. The woman whispers to me that no one lives up there and it must be an incredible experience to go there.

"Now all accelerates as image upon image flood the screens around us. The new woman and I are overwhelmed by the multi-layered radiance of these beautiful natural scenes. As I become lucid that I am now waking from a dream, I 'hear'– seemingly, but surely not physically – high-pitched bells, the shimmering light-energy becoming music!"

– from David's "Snowy Natural Bridge" dream,
half a year before meeting Kelly (Chapter 9)

"[Kelly] knows she has to make a choice. She has already made it, but the timing of the choice bothers her. Things will happen as they are for a time. There's a point, not far distant, where all these things will come together. Basically, that point will be the centre of this life as far as happenings are concerned. That will be the pivot point here. It will be *unmistakeable*. There will be no doubt. Circumstances will force things to that point, circumstances that have already been laid out. It *is* fast approaching. From that point onward, many things will open, and many things will fall away."

– Moita speaking for the first time (Chapter 10)

"I hope I have shown that those from *here* are nothing to fear – that we just are another form of this existence, the same as you; and that we hope all of you find your own centre of joy and let that flow out, because life is here to be loved, not to be destroyed. And we are in everything that you see. You can never be alone, none of you, because the force of love that has created this world lives in it still and flows out to anyone who will receive it."

– Moita speaking to our first workshop group (Epilogue)

෨   ෨   ෨

TO HELP FOUND A NEW WORLD

"Evolution happened from the 'top' down, not from the 'bottom' up. Spirit is cause; matter is effect. Scientists look from the physical only. They have not yet identified the unifying principle that is in all matter, but they also do not recognize the power of creation. They will never find a 'missing link'. There *is* none."

"Pressures within the Earth are building because man has chosen to ignore and to use. He has created this world, and he is trying to uncreate it because he cannot cope with its beauty as a reflection of himself.

"The Earth has been unrecognized as a soul in its own right, as a Being you are sharing. It will be your greatest disruptive influence. The Earth has great power, and it will use it because it has no choice. It is either disrupt, or die.

"The future is still fluid. As yet, there is time to change what can be, or what may be. We can stall the devastation some time yet."

"It is no easy task that we undertake – to turn about the destiny of the world when it is running headlong into disaster. If it was something we could accomplish alone, it would have been done eons ago.

"The key is within. You hold it in your hand. I cannot turn the lock. There are still many universes to choose from. Will you make a world of light, or one of darkness? You are at a crossroads, and time is short."

"There is no doubt there will be 'cosmic' influences. The Earth is not travelling through a vacuum. A long cycle is coming to a close, and we are preparing for the arrival of some others, to return.

"We have called them 'the High Ones'. The addition of their energy to the Earth will help to bring about a great many of the changes that have been foretold. The added energy of their presence will bring things to a crisis point so that there can be a breakthrough into a new reality."

"Some will not be able to accept newness and change. They will be given an opportunity to develop in another place, on another Earth, and start the cycle again. By giving themselves this doorway, those of you who have chosen to be here through this time and afterwards to help remake man's awareness and to heal the Earth will be freer to do so."

"Of all my children, man is the only one who has ever treated me with pain and fear. All of Earth's history man has created in his dream. And the end of Time will come when man wakes up and realizes he has been dreaming.

"Do you understand? You have been asleep! It is time to wake up! And yet you will still be here with the other dreamers. You must learn to flow in their dream and help them wake, so the dream may end [and] we may all be reborn together...

"So we begin a little early, trying to stack the deck."

"It is not lightly I tell you these things. That is how a path is born: in a single moment of choice. So I have followed it here, to help others find their way out of the maze I helped to create."

ဆ   ဆ   ဆ

(Comments from Lisa after, and Mike during, their sessions; then Moita's reply:)

Lisa: "That is truly a mind-blowing experience. There were a few moments there where I could just feel my consciousness being totally drawn in. 'What's going on here?!' *Neat.* I really didn't expect it to be as intense. It felt like somebody who's been helping you all your life behind your back, and you don't know it, all of a sudden stands in front of you and says, 'Here I am.'"

Mike: "Your presence gives a lot of hope, and love. It's almost like a dream. You grow up and you always know or have the feeling that something else is there. When it starts happening in front of you, it's . . . Well, I'm really thankful for it, and I hope I can give back, instead of just receiving."

MOITA: "That is why, when love is freely given, nothing is ever lost. It generates feelings such as that. We always get back more than we anticipate."

Appendix A

INDEXES OF DREAMS AND REGRESSIONS*

– DREAMS –

Date	Dream Title	Dreamer	Pages
1971-11-06	New Being Evolved Out of Rose	David	326-327
1972-05-13	Flight to Space Station	David	122
1972-12-14	Game of Identity	David	150
1973-01-10	Who Let the Cat Out?	David	151-152
1973-07-11	Escaping Ancient Catacomb	David	11
1974 summer	Lotus Meditation Being	David	98-99
1975-04-10	Elevator of Consciousness	David	123-124
1975-09-12	Shaking of the Firmament	David	265-266
1975-11-25	Deformed, Split Fetus	David	56
1976-01-07	1845 Chesterfield Woodcut	David	74-76
1976-02-12	Inner Onto the Outer	David	268
1976-02 or 03?	Flying Pig and Blazing Lamb	Ruth	325
1976-03-15	Advocating Own Water Source	David	173-174
1976-04-07	First Direction that Comes to Mind	David	15
1976-06-08	Pregnant and Celebrating	Ruth	13
1976-06-17	Discovery of My Deep Centre	David	174
1976-06-21?	Floating Lovers View Himalayas	Ruth	13
1976-09-11	If You Meet the Buddha	David	13-14
1976-10-17	A Place to Stay	David	239
1976-11-06	Power of Evocation	David	268
1976-11-15	Healing Tea at Mountain Lake	David	268
1976-11-19	Shansa National Park	David	269
1977-09-08 to 12?	Snowy Natural Bridge	David	15; 239; 293; 356
1978-01-??	Holographic Pyramid Cornerstone	Ruth	292
1978-03-01	Book of Birth Experiences	David	237
1978-04-12	Teacher Cries "S/He's Come?!"	David	233; 239
1978-05-15 to 16?	Rose Crystal with Spokes	David	293
1978-07-11a	Eye-Opening False Labour	David	341
1978-07-11b	I Have My First Contractions	David	341
1978-07-21	Steiner and Skydiving	David	233-234
1978-07-29a	Spirit Rays and the Next Step	David	15; 233-234
1978-07-29b	Chair-Tipping Miracle	David	15

* Page entries locate the most complete account, summary or reference, or more than one partial account, for the experience. The great majority of dreams occurred in the early a.m. hours of the date given. Exceptions are described in the text as happening in the evening or daytime of the given date. Entries without any date are in Part One, where material is undated.

Date	Dream Title	Dreamer	Pages
1978-07-31	Psychological Tests	Kelly	204
1978-08-03	Ship Must Land Tomorrow	David	234
1978-08-12a	A Spirit Takes Control	Kelly	204
1978-08-12b	Becoming Trance Medium	Kelly	204
1978-10-11	Dry Prairie or Forest Streams	David	349
1978-10-12	Haunting Indians Seek Partner	David	233
1978-10-16a	Election of New Pope	David	231
1978-10-16b	Greetings to My Created Earth!	David	232
1978-10-29	House Near Garbage Dump	Kelly	217
1978-11-02a	The Trouble with Hell	Kelly	221
1978-11-02b	Absolution to Murdered Monk	Kelly	221
1978-11-02c	The Energy Beyond Death	David	221
1978-11-03 to 07?	The Eagles Are Coming!	David	240
1978-11 (mid)	Communicate Thru Top of Head	David	224-225
1979-01-09	Old Book about Loria	David	323
1979-10-27	Scared by Doppelgänger	David	144
1980-06?	Mary Teaching How to Channel	Joan	316
1982-07-10a	Earthy Unwed Reunion	David	342
1982-07-10b	Family Reunion with Ruth & Kelly	David	342
1982-07-11	Ruth Merging with Kelly and Me	David	342
---------	Closing Door Blocked by Bear	Sara	48
---------	Teaching Men How to Die	Jane	129
---------	Moita Accepting, Humans Hostile	Ike	160

– REGRESSIONS –

Date	Regression summary	Subject	Pages
1978-06-27	Visionary country girl	Kelly	234; 324
1978-09-15	Earth and Sun, and thereafter	Kelly	257-258; 319-321; 337
1978-12-03	Musili (in her room, Moita appears)	Kelly	289-290
1979-01-19	Kyrionis (and journey to Musili)	Kelly	280-286
1979-02-04	Musili (lives of group members)	Kelly	287-293

Appendix B

INDEX OF COMMUNICATIONS, PART ONE*

* Chapter and page numbers locate all Moita session excerpts and/or references included in the main text. Only the primary participants related to the key phrases are given. If there is more than one primary participant, a key phrase may be given for each on a separate line. Bracketed entries under "Key phrases" provide summaries instead of quoting words.

Participants	Moita sessions – key phrases	Pages
	Chapter 6 – Entering Other Realities	
------	I would like to take you all on a trip!	125-126
David	Giving life to characters, Kelly lets them develop	126
------	Both are becoming very open to me in dreams	126
Hazel	Experiencing a person travelling in dream world	127
David	One of those instances of meeting another	127
C.	A world of your own creation, as when you die	127-128
Steven	Many teaching places in out-of-body experience	128
Jane	You teach others to be more aware of dreaming	129
Tim	You create your reality in life and in death	129-130
Peter	A soul sends out parts of itself to be born	130-131
Marcia	Each makes his own heaven and hell	131-132
Barb	You can make as many mistakes as you wish	131-132
Dorothy	If not understanding, a soul will punish itself	132-133
David	This is what it means to have fluid time	133
Leslie	For me, there are no gaps between sessions	134
Rita	For me, your past and future are the same now	134
David	Like parts of a jellyfish, I can shift my focus	134-135
Bill	Simultaneous lives are like rows of movie reels	135-136
Jim	All your lives and possible lives occur at once	136-137
Todd	Choices decide which future you make physical	137
Ivan	Your "now" is where your conscious focuses	137-138
David	Period of great adjustment in first years of life	138-139
Joel	Child more open to influences from other levels	139
Jane	Child sees other worlds till knows it shouldn't	139
Owen	You view past lives through your present lens	139-141
Steven	You bring energy of past "high" lives into now	139-141
C.	It's not always wise to dwell on destructive past	141-142
Shelley	When die, have "tea party" for all possible lives	142-144
David	Doppelgänger is opposite of ideal blueprint	144-145
Mike	Fear at brilliant light of oneself being created	146-147
-------	As many universes as souls to perceive them	147
Ivan	We are all part of the central consciousness	147-148
-------	Danger in naming things is missing many points	148
-------	Truth must be discovered for oneself	148-149
Gail	Going too far too fast, you can lose your focus	149
	Chapter 7 – The Art of Discretion	
Anne	You are contacting your own higher self	153-154
Mary	There is a depth to everyone's soul	154
Norman	By having expectations, you place blocks	154-155
Amelia	Let your heart open and become more accepting	155-156
Will	Means of communication vary by the individual	156
Lisa	Each soul has affinity for a kind of channeling	156-157
Margaret	Any experience is a potential mirror into self	157
Alice	There was a special feeling with your guide	157-158

Appendix C

INDEX OF COMMUNICATIONS, PART TWO*

Sources and respective mediums:
Moita, Amar, [???] ....Kelly
Loria...............................Ruth, David
Topling......................................Kitty

Date	Source	Key phrases	Pages
1976-10-21	Loria	Do you recognize what's been said?	267
1976-11-23	Loria	You were once a poet in Musili	269-270
1976-12-03	Loria	Others were part of circle in Musili	270
1977-07-24	Topling	Musili founded by part of larger group	271
1977-07-25a	Loria	[Explains splitting of Kyrionis group]	271
1977-07-25b	Topling	Bleed-through from Lumania	286
1977-08-09a	Loria	Meeting with our group entity	267
1977-08-09b	Loria	Community's group entity to speak	271
1977-08-09c	Loria	Lumania settled by groups' descendants	286
1977-08-18	Loria	The last time the six of you . . .	271-272
1978-06-27	Moita	That will be the pivot point here	232-233
1978-07-06	Moita	A highly individualized experience	201
1978-07-10	Moita	Follow the fleeting thought	201-202
1978-07-11a	Moita	Feelings are far more accurate	202
1978-07-11b	Moita	Those who remember beginnings	257
1978-07-12	Moita	Rare to spend so many lives together	318
1978-07-15a	Moita	Each of you adds my part back	273-274
1978-07-15b	Moita	I see the group on a different plane	302
1978-07-17	Moita	Learn to roll with the punches	214
1978-07-26a	Moita	It is not Kelly with whom you speak	203
1978-07-26b	Moita	Secret to changing your reality	215
1978-07-26c	Moita	It is not easy to be a group	274
1978-07-27	Moita	My energy is constantly changing	274
1978-08-01a	Moita	Tests important for both of you	204
1978-08-01b	Moita	You and Kelly stand back to back	318
1978-08-03a	Moita	Take step not knowing where it leads	214
1978-08-03b	Moita	Only you can decide what applies to you	351
1978-08-11a	Moita	Competitiveness in past not felt equally	273
1978-08-11b	Moita	You have different ideas of community	274
1978-08-12a	Moita	Many changes, physical and spiritual	252-253
1978-08-12b	Moita	There will not be forgetfulness	257

---

* Page numbers locate all session excerpts and/or references included in Part Two, plus the 5 excerpts from dated sessions in Chapters 7 and 8. Separate references to one session are identified by letters after a repeated date ("1976-08-06a"). Bracketed entries under "Key phrases" provide descriptions instead of simply quoting the source's words.

Date	Source	Key phrases	Pages
1978-08-12c	Moita	Kelly and Moita were together in Mu	276-277
1978-08-12d	Moita	[Moita as Virgin: blue-eyed blond]	314
1978-08-13	Moita	My teachings are not complicated	204-206
1978-08-16	Moita	Losing the thread of consciousness	207-208
1978-08-21	Moita	Your growth to discover workings	215
1978-09-early	Moita	Changing the structure of your universe	259
1978-09-15a	Moita	It is the world discovering itself	257-258
1978-09-15b	???	I exist in another time period	257-258
1978-09-15c	Moita	There is much fear of joy in the world	321
1978-09-20	Moita	Only you can decide what is truth	206-207
1978-10-11a	Moita	Communications are continuous	213
1978-10-11b	Moita	Everyone is taught differently	216
1978-10-11c	Moita	Contrast very often brings out much	349
1978-10-16a	Moita	I repeat myself 1000 times a day	209-210
1978-10-16b	Moita	Decision to be made on another level	235-237
1978-10-16c	Amar	I am obviously someone else	235-237
1978-10-16d	Moita	Hiding as big reason for reincarnation	254
1978-10-18a	Moita	Forming a group creates a new being	267
1978-10-18b	Moita	Not all things hoped for come to pass	275
1978-10-18c	Moita	A better explanation of what I am	277-279
1978-10-18d	Moita	Difference between Loria and I	322
1978-10-25	Moita	You all have done evil in your time	211
1978-10-29a	Moita	Warnings about power in every age	217-218
1978-10-29b	Moita	There are always more than just me	238-239
1978-10-29c	Amar	Your inner and outer, together	238-239
1978-11-01a	Moita	Your searching for a question	209
1978-11-01b	Moita	House located on minor power point	219-220
1978-11-02	Moita	Much work needs to be done here	221-224
1978-11-07a	Moita	Many things are being dealt with	224
1978-11-07b	Moita	Revelations must be worked for	240-241
1978-11-07c	Amar	Arrival of High Ones on your plane	240-241
1978-11-07d	Moita	All weaves together in a whole	275-276
1978-11-11a	Moita	Kelly feels my concentrated energy	187-188
1978-11-11b	Moita	Power draws power	225-226
1978-11-11c	Moita	Universe is willing to give anything	349
1978-11-14a	Moita	What constitutes proof of existence?	227-228
1978-11-14b	Amar	Purification of place not complete	242-243
1978-11-14c	Moita	He was afraid of doing damage	242-243
1978-11-17	Moita	[Moita says she is "being present"]	203
1978-11-21	Moita	My presence is more important	211
1978-11-24a	Moita	How do you experience our energy?	188-189
1978-11-24b	Loria	You must learn to relax more	188-189
1978-11-24c	Moita	Everyone knows you are here	225
1978-11-27a	Moita	Something's happening tomorrow	250-251
1978-11-27b	Moita	One of the changes towards our level	251-252
1978-11-27c	Moita	A long cycle is coming to a close	254-255

Date	Source	Key phrases	Pages
1978-11-27d	Moita	Our influence will be drawing close	259-260
1978-12-02a	Moita	Force of love created this world	200
1978-12-02b	Moita	The Earth has had many faces	249
1978-12-02c	Moita	You will make the difference	250
1978-12-02d	Moita	My particular level of vibration	312
1978-12-03	Moita	Thoughts have their own reality	253-254
1978-12-08	Moita	Distance as rebound from energy change	260
1978-12-10	Moita	All things have a consequence	260-262
1978-12-13a	Moita	Time compressed for a reason	243-245
1978-12-13b	Amar	Fitting yourself into your scheme	243-245
1978-12-19a	Moita	You are selector of the information	211-212
1978-12-19b	Moita	Good to put this point to use	245
1978-12-19c	Moita	World changes and pressures	262-263
1978-12-19d	Moita	In life you lived with Earth and Sun	321-322
1978-12-26a	Moita	You have released & created doubts	328-331
1978-12-26b	Loria	How unlimited is Loria	328-331
1978-12-26c	Moita/ Loria	How compatible we are	335
1979-01-09a	Moita	Competition among all 3 of you	294-295
1979-01-09b	Moita	We have conspired together	322-324
1979-01-09c	Moita	You represent the meeting of the worlds	328
1979-01-09d	Moita	You have intermingled your sameness	337
1979-01-11	Moita	Inside this bud is the memory of you	255
1979-01-13	Moita	Buds will begin to open for many	256
1979-01-16a	Moita	Planet covered with tides of change	247
1979-01-16b	Moita	You have had unusual cooperation	350
1979-01-26a	Moita	Bringing yourself out of solitude	248
1979-01-26b	Amar	Day of reckoning is not far off	248
1979-01-26c	Moita	Thought is a powerful thing	263-264
1979-02-06a	Moita	You are only one part of the play	199
1979-02-06b	Moita	You only see me when I am here!	294
1979-02-06c	Moita	I am the closest you will come to it	295-296
1979-02-06d	Moita	You are at the centre of the hurricane	318
1979-02-09	Moita	We have an interfering influence	304-305
1979-02-12	Moita	I act as a focus on a number of levels	305-307
1979-02-17	Moita	You have met him, have you not?!	296-297
1979-02-24	Moita	One pattern that is easily disrupted	263
1979-02-27	Moita	Out here, there are so many universes	303
1979-03-01	Moita	To speak, he must be solid	237
1979-03-05	Moita	Imagine our touch as warm mantle	346
1979-03-29	Moita	There are no such things as secrets	264-265
1979-05-13	Moita	The energy you felt has no name	335
1979-05-20a	Moita	The words should come without thought	189-190
1979-05-20b	Moita	Free a person within yourself	228-229
1979-06-06	Moita	You could say I am that larger entity	297-298
1979-07-28	Moita	Physical and spiritual deception happens	162-164
1979-08-11	Moita	The group entity has always been here	308-311

Date	Source	Key phrases	Pages
1979-09-13	Moita	The city was a being in its own right	298-302
1979-11-18	Moita	Interpreting our energy into words	190
1980-01-01	Moita	The art of communication	308
1980-02-13	Moita	A few have been created like Loria	332
1980-02-24a	Moita	That loss becomes a gift, a teacher	332-334
1980-02-24b	Amar	I can come through more than one	332-334
1980-05-13	Moita	The manifesting of such a Presence	325
1980-07-04	Moita	I have been called "Mary" before	316-317
1980-08-16	Moita	We decide what is best said/unsaid	304
1980-12-21	Moita	Three planets and one star in alignment	339
1980-12-28	Moita	People will not need to miss us	315
1981-01-04	Moita	I have radiated out to many beings	315-316
1981-01-17	Moita	Someday you will see all of me	317
1982-07-24	Moita	My function to weave together levels	314

ABOUT THE AUTHOR

David W. Letts was born in 1947 in New York City. He grew up in a Lutheran minister's family with his older sister and brother. David entered college to study music, but in the shadow of the Vietnam War switched to history and sociology. He filled his extracurricular hours with peace education/activism and, after being rejected for conscientious objector status, became a war resister by publicly returning his draft card to the government in 1968.

David later graduated Phi Beta Kappa from the University of Oregon, majoring in psychology and minoring in philosophy. He earned his M.A. at the University of Saskatchewan (Regina), Canada, with a holistic critique of the typical textbook introducing psychology to university students.

As a Ph.D. student, David's research on lucid dreams led to "midwifing" two women's openings to psychic-spiritual communication. He was a regular participant and transcriber for over 300 of these individual and group sessions, shared with hundreds of participants from 1976 to 1985. He also edited the journal *Rays* devoted to selected transcripts and related experience.

David has applied his holistic outlook in his writings and in teaching a variety of university psychology courses. He has led or co-led dream workshops, among other groups, and guided past-life regressions, across western Canada.

Since the mid-1980s, David has also worked as an editor in two Canadian provincial governments, including several years for a New Democratic Party caucus and premier. David notes this proves that exploring non-ordinary realities need not impair one's social, rational (even pedantic) side. "Editing government legal publications is as far from the intuitive psyche as one human mind would ever want to stretch. Yet it has balanced me in useful ways."

A new, fulfilling phase of life began in 1986 when David met his soon-to-be wife Margi. Since 1987 they have lived in Victoria, British Columbia. As retirement from full-time government work beckons, David looks forward to engaging more actively again toward transformative change on levels from global to local to individual.

Readers are encouraged to contact the author through Trafford Publishing (www.trafford.com) with feedback on this book and/or interest in arranging talks, seminars, past-life regressions, dream workshops, etc.

ABOUT THE CO-AUTHORS

Siofra Bradigan (a.k.a. Kelly) has consulted on aspects of the *Mind Leap* series but prefers to continue her healing work (which no longer involves extensive Moita sessions) without a public profile of this kind. Meanwhile Moita undoubtedly continues her own joyful work – under many names, or none.

ACKNOWLEDGMENTS

I wish to thank the hundreds of participants in our Loria and Moita sessions for sharing their energy and curiosity, their experiences and heartfelt concerns. They contributed greatly to the variety and deep relevance of this material.

I also thank Elihu Edelson, editor/publisher of *Both Sides Now*, for assisting with publication of our journal *Rays* (where many chapters of this series first appeared) during the 1980s. It is a pleasure to be connected still with this beacon of the New Age.

And I am grateful to my wife Margi for choosing to be my companion through these past twenty-five changeful years and for continuing to sustain me, during this writing, in all the ways that she does.

I acknowledge the following sources regarding included excerpts:

Illustration reproduced from "2009 – Crop Circle Communication" (web article), courtesy of Bert Janssen [www.CropCirclesandMore.com].

The Ages of Gaia by James Lovelock (NY: Norton, 1988).

"Allegations of Sexual Misconduct, Cruelty at Ranch Stir Controversy" by Henry Fuentes, San Diego Union (Sept. 2, 1979).

"Amchitka" (web article) [http://en.wikipedia.org/wiki/Amchitka].

Black Elk Speaks by John G. Neihardt (Richmond Hill, Ontario: Simon & Schuster), reprinted by permission of the John G. Neihardt Trust.

Earth Mind by Paul Devereux, John Steele and David Kubrin (NY: Harper & Row, 1989).

"In Search of Mary: Handmaid or Feminist" by Richard Ostling, Time (Dec. 30, 1991).

Knowledge of the Higher Worlds and Its Attainment by Rudolf Steiner (Spring Valley, NY: Anthroposophic, 1947).

The Inner World of Choice by Frances G. Wickes (Englewood Cliffs, NJ: Prentice-Hall, 1963).

The New Webster Encyclopedic Dictionary of the English Language (NY: Delair, 1971).

The Origins and History of Consciousness by Erich Neumann (Princeton, NJ: Princeton University Press, 1970).

The Return of the King (Third Part of the Lord of the Rings) by J.R.R. Tolkien (London: Unwin Paperbacks, 1966).

The Wheel of Life by Elisabeth Kübler-Ross (NY: Simon & Schuster, 1997).

Webster's Seventh New Collegiate Dictionary (Springfield, MA: Merriam, 1965).

PHOTOGRAPHS

Front cover photo –
East Sooke, British Columbia:
David W. Letts

Author photo: Margi V. Letts

BIBLIOGRAPHY

Andrews, Synthia and Colin. 2008. <u>The Complete Idiot's Guide to 2012</u>. NY: Penguin.

Ardagh, Arjuna; Argüelles, José; and 24 other contributors. 2007. <u>The Mystery of 2012: Predictions, Prophecies & Possibilities</u>. Boulder, CO: Sounds True.

Association for the Understanding of Man. 1974. <u>Fatima Prophecy: Days of Darkness, Promise of Light</u>. TX: Association for the Understanding of Man.

Barfield, Owen. 1965. <u>Unancestral Voice</u>. Middletown, CT: Wesleyan Univ. Press.

Bock, Emil. 1955. <u>The Three Years: The Life of Christ Between Baptism and Ascension</u>. London: Christian Community Press.

Booth, Teena. 2009. <u>Unfinished Evolution: How a New Age Revival Can Change Your Life and Save the World</u>. Phoenix, AZ: Scotalyn Press.

Carter, Mary Ellen. 1968. <u>Edgar Cayce on Prophecy</u>. NY: Warner.

Castaneda, Carlos. 1968. <u>The Teachings of Don Juan</u>. NY: Simon & Schuster.

_____. 1971. <u>A Separate Reality</u>. NY: Simon & Schuster.

Challoner, H.K. <u>The Wheel of Rebirth</u>. 1976. Wheaton, IL: Theosophical Publishing House.

Churchward, James. 1968. <u>The Lost Continent of Mu</u>. NY: Paperback Library.

Cooke, John Starr. 1969. <u>T: The New Tarot for the Aquarian Age</u>. Kentfield, CA: Western Star.

De Chardin, Teilhard. 1976. <u>The Phenomenon of Man</u>. NY: Harper Perennial.

Devereux, Paul; Steele, John; and Kubrin, David. 1989. <u>Earth Mind</u>. NY: Harper & Row.

Edinger, Edward F. 1973. <u>Ego and Archetype</u>. Baltimore, MD: Penguin.

Eliot, T.S. 1939. <u>The Family Reunion</u>. NY: Harcourt, Brace & World.

_____. 1943. <u>Four Quartets</u>. NY: Harcourt, Brace & World.

Faraday, Ann. 1974. <u>The Dream Game</u>. NY: Harper & Row.

Findhorn Community. 1975. <u>The Findhorn Garden</u>. NY: Harper & Row.

_____. 1980. <u>Faces of Findhorn: Images of a Planetary Family</u>. NY: Harper & Row.

Fisher, Joe K. 1991. <u>Hungry Ghosts</u>. Toronto, ON: McClelland & Stewart.

Fuentes, Henry. "Allegations of Sexual Misconduct, Cruelty at Ranch Stir Controversy". <u>The San Diego Union</u> (September 2, 1979).

Glickman, Michael. 2009. <u>Crop Circles: The Bones of God</u>. Berkeley, CA: North Atlantic.

Hawken, Paul. 1975. <u>The Magic of Findhorn</u>. NY: Harper & Row.

Hesse, Hermann. 1975. <u>The Glass Bead Game</u>. NY: Penguin.

Hinshaw, Lerner. 2006. <u>The Magnificent Potential</u>. Whitefish, MT: Kessinger.

<u>Holy Bible, The</u>. Authorized or King James Version. Philadelphia, PA: Winston.

Janssen, Bert. 2004. <u>The Hypnotic Power of Crop Circles</u>. Netherlands: Frontier.

Jenkins, John Major. 2002. <u>Galactic Alignment: The Transformation of Consciousness According to Mayan, Egyptian, and Vedic Traditions</u>. Rochester, VT: Bear & Co.

Jung, C.G. 1962. "Introduction" to <u>The Secret of the Golden Flower</u> by Richard Wilhelm. NJ: Princeton Univ. Press.

_____. 1979. <u>Flying Saucers: A Modern Myth Seen in the Skies</u>. NJ: Princeton Univ. Press.

Kübler-Ross, Elisabeth. 1970. <u>On Death and Dying</u>. NY: Macmillan.

_____. 1977. "Death Does Not Exist", <u>Co-Evolution Quarterly</u> (Spring 1977).

_____. "Playboy Interview with Dr. Elisabeth Kübler-Ross". <u>Playboy</u> (May 1981).

_____. 1997. <u>The Wheel of Life: A Memoir of Living and Dying.</u> NY: Simon & Schuster.

Letts, David W. 1974. "Objective" Psychology – the Holistic Alternative. M.A. thesis, University of Saskatchewan (Regina).

Lewis, C.S. 1980. The Last Battle. London: Collins.

Lovelock, James. 1979. Gaia: A New Look at Life on Earth. UK: Oxford Univ. Press.

_____. 1988. The Ages of Gaia. NY: Norton.

Mack, John. 1995. Abduction: Human Encounters with Aliens. NY: Simon & Schuster.

_____. 2000. Passport to the Cosmos. London: Thorsons.

MacLaine, Shirley. 2000. The Camino: A Journey of the Spirit. NY: Pocket Books.

Miller, Pam. "Nuclear Flashback: Report of a Greenpeace Scientific Expedition to Amchitka Island, Alaska". Referenced under "Amchitka" in online Wikipedia.

Monroe, Robert. 1971. Journeys Out of the Body. NY: Doubleday.

_____. 1985. Far Journeys. NY: Doubleday.

Montgomery, Ruth. 1978. Strangers Among Us. NY: Coward, McCann & Geoghegan.

Moore, Marcia. 1976. Hypersentience. NY: Crown Publishers.

Neihardt, John G. 1972. Black Elk Speaks. Richmond Hill, ON: Simon & Schuster.

Neumann, Erich. 1970. The Origins and History of Consciousness. NJ: Princeton Univ. Press.

Ostling, Richard. 1991. "In Search of Mary: Handmaid or Feminist". Time (Dec. 30, 1991).

Perls, Frederick S. 1969. Gestalt Therapy Verbatim. Lafayette, CA: Real People Press.

Picknett, Lynn, and Prince, Clive. 1997. The Templar Revelation. NY: Simon & Schuster.

Pinchbeck, Daniel. 2007. 2012: The Return of Quetzalcoatl. NY: Tarcher/Penguin.

Porter, Eliot. 1962. "In Wildness is the Preservation of the World". NY: Sierra Club-Ballantine.

Ram Dass, "Egg on My Beard". Yoga Journal (Nov. 1, 1976).

Roberts, Jane. 1970. The Seth Material. Englewood Cliffs, NJ: Prentice-Hall.

_____. 1994. Seth Speaks: The Eternal Validity of the Soul. San Rafael, CA: Amber-Allen. (Original publication, 1972; Englewood Cliffs, NJ: Prentice-Hall.)

_____. 1973. The Education of Oversoul 7. Englewood Cliffs, NJ: Prentice-Hall.

_____. 1976. The Coming of Seth. NY: Pocket.

_____. 1979. The Further Education of Oversoul 7. Englewood Cliffs, NJ: Prentice-Hall.

Roszak, Theodore (editor). 1972. Sources. NY: Harper & Row.

Rudhyar, Dane. 1936. The Astrology of Personality. NY: Lucis Publishing.

Sharman-Burke, Juliet, and Greene, Liz. 1986. The Mythic Tarot. NY: Simon & Schuster.

Spangler, David. 2010. Subtle Worlds: An Explorer's Field Notes. Everett, WA: Lorian.

Stearn, Jess. 1968. Edgar Cayce – The Sleeping Prophet. NY: Bantam.

Steiner, Rudolf. 1947. Knowledge of the Higher Worlds and Its Attainment. Spring Valley, NY: Anthroposophic.

Stewart, Kilton. "Dream Exploration Among the Senoi". Included in Roszak [1972].

Storm, Hyemeyohsts. 1972. Seven Arrows. NY: Harper & Row.

Stray, Geoff. 2005. Beyond 2012 – Catastrophe or Ecstasy: A Complete Guide to End-of-Time Predictions. UK: Vital Signs.

Thoreau, Henry David. 2009. The Journal of Henry David Thoreau. NY: NYRB Classics.

Tolkien, J.R.R. 1966. The Lord of the Rings. 2nd ed. London: Unwin.

Webster Encyclopedic Dictionary of the English Language, The New. 1971. NY: Delair.

Webster's Seventh New Collegiate Dictionary. 1965. Springfield, MA: Merriam.

Wickes, Frances G. 1963. The Inner World of Choice. Englewood Cliffs, NJ: Prentice-Hall.

ENDNOTES

1   *The Mystery of 2012: Predictions, Prophecies & Possibilities* (Ardagh, Argüelles, et al. 2007); *Galactic Alignment: The Transformation of Consciousness According to Mayan, Egyptian, and Vedic Traditions* (Jenkins 2002); *2012: The Return of Quetzalcoatl* (Pinchbeck 2007); *The Complete Idiot's Guide to 2012* (Andrews and Andrews 2008); *Beyond 2012 – Catastrophe or Ecstasy: A Complete Guide to End-of-Time Predictions* (Stray 2005); and others.

2   One excellent, long-time example of this relationship is *Both Sides Now,* edited by Elihu Edelson. Go to [http://bothsidesnow.freeservers.com] or write Both Sides Now, 10547 State Hwy 110N, Tyler, Texas, U.S.A. 75704-3731.

3   Spangler [2010], pp. 8-10, 18. Like Spangler, I will almost interchangeably use "non-physical", "subtle", "other-worldly", "higher dimensional" – and "inner" (meaning accessed by inner, non-physical means) – to refer beyond our normal 3-dimensional space plus linear time. I try only to use "spiritual" to describe the presence of sacredness, unconditional love, etc., on whatever level it shows itself. Regarding the evaluation of messages between levels, also see the third of the "Three Clarities" in *Mind Leap*, pp. 23-25, particularly the "pointers" to good-quality communications.

4   Janssen [www.CropCirclesandMore.com/thoughts/200902ccc.html]. On this website, see especially the article "2009 – Crop Circle Communication". It refers to a workshop co-led by Bert Janssen on May 16, 2009 in the Netherlands entitled "Meet the Circlemaker", aimed at coming as close as possible to the energy/mind behind crop circle creation. One activity was constructing a mandala starting from the design of a May 2008 crop formation dubbed "Yin Yang Yang", involving 3 adjoining yin/yang symbols. It was another evidence of likely intercommunication between humans and the "circlemaker" that the *next three* English crop circles to appear that month were geometrically related to the mandala produced in Janssen's workshop. The third of these formations – the most obvious yin/yang/yang – is shown on our title page.

5   An ellipsis representing the omission of text from a quotation appears as three closely spaced dots (...). On the other hand, three dots spaced apart (. . .) indicate a pause, interruption or unspoken conclusion. Two exceptions to the above: omitted or reordered text in the centred, italicized quotations from Moita and in the Afterword is *not* indicated by ellipses, in order for the quotes to flow without interruption. And while the text of all other channelings is shown precisely, with ellipses at any gaps, the words of session participants are occasionally abridged without notice.

6   Kelly's account of her earlier life can be found in Chapter 8 of *Mind Leap: Intimate Changes and Communication Between Worlds* (2010).

7   See the transcript at the end of Chapter 10, *Mind Leap*, from which the excerpt was taken under "Previews of the *Mind Leap* Series" in the present book.

8   This "rarest exception" is described in Chapter 9 of the present book.

9   See stepping-stone #5 in Chapter 1, *Mind Leap*.

10 Letts [1974].

11 Roberts [1970, 1972]; Findhorn Community [1975].

12 Since "psychic-spiritual communication" acknowledges the two-way cooperation of source and medium, I preferred this phrasing over "channeling" in *Mind Leap*. But "channeling" is the more prevalent term and so the natural one for Kelly and Moita to have adopted. Thus "channeling" will appear often in this and later books. As Kelly's letter has made clear, the same participatory meaning is intended.

13 See "Psychic Communication and the 'New Age'" in *Mind Leap*, pp. 331-335.

14 See the "If You Meet the Buddha" dream in Chapter 5 of *Mind Leap*, p. 100. The "Snowy Natural Bridge" dream can be found in Chapter 9 of *Mind Leap*, pp. 171-172, and is excerpted under "Previews of the *Mind Leap* Series" in the present book.

15 As in *Mind Leap*, Loria's words are paraphrased very closely to the original in meaning and style, since permission has not been sought for their verbatim publication.

16 See Chapter 9 of *Mind Leap*.

17 Jane Roberts's novel *The Education of Oversoul 7* (1973) gives many illustrations.

18 See the Epilogue, *Mind Leap*.

19 Faraday [1974], drawing on "topdog" and "underdog" concepts in Perls [1969].

20 The "Kentucky life" is mentioned in Chapter 7, *Mind Leap*. This life began in the early 1800s, moving from the eastern seaboard to the Appalachians. After the Civil War, it continued across the Great Plains and Rocky Mountains to the Pacific coast.

21 Historical notes: While the town of Chesterfield has existed in northeastern New York since 1802, the dream may simply have concocted the name from Chester, the middle name of my father, who grew up in upstate New York. Loria did state that I and my wife travelled to New York state in the interests of our Kentucky dairy farm.

The American National Biography confirms that the famous Lakota war leader Crazy Horse was bayonetted to death while under military guard in Nebraska in 1877. But, needless to say, many other Indians would have been killed across the West in not dissimilar circumstances.

22 Kilton Stewart, "Dream Exploration among the Senoi" in Roszak [1972]. Though Stewart's anthropology is controversial, the dream wisdom stands on its own merits.

23 Hesse [1975].

24 Lewis [1980].

25 Kelly's novel is as yet unpublished.

26 Kübler-Ross [1976].

27 Steiner [1947].

28 See the relevant quotation in "Previews of the *Mind Leap* Series" in the present book.

29 Cooke [1969].

30 See Chapter 8 of *Mind Leap*.

31 Kübler-Ross [1997]. Preceding paragraphs draw from the early chapters of this book for their summary of Elisabeth's life, up to her husband's request for a divorce (p. 205).

32 See Chapter 6, *Mind Leap*, pp. 118-120.

33 Fuentes [1979].

34 *Ibid.*

35 Ram Dass [1976].

36 Kübler-Ross [1997], pp. 227-229.

37 *Ibid.*, p. 203.

38 Kübler-Ross [1981].

39 Kübler-Ross [1997], pp. 230-235.

40 *Ibid.*, p. 240.

41 See Epilogue, *Mind Leap*, pp. 311-312. But Moita explains her origin and connection to Kelly in more detail in Chapter 13 of the present book.

42 Stearn [1968].

43 Roberts [1979].

44 See "Ship Must Land Tomorrow" dream, Chapter 12, *Mind Leap*, pp. 262-263.

45 A full account of this EEG effect, first included in an endnote to *Mind Leap*, is repeated in the early pages of Chapter 9 of the present book.

46 Roberts [1972/1994], pp. 357-361.

47 Webster's [1971]. Then there are the more usual denotations of "conspire" ("to agree by oath, covenant, or otherwise to commit a crime; to form a secret plot; to hatch treason") and "conspiracy" ("a secret combination of men for an evil purpose").

48 The numbering of these sessions matches the listing of transcripts in our binders, including Moita sessions and regressions – all numbered consecutively without distinction. The #4 does not mean it is Moita's fourth written communication (actually, it's the second in writing), but rather that it is our fourth transcript overall.

49 See the June 27, 1978 session, Chapter 10, *Mind Leap*, p. 219.

50 Steiner [1947], p. 69. The quotation reads: "For every one step that you take in the pursuit of higher knowledge, take three steps in the perfection of your own character."

51 Hawken [1975], pp. 42-89.

52 See Chapter 13, *Mind Leap*.

53 Hawken [1975], pp. 93-95.

54 See Chapter 8, *Mind Leap*.

55 Tolkien [1966].

56 Castaneda [1971], pp. 51-58.

57 Tolkien [1966], *The Return of the King (Third Part of The Lord of the Rings)*, p. 272.

58 Also quoted in "The Transitus and the Medicine Wheel" in *Mind Leap*, p. 16.

59 Wickes [1963], pp. 152-153.

60 See Chapter 10, *Mind Leap*, p. 219.

61 See Chapter 13, *Mind Leap*, p. 287.

62 See Chapter 9, *Mind Leap*, pp. 178-179.

63 See Chapter 13, *Mind Leap*, pp. 281-282.

64 See Chapter 12, *Mind Leap*, for all three dreams.

65 Bock [1955].

66 Picknett and Prince [1997].

67 Barfield [1965], pp. 39-48.

68 Looking back since the 21st century death of this pope, I would say that John Paul II certainly embodied and communicated spiritual devotion (in particular, for the Virgin

Mary) to billions of humans, and so will undoubtedly have played a role in preparing humanity for planetary transformation. But the adherence throughout his papacy to traditional Catholic doctrines and practices was certainly, to my mind, an opportunity squandered. One can only hope his unremitting patriarchal conservatism will soon be seen by most for the anachronism it was, underscoring the need for a true revolution in our minds and hearts.

69 See Chapter 9, *Mind Leap*.

70 See "Place to Stay", "Snowy Natural Bridge" and "Teacher Cries S/He's Come?!" dreams in *Mind Leap*, pp. 105, 171-172 and 178-179.

71 Neihardt [1972]; Fisher [1991], p. 70.

72 See Chapter 12, *Mind Leap*, pp. 247-249.

73 Devereux, Steele and Kubrin [1989], pp. 63-87 & 135-143, which in turn references works of de Chardin [1976] and Lovelock [1979, 1988].

74 Associations of the Light Morning [1974].

75 The mass suicide and/or murder of the People's Temple group in Jonestown, Guyana, occurred during the week preceding this session. Many temple members were drawn from the San Francisco area, where another very public act of violence occurred in the past few days. As depicted in the 2008 movie *Milk*, the city's liberal Mayor Mosconi and Alderman Harvey Milk, leader of the city's gay community, were assassinated by a former member of city council described as feeling extreme pressure leading up to the murders. The city responded in a huge, emotional candlelit march.

76 Churchward [1968]; Stearn [1968].

77 See Chapter 7. *Mind Leap*, pp. 134-135.

78 Quoting Topling, a masculine entity speaking through friends in Regina. See Chapter 12, *Mind Leap*, p. 247.

79 See Chapter 5, *Mind Leap*, pp. 110-111.

80 The second part of the "Reflections" section at the end of *Mind Leap* recounted this "Inner Onto the Outer" dream in its relation to my earlier "Raven Transformation" dream. Omitted in that telling were these next-quoted words uttered by my professor/therapist.

81 "Evocation" is defined as the act of calling forth or summoning, as of a spirit or in "imaginative recreation"; as initiation into a vocation, a calling; and in biology, as the "initiation of development of a primary embryonic axis. Each of these meanings certainly fits our situation, especially since this is the period in which Ruth and I are beginning to try to conceive a child together. All in all, it is a very evocative word! (Definitions in this chapter are taken from Webster's [1965].)

82 Spelling is, of course, only an approximate translation from an unknown source. The existing word closest to the sound I dreamed (according to a recent web search) is "niramata", apparently a somewhat common East Indian name. On October 21st, Ruth uttered "naramata", which happens to be the name of a present-day town in the Okanagan Valley of British Columbia. Interestingly, the town was named in honour of "Naramattah" [meaning "smile of the Manitou" (Great Spirit)], who was the wife of an important Sioux Indian Chief, Big Moose. Though the town Naramata wasn't known

83   to me in 1976, I presume its name was familiar to Ruth from living previously in B.C. It is conceivable that this knowledge affected her reception on October 21st, changing a similar-sounding ancient word into one more familiar.

83   The "Snowy Natural Bridge" dream can be found in Chapter 9 of *Mind Leap*, pp. 171-172, and is excerpted under "Previews of the *Mind Leap* Series" in the present book. For the Arrow Mountain trip, see Chapter 10, *Mind Leap*, especially pp. 202-205.

84   Many years later, I will read Shirley MacLaine's *The Camino* (2000). Despite the major earth changes that separate pre-Atlantean times from today, I will still wonder whether there could possibly be a connection between Musili and the famous Camino pilgrimage route, from the Pyrenees across northern Spain to Santiago de Compostela on the Atlantic coast, reputed to follow major ley lines.

85   See Chapter 5, *Mind Leap*, pp. 110-111.

86   See Chapter 6, *Mind Leap*, p. 119.

87   See Chapter 11, *Mind Leap*, pp. 237-239.

88   The possibility of perceiving, even communicating with, the entities of different nations has become familiar to us by this point through H.S. Challoner's unique reincarnational autobiography, *The Wheel of Rebirth*.

89   A more general statement of this information appeared in the workshop session comprising the Epilogue to *Mind Leap*, though that was delivered on December 2, 1978, later than the sessions excerpted here.

90   Rudhyar [1936], pp. 217-220. This clock, with 12 meaning outward, and 6 inward, corresponds to the pattern of houses in astrology, which begin at 9 o'clock and move counter-clockwise. Here the parting of groups is visualized to be at 3 o'clock. One group seeks inward, travelling clockwise, back through the houses of the astrological clock toward the point of origin (9 o'clock position), toward intuitive oneness at the beginning. It travels east to what will become the Himalayas. In travelling west, the other group moves outward, continuing counter-clockwise, forward through the astrological houses toward the same point, which for it is the final goal, the fullness of spirit in creative expression. Does this not correspond to the polar tendencies of traditional Oriental and Occidental cultures lingering even today?

91   Roberts [1972/1994], pp. 215. Originally published in 1972, but the 1994 release may be more accessible today.

92   Roberts [1973], pp. 30-31.

93   See "Rose Crystal with Spokes" dream in Chapter 9, *Mind Leap*, p. 193.

94   The ensuing discussion appears in Chapter 6 of the present book (Steven's question).

95   Ostling [1991], pp. 52-56.

96   See "A Letter from Kelly" and "David's Introduction" in this book, or the most complete original description in Chapter 8, *Mind Leap*, p. 161.

97   See Chapter 10, *Mind Leap*, pp. 217-219.

98   Association for the Understanding of Man [1974], pp. 9-50.

99   *Ibid.*, pp. 52-56. It is true that these latter qualities of autonomous, earthy feminism, linked to ancient Goddess worship, have been associated by prominent Christian "heretical" traditions with Mary Magdalene rather than the Virgin Mary – see, for

100   example, Picknett and Prince [1997].

For Ruth's "Flying Pig and Blazing Lamb" dream, see Chapter 3, *Mind Leap*, p. 66.

101   Loria's explanation of the symbol came in Chapter 4, *Mind Leap*, p. 85.

Jung [1962], pp. 101-102. This is Jung's famous introduction to Richard Wilhelm's *The Secret of the Golden Flower*.

102

103   Jung [1979].

Compare the erect "ant-like" aliens I perceive in this dream with the way some who perceive themselves abducted by UFOs describe their insect-like ET abductors: an erect praying mantis. (John Mack, *Abduction: Human Encounters with Aliens*, pp. 37, 207, 211, etc.; and *Passport to the Cosmos*, pp. 19, 57, 230). I believe most UFO abduction reports are honest experiential descriptions, but likely involving interaction with other-dimensional energies that take on forms suitable to our space age.

104   Quoted from Wikipedia article on "Amchitka", citing this report among others: Pam Miller, *Nuclear Flashback: Report of a Greenpeace Scientific Expedition to Amchitka Island, Alaska – Site of the Largest Underground Nuclear Test in U.S. History*.

105   Interestingly, one of these high school girls is how the mysterious woman will first appear in my "Game of Identity" dream a year later. Riding beside me on a school trip, this girl once said quite out of the blue: "If you ever get bored, just look around you at what there is to see." I suspect this is why my dreaming mind has adopted her image.

106   These last words, originally recorded as such, were familiar to me as quoted in Porter [1962], from *The Journal of Henry David Thoreau* (January 26, 1853).

107   This is the same sensation as in my dream of August 3, 1978, given in Chapter 12, *Mind Leap*, pp. 262-263.

108   See Chapter 10, *Mind Leap*, p. 197.

109   See Chapter 12, *Mind Leap*, pp. 247-248.

110   See Chapter 9, *Mind Leap*, p. 190.

111   See Chapter 11, *Mind Leap*, p. 231.

112   See Chapter 9, *Mind Leap*, p. 190.

113   Neihardt [1972], pp. 35-36.

114   Wickes [1963], p. 153.

115   Neumann [1954], p. 133.

116   Lovelock [1988], quoted in Devereux [1989], p. 153.

117   Ruth's and my reconciliation in 1981-1982, including Mark and Michael's stay in Kelly's and my home during the earlier summer, brings closure to the events of 1978 crucial to Kelly, Moita and me coming together. Accordingly, I will not write further of subsequent relations with Ruth and the children, for the privacy of all concerned.

118   I've found parallels between the story in *Mind Leap* and all 22 of the Tarot's Major Arcana, especially as amplified with Greek mythology by Sharman-Burke and Greene in their masterful *The Mythic Tarot: A New Approach to the Tarot Cards*.

119   Sharman-Burke and Greene [1986], pp. 81-83.

120   Edinger [1973], pp. 20-21.